THE HUMAN RESOURCE FUNCTION IN EDUCATIONAL ADMINISTRATION

SEVENTH EDITION

William B. Castetter

Professor Emeritus
Graduate School of Education
University of Pennsylvania

I. Phillip Young

William & Marie Flesher Professorship
in Educational Administration
The Ohio State University

MERRILL
an imprint of Prentice Hall
Upper Saddle River, New Jersey • *Columbus, Ohio*

Library of Congress Cataloging-in-Publication Data

Castetter, William Benjamin
    The human resource function in educational administration   /
    William B. Castetter and I. Phillip Young.—7th ed.
        p.   cm.
    Includes bibliographical references and indexes.
    ISBN 0–13–927112–0
    1. School personnel management—United States.   I. Young, Ila
Phillip.   II. Title.
LB2831.58.C37   2000
371.2'01'0973—dc21   99-21248
                                                                              CIP

Cover/photo: © Photo Bank
Editor: Debra A. Stollenwerk
Editorial Assistant: Penny S. Burleson
Assistant Editor: Heather Doyle Fraser
Production Editor: Linda Hillis Bayma
Production Coordinator: Betsy Keefer
Design Coordinator: Diane C. Lorenzo
Text Designer: Gary Gore
Cover Designer: Tope Grafix
Production Manager: Pamela D. Bennett
Illustrations: Carlisle Communications, Ltd.
Director of Marketing: Kevin Flanagan
Marketing Manager: Meghan Shepherd
Marketing Coordinator: Krista Groshong

This book was set in Photina by Carlisle Communications, Ltd., and was printed and bound by R. R. Donnelley & Sons Company. The cover was printed by Phoenix Color Corp.

Printed in the United States of America

10 9 8 7 6 5 4 3 2 1

ISBN 0-13-927112-0

Prentice-Hall International (UK) Limited, *London*
Prentice-Hall of Australia Pty. Limited, *Sydney*
Prentice-Hall of Canada Inc., *Toronto*
Prentice-Hall Hispanoamericans, S. A., *Mexico*
Prentice-Hall of India Private Limited, *New Delhi*
Prentice-Hall of Japan, Inc., *Tokyo*
Prentice-Hall (Singapore) Pte. Ltd., *Singapore*
Editora Prentice-Hall do Brasil, Ltda., *Rio de Janeiro*

To Roberta, with Affection—W.B.C.

To My Wife, Karen
My Daughter, Rebecca
and
My Son, Phillip—I.P.Y.

PREFACE

As the world passes from one century to another, its well-being depends upon the resolution, by all forms of organizations, of old problems ever new, as well as challenges brought about by emerging social, political, moral, governmental, and technical developments. While organizations span the entire spectrum of products and services, those devoted to educating current generations of children and youth have become exceptionally prominent.

One of the verities of school systems, as well as all forms of organizations, is that they are managed by, staffed by, and dependent upon people whose effectiveness determines whether the established mission of the system will be achieved.

The seventh edition of this text is organized into three parts, containing eleven chapters, an appendix, and a glossary.

• *Part I.* Addresses the foundations of the human resource function, strategic planning and its linkage to mission, and the role of an information system in strategic planning and its importance in the information-communication connection.

• *Part II.* Describes the building blocks on which the continuing operation and sustainability of the school system are based. These include the recruitment-selection, induction, staff development, performance appraisal, and compensation processes.

• *Part III.* Contains three chapters focusing on employment continuity, employment justice, and unionism. Included is a design for the employment continuity process, plans for implementing an organizational justice system, and linking unionism to strategic planning.

• *Appendix.* Portrays the organizational purpose, potential, and reaches of a school system mission.

What the Seventh Edition Brings To You

This seventh edition provides new concepts, knowledge, tools, and technology to design, implement, and monitor a complete human resources program in readable and understandable language by:

• Placing in perspective the nature, dimensions (mission, human, technical, environmental, culture, and ethics) and significance of the human resource function. (Chapter 1)

• Treating the function foundations in terms of their boundaries and linkage to other school system functions in order to make sense of the changing world of contemporary human resource management, development, and utilization. (Chapter 1)

• Focusing on the school system mission as the guiding star in the design and direction of the human resource function. (Chapter 2 and the Appendix)

- Explaining the importance of system strategic intent as the foundation for human resource planning. (Chapter 2 and the Appendix)
- Providing models, policies, procedures, practices, and checklists for administering the eleven processes of the human resource function. (Chapters 1–11)
- Establishing approaches for dealing with employment continuity and employee justice. (Chapters 9 and 10)
- Considering the significance of unionism as a force in strategic planning and implementation. (Chapter 11)
- Advancing an overview of relevant employment laws, court decisions, and vulnerable human resource practices. (Chapters 1, 4, 5, 9, 10, and 11)
- Bringing into focus the crucial importance of six human resource processes (recruitment, selection, induction, development, performance appraisal, and compensation) as a contributory basis for the daily and annual system operation. (Chapters 4–8)
- Indicating guidelines for designing and implementing an automated information system and modern records management. (Chapter 3)
- Including a comprehensive glossary designed to explain terms and concepts that apply to the human resource function. (Glossary)
- Suggesting the development and employment of four personnel manuals as communication and control instruments in human resource management (policy, employee, job description, and records system). (Chapters 2, 3, and 10)

Finally, it is our intent, belief, and sincere desire that the timeliness of the additions, revisions, changes, and contemporary practices and features of the seventh edition give credence to the concept that effective employees are the system's most important and imperative resource.

Acknowledgments

The authors express their sincere appreciation to those who gave so freely of their time and counsel. Their contribution has enriched this book in many ways. In particular, we are most grateful to the following reviewers of the seventh edition: Robert E. Anderson, Wichita State University; David C. Bloomfield, Teachers College, Columbia University; Jane Clark Lindle, University of Kentucky; Margaret Grogan, University of Virginia; P. Lena Morgan, Valdosta State University; Cynthia J. Norris, University of Houston; and A. P. Wilson, Kansas State University.

In addition, we gratefully acknowledge the contribution of Dr. Richard S. Heisler, University of Pennsylvania, personnel of the Bryn Mawr and Gladwyne Libraries for their expertise in guiding us to sources and indispensable information, and the following doctoral students at The Ohio State University for their assistance: Kimberley Miller-Smith, LeRoy Johnson, Mark Gooden, and Dane A. Delli.

Finally, we regard highly the support and encouragement of our editor, Debbie Stollenwerk, as a vital participant in exercising a gifted pencil to the editorial process.

W. B. C.
I. P. Y.

BRIEF CONTENTS

CONTENTS

3   *Information Technology and the Human Resource Function*   76

PART I

FOUNDATIONS OF THE HUMAN RESOURCE FUNCTION

Part I introduces the reader to the content and context of the human resource function in the management of educational institutions. The intent of Part I is to:

• Provide an overview of the human resource function, its linkage to other organizational functions, and key function elements and their management implications.
• Describe the nature of strategic planning and discuss ways in which it can be employed to enhance attainment of strategic objectives.
• Emphasize the vital importance of the information–communication connection and its power to impact on the efficacy and efficiency of human resource outcomes.

1 The Human Resource Function in Perspective

CHAPTER OBJECTIVES

Place in perspective the nature, dimensions, and significance of the human resource function.

Establish the purposive nature of educational institutions.

Stress the considerable impact of the endless and sometimes dramatic rapidity of social change and the role of the human resource function in resolving the challenges it represents.

Support the proposition that everything that goes on in a school system is linked to its human resources.

Identify major current and emerging problems confronting modern school systems and associated environmental forces that both hinder and enhance educational change.

Provide a foundation for improving the system's ability to close the gap between the actual and desired state of individual, work unit, and system effectiveness.

CHAPTER TERMS

Affirmative action	Ethics
Culture	External environment
Equal employment opportunity	Human resource function

Internal environment   Regulatory environment
Mission   Values
Organization structure

This book deals with the human resource function in educational institutions. Its aim is to bring a broad perspective to the subject matter under consideration—to provide insights into the purposes, policies, plans, procedures, and projects, and their impact on work, working arrangements, and work motivation of school administrative, teaching, and support personnel. The intent of this book is expressed by providing a framework that:

• Places in perspective the nature, significance, scope, and dimensions of the function.
• Emphasizes the purposive aspect of school systems and its potential power by internalizing its application.
• Considers the interlocking triad of three organizational variables—social change, education reform, and the human resource function—as factors either hampering or enhancing the process of school improvement.
• Identifies six dimensions of the human resource function and their potential for affecting individual, work unit, and system performance.

Nature and Characteristics of the Human Resource Function

The broad purpose of the **human resource function** in any educational institution is to attract, develop, retain, and motivate personnel in order to achieve the system's mission; assist members to achieve position and work unit standards of performance; maximize the career development of every employee; and reconcile individual and organizational objectives. This general purpose must be translated into operational terms to give direction to those responsible for achieving the overall intent of the human resource function.

As this nation enters the twenty-first century, these proposed outcomes for the human resource function are yet to be realized in the majority of school systems. Impediments to their achievement, including institutional rigidity and inertia; failure to achieve individual and organization purposes; reluctance or inability to apply technical rationality to human and organizational problems; and internal and external forces (governmental, political, school system culture, unionism, community) that require the most creative school system inventions for their resolution.

Underlying analysis of the human resource function is the notion that organization presupposes the existence of interrelated parts. This concept is illustrated in Figure 1.1, which portrays administrative functions and subfunctions of the hypo-

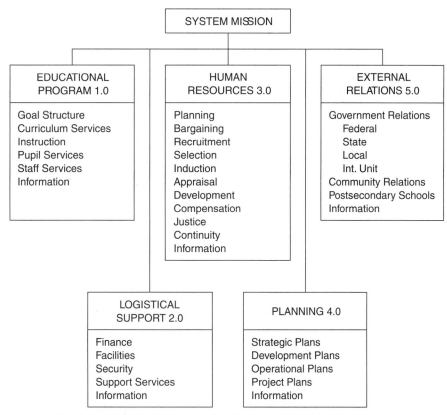

Figure 1.1   Major administrative functions and subfunctions of the Goodville school system.

thetical Goodville school system. The purpose of a portrayal such as that in Figure 1.1 is to identify, classify, and interrelate major functions and subfunctions that must be performed somewhere in the system if the mission is to be fulfilled. The human resource function, it should be noted, is divided into eleven areas: planning, information communication, recruitment, selection, induction, development, appraisal, compensation, justice, employment continuity, and unionism. These processes form the foundation of subsequent chapters.

Function Significance

From the preceding summary of the human resource function, one can examine the significance of this important subsystem of a school organization. For example:

•   In contrast to other major functions, human resource is concerned with activities primarily related to people.
•   The scope of the function, as can be judged from the activities listed in Figure 1.1, is extensive. These functional activities exercise a pervasive influence on the careers of system personnel.

• Design and operation of the function can have positive or negative effects on the individual, the work unit, and the system. Individuals' behaviors, as well as combined behaviors, influence organizational effectiveness. A proactive role of the function is to develop a structure within which individuals and work units are able to work cooperatively and perform productively.

• In the maelstrom of contemporary challenges posed by external and internal governmental, political, educational, economic, and social change, the function needs to be shaped so that it occupies a pivotal position to link system purposes to human resource practices. This point provides a preamble to the forthcoming discussion on the purposive aspects of the human resource function.

Purposive Aspects of the Human Resource Function

A school system is one of the most important purposive social institutions. Although there are contrasting views on the school's role as a social institution, a statement by George S. Counts regarding public education in the United States represents a consensus of the purposes of education in a democracy:

> Education for individual excellence.
> Education for a society of equals.
> Education for a government of free men.
> Education for an economy of security and plenty.
> Education for a civilization of beauty and grandeur.
> Education for an enduring civilization.[1]

In a call for a thorough reexamination of what schools are for, Goodlad amplifies Counts' statement of purposes. According to Goodlad, the goals of schools are to develop

• Mastery of basic skills or fundamental processes.
• Career or vocational education.
• Enculturation.
• Interpersonal relations.
• Autonomy.
• Citizenship.
• Moral and ethical character.
• Self-realization.[2]

The goals cited above by Counts and Goodlad are illustrative of those to be considered for their meaning, significance, and implications for educational practice. In subsequent chapters, one of the objectives is to consider ways in which the system mission is converted into derivative goals, programs, processes, practices, and projects that undergird activities with potential for enhancing the growth and development of human beings for whom school systems are created.

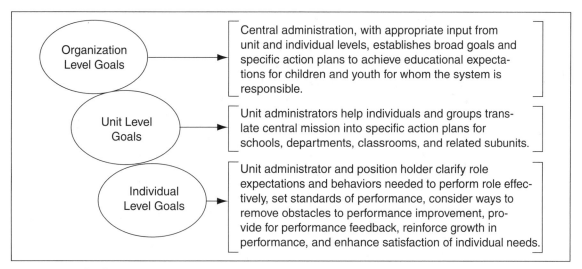

Figure 1.2   Trilevel interlocking goals: antecedents to the human resource function.

If the proposition is accepted that a school system is a purposive organization whose members seek through common effort to attain goals such as those just cited, then it becomes clear that the long-range strategy of personnel administration is to help the school system attract, retain, and develop the kinds of human resources needed to achieve its overall goals. The personnel envisioned here are those who will have the ability, motivation, and creativity to (a) enable the system to surmount its infirmities; (b) adjust the educational program continually to the needs of individuals living and competing in a dynamic society; (c) provide leadership that shapes the human organization in such a way that there will be congruence between the individual and the system; (d) create conditions and a climate conducive to maximum voluntary growth and individual effectiveness; and (e) influence ordinary personnel to perform in extraordinary fashion.

This kind of personnel strategy calls for a leadership focus that is intent upon achieving the goals of the organization; that provides opportunities for its members to bring initiative and creativity to their tasks, which will result in both individual satisfaction and effective position performance; and that will mesh administrative processes so that greater congruence between organizational ends and individual efforts becomes a reality.

Educational organizations are created and maintained to achieve purposes such as those previously noted. It is important to understand the significance of the relationship between organizational purposes and the human resource function. Figure 1.2 will enable the reader to visualize the interaction among three types of goals and the personnel function.

System Purposes and the Human Resource Function

Modern thought in all forms of organizations emphasizes the human resource function, as well as its human aspects, as bases for dealing with human workplace problems. This viewpoint includes, among other values, careful attention to purpose formulation, clarification, adherence, and internalization, as well as development of plans within the human resource function for improving interpersonal relationships, for seeking better methods of resolving conflict, and for increased mutual understanding among system personnel.

Goal setting and goal achieving are emerging as significant modern organizational activities. Their growing acceptance is the result of a number of factors, including the need for greater unity of direction in all organizations, pressure to clarify system and individual roles, and the importance of feedback to close the gaps between both individual and organizational plans and actual performance.

Considerably less attention has been paid, however, to the behavioral aspects of goal setting as they apply to members of a school system. Although it is clear that numerous benefits can be derived from goals established at the top level of the system for the total organization and at successively lower levels to engage the interests and energies of personnel in every position, it is equally manifest that unless members of the system are committed to general organizational goals and specific position objectives, the intended outcomes will not be realized. As will be stressed in subsequent chapters, setting organizational goals involves consideration of the impact of this process on the people it will affect and attention to internalizing organization goals so that they become part of the individual's value system. As indicated in the diagram that follows, the gap between the actual and anticipated levels of achievement represents the motivational potential for both organizational and individual improvement.

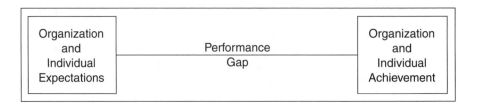

One of the major tasks of personnel administration is to understand human responses to system processes designed to achieve organizational goals. It is then possible to modify those processes when it is apparent that there is incompatibility between goals and human reactions to mechanisms for their attainment. Goal acceptance, commitment, and internalization are behavioral aspects involved in and essential to the outcomes of the goal-setting process. When carried out in isolation from, or with indifference to, the people responsible for intended outcomes, this process is not likely to result in either high levels of personnel motivation, fulfillment of organization plans, or self-actualization for the school staff.

There is a kernel of truth to the criticism that educational establishments suffer from "purpose ambiguity." Clarification of the hierarchical goals of the school system, from the very broad ones at the top to the specific, limited objectives pertaining to the staff member at the lowest organization level, can become the basis for voluntary cooperation. Not only does clarification of organizational expectations for the individual contribute to security and to position orientation, but achievement of both organizational and individual goals gives the individual a significant sense of accomplishment. The attempt by administrators to motivate their subordinates to achieve unknown or ambiguous goals is, of course, futile. The more clearly individuals understand what they are expected to do, the more likely they are to achieve expectations. The clearer the organizational expectations of individuals, the easier it is to evaluate progress in attaining the goals. In fact, individuals cannot know where they are going or what they are doing until the school system knows where it is going. If the goals of the system are known and the individual has an opportunity to participate meaningfully in meeting these objectives through activities contributing to self-actualization, attainment of both system and individual goals will be enhanced.

Defining and Articulating Strategic Intent

Part of the leadership responsibility of a school system is defining, articulating, and implementing the strategic intent. Explicating and implementing this intent begins with ongoing staff development programs for system members to acquire full understanding about utilizing a group of unifying intentions. These components include the mission, purposes, goals, aims, objectives, strategies, and values. Each varies somewhat from the others in direction and degree of intent. For our purpose, these components are defined as follows:

Mission

The mission establishes what the school system is charged statutorily with doing or is expected to achieve. The mission specifies its future direction.

Purposes and Goals

The terms *purposes* and *goals* are used interchangeably and draw on the system's mission to indicate such matters as what work and what work activities are to be undertaken and what competencies are needed to accomplish the core activities expressed in a position description. In addition, purpose and goals lead to consideration of performance requirements for the work and for determining the structure most appropriate to facilitate achievement of core tasks.

Aims and Objectives

Aims and objectives are time-bounded specific targets identifying what is to be accomplished, by whom, during what time period.

Strategy

Strategy involves development or employment of overall plans, sometimes referred to as grand designs, in order to achieve goals, planned effects, or desired results. Strategy is considered to be a technique of total planning that encompasses the overall purposes of the system and establishes functional strategies (e.g., educational program, human resources, logistics, and environmental relations) to achieve them. Each of these functional areas is shaped into individual modules to create an overall plan for guiding the system's future direction.

Values

Values form the framework for a school system's culture, beliefs, and operational style.

The Power and Promise of System Purpose

The foregoing review of the purposive aspects of school systems leads to the realization that planning goals are more likely to be accomplished when human resource plans and practices are focused on critical issues and problems to be solved. Attainment of strategic system ends is enhanced when human resource practices are focused on strategic intent, prioritized, and translated into plans of action capable of being assessed in terms of their outcome.

In sum, it can be said that careful attention to the purposive aspects of a school system may be viewed as the rippling or undulating effect on water agitated by a breeze or the impact of an object. It would be senseless, for example, to make decisions about recruitment, selection, induction, compensation, appraisal, and tenure of system members without connecting these planning components to the goals, purposes, and outcomes of the system. Here are some reasons to support the contention that purposeful planning is an empowerment tool for meeting some new as well as old human resource challenges.

- School system goals are arranged hierarchically.
- Goals define the final purpose and direction of members' activities.
- Goals create unit, system, and individual subgoals.
- Goals affect virtually all types of plans relating to system membership, from the quantity and quality of personnel to their recruitment, selection, and related processes identified in Figure 1.1.
- Goals provide the basis for coordinated effort.
- Failure to achieve individual objectives adversely affects unit and system objectives.
- Human beings are goal directed. Clearly established goals provide meaning for work and workers throughout the organization.
- Goals provide standards against which to evaluate not only system parts but the total system as well.
- Goals are conductive to self-regulated behavior.

• Goals set the tone of members' behavior.

• Goals are antecedents to human resource policies, procedures, rules, methods, and strategies.

• Organizational effectiveness is enhanced when individual, system, and unit goals are compatible.

Social Change, Education Renewal, and the Human Resource Function

In the dawn of a new millennium there are numerous concerns, expressed in various ways, regarding the quality of public education in the United States. Surprisingly, surveys have tended to blame the state of American education not on teachers, but on the state of American home and family life.[3]

As reported in various media, there are both achievements and problems in our schools. It is said that the only certainty in life is change, and education is no exception. One very important factor creating both problems and challenges in educational systems is contemporary social change in both the internal and external environments in which education is conducted. Figure 1.3 demonstrates that there are a host of external environmental factors over which educational institutions can exert little control but that pose extensive challenges for education reform in order to improve what is deemed to be wrong and unsatisfactory in both system and human resource management.

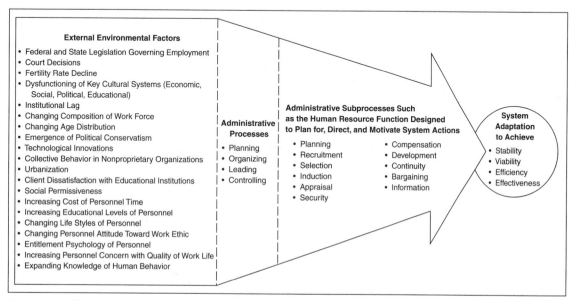

Figure 1.3   Illustration of the relationship among environmental factors, administrative processes and subprocesses, and school system adaptation.

Whether school officials favor or oppose emerging social developments is largely irrelevant. School administrators must operate within parameters not of their own making and not necessarily to their own liking. What is equally evident is that if the viewpoint is accepted that effective human resource management is the foundation of any well-managed organization, then educational institutions must face the reality of change by strengthening those entities designed to aid the system to move from where it is to where it should be.

Those responsible for managing school systems in the twenty-first century face diverse pressures. These include union activism, regulatory controls, personnel litigation, competition for qualified personnel, career development issues, modernizing information systems, and changes in the work, the worker, and the work environment. Tomorrow's school officials (regardless of system size) will face additional challenges as they address pressing social needs. Judging from current indications, the twenty-first century is shaping up as a time when educational systems will be forced to deal with problems that have extensive implications for the human resource function.

Demands for education reform in the years ahead, according to Sharp and Sharp, will involve ten changes relating to decentralization of power and shared decision making; increased demands on schools; ambivalent or hostile publics; altered school structures and programs; a diverse school populace with a variety of needs; the concept of choice in education; the further expansion of technology into schools; increased emphasis on member performance; and early retirement of teachers and administrators.[4]

These challenges are among many others cited in the educational reform literature. They provide a point of departure for (a) understanding the forces, factors, and conditions involved in giving direction to the human resource function; (b) emphasizing the importance of appreciating the nature, extent, and causes of workplace problems; and (c) establishing a supportive framework on which to fashion strategies, policies, and processes that enable the human resource function to contribute more effectively to a school system's established purposes.

Social Change and the Human Resource Function

Consideration of social change helps to illustrate that the challenges are compelling enough to warrant redesign of strategies directed to greater resource productivity. Among various criticisms leveled at school system management, one gaining credence is that traditional models have yet to develop comprehensive approaches to cope satisfactorily with changing internal and external environments. In large measure, present models fail to reflect the degree to which emerging developments are shaping the nature and needs of a human resource function whose force is vital to achieving organizational purpose. For example, changes in the internal and external environments have outstripped our full understanding of their organizational implications. Most current models have yet to bring together two elements critical to improving the human resource function. The first element consists of plans to cope with political, economic, and technological forces; regulatory provisions; unionism; generational culture; and an increasingly litigious society. The second element includes incorporation of new ideas, strategies, policies, and processes generated by academicians from a variety of disciplines, as well as those developed by practicing administrators. The above statements lend credence to a viewpoint expressed by Richard McAdams in an instructive review of school reform. He has this to say about the need for different models to engage the challenges of school reform:

> Repeated failed attempts at reform suggest that our standard approach to reform is fundamentally flawed. Substantive reform in a complex system such as a school district requires a level of sophistication and unity of purpose that is seldom attainable under our prevailing model of school governance. Moreover, leading educational researchers and theorists typically focus on narrow slices of the reality of school systems and ignore the relationships between their area of expertise and other relevant phenomena in school district operations.[5]

Successful reform, according to McAdams, requires an understanding of the interplay of five factors and the ability to integrate this knowledge into a systemic reform effort. These factors are leadership theory, local politics, and governance; state and national politics; organizational theory; and change theory. In capsule form, the characteristics of a school system that would be amenable to reform are an effective superintendent; a politically stable school district; a long-term relationship between the superintendent and the school board; ongoing state-level reform initiatives; understanding of change theory; and knowledge of school systems as loosely coupled systems.[6]

An important message can be derived from the foregoing discussion of social change and its relevance to the management of school systems and their human resources. The world is undergoing a sea change—globally, governmentally, technologically, socially, legally, economically, politically, morally, and ethically. Therefore, challenges are presented to all types of organizations, are highly complex, and will tend to require concentrated planning efforts over time. School systems in the United States are one of our most valued social institutions. If we are determined to pass on to future generations a better country and better school systems, and to achieve the general purposes of education, continued improvement of educational institutions—public, private, and parochial—is central to the task. In the section that follows, six dimensions of the human resource function will be discussed to provide foundation for understanding the challenges of social change, the need for a systems approach to substantive management of the interaction between processes and functions, and the need to forsake the myth that government must guarantee the right of all school systems to stay in business, regardless of ineptness and ineffectiveness.

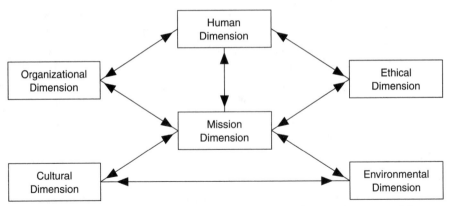

Figure 1.4   Dimensional elements that define and influence the design and operation of the human resource function.

Dimensions of the Human Resource Function

Any attempt to understand the scope and significance of the human resource function and its role in facilitating individual, group, and system effectiveness requires some understanding of its *dimensions.* The text that follows highlights key dimensions of the human resources function and their implications for designing, implementing, controlling, and correcting courses of action so that desirable results are achieved within the bounds of established standards.

Figure 1.4 identifies major dimensional elements that have an impact on the operation of the human resources function. It is clear that management of a school system involves many interdependent activities, governance of which is influenced by various forces, factors, and conditions. Because each of those forces has potential to affect organizational performance, each must be understood to appreciate fully how they pervade the decision-making process. In the context of decision making, the dimensions noted in Figure 1.4 can be considered as a framework for bringing about school system improvement in a mission-oriented and *ethically appropriate* manner. The first of these dimensions—the *system mission*—is the subject of the following discussion.

Mission Dimension

The **mission** of a school system identifies the purposes for which it has been created, its boundaries, and its activities, as well as its governmental and collateral purposes. The mission represents the foundation for providing an educational program and supporting services that will enhance the mental, moral, social, and emotional development of children, youth, and adults served by the school district. To illustrate, Joyce, Hersh, and McKibbin define system mission as follows:

The mission of the school can be defined by how it enters into the lives of students. Formal education is an organized attempt to enter into and change students' lives to help them develop the capacity to respond to reality in new ways. The primary task in selecting the mission is to identify how the school can enter the lives of students in order to change their responses to living in the world. Three domains that can be greatly enhanced by organized schooling include:

- Personal domain—personal capabilities such as creativity, intelligence, and motivation.
- Social domain—interactive social and economic skills.
- Academic domain—skills that comprise an academic subject area such as mathematics or English.[7]

To some educators, developing a mission statement to guide school system planning and selecting from among the multitude of underlying choices that must be made to coordinate diverse system activities represents a meaningless exercise in academic nonsense. As we examine mission statements, however, such as those in Figure 1.4, the mission is arguably the most basic property of a school system and one possessing considerable practical utility.

The mission is the system's overarching plan from which a set of subplans derive. These subplans include definition of the kinds of work to be done, division of labor, specification of the number and kinds of jobs needed and how they are structured, how resources are allocated, and articulation of system **values** and their content through such processes as personnel involvement, goal acceptance, and commitment, as well as member induction and socialization.

Mission-anchored Planning

Examination of various mission statements leads to the realization that they embody the potential for:

- Clarifying the core purpose of school system existence.
- Identifying services that the public expects the system to deliver in exchange for financial support.
- Providing a framework for judging the extent to which the mission is being realized.
- Creating a focus for defining the scope and limitations of the system's endeavors.
- Establishing a point of departure for deciding which key activities need to be performed.
- Deciding how financial, technical, human, and organizational resources will be allocated.
- Focusing on the end state rather than on the means of getting there.
- Developing a frame of reference by which controls are generated to implement the mission (strategies, policies, programs, projects, rules, and regulations).

Another important value of a clearly defined mission statement is that it serves as a boundary guide, determining what it should not do as well as stating what it intends to do. There is, for example, a hierarchy of laws, rules, and decisions in each state that have operational meaning for school systems. These include such elements as the state constitution; statutes; state board of education rules; department of education regulations; court decisions; and system policies, contracts, and rules.

Consequently, these governing influences eliminate discretionary consideration of certain decisions while also leaving important permissive decisions to the school system. A reality-based mission statement serves as an important contemporary base for defining the scope of acceptable choices regarding such current education issues as fitting religion into the public schools, sex education, preschool day care, pressures for extensive extracurricular programs, the extent of special education and pupil disability arrangements, various types of age-group plans, continuing education classes for pregnant teenagers, desegregation, bilingual education, and issues relating to cultural diversity, quality of work life, and restructuring the system.

Viewed in the context of this discussion, the mission plan is important because it provides a focal point for debating, discussing, and arriving at a consensus among system members concerning their expectations and beliefs, as well as to their expressed wishes about what the organization's common purpose should be.

For all of these considerations, the system mission, if clearly understood, can be conducive to internalizing commitment and even dedication to an explicit set of values. The school system is ill served when officials fail to appreciate the interactive potential of a system mission and to use it consistently as a standard in making decisions regarding transformation from the present to a desired state. Creation and application of a unified purpose through a mission statement is frequently hindered by short-term perspectives and obscured by the business at hand.

Human Dimension

The term *human resources* refers to those individuals who comprise the school staff and contribute to the operation of the school system. This staff includes members who vary in such characteristics as quantity and quality of position preparation; gender, age, and personality; work experiences, learning styles, work expectations, and assignments; temperaments, attitudes, aptitudes, and stress tolerance levels; and skills, interests, and motivation.

As we strive to learn about the human dimension and its significance for school system effectiveness, one actuality is worth recognizing: *individual performance is the core element fundamental to any organizational endeavor.* Individuals carry out the instructional process; decide what, when, where, how, and by whom school work is done; and decide which employees enter and leave the system.

In the following discussion, several aspects of the human dimension are included to illustrate how they fit into the context of meeting expectations of individuals, groups, and the system.

Humanistic Perspective

Humanism is defined as an expression of human values and a means of developing the free, responsible individual. Humanism is based on the incontestable principle of the inalienable and sacred rights of the individual.[8] For centuries the rights of the individual have been given compelling expression through (a) the Magna Carta (1215); (b) the Declaration of the Rights of Man and the Citizen adopted by the French National Assembly (1789); (c) the U.S. Bill of Rights and Amendments (1791); (d) the Emancipation Proclamation (1863); (e) the Women's Suffrage Act (1920); and (f) the Universal Declaration of Human Rights adopted by the United Nations General Assembly (1948).[9] How the force of these documents are relevant to shaping the human resources function of a school system is exemplified in Article 23 of the Universal Declaration of Human Rights.[10]

Article 23

1. Everyone has the right to work, to free choice of employment, to just and favorable conditions of work and to protection against unemployment.
2. Everyone, without any discrimination, has the right to equal pay for equal work.
3. Everyone who works has the right to just and favorable remuneration ensuring for himself and his family an existence of human dignity, and supplemented, if necessary, by other means of social protection.
4. Everyone has the right to form and to join trade unions for the protection of his interests.[11]

"Other means of social protection" currently include a canopy of safeguards for educators that have evolved over time. Illustrative are academic freedom; tenure; formal grievance and concern-complaint procedures; union contracts; personnel policies; codes of ethics; various local, state, and federal regulatory provisions; and the judicial system of the United States (see Chapter 2).

Figure 1.5 presents a personnel bill of rights whose intent is to define the human standards the system aspires to and intends to observe in the individual–organization relationship. It sets forth expectations the system has for its personnel and provides a foundation for maintaining modes of thought or action in which human interests, values, and dignity predominate.

If the ideals of human dignity and worth are to permeate organization culture, it is clear that they must have a significant role in the conduct of the human resource function. Adoption of and adherence to a set of guidelines that are ethically oriented is a way of committing system authorities to a position for enhancing individual–organization relationships. The intent of these guidelines is to provide guarantee to members that they will enjoy the same rights as position holders as they do as ordinary citizens. They create a framework for gaining commitment of individuals to pursue their personal, position, group, and organization goals. In addressing the value of the individual personality, the system extends to

- The right to give and receive feedback.
- The right of fair treatment in every area of work experience.
- The right to basic dignity, respect, and personal identity as a human being.
- The right to a style of management that enhances self-esteem and dignity as a person.
- The right to have the opportunity for a meaningful job for which they are qualified.
- The right to be consulted and involved in those decisions that relate to the employee's job.
- The right to be involved in social action programs.
- The right to set their own work goals.
- The right to set their own lifestyle.
- The right to be creative in the performance of the task and in the fulfillment of the daily goals.
- The right to fair compensation for their efforts.
- The right to work hard to develop in a way that enables them to meet new challenges.
- The right to be coached, assisted, and helped in the achievement of their goals.
- The right to an optimistic, trusting, and caring relationship in their work environment.

Figure 1.5　A personnel bill of rights.
Source: Reprinted, with permission of the publisher, from *Tough-Minded Leadership*, by Joe D. Batten © 1989 AMACOM, a division of the American Management Association, New York. All rights reserved.

the workplace the principles of fair and reasonable treatment in exchange for outcomes such as high productivity and improvement in work motivation.

Organizational Dimension

The formal organization, as represented in Figure 1.1, is one of the forces in the system infrastructure influencing the design and operation of the human resource function. Organization derives from the system mission, which in turn emanates from the external environment (state system of education). As considered in the following discussion, three basic elements of educational institutions include system purpose, leadership, and organization structure.

Purpose

As noted previously, a well-developed and extensively promulgated sense of common purpose is fundamental to unification of the talents, education, experience, and motivation of individuals and groups to achieve the goals of the system's existence. Statements of mission originate from various sources, including state education laws, state mandates requiring school systems to establish a mission statement, or strategic plans developed independently by local school districts.

Because a mission statement represents the system's strategic aim and provides a means of establishing outcomes it intends to achieve, the educational impact it intends to create, and client expectations it aims to satisfy, its articulation and communication are highly important. The following discussion focuses on the role of leadership in organizing the school system to carry out its mission effectively.

Leadership

A number of leadership elements enter implementation of the system mission, but the single most important requisite is deciding multiple issues on the basis of the extent to which they support and enhance values and expectations set forth in the mission statement. Because missions are stated in broad terms, they are frequently subjected to various interpretations by various interest groups. Securing mission acceptance and adhering to its sense of purpose, however, is fraught with issues and pressures from religious groups, politicians, and social activists to incorporate their interests within the framework of broad system purpose. Hard as it may be, every decision made by leadership needs to be viewed in terms of whether its impact will be instrumental in furthering the strategic intent of the mission statement.

In seeking to remedy selected negative circumstances within the system, leadership is constantly faced with challenges from both internal and external sources. In advancing school system interests as well as the status of the human resource function, these complex problems are among the more compelling to be noted:

• Finding solutions to problems associated with the growing diversity of the work force.
• Dealing with the question of whether the system's present priorities should be its basic priorities in the future.
• Resolving internal, external, and professional problems that are barriers to desired personnel performance.
• Deciding how best to employ structure, leadership styles, rewards, money, power, authority, recognition, incentives, and controls to improve the contributions of individuals and groups.
• Fostering union–system relations in such a manner that collective bargaining becomes a positive force for system unity and goal orientation.

Structure

What is important to remember is that to challenges such as the foregoing, few proven solutions are universally applicable in large, medium-sized, and small school systems. With these thoughts in mind, we will now consider ways in which the **organization structure,** an inescapable characteristic of organizations, is

Purposes	Every organization has a structure—a plan for linking positions and people to purposes. The purposes of an organization form the starting point of structural planning because all activities flow from purpose.
Activities	Activities are divided into positions; positions are grouped into major functions; functions are grouped into organizational units.
Superior–subordinate	Every structure has a hierarchy to coordinate organizational activity. The essence of a hierarchy is the superior–subordinate system in which certain positions are granted authority to direct the work of subordinate positions. The number of subordinates reporting to a superior is referred to as the span of control. Degrees of responsibility and authority are referred to as levels or layers of administration in the hierarchy.
Line and staff relationships	Most organizations have line and staff positions. Line positions are those that have the authority to initiate and carry through the basic activities of the organization that are essential to goal attainment. Collectively, line positions form the chain of command in an organization through which decisions are made, information communicated, and activities coordinated and controlled. Staff positions are those responsible for rendering advice, service, and counsel to individuals and groups within the organization.

Figure 1.6   Elements of an organization structure.

shaped to meet challenges posed in implementing the system mission in contemporary society.

Every organization has a structure—a plan for linking positions and people to purposes. The structure may be one that has been formally adopted by the board of education and described by organizational charts, position guides, and organizational manuals. Or it may be an informal structure, without documentation or evidence of any kind to describe its characteristics. In any case, organizations are composed of people who occupy positions, interact with each other, and are vitally concerned that they be compensated, both for responsibilities inherent in the work they perform and for their individual contributions to organizational effectiveness.

As illustrated in Figures 1.6 and 1.7, elements of a structure include purposes, people, activities, and relationships. One of the inferences that can be drawn from analysis of an organization structure is that its design and implementation involve individual and group participation through which system purpose is transformed into policies, functions, processes, activities, operations, and control mechanisms aimed at achieving perceived organizational outcomes. Another inference is that

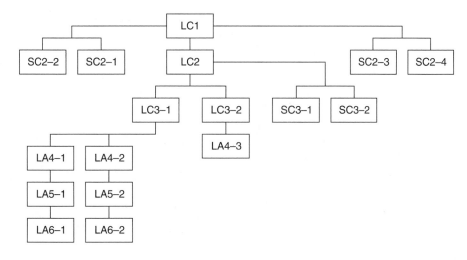

Central Administration

A. Line Positions

LC1	Superintendent
LC2	Deputy Superintendent: Instruction
LC3–1	Director: Secondary Education
LC3–2	Director: Elementary Education

B. Staff Positions

SC2–1	Assistant Superintendent: Business
SC2–2	Assistant Superintendent: Personnel
SC2–3	Assistant Superintendent: Research
SC2–4	Assistant Superintendent: Planning
SC3–1	Coordinator: Pupil services
SC3–2	Coordinator: Curriculum Services

Attendance Units

A. Line Positions

LA4–1	High School Principal
LA4–2	Middle School Principal
LA4–3	Elementary School Principal
LA5–1	Assistant Principal
LA5–2	Assistant Principal
LA6–1	Department Head
LA6–2	Department Head

Explanation of Position index

First Letter Indicates Line or Staff Position

    L = Line Position
    S = Staff Position

Second Letter Indicates Location of Position

    C = Central Administration
    A = Attendance Unit

First Number Indicates Structural Level of Position

1. Superintendent
2. Assistant Superintendent or Deputy Superintendent
3. Director or Coordinator
4. Principal
5. Assistant Principal

Second Number Indicates one of several similar positions at same level

Example: LA4–3 indicates a line position in an attendance unit at fourth level, elementary school principal.

Figure 1.7   Position index system designed to clarify school system organization structure and to develop a uniform system of titles.

there are compelling questions to be answered about the design of the organization structure such as these:

• What are the key activities that need to be performed to serve the interests of our students, human resources, regulatory agencies, community groups, parents, and the school system?
• What is the most appropriate way to group these key activities into positions?
• How shall positions be grouped into attendance units, departments, administrative and supervisory groups, support services, and temporary personnel requirements?
• What number of positions should be in the structure? What major tasks, authority relationships, and performance criteria should be established for each position?
• To what extent should the system be decentralized or centralized for decision-making purposes?
• What integration devices such as communication and coordination are most suitable for bringing together positions, position holders, and work units into a cohesive whole for system betterment?
• What chain of command should be established? How many levels of management are needed in large systems? A few? A moderate number?

Structural questions such as these force designers to focus on how best to utilize the structure, choosing from among the feasible options the ones most likely to improve individual, group, and system performance. One of the inescapable circumstances of school management in the late years of the twentieth century is that the complexity, as well as the politically and intellectually demanding tasks associated with school restructuring, require an appreciation of a host of factors that must be taken into consideration.

Despite all the criticism about school system structures that has surfaced in the long-running debate about restructuring schools, especially regarding hierarchies, levels of management, close supervision, and top-down decision making, some mode of procedure, of fusing human and nonhuman resources into a cohesive effort toward purpose attainment, is inescapable. An arrangement of authority is essential to implement system improvement through direction and coordination. Without a chain of command, power becomes unbridled.

Controls

Control mechanisms are essential to any and all forms of human resource planning. One compelling reason is that every plan that the school system initiates, and allocates resources for, should have built-in means for judging its effectiveness. There are numerous other justifications for control mechanisms, such as preventing and correcting deviations from standards; curbing turnover, absenteeism, sick leave, and other benefit abuses; and minimizing behaviors that are antiorganizational, self-serving, defiant, rebellious, or in violation of the system's code of ethics.

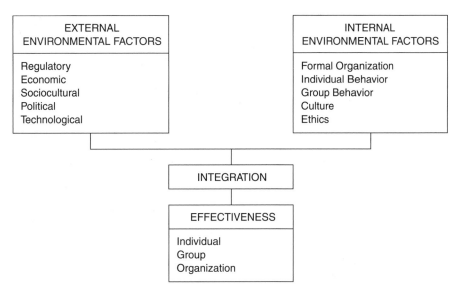

Figure 1.8   Environmental interactions that influence performance effectiveness.

Two kinds of controls should be mentioned: system and functional. System controls are focused on the total organization and include policies, position descriptions, strategic plans, and mission statements. Functional controls pertain to those measures that guide the human resource function, such as the 11 human resource processes identified in Figure 1.1.

Employing this discussion as background for a broad view of the organization structure, the reader is advised that each of the remaining chapters contains content relating to the significance of the structure within the various processes of the human resources function.

Environmental Dimension

School systems are created by and intended to serve the society that sustains them. Those persons performing or aspiring to managerial roles in school systems need an effective working knowledge of the relationship of the environmental dimension to the operation of the human resource function. Consequently, a model for understanding the interaction of the school system environment and its influence on individual, group, and organizational behavior is presented in Figure 1.8. This schematic portrayal of the environmental dimension consists of two types of environments: external and internal. To give the reader more specific insights into the pervasive influence of environmental forces on social, organizational, functional, and position-holder objectives, the following discussion provides a brief summary of their significance.

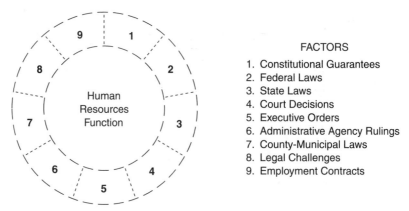

Figure 1.9   *Regulatory environment of the human resources function.*

External Environment

Much of the evolution of the human resource function, in both the public and private sectors, has been brought about more by the **external environment** than by practitioners. Major external forces that affect the human resource function have been grouped arbitrarily into five clusters (as outlined in Figure 1.8) in order to establish a framework for analyzing the complex interaction between environmental factors and the human resource of a school system. Environmental–organizational interaction suggests that there are constraints, forces, and options to which a system must respond in order to achieve stability and viability. The human resource function plays a vital role in helping the system to live within economic strictures, meet legal mandates, honor contractual obligations, deal with pressures of special-interest groups, adapt to emerging technologies, and uphold ethical standards while maintaining centrality of purpose. Striking this balance requires considerable organizational effort. For this reason, the aims of the discussion that follows are to (a) note the political, economic, technological, and environmental forces referred to earlier about the human resource function; (b) indicate the importance of understanding their potential for strategic and operational planning for human resource (to be discussed in Chapter 2); and (c) point out the organizational significance of forging proactive personnel policies in response to evolving social phenomena such as changing environmental patterns, educational retrenchments, an environment with fewer resources, and evolving ethics of the work force.

Regulatory factor.   Education in the United States operates within a framework of regulatory controls of varying degrees. As indicated in Figure 1.9, these elements include the Constitution; federal laws; state, county, and municipal laws; court decisions; executive orders; administrative agency rulings; legal challenges; and employment contracts. It is generally agreed that provisions governing employment in both the public and private sectors have far-reaching influence on the operation of the human resource function. Each state system controls the school curriculum and supporting services, who shall teach, how schools are financed, and school board policy-making authority. In addition, there are regulatory controls governing taxation limitations, salaries, benefits, collective bargaining, performance appraisal, tenure, grievance procedures, and budgetary requirements.

This **regulatory environment** extends to the federal government and the judicial system, which influence virtually every aspect of the human resource function, including discrimination, hiring practices, compensation, benefits, and unjust dismissal. Beckham and Zirkel, in their analysis and review of legal issues in public school employment, indicate that the relationship between public schools and their employees is one of the most frequently litigated aspects of American education. Prominent employment disputes include discrimination, First Amendment rights, due process, collective bargaining, performance appraisal, dismissal, and staff reductions.[12]

A 1988 study of United States Supreme Court decisions affecting education brings into focus the regulatory influence on employee rights and responsibilities. Decisions relate to compensation, residency requirements, strikes, age of retirement, due process, right to teach, involuntary transfer, leaves of absence, continuing education, loyalty oaths, union-related matters, tenure, contract renewal, and at-will dismissal.[13] More indications of the regulatory environment for the human resource function are provided by Zirkel. In a review of state legislation, related policies and guidelines, and the law on teacher evaluation, the author concludes that the legal boundaries for performance evaluation of professional educators in public schools are much broader than the typical evaluator realizes.[14]

Because school systems operate within an environment external to their existence, and over which they exercise little control, knowledge of the present environment, especially its direction and organizational impact, is an essential aspect of human resource management. In addition to the regulatory factor, there are four other factors noted in Figure 1.8 (economic, sociocultural, political, and technological) that affect conditions in the workplace. Following are some indicators illustrating the external environmental impact on people, positions, and direction of the human resources affairs.

Economic factor. Virtually all funds needed to operate a public school system are derived from public education policy in the external environment. About four-fifths of the annual school budget is devoted to system member requirements. Economic conditions shift rapidly with governmental actions, which in turn influence the extent to which school systems are able to realize organizational and human resource goals.

Sociocultural factor. Included in the growing challenges facing managers of the human resource function are those stemming from a combination of social and cultural elements. Worthy of note are such matters as political correctness, pressures for religious accommodation, drug/alcohol testing, AIDS, taxpayer resistance to the increasing costs of education, changing values of system members, assaults on school personnel, privacy rights, the Family Rights Act of 1991, employees speaking out, and external demands for school reform.

Political factor.   Numerous groups in the external environment (political, religious, ethnic, antitax, reformist, business, and governmental) have the potential to influence public education policy regarding school reform, discrimination, desegregation, health care, sexual harassment, gay rights, bilingual education, teacher certification, vouchers, school choice, and so forth. For example, a Pennsylvania school district, ending a dispute with its teachers' union, voted to provide health care coverage for same-sex domestic partners of school district employees, obeying an order from the American Arbitration Association based on the point that the system's equal opportunity policy forbids discrimination because of sexual orientation. One taxpayer noted that the action "used taxpayer money to make social policy."[15] Among the foremost issues in recent local, state, and federal elections (crime, taxation, health, and schools) is the crisis in public education.

Technological factor.   *Technology,* in terms of the human resource function, refers to the sum of ways in which the school system attains the material means needed to carry out the processes, mechanisms, and techniques it employs to deliver educational services and to extend its potential for doing so. Among the emerging challenges for the human resource function created by the advent of modern technology and the quickening pace of its development are these pressing agenda items:

• *Technology assimilation*—Ensuring that technology is available for and used to best advantage by the system and its members.
• *Comprehensive information system*—A modern, systematic plan designed to acquire, store, maintain, protect, retrieve, and communicate data in a valid and accurate form, employing computer and noncomputer approaches.
• *Staff development*—With advances in electronic technology, a critical shortage of computer-literate support staff has developed. Programs for assisting personnel, especially those in the temporary category, are necessary to acquire the skills needed to satisfy burgeoning demands for information.
• *Office operations*—An information-driven school system requires application of new technology to increase the efficiency and effectiveness of office operations.
• *Computer applications*—Examples of computer applications to the human resource function include recruitment and selection tracking, attendance tracking, training and development management, position control, compensation (including benefits), regulatory adherence, payroll, forms management, record center operations, and computer-assisted instruction.

Internal Environment

Internal as well as external forces affect the human resource function in overt and covert ways. Interaction of these influences creates administrative challenges, especially concerning their impact on individual and group behavior, as well as the need for strategies to cope with the inexorable tendency toward environmental change. Among the key of the **internal environment** factors in Figure 1.8, the five that follow are noteworthy.

Formal organization.   The formal organization of a school system, identified in Figure 1.8 as one of the forces influencing the design and operation of the human resource function, derives from the system, which in turn emanates from the external environment. These forces also include the organizational structure, purposes of the school system, work (roles) to be performed, and technology for performing the work such as curriculum, instructional system, teaching-learning tools, and facilities.

Individual and group behavior.   Dealing with personnel problems in the workplace is something all administrators have to do. How it is done may result in productive, nonproductive, or counterproductive behaviors. Individual and group behaviors are two forces that shape human issues in every organization and give such matters system, legal, social, and economic significance. Implications for those responsible for dealing with behavioral problems are considerable. The following points are relevant:

• Previously, it was mentioned that modern school systems employ personnel whose mental, physical, intellectual, and emotional characteristics vary extensively. Approaches for dealing with human diversity involve a system orientation to understand the psychological makeup of individuals so that the underlying needs of the system and its members can be accommodated.

• The leadership style employed to relate to varying personalities depends upon characteristics of the leader, the followers, and the situation. These factors influence which of several leadership styles (directive, participative, free-rein, or a combination of these) will enhance personnel cooperation and performance.[16]

• Grouping is an integral component of any organization. Groups have been categorized as formal (command and task) and informal (interest and friendship). Unions are accorded formal status because they are officially and legally organized.

• Work involved in implementing the school system's mission is divided into segments or units to which work groups are assigned. Work is usually organized by functions (finance, human resource); programs (preschool, elementary, intermediate, secondary, postsecondary); geography (school attendance units); departments (mathematics); and committees (standing, such as board of education finance committee).

• Productive groups share several characteristics: members tend to make valuable contributions to group effort; formal and informal goals of the group are achieved; group members share a sense of satisfaction and high morale; and productive groups have an appropriate mix of skills and background, an effective group structure, and a good communication process.[17]

- Work expectations are created not only by the individual and the organization but also by group norms, standards, structure, and goals.

The reader should note that Figure 1.8 includes two internal environmental elements, namely **culture** and **ethics,** which are linked to group behavior. Such terms as *norms, values, sanctions, disciplinary action, behavior patterns, shared meanings,* and *habits of thinking* are commonly used to describe group and organization culture. Ethics of individuals, groups, and organizations are intertwined with group culture because they involve concerns about rights, obligations, expectations, and justice. Leadership implications of culture and ethics are several and form the basis for the sections that follow.

Culture Dimension

Every school system has a culture—a set of interrelated values and priorities, norms and expectations, and ideas and ideals. Norms, according to Smither, serve a variety of useful functions, such as (a) establishing standards and shared expectations that provide a range of acceptable behaviors for group members; (b) providing guidelines for unsocialized individuals to fit into the ongoing group; and (c) establishing standards for behavior that facilitate interaction between members and are a means of identifying with one's peers.[18]

The culture of an organization encompasses many factors and forces, and according to Ellis, most of them are transitory or intangible. Examples include changing values, social trends, authority, needs, rights, obligations, and expectations of both system and its personnel groupings.[19]

One of the important questions about school system culture is, What is its relationship and significance to the human resource function? One response is that to a considerable extent culture is tied to the impact of change in the workplace. There are shifting human values and changes in the demographics of the work force (in ethnic background, in cultural diversity, and in graying of the instructional cadre).

There is another set of forces that are culture laden with the potential for affecting individual and group behavior. This category includes regulatory agencies, community groups, boards of education, school management, unions, standing committees, work units (such as elementary schools), and support groups (maintenance, operation, clerical, food service, security, and transportation). In one way or another, each of these system entities and their constituents is affected by changes that have personal, organizational, legal, state, national, and international causes.

Culture and Need Satisfaction

The need to balance organizational imperatives with individual and group expectations has always been a challenging managerial endeavor. Contemporary forces of change have rendered traditional approaches to resolving workplace problems irrelevant.

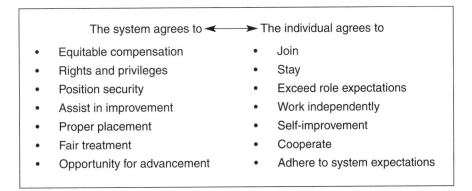

Figure 1.10   Conceptualization of the employment exchange theory.

One way of viewing employment in a school system is as an exchange between the individual and the organization in which each gets something in return for giving something. Figure 1.10 conceptualizes the exchange theory of employment (referred to in the literature as a *psychological* or *social contract*).[20] The psychological or social contract is unwritten, but it is constantly in operation as the means through which both parties seek to have certain conditions of work satisfied.

In summary, both workers and management recognize that job satisfaction hinges on *nonmonetary* rewards, as well as the actual paycheck. So, smart managers offer those intangibles as relatively cost-free incentives to maintain a happy, productive work force.

Cultural factors in the human resource function that can be changed by those in leadership positions include envisioning, bringing to life, reinforcing, rewarding, and embedding constructive behavior. Beyond helping members to understand their culture, creating means to enhance its positive features aids in neutralizing tendencies toward system instability, and breakdown of standards and values, as well as alienation and uncertainty that come from a lack of purpose or ideals. A set of indicators derived from several human resource processes creating and managing culture include:

- *Induction*—Develop socialization programs focusing on the system culture.
- *Appraisal*—Change the traditional performance culture from a measurement process to a communication process.
- *Planning*—Focus on neutralizing change-restraining forces.
- *Justice*—Maintain the justice system for prompt and effective treatment of problems involving personnel rights and responsibilities.
- *Recruitment*—Locate and attract candidates suitable by nature to accept, commit, and further the desired system culture.

Cultural aspects inherent in each of the eleven personnel processes will be considered in succeeding chapters as they pertain to understanding and nurturing a proactive cultural foundation.

Values	Ethics
• define the individual	• translate values into action
• are constant	• are changing
• are internally derived	• are situationally determined
• are concerned with virtue	• are concerned with justice
• are general	• are highly specific
• are stated morally	• are judged there or absent
• are judged good or bad	• set boundaries for appropriate behavior
• set priorities	

Figure 1.11   The relationship between values and ethics.
Source: H. B. Karp and Bob Abramms, "Doing the Right Thing," in Mary F. Cook, Editor, *The Human Resources Yearbook, 1993–1994 Edition* (Englewood Cliffs, NJ: Prentice-Hall Inc., 1993), 8–19. © 1993, reprinted by permission of the publisher, Prentice Hall/A Division of Simon & Schuster.

Ethics Dimension

It is an inescapable fact that decisions give life to a school system and that most decisions are permeated by ethics. Consequently, a broader understanding of ethical behavior in the workplace, especially as it applies to the human resource function, is an important step in dealing with personnel problems and enhancing system betterment.

Ethics, according to a dictionary definition, refers to the rightness or wrongness of certain actions, and to the goodness or badness of the motives and ends of such actions. What is or is not ethical, however, is a matter of personal interpretation.

Three characteristics of the relationship between values and ethics, as depicted in Figure 1.11, are that they are value driven, action oriented, and situational.

Ethics and Decision Making

For those who run school systems, including board members, superintendents, principals, supervisors, department heads, and other instructional leaders, the ethics dimension has some clear implications. The relationship between ethical sensitivity and the human resource function is an intimate one, as the following concepts demonstrate.

• Leadership is involved with decisions about such matters as organizational purpose, goals, objectives, strategies, and their implications.
• Ethical considerations, when factored into the decision-making process, uphold human dignity as a contributor to positive personal and organizational behavior.
• Decisions made by leaders have a direct impact on both the internal and external environments.

• The task orientation of individuals and groups is influenced by ethical sensitivity to their expectations, aspirations, well- being, conditions of work, compensation equity, and the reward system.

• Decisions and power are inseparable. Those who have authority to make decisions are able to exert control over others, either directly through position power or indirectly through various forms of expertise.

From the foregoing points, it can be assumed that power to decide can influence member behavior. As we examine the eleven personnel processes in forthcoming chapters, attention will be focused in part on decisions with ethical connotations, especially in such areas as recruitment, selection, appraisal, compensation, development, and justice.

Exercise of authority through the decision-making process includes consideration of its ethical implications. Some of the reasons for providing a foundation for judgments based on organizational values and implemented by ethical actions will now be considered.

Guidelines for Ethical Standards

It is generally assumed that educators and educational systems are the principal guardians of the nation's culture. Enhancement of this assumption by a school system requires various underlying strategies for strengthening and maintaining standards of ethical behavior among those in its employ. Following are some suggestions.

Social change and ethics issues.   Social change and its evolving attitudes have brought the matter of ethical conduct in public organizations to the forefront of leadership concerns. Emerging regulatory plans and practices, the power of human resources to contest management actions, and the changing composition of school staffs are illustrative of forces influencing greater attention to policies and other plans that define ethical standards to aid personnel in understanding and avoiding unethical situations.

Identification of system ethical issues.   Reports of unethical behavior by school employees are common. One action for dealing with personnel misconduct is identification of the presence, nature, and extent of current unethical situations. In brief, leadership in resolving unethical practices requires the presence of an information base for planning the system's approach to resolving behavioral dilemmas.

Ethical standards.   Ethical standards to which a school system is committed need to be clearly and extensively communicated. Mechanisms for this purpose include personnel handbooks, policy manuals, codes of ethics (Figure 1.12), adherence to the psychological contract, enforcement provisions governing unethical behavior, and staff development programs for all categories of personnel. Such approaches are among those aimed at communicating, interpreting, and enforcing

- Maintain the highest standards of professional and personal conduct.
- Strive for personal growth in the field of human resource management.
- Support the Society's goals and objectives for developing the human resource management profession.
- Encourage my employer to make the fair and equitable treatment of all employees a primary concern.
- Strive to make my employer profitable both in monetary terms and through the support and encouragement of effective employment practices.
- Instill in the employees and the public a sense of confidence about the conduct and intentions of my employer.
- Maintain loyalty to my employer and pursue its objectives in ways that are consistent with the public interest.
- Uphold all laws and regulations relating to my employer's activities.
- Refrain from using my official positions, either regular or volunteer, to secure special privilege, gain or benefit for myself.
- Maintain the confidentiality of privileged information.
- Improve public understanding of the role of human resource management.

Figure 1.12   Code of Ethics for the Society for Human Resource Management.
Source: Reprinted by permission of the Society for Human Resource Management, Alexandria, VA.

ethical and legal behavioral standards that will lead to emergence of organizational settings conducive to improving workplace behavior.

Categories of ethical concern.   Issues of ethical concern for the school system include obligations as well as various kinds of responsibilities. For example, system and member obligations, such as those following, have the inherent potential for unethical conduct when behavioral obligations and responsibilities are unfulfilled:

- Member ethical obligations to the school system.
- System ethical obligations to its members.
- Teacher ethical obligations to students.
- System ethical obligations to the public.
- Personnel obligations to the profession.
- System and personnel obligations to adhere to the psychological contract.
- System and member commitment to professional employment practices.
- System and member obligations and responsibilities to *claimants* in the external environment such as taxpayers, creditors, suppliers, governments, unions, accrediting agencies, and recruitment sources (colleges and universities, other school systems, and placement agencies).

It is worth noting here that system indifference and inattention to, as well as nonenforcement of, behavioral rules generate organization disrupters that undermine cultural stability and the ability to carry out the system's mission effectively. Some examples of common behavioral dysfunctions are engaging in off- duty crime, covering up discriminatory employment practices, condoning gender discrimination, engaging in sexual harassment or sexual relationships with students, abetting employment intrusion by political interests, lateness and absenteeism, and abuse of leave and workers' compensation benefits.

Human Resources and Otherness in the Workplace

Of all of the problems in managing the human resource function in the twenty-first century, none are more formidable, and none show fewer signs of abating in intensity, than those posed by **affirmative action, equal employment opportunity,** and workplace diversity variables. Figure 1.13 indicates that the legal context includes a variety of forces shaping the environment in which decision making concerning the human resource function takes place. Other factors over which the school system has little or no control include unionism, cultural differences, emerging technology, and human diversity (educational levels, race, sex, age, changing attitudes, diverse viewpoints, racial and ethnic composition of communities). To this list should be added deep-seated prejudices and biases in regional, social, economic, religious, and political interests. It is important to note here, however, that the school system does play a part in dealing with diverse forms of workplace behavior not generally subject to antidiscrimination laws (progressive discipline and abrasive, or malcontented employees).

In effect, environmental forces, both internal and external, with which management must contend are ever present, such as political, social, community, regulatory, governmental, and union forces. Their impact must be anticipated, and approaches must be developed to act accordingly.

As forthcoming chapters will demonstrate, discrimination is most likely to occur in the areas of personnel acquisition, continuation, and employment termination. A secondary area for unequal treatment of personnel include performance appraisal, justice, compensation, staff development, and collective bargaining.

Ethical implications for managing diversity in the workplace and ensuring fair and equal treatment of personnel involve adherence to ethical concepts of rights, obligations, and justice. Forthcoming chapters will explore these concepts.

The human resource approach to resolving improper conduct by members of the system, according to Levesque, is to recognize and use three action stages:

• *Prevention*—To work toward proactive measures that resolve potential problems before they occur.
• *Control*—To establish specific, realistic, and understandable standards that reinforce mutual needs between employees and the organization and thereby reduce the likelihood of serious discontinuities.

Affirmative Action

- *Definition.* Actions designed and taken by an organization to eliminate present effects of past discrimination practices in employment and education.
- *Employment implications.* The entire span of human resource processes is affected in some way by affirmative action and equal employment legislation.
- *Legal vulnerability.* Policies designed to carry out affirmative action plans have been and continue to be subject to legal challenge by arbitrators, compliance agencies, and courts. Demands of affirmative action must be reconciled with those of seniority. Costs of staff development for new immigrants must be considered when education budgets are at risk.
- *Human resource approach.* Reviewing personnel policies and operational practices for potential discriminatory effect. The strategic system aim is to employ any individual who demonstrates desired abilities. Employment and retention decisions should be in keeping with hiring and retaining people who can and should be doing the work in terms of achieving strategic results.

Equal Employment Opportunity

- *Definition.* Plans to prevent employers from discriminating against any employee or job applicant because of color, race, religion, national origin, sex, physical or mental handicap, or age.
- *Employment implications.* Equal employment laws have considerable impact on the human resource function and how it is managed. These laws compel the system to address societal, legislative, and organizational objectives through various processes of the human resource function.
- *Legal vulnerability.* Crucial personnel decisions subject to legal vulnerability include discrimination in any form, such as employment at will, tenure, behavioral conduct, just cause termination, privacy violations, performance appraisal, and leave return rights.
- *Human resource approach.* Management must gain full understanding of discrimination laws and their effect on employment practices. This avoids barriers to employment applicants.

Employee Diversity

- *Definition.* Composition of a heterogeneous workforce in terms of differences in position, race, ethnicity, national origin, gender, age, values, religion, pregnancy, language skills, disabilities, aspirations, personal idiosyncracies, and lifestyles. Diversity management involves plans to resolve workplace problems relating to staff improvement, organizational conformity, and behavioral dysfunction.
- *Employment implications.* Employers set and abide by reasonable standards of conduct. This requires structuring of human resource plans that enhance individual behavior conducive to organizational aims.
- *Legal vulnerability.* Diversity management has legal vulnerability pertinence but focuses more on discretionary operational matters such as behavioral standards and dysfunctions as they apply to all system personnel. It differs from equal employment opportunity and affirmative action in that compliance is more an organization than a statutory concern.
- *Human resource approach.* Managing diversity in the workplace requires management and employee understanding of what diversity management means, why it is to be valued, and what practices and policies are needed to achieve strategic results.

Figure 1.13   Characteristics of three human resource variables: affirmative action, equal employment opportunity, and employee diversity.

• *Correction*—To initiate timely, effective, and appropriate measures when deviations arise that might otherwise create a detrimental organizational consequence.[21]

In sum, there is considerable support for the proposition that prevalence of moral rectitude contributes to the desired image, wellness, and effective operation of the entire school system. Establishment of a set of rules governing member behavior, and utilization of a model for applying performance standards, are indicative of approaches needed in the quest for rightness of principle or practice in the workplace.

Review and Preview

One of the main purposes of studying the human resource function of a school system is to develop a broader understanding of the forces, factors, conditions, and circumstances that shape its role as a contributor to organizational effectiveness. The intent of this chapter is to convey the viewpoints that follow.

Evolving models of the human resource function extend well beyond traditional tasks of record keeping, social work, and collective bargaining. Today's designs consider the human resource function to be a vital unit in any organization. The organized and unified array of system parts interact through human performance to establish a productive public institution. The eleven personnel processes within the human resource function (Figure 1.1) are linked to the organization infrastructure (Figure 1.4). Dimensions of the infrastructure include system mission, human resources, regulatory requirements, environmental factors, and ethical presence.

The chapter that follows examines the planning process as a component of the human resource function and its linkage to the elements in the organizational infrastructure referred to in this chapter.

Social change and educational reform movements brought about by a combination of sociological, political, economic, regulatory, technological, and human resource forces require changes in models for enhancing the potential of the function to clarify problems and to develop plans for their solution.

Discussion Questions

1. Since school systems are influenced by the internal and external environments, respond to the following questions:

a. Can you cite three examples, drawn from your personal experience, of the influence of the external environment on a school system?

b. Can you cite three examples of the influence of the internal environment on a school system?

c. Can you cite three examples of the influence of the external environment on a school system?

2. What does the term *technology factor* mean to you? How does this factor affect the operation of a school system?

3. Courts interpret laws and how they will be enforced. This type of law is referred to as *case law*. Give three illustrations of case law applicable to school systems (e.g., sex discrimination, seniority).

4. Give three illustrations of *ethical* issues in the workplace and their implications for the human resource function (e.g., falsification of records).

5. In what manner and to what extent does the organizational structure of a school system influence its efficiency? Its effectiveness? What factors should be considered in designing a school system's organization structure?

Notes

1. George S. Counts, *Education and American Civilization* (New York: Bureau of Publications, Teachers College, Columbia University, 1952), 311–430.

2. John I. Goodlad, *What Schools Are For* (Bloomington, IN: Phi Delta Kappa Educational Foundation, 1994), Chapter 3.

3. Ellen Graham, "What's Wrong—and Right—With Our Schools." "American Opinion," *Wall Street Journal* (March 14, 1997), R1.

4. Helen M. Sharp and William L. Sharp, "Preparing for the Future in the Next Stage," *National Forum of Educational Administration and Supervision Journal* 13, 1 (1995), 25–33; B. W. Nelan, "How the World Will Look in 50 Years," *Time* Magazine, Special Issue: *Beyond the Year 2000* (Fall 1992), 36–38.

5. Richard P. McAdams, "A Systems Approach to School Reform," *Phi Delta Kappan* 79 (October 1997), 138.

6. Ibid., 139–142.

7. Bruce R. Joyce, Richard M. Hirsh, and Michael McKibbon, *The Structure of School Improvement* (New York: Longman Publishing Company, 1983).

8. Grolier, Inc. (Danbury, CT: 1990), Author, Vol. 7, 415.

9. *The World Book Encyclopedia* (Chicago: World Book Company, 1990), Vol. 9, 415.

10. Ibid.

11. Ibid.

12. Mary M. McCarthy, "Discrimination in Employment," in Joseph A. Beckham and Perry A. Zirkel, eds., *Legal Issues in Public School Employment* (Bloomington, IN: Phi Delta Kappa, 1983), 45–47.

13. Perry A. Zirkel and Sharon Richardson, *A Digest of Supreme Court Decisions Affecting Education* (Bloomington, IN: Phi Delta Kappa Educational Foundation, 1989), chapters 4–6.

14. Perry A. Zirkel, *The Law of Teacher Evaluation* (Bloomington, IN: Phi Delta Kappa Educational Foundation, 1996).

15. *Philadelphia Inquirer* (October 22, 1997), R1–R4.

16. John M. Ivancevich and Michael Matteson, *Organizational Behavior and Management*, 3rd ed. (Homewood, IL: Richard D. Irwin, Inc., 1993), 451.

17. Dennis Middlemist and Michael A. Hitt, *Organizational Behavior* (St. Paul, MN: West Publishing Company, 1988), Chapters 3 and 4.

18. Robert D. Smither, *The Psychology of Work* (New York: Harper & Row, 1988), 363.

19. Robert J. Ellis, "Using Human Resources Programs to Support Cultural Change," in Mary F. Cook, ed., *The Human Resources Yearbook, Inc.,* (Upper Saddle River, NJ: Prentice-Hall, Inc., 1993–1994), 2.2.

20. For a detailed treatment of the psychological contract, see Mary Coli Meyer, "Motivation," in William R. Tracey, ed., *Human Resources Management and Development* (New York: AMACOM, 1995), 201–204.

21. Joseph O. Levesque, *The Human Resource Problem Solvers Handbook* (New York: McGraw-Hill, Inc., 1991), III. 3.81.

Supplementary Reading

Arenofsky, J. "Information Age: "How It Affects the Way We Work." *Career World* 25 (March 1997), 6–11.

Ball, Carl G.; and Steven Goldman. "Improving Education's Productivity." *Phi Delta Kappan* 79, 3 (1979), 228–233.

Consortium on Productivity in the Schools. *Using What We Have to Get the Schools We Need.* New York: The Consortium, 1995.

"Defining Affirmative Action." *Wall Street Journal* (April 1998), A18.

Digh, Patricia. "Coming to Terms with Diversity." *HRMagazine* 43, 12 (November 1998), 117–120.

Education Commission of the States. *The New American Urban School District.* Denver: The Commission, 1993.

Education Commission of the States. *Education Accountability Systems in the Fifty States.* Denver: The Commission, 1993.

Galphin, Timothy. "Connecting Culture to Organizational Change." *HRMagazine* 40 (June 1995), 98–104.

Greene, Robert J. Culturally Compatible HR Strategies." *HRMagazine* 40 (June 1995), 115–123.

Heller, Robert; and Tim Hindle. "Changing Culture." In *Essential Manager's Manual.* New York: DK Publishing, Inc., 1998, 742–747.

Kaplan, Robert D. "Travels Into America's Future." *Atlantic Monthly* 282, 2 (August 1998), 37–61.

Kreyche, G. F. "Public Education's Intractable Problems." *USA Today* 126 (July 1997), 82.

Kritsonis, William. "The Psychology of Leadership in Educational Institutions." *Record* 17, 172 (1997), 11–14.

Ladenson, R. R. *Ethics in the American Workplace: Policies and Decisions.* Horsham, PA: LRP Publications, 1996.

Leider, Richard J. *The Power of Purpose.* San Francisco: Berrett-Koehler Publishers, Inc., 1997.

Morgan, Gareth. *Images of Organization.* San Francisco: Berrett-Koehler Publishers, Inc., 1998.

Pell, Terence J. "Does 'Diversity' Justify Quotas? The Courts Say No." *Wall Street Journal* (November 24, 1998), A22.

Schuler, Randall S. *Managing Human Resources,* 6th ed. Cincinnati: South Western College College Publishing, 1998.

Shlaes, Amity. "The Saving Grace of School Reform." *Wall Street Journal* (February 6, 1997), A14.

Sheridan, J. E. "Organization Culture and Employee Retention." *Academy of Management Journal* 36 (1992), 1036–1056.

Shields, Patrick M.; and Michael Knapp. "The Promise and Limits of School-Based Reform." *Phi Delta Kappan* 61 (1979), 288–294.

Steinhauser, Sheldon. "Is Your Corporate Culture in Need of an Overhaul?" *HRMagazine* 43, 8 (July 1998), 87–91.

Stutz, Jonathan; and Randy Massengale. "Measuring Diversity Initiatives." *HRMagazine* 42 (December 1997), 85–90.

Terry, C. C., ed. *Dictionary of Principles in the Workplace.* Chicago: DeAcklen-Terry Publishing Company, 1990.

Time Magazine Special Issue 3. *The New Face of America: How Immigrants are Shaping the World's First Multicultural Society* (Fall 1993).

2

Strategic Planning and the Human Resource Function

CHAPTER OBJECTIVES

Introduce the concept of strategic planning and discuss its relationship to the human resource function.

Emphasize the importance of developing system visions, values, goals, ideas, and initiatives to implement human resource plans.

Highlight key stages of the strategic planning sequence, major components, and their linkage.

Stress that strategic plans are temporary, subject to changes as internal and external challenges emerge.

Gain greater understanding of the need to motivate all personnel, from the top to the bottom of the system, to perform their roles effectively in the interests of strategic expectations.

CHAPTER TERMS

Effectiveness	Policy
Goal structure	Position guide
Information system	Program structure
Organization chart	System
Organization manual	Work analysis
Organization structure	

Contrivance of Organizational Change

This chapter introduces the reader to the broad framework around which a human resource planning system is developed to influence personnel behavior toward achievement of system, work unit, and individual goals. The focal point of analysis is the family of plans employed to make the function an effective part of the entire school system. In subsequent chapters, the primary intent of each of the human resource processes is to emphasize plans for employing people most efficiently and effectively in the pursuit of the system's strategic goals.

Every school system, regardless of its size or pattern of organization, performs a human resource function. People must be recruited, selected, inducted, compensated, appraised, directed, developed, disciplined, motivated, counseled, and accorded those rights accruing to individuals who perform organization work in modern society. These tasks are ongoing and pervasive, and are performed whether their responsibility is allocated to a work unit within the central administration or assigned to various system administrators. In addition to solving human problems that daily confront every kind of organization, executives must be concerned with change—with anticipation of problems, issues, and challenges that emerge from both internal and external environments and are apt to affect system strategy. Devising plans to deal with environmental conditions becomes a critical strategic element.

Throughout history the concept of systematic plans for achieving goals has been an intellectual luxury, generally without relevance to ordinary affairs of people and nations. During the last half of the twentieth century, however, it has become increasingly apparent that the complexities of organizational and ordinary life are so pressing that planning is no longer a luxury but a practical necessity. Instances of the lack of planning in educational institutions relative to the human resource function are abundant. For example:

- Failure to incorporate the function effectively within the total organization structure.
- Absence of administrative rationality in planning for human resources.
- Failure to link organizational expectations to human needs.
- Viewing personnel as ends rather than means.

- Failure to staff the function adequately (numerically and qualitatively).
- Failure to develop accurate and realistic staffing specifications.
- Failure to maintain aggressive, imaginative, and well-designed recruiting programs.
- Creation of psychic anxieties in personnel as a result of ineffective ideologies, plans, procedures, and rules.
- Failure to use collective bargaining positively to resolve human problems.
- Persistent adherence to obsolete performance appraisal systems.
- Failure to anticipate personnel shortages and surpluses.
- Unresponsiveness to legislation governing fair employment, compensation, and related conditions of work.

The growing realization that goal attainment in organizations is closely linked to effective behavior of human resources has important implications for administration. For boards of education and school administrators it means, for one thing, greater attention to immediate- and long-range planning that will encompass the entire range of activities involved in administering the function. Building a dedicated staff competent to direct the education of children and youth, fostering a climate wherein staff members will release their creative energies, and stimulating staff members to contribute their skills to human betterment are all organizational activities that require planning.

The following section examines the relationship between the planning process and the behavior of system members. In setting forth these ideas we will

- Consider the relationship between planning and the resolution of human performance problems.
- Examine human resource planning in the context of educational system planning.
- Review the systems approach to human resource planning.
- Identify the elements of a human resource planning process.
- Portray planning outcomes as a system of plans.
- Analyze the interrelationship among system, unit, and position plans and the personnel function.
- Review the connection between planning and the time dimension.
- Depict the significance of planning to individual and organizational change.

Human Resource Planning in the Context of Educational System Planning

Planning is humanity's way of projecting intentions. Because it deals with concepts of the future, with problems requiring imagination and choice, with deliberate forethought, with attainment by design, it represents a most appealing and challenging endeavor. It is recognized as an organization's most reliable way of realizing its goals. It is the antithesis of expediency, laissez faire, and indirection. It is an effort to set a course of action and to guide the action toward a set of expectations. Ackoff, in defining the nature of planning, notes that although planning is a decision-making process, it is a special kind of decision making:

(1) planning is something we do in advance of taking action, that is, it is anticipatory decision making; (2) planning is required when the future state that we desire involves a set of interdependent decisions, that is, a system of decisions; (3) planning is a process directed toward producing one or more future states that are desired and that are not expected to occur unless something is done.[1]

A working definition of a **system** is that it constitutes an assemblage of correlated parts acting together to form a unitary whole for the purpose of achieving institutional goals. An organizational system, such as a school system, is made up of a number of subsystems, each having a function such as instruction, personnel, and logistics. These subsystems, in turn, are composed of a number of sets of facilitating processes. The personnel subsystem, for example, includes such processes as planning, recruitment, selection, induction, and development. What this means to school officials responsible for the personnel function is simply this: In order to design plans (which include processes) to administer the personnel function, the designer must understand how the total system functions; the nature and purposes of the parts; the ways in which the parts are related to each other and to the total system; and the ways in which the parts interact to facilitate achievement of goals.

Strategic Planning Process

In order to prepare students to be effective in current and future environments replete with continually changing conditions, school systems must change because of their role as major social institutions. This challenge requires a strategic planning process in order to refine or redefine institutional *goals, initiatives* needed to implement *goals,* and *outcome measurements* and *assessments* to determine the extent to which *outcomes* related to the *initiatives* set forth have been achieved.

Previously, it was observed that strategic planning should set broad directions for achieving system goals, including a set of comprehensive plans for their accomplishment. Let us look at one kind of planning tool in the family of strategic plans, referred to here as a *process,* and see how it can be employed in dealing with the complexities of strategic planning as the system is guided from the present into the future.

Process, as the term is used here, refers to a series of progressive and interdependent steps designed to (a) enhance actions to bring about positive change in the human resource function, (b) establish a systematic approach for coping with routine and nonroutine human resource problems, and (c) improve human resource problem solving.

Stage	Activity
One	Define, clarify, articulate, and communicate expectations for the system's human resources.
Two	Assess the overall state of the human resource function in the context of the current school system's needs and aspirations.
Three	Develop a strategic plan.
Four	Implement the strategic plan.
Five	Monitor, evaluate, and adjust the strategic plan.

Figure 2.1   Sequential model of the human resource planning process.

An example of a planning process for the school system's human resource is illustrated in Figure 2.1. It should be noted that the process consists of a series of steps or activities that serve to systematize the manner in which managerial judgments are made relative to people plans and people planning. The ultimate ends toward which the process is directed include (a) heightening the impact of the human resource function on organizational purpose, (b) contriving ways to bring about desired changes in system performance, (c) orienting the planning process beyond short-term needs, and (d) assessing the internal and external environments likely to influence planning choices. The first step in the process, articulation of a mission statement, is the subject of the discussion that follows.

Stage One: Defining System Expectations, Values, and Strategy

In an age of budget limitations, an increasingly diverse society, changing social mores, and confusion regarding ends, means, and methods of improving public education in the United States, as well as a growing chorus of system critics, the task of developing plans for educational reform appears to be a rather daunting undertaking. It is essential, however, for every institution seeking to improve teaching and learning through the human resource function to develop a set of plans and administer its affairs in an orderly and humane manner in accordance with a set of beliefs and values to guide its human resource planning efforts.

As noted in Figure 2.1, Stage One of the human resource planning model includes definition and articulation of the system's expectations for its human resources.

Articulation of Mission Statement

A mission statement, as well as the entire human resource planning process, involves consideration of the following questions:

- What is the school system *expected to do?*
- What is the system *currently doing or not doing* to achieve its expectations?
- What *should the school system be doing* to achieve its expectations?

The question of what the school system is expected to do provides the source from which the system creates its strategy to carry out the mission. In giving thought to the school system's expectations, the following statement by Goodlad, as well as examples provided in Chapter 1, are helpful. Goals that have emerged in the United States may be placed conveniently into four categories: (a) academic—early emphasis was on sufficient schooling to learn principles of religion and the laws of the land (sometimes referred to as *functional literacy*); (b) vocational readiness for productive work and economic responsibility; (c) social and civic—socialization for participation in a complex society; (d) personal—the goal of personal fulfillment, which is a fairly recent development.[2]

Mission as a Frame of Reference

The mission statement can be conceived as a frame of reference by which to assess program options, communicate ideas, shape system performance culture, and coordinate system functions such as human resources with system strategic aims.

In establishing school system expectations on the basis of a mission statement, it is important to consider several factors for incorporation into strategic planning for human resources. These factors include claimant interests, strategy levels, scope, and school system individuality.

Claimant Interests

There are various interests that human resources planning must satisfy, including societal interest (governmental); system interest (strategic aims); functional interest (human resources); and personal interest (economic, social, and psychological objectives of position holders).

Strategy Levels

The system strategy is designed to accomplish broad system purposes; a functional strategy, such as human resources, is created to serve, support, and enhance the system strategy.

Scope

The scope of the mission is to provide a foundation for systemwide planning and to implement plans aimed at achieving primary expectations; to set planning boundaries; to alter, remove, add, or extend existing programs and practices; and to channel available resources into plans most likely to produce intended results.

School System Individuality

Individuality refers to the set of characteristics that should be taken into consideration in utilizing the mission for school improvement purposes. School systems differ profoundly from other organizations. Schools are, for example, small, medium, and large; urban, suburban, and rural; year-round and academic year; those whose student population is largely homogeneous; those where most students' first language is not English; those where a dozen or more languages are spoken; and those for children of military personnel. Thus, the human resource planning process, in concert with the system mission, are tools through which plans are made to accommodate the unique and special characteristics that form the fabric of a particular school system.

Strategic Planning

A strategic school system plan may be described as a planning tool to do the following:

- Move the system from its current state to a desired state.
- Establish the basic system purpose, goals to be pursued, and the general means (tactical plan) by which they will be sought.
- Address fundamental questions about the structures needed to develop the system's purpose, direction, and future generations of educational programs and services.
- Make planning and tactical decisions within the framework of the system mission, goals, policies, and human resource values.
- Provide a point of departure to assess the impact of future environments on strategic plans.
- Link functional goals (e.g., educational programs and services, human resources, logistics, and external relations) to the goals of the strategic plan.
- Assess social, legal, technological, political, economic, educational, and governmental factors that may create opportunities for or obstructions to strategic plans.

Figure 2.2 provides an illustration of the anatomy of the strategic planning process as conceived by the Riverpark school system. Through this process the system intends to address and explore the range of options, opportunities, and strategies through which to enhance the system's future condition.

Perhaps the most appealing aspect of strategic planning is that it provides a unique opportunity to pull back from the immediate details of everyday school system life, important though they are in their own terms, in order to examine what is at stake in efforts to move the system from where it is to where it should be. Contemporary times are full of animation and activity regarding the resolution of problems confronting educational systems. Redesign efforts through instructional and organizational reform, restructuring, decentralization, comprehensive care for children from birth to graduation, and site-based management are commonplace. The appeal of strategic planning is that it serves as a mechanism for weaving the fabric of a school system, through an ongoing process involving position holders working with each other to make school improvement an aggressive movement for dealing with a social failing.

The future status Riverpark school system desires for its human resources is based upon these common premises for action:

Goals. The primary aim of the system is to achieve teaching and learning outcomes beyond those established by state regulations and those proposed by the federal government.

Planning focus. The underlying intent of the system's strategic planning process is to identify conceivable opportunities, favorable and unfavorable relevant changes, regulatory trends, economic conditions, union initiatives, and sociocultural factors that impact on attainment of our desired future status.

Planning priorities. The following priorities have been identified through systemwide review and given primacy as human resources objectives during the time frame portrayed below:

- Develop and implement a strategic planning model to serve the system's interests effectively and efficiently.
- Take steps to achieve our strategic aims through the collective bargaining process.
- Enhance the recruitment process to attract and retain the quality of personnel needed to improve teaching and learning outcomes.
- Identify anticipated changes in the educational program and their impact on the future work force.

Time frame. The time frame shown below represents one of the components of the strategic planning process. Current and strategic plans are reviewed, revised, and recast each year and adjusted as necessary.

Strategic Planning Time Frame							
Current	2	3	4	5			
	Current	2	3	4	5		
		Current	2	3	4	5	
			Current	2	3	4	5
				Current	2	3	4	5

Planning involvement. A planning council is established to ensure system-wide participation for developing current and strategic plans. Council members are representative of and accountable to work units (central, teaching, support) for input regarding decisions affecting their work and working conditions. One aim of the planning process is to avoid management exclusivity—unwritten, temporal, and intuitive approaches borne of individual experience rather than of system implications of current developments and trends.

Figure 2.2   Elements of Riverpark school system's strategic planning process for its human resources.

- *Planning.* Refine current human resource strategic plan on the basis of assessments of the process outcomes. Take steps to internalize human resource goals and initiatives at every system level and for every current position.
- *Recruitment and selection.* Attract, develop, and retain the finest staff to improve and enhance instructional programs.
- *Information.* Improve the system's information management system and record center operation and update its information technology.
- *Communication.* Improve and expand communication with internal and external communities.
- *Unionism.* Further the strategic aims of the system and its human resource function through the collective bargaining process.

Figure 2.3   Illustration of types of strategic goals of the human resource function.

Values and Human Resource Planning

Assuming that a strategic plan is a framework that sets forth what a school system is expected to do, what it chooses to do, and what it intends to be like in a desired future strategic position, a set of value-driven influences is essential to guide decisions aimed at having a positive effect on the performance of the system's human resource. Figures 2.2 and 2.3 illustrate tools that serve a most important function in this regard. The intention of these goals and policies of human resources is to define the human standards the system intends to observe in managing the human resources function; to create a conditional covenant, declaration, or promise between two parties to develop certain conditions regarding work, workers, and working conditions; and to provide the moral impetus for doing the right thing in resolving matters relating to those who serve the system.

Given ideals for system personnel relating to dignity and worth such as those proposed in Figures 2.2 and 2.3, it can be seen how important they are to administration of the human resource function. They commit school leadership to a set of values for guidance in relationships among individuals. They represent a promise to organization members that they will enjoy the same rights as they do as ordinary citizens.

Knowledge of broad system and human resource function goals is used to engage Stage Two of the human resource planning process (as shown in Figure 2.1). This stage is frequently referred to as *organizational diagnosis.* As detailed in the section that follows, Stage Two involves formation of data bases relating to key planning areas in the internal and external environments. This derivative information provides a context within which to arrive at what is known about the present condition of the system's human resources, and to consider options and develop assumptions about conditions that need to be created to achieve the desired end results.

Stage Two: Assessment of the Human Resource Condition

As the educational reform movement becomes a reality, there is little disagreement about the conditions of schooling in the United States:

• School systems, whether small, medium, or large, are in need of considerable improvement in both efficiency and effectiveness.
• All systems engage in some form of planning, whether sophisticated or unsophisticated, formal or informal, piecemeal or holistic.
• A systematic approach to planning enhances the likelihood of educational improvement.
• School systems with the biggest problems tend to be located in large cities with poor populations, to have entrenched bureaucracies, and to have a pervasive union influence.
• There is no one best approach to human resource planning. Each system, regardless of its size, must develop its own blend of strategies, purposes, policies, programs, and practices that work within the context of system culture and the realistic expectation of meeting current and future expectations.
• Small school systems can expect planning advantages deriving from either short-term fixes or long-term overhaul.

Probing for Strategic Direction

The planning process model shown in Figure 2.1 indicates that Stage Two is aimed at assessing the current condition of the system and its linkage to the human resource function. This step is basic to enabling the function to play a pivotal role in creating a performance potential to confer desired outcomes on the system, its members, and those for whom it renders service. This responsibility means shaping the system to be able to perform effectively under conditions of continuous change, unanticipated schooling requirements, and scarcity of resources, as well as demographic, political, and governmental uncertainty. Meeting these requirements will require close scrutiny of questions such as:

• How can human resource planning be linked more closely to the school system's strategic plan?
• What is the system's current situation regarding attainment of our educational expectations?
• Which are our strongest educational programs? Our weakest?
• What informational inputs are needed to develop the strategic plan?
• What will the future external environment represent in terms of demand for school system services?

Adequacy of current system strategic aims.
Adequacy of human resources function aims.
Analysis of present system and function performance.
Analysis of past system and function performance.
Adequacy of mechanisms for strategic review plans.
Problems with current system and function goals.
Adequacy of current programs, policies, and structures.
Adequacy of current planning information.

Figure 2.4   Guidelines for evaluating current system conditions.

- What conditions must the system create to deal with present infirmities and anticipated future conditions?
- What priorities should be established for the allocation of anticipated resources? What current basic priorities should be questioned?
- What factors, both internal and external, might inhibit attainment of the system's education aims?

Strategic Planning Considerations

Assuming that a school system has settled on its *educational goals,* as well as the *social purposes* (often in the form of laws) it is called upon to serve (see Chapter 1), the purpose of Stage Two of the human resource planning process is to provide a forum for the system to examine questions such as those mentioned in the preceding list, resolution of which requires dealing with challenging, complex, and unapparent issues. One of the key organizational resources essential to examination of the current state of the system is *information* because selected forms of this planning mechanism are basic to decisions for bridging the gap between *standards* and *norms.* Closing the breach between practice and purpose involves balancing the system's ideological commitment with omnipresent political, governmental, and special interest demands, which when in imbalance is fraught with the potential for diminishing educational expectations.

Development and maintenance of a human resources **information system** will be addressed in Chapter 3. The role of information in conducting an evaluation of organization strengths and weaknesses is the focus of the discussion that follows.

As indicated in Figure 2.4, determination of the school system's current condition in relation to its strategic aims involves delineation of key factors that need to be evaluated. Moreover, decisions regarding the conduct of the evaluation include such matters as what is to be evaluated; means of evaluation; information needed; membership participation; and how data will be collected, refined, stored, communicated, and utilized to implement the strategic plan.

Strategic Planning Areas and Data Sources

In recent years many school systems have come to realize that information is one of their key assets, along with building and equipment, human resources, and fiscal resources. Various terms are used to describe information, such as *computer-based* and *nonautomated; external* and *internal;* and *centralized* and *decentralized* data bases. The term *human resource information system* refers to the integration of a variety of data bases that have a bearing on the human resource function. For example, managing the 11 subprocesses of the human resource function effectively and efficiently requires information from both the internal and external environmental forces that influence human resource decisions. Among the major classes of information essential to human resources planning are:

- *Purpose information*—Includes the system purpose hierarchy of mission, objectives, goals, strategies, and policies.
- *Program structure information*—Components of the educational program that interact with the human resource function.
- *Pupil information*—Present and future school enrollees for whom the educational program is designed.
- *Position information*—Number, types, work content, and structural location of present and future positions.
- *Position-holder information*—Information about present and future position occupants.
- *Organization structure information*—Assignment of tasks, responsibility, and authority of the human resource function.
- *External environment information*—Economic, governmental, legal, union, and public influences affecting personnel decisions.
- *Internal environment information*—Work force, negotiated contracts, budgets, audits, structure, technology use, planning efforts, legal compliance, and system culture.

The foregoing classes of system information underscore the need for a comprehensive set of information-gathering tools to collect data for improving strategic planning and performance. The most common mechanisms for gathering strategic planning data are listed in Figure 2.5. With such data at hand, the system can focus on plans to upgrade priority activities. In the text that follows, each of the classes of information noted in the preceding list will be examined to illustrate its importance in identifying effective programs and practices and for improving those that are less than satisfactory.

Accounting reports	Plans
Accrediting agencies	policies
Audits	programs
Budgets	projects
Computer bases	Self assessments
Contracts	Services (personnel)
Enrollments (system)	System culture
Environmental data	Technology use
Files (personnel)	Statistical data
Forecasts	absenteeism
Interviews (exit)	deaths
Inventories (skill)	grievances
Job analyses	polls
Job specifications	promotions
Observation	questionnaires
techniques	recruitment
Organization	retirement
charts	selection
documents	surveys
records	transfers
structure	turnover

Figure 2.5   Sources of data for human resources planning.

Purpose Information

We have observed that the human resource function, like all broad administrative functions, is determined largely by the school system's purpose structure. Purpose determines the **program structure,** the number and types of positions, the quantity and quality of persons needed to implement the educational program, and administrative processes and relationships employed to maintain the system. Hence, determination of educational aims and expectations is an imperative planning task, one that precedes all other organizational activities. It is evident to even the most casual observer that the abilities and values that enrollees are expected to acquire under the guidance of the school affect the size and characteristics of the school staff. Purposes are the ends toward which the educational program structure is directed. They determine which educational opportunities are provided and, in turn, affect the size and composition of the school staff. It is worth restating here that purposes have little value unless they can be translated into attainable objectives. As the purpose structure is shaped and clarified, the likelihood increases that better decisions can be made on what should be taught, how it is to be taught, who should do the teaching, what outcomes are anticipated, and how they should be measured.

After the overall purposes of the school system have been established, additional planning decisions need to be made before the organization structure best suited to meet future institutional needs can be visualized. These decisions include assumptions or premises derived from the broad purpose hierarchy, which are essential to preparation of specific forecasts, master plans, policies, programs, and budgets. Figure 2.6 contains a series of questions that will elicit the types of purpose-related information on which planning assumptions can be based. Planners need to know, for example, the bases on which pupil forecasts will be made, the number of school attendance units needed, the educational programs and supporting services each school will accommodate, and the professional and supporting staff arrangements that are envisioned. The implication of this line of analysis is that projection of the future organization begins not with the status quo, but instead with purpose information that clarifies educational and human problems and ways in which they can be solved.

The reader is advised to review the idealized personnel objectives shown in Figures 2.2 and 2.3 in conjunction with Figure 2.6. Figures 2.2, and 2.3 present purpose-related illustrations, providing an overview of the nature of current purpose information that is gathered and analyzed in order to form a data base for strategic planning.

Program Structure Information

It is reasonable to assume that school officials who make personnel decisions will be better equipped to do so if they are fully versed in the organizational ramifications of two key aspects of the educational program: *organization of instruction* and *instructional grouping.*

Organization of Instruction

Broad goals of the system are implemented through some form of instructional organization. Assumptions are made by the system as to the breadth and depth of learning experiences to be included in the curriculum, where the experiences will be provided, when they will be offered, by whom, in what manner, in what grouping arrangements, and for what purposes. Decisions such as these have considerable influence on the quality and quantity of personnel needed to staff the educational program. Arriving at such decisions is no easy matter because it involves consideration of conflicting philosophies of education; theories of curriculum development; psychologies of learning; and needs of the individual learner, the local community, the state, the region, and the nation. One of the inferences to be drawn from Table 2.1 is that the choice of alternatives relating to the instructional program affects the number, types, and levels of sophistication of personnel employed. An instructional program organized around the assumption that the subject matter of the past is the basis for developing a satisfactory curriculum will be staffed differently than one based on the assumption that encourages the fullest development of every individual for whom the school is responsible.

Instructional Grouping

Class or *group size* refers to pupil membership in a group organized for instructional purposes. The question of how many pupils should be assigned to an instructional

- What persons in what age groups should be educated at public expense? Within what age limits should pupils be compelled to attend school? What pre- and postcompulsory age groups should be included in the educational program?

- What purposes are schools expected to achieve? What should be the range and nature of educational experiences provided by the school system to achieve its purposes?

- How should the educational program be structured? Should it be similar to or different from the following pattern?

	Age Groups
Prekindergarten	1–5
Kindergarten	5–6
Elementary school	6–12
Middle school	12–15
Senior high school	15–18
Junior college	18–20
Adult education	16 years and more

- What are the most effective ways of organizing instructional groups?

- What methods, materials, and services should be used to make educational experiences meaningful to learners?

- What should be the size and composition of the professional instructional staff? The administrative staff? The support staff? To what extent should the staffing of each attendance unit be decentralized?

- What special services should be provided in each of the school attendance units? In the central administration?

- What systemwide services to teachers—for example, continuing education, supervision, professional library, and curricular and instructional aids—should be provided?

- What central administrative services—for example, pupil personnel, staff personnel, logistics, plant, research, planning, external relations, and coordination—are necessary?

- What should be the size and deployment of the support staff—for example, custodial, maintenance, transportation, food, clerical, and security services?

- What positions should be retained in the future organization structure? Added? Dropped? Modified?

- To what extent should existing personnel comprise the future organization structure? New personnel?

- How can the future structure be organized to satisfy member needs more effectively?

Figure 2.6   Considerations involved in developing human resource planning assumptions.

TABLE 2.1
Illustration of Instructional Program Options That Influence Human Resource Plans

Program Component		Illustration of Alternatives
Program focus	or	Central purpose is to develop the intellect.
		Central purpose is to develop individuals for effective social living.
Program content	or	Rigid, grade-sequenced learning experiences.
		Flexible-sequenced learning experiences determined by learner readiness, interest, and/or needs.
Program breadth and depth	or	Program limited to time-tested elements of our social heritage.
		Program planned to encompass breadth and depth of educational opportunities.
Program location	or	Within attendance units of system.
		Within and outside of system.
Program staff	or	Conventional: one instructor per group.
		Nonconventional: variable staffing at different levels of the system, including volunteers, part-time personnel, aides, and peer instructors.
Program time	or	Uniform schedules (day only).
		Variable schedules (day, evening, summer).
Program flexibility	or	Pupil moves through program experiences at a uniform rate (one grade per school term).
		Pupil moves through system depending on achievement.
Pupil grouping	or	Graded (learning groups closed).
		Nongraded (learning groups open).
Program control	or	Program decisions restricted to professionals.
		Program decisions unrestricted (staff, parents, pupils, and/or community groups involved).
Program instructional methods	or	Conventional forms of instruction.
		Augmented forms of conventional instruction.

group has been and still remains a subject of serious concern to all who are interested in the nation's schools. It should be noted that assumptions regarding class size are of vital significance to human resource planning. There are several reasons why so much significance is attached to the question of class size. The first is the educator's quest to provide grouping arrangements most conducive to learning and study. Although it is clear that a given class size is no absolute guarantee of the educational progress of all children, many educators are convinced that the grouping plan is an important contributor to educational attainment.

The second reason is cost. There is a considerable difference between the budgetary requirements of a school system that decides it needs one classroom teacher for every 20 pupils and one that sets the class size at 40 pupils.

The major share of current expenditures in a school budget for any fiscal year is allocated to staffing requirements. In searching for the maximum return for every dollar invested, assumptions about class size are always open to question. If a class of 25 is as effective for educational purposes as a class of 20, is adherence to the latter figure educationally and fiscally defensible?

The rapid growth of collective bargaining in public education is another reason why planning assumptions must include consideration of class size. The matter of class size has become a negotiable item in many contracts between teachers and boards of education, a development that, some observers suggest, may prove to be an impediment to new forms of instructional grouping and staff utilization.

Despite experimentation with new forms of instructional grouping, educational technology, and staff utilization and deployment, the question of class size cannot be dismissed as irrelevant when developing human resource planning assumptions. In making assumptions, consideration must be given to the purpose for which instructional groups are formed (the type of learning desired), the intellectual and emotional needs of pupils, the skills of the teacher, and the nature of the subject matter.

Research into the class-size question and related policy and budgetary implications began late in the nineteenth century. Since then, through periods of declining and expanding enrollments, researchers have tried to resolve relevant questions such as: Is there an optimum class size? Do small classes make an impact on teacher morale? Does class size affect the kinds of instructional procedures used in the classroom? Recent reports on these questions are contradictory and do not answer conclusively many of the important questions relating to the effects of class size on pupil learning, the teaching process, teacher morale and job satisfaction, and cost–quality relationships.[3]

Resolution of critical issues relating to class size (including the economics of achieving smaller instructional groups, increasing teacher contact with pupils, and schedule reorganization) involves, directly or indirectly, most of the personnel processes. So central and pervasive is the matter of class size to improvement of pupil performance that the design and operation of the personnel function should be considered as a key factor in increasing the learning level of students and their effectiveness in learning in terms of time and effort expended.

Grouping schemes, it should be noted, should not be viewed as substitutes for excellence in teaching, for adjusting methods and materials of instruction to individual pupils, or for making provisions for those children whose adjustment will be difficult under any organized plan of instruction. It is equally plain that regardless of the grouping plan, every school system needs a staff that is adequate in size and composition—one that is deployed and balanced properly—to provide all pupils with essential instructional services. Although *class size* is important, a concept of equal significance in developing human resources planning assumptions is *staff size.*[4]

Pupil Information

Pupil information is of major importance to school organizations, especially when viewed from the standpoint of specific effects of declining or increasing enrollments. A survey by the National School Boards Association indicated the following aftereffects of declining enrollments: reduced state aid; hiring freezes or

reductions in staff; smaller class sizes; redistricting of school boundaries; and closing, modifying, leasing, or selling of school facilities. Increasing enrollments, in
contrast, may create double sessions, overcrowded classrooms, and a need for
rapid staff expansion.[5]

Consequently, accurate enrollment projections are vital to staff planning
strategies. Literature models employed by school districts to project enrollments
are numerous and varied. A review of enrollment projection models indicates that
at least four practical methods are available: *census class projection, ratio retention
projection, housing projection,* and *total population forecast.* Of the various techniques employed in enrollment projections, the most commonly used procedure is
the *ratio retention* or *cohort survival* method. A 1989 report by Phi Delta Kappa on
enrollment projection concluded that the cohort survival method, when adapted
to a specific environment, provides results that are sufficiently accurate to permit
planning for school staff requirements.[6] It should be noted that in addition to
birth and enrollment data, external environmental information is essential to
making enrollment projections as consistent as possible. Examples of such information include:

- Local and statewide birth rates
- Ethnic composition of the community population
- Emerging communities
- Changing community population patterns
- Nonpublic school enrollments
- Changing transportation patterns
- Integration mandates
- Open school enrollment policies
- School census data
- National census data
- Zoning regulations
- Utility connections and plans
- Bank deposits
- Building permits
- Initiation of voucher plans
- A material event, such as the loss by a city or town of a major employer
- External pressure for school system adoption of a "multiracial, multicultural,
gender, education" policy
- Industry mobility
- Changes in employment patterns
- Family mobility
- State, regional, and community planning data

Investigations of the reliability of enrollment forecasts indicate that the following guidelines deserve consideration:

- Adopt two separate forecasting methods: one at the district level and one at the building level.
- Employ a district level method, such as the cohort survival technique, to account for enrollment trends and community variables.
- For comparative purposes, develop enrollment forecasts for each school attendance unit.
- Take into account rapid enrollment changes. This kind of development may require a housing survey or a school census in addition to or in combination with standard projection procedures.[7]

School System Jobs: Information, Projection, Communication

After the school system's **goal structure** has been established, the task of categorizing the work evolving from the structure into work units, job categories, jobs, job descriptions, and job specifications can be undertaken. The foundation of any educational enterprise is the work or input needed to accomplish the purpose for which it exists. Accordingly, the system's long-term educational and human resource aims represent the basis on which a host of personnel-related activities are determined. This needed information includes the number and types of positions to be included in the budget; who does what kind of work, in what groups, and in what locations; who coordinates the work; how the work is to be done; and how the work expectations are to be judged. **Work analysis,** job classifications, job descriptions, and job communication are illustrative of essential types of planning information.

Employment Analysis Information

One way to gather information about the work to be undertaken in a school system is shown in Table 2.2. The intent of the display is to characterize the nature and scope of school system work, job clusters evolving from the required work activities, and the structural settings in which the work takes place.

As indicated in Table 2.2, instructional and related tasks are assigned to attendance units (individual schools), whereas general administrative work is allocated to the administrative unit. Various types of positions are essential both at the central level and in the attendance units.

The text that follows presents in summary form information about the breakdown of school system work into its components and their distribution among different persons or groups. The work and the jobs referred to derive from the system mission. Four closely related topics are discussed in terms of their singular importance to system jobs and division of work. Applications of job information, as portrayed in Table 2.3, have significant value in nearly every phase of human resource administration.

Position Description—Specifications Information

Two of the important products deriving from employment work analysis are position descriptions and position specifications. A *position description* is a document

TABLE 2.2
Nature and Scope of School System Work, Positions, and Structural Settings

Types of System Work	Types of Positions	Structural Setting	Hypothetical Proportion of Total System Personnel (%)
Planning, organizing, leading, controlling total system	Professional administrative: superintendent, assistant superintendent, associate superintendent, directors, assistants to higher-level personnel	Central administration	1
Planning, organizing, leading, controlling individual school attendance units	Professional administrative: principals, assistant principals, department heads, team leaders	Individual client service units (schools)	3
Instructional programs (regular, special)	Professional teaching: classroom teachers. Professional specialists: art, health, library, guidance, music, physical education, psychological service, reading, speech correction, home–school visits, audiovisual	Individual client service units (schools)	62
Instructional support programs: operation, maintenance, food service, transportation, health, security, secretarial, clerical	Classified: skilled, semiskilled, unskilled	Certain personnel work under direction of central administration; others work in attendance units under direction of principal	34

TABLE 2.3
Administrative Uses of Job Information

- Provide the basis for recruiting and interviewing job candidates and for personnel planning and budgeting.
- Clarify duties and responsibilities.
- Help staff members see their roles and contributions in relation to other employees.
- Help staff members see how their jobs relate to the school system's goals and objectives.
- Help set fair and objective standards for supervising and evaluating job performance.
- Help maintain equity in the job classification program.
- Provide data for wage and salary administration.
- Serve as guides for part-time help and substitutes.
- Indicate inconsistencies, inefficiencies, ambiguities, and overlap in job assignments and work flow.
- Clarify lines of authority and communication.
- Provide guides for the orderly expansion and contraction of the work force.
- Provide the board and public with information about what school team members actually do.
- Provide legal safeguards for dealing in a just manner in cases of employee termination.
- Identify essential and marginal duties for compliance with ADA [Americans with Disabilities Act].
- Identify exempt and non-exempt status to meet U.S. Department of Labor regulations.

Source: National School Boards Association, *The School Personnel Management System* (Alexandria, VA: The Association, 1996), Chapter E, 152.

Goodville School District

Position Guide

Part A: Position Requirements

Position Title: Instructor of Mathematics, Senior High School

Position Code: T68

Primary Function: To participate, as a member of the instructional staff, in directing learning of all students in the area of mathematics. Such participation shall be directed toward attainment of general and specific behavioral objectives of each course, of the school, and of the school district.

Major Classroom Responsibilities: (1) Planning for teaching, (2) motivating pupils, (3) developing classroom climate, (4) managing the classroom, (5) interacting with pupils, (6) evaluating pupils.

Illustration of Key Duties: (1) *Planning for teaching:* within the framework of goals established by the school system, plans the long- and short-range objectives for each assigned course; collects and utilizes a wide variety of information to aid in guiding the growth and development of individual pupils; selects meaningful subject matter and related learning experiences appropriate to various stages of pupil's development; selects and utilizes teaching procedures appropriate to attainment of short- and long-range objectives; selects teaching materials considered to be conducive to attainment of intended goals; (2) *Motivating Pupils:* establishes standards for individual pupils in terms of ability level of each; uses a variety of activities to develop pupils' curiosity and discoveries; (3) *Developing a classroom climate:* creates a classroom climate conducive to pupils' intellectual, social, emotional, and moral development; (4) *Managing the classroom:* controls pupils' behavior and activities so that they contribute positively to accomplishment of goals; (5) *Interacting with pupils:* utilizes concept formation, principles, and generalization in helping pupils understand subject matter; (6) *Evaluating pupils:* evaluates pupils' performance continuously to determine nature and extent of direction needed to attain goals.

Figure 2.7 Illustration of position guide for teaching position.

that describes the cluster of related tasks carried out by one person in a specific work unit, such as a mathematics teaching position in a senior high school (see Figure 2.7). A *position specification,* which describes the qualifications needed by the incumbent occupying the position, includes the following information: job purpose; what the incumbent should know; what the incumbent should be able to do; what the major duties and responsibilities are; and related qualification requirements such as education, experience, and skills needed; knowledge needed; licenses required; physical and medical specifications; terms of employment; performance standards and evaluation; approval by the supervisor; and the incumbent's signature. The National School Boards Association, as shown in Table 2.4, believes that a position description should meet 11 criteria. Some of the tools employed to gather information for position descriptions include questionnaires for current incumbents; job descriptions from the *Dictionary of Occupational Titles;*

Special Assignment: Sponsor of the Square Club, a voluntary organization designed for students who wish to further their knowledge, interest, and skill in mathematics.

Organizational Relationships: (1) is accountable to department chair for performance of assigned responsibilities; (2) coordinates work with members of mathematics department; (3) relates role to building systemwide programs and objectives.

Performance Standards: Performance in this position is considered satisfactory when: (1) *in-class behavior:* there is evidence that the pupils assigned to courses for which the instructor is responsible have achieved the established behavioral objectives as specified by course criteria for acceptable performance; (2) *out-of-class behavior:* there is evidence that the instructor has developed out-of-class behavior that results in effective cooperation with colleagues and laypersons, and in effective self-development.

Part B. Position-Holder Qualifications

Position-Holder Qualifications: (1) *Education:* (a) graduate of a four-year accredited college; (b) professional preparation; (c) academic major in mathematics; (2) *Skills, knowledge, abilities:* (a) functions effectively as a member of an instructional team; (b) organizes and works effectively with small seminar groups; (c) maintains strong commitment to mathematics program and to team teaching; (d) has ability to develop program plans in cooperation with students, parents, staff; (e) works effectively with laypersons in community; (f) has ability to adapt to differences and changes in pupil characteristics, program characteristics, leadership characteristics, colleague characteristics, and community characteristics; (g) has desire and ability to make decisions that go beyond directions from curriculum and instruction guidelines; (h) has desire and ability to achieve close relations with students without emphasis on the authority relationships; (3) *Experience:* three years of experience in teaching mathematics in a secondary school.

Figure 2.7   continued.

TABLE 2.4
Illustration of Job Description Criteria

A job description should:
- Specify the job's title.
- Indicate the kind and extent of skills, knowledge, and abilities required by the job.
- Make clear the job's position in the chain of supervision.
- Relate the job to its ultimate client—the student—and to the objectives of the educational program.
- Outline the major performance responsibilities that make up the job's content.
- State the terms of employment and refer to evaluative criteria for the job.
- State how often the incumbent's performance will be evaluated according to the job description's evaluative criteria.
- Provide the incumbent's acknowledgement of the details of the job description.
- Specify the goal, mission, or purpose of the job.
- Identify essential and marginal duties for compliance with ADA.
- Identify exempt and nonexempt status to meet the regulations of the U.S. Department of Labor.

Source: National School Boards Association, *The School Personnel Management System* (Alexandria, VA: The Association, 1996), Chapter F, p. 152.

similar job descriptions employed in other organizations; incumbent job descriptions; supervisory descriptions of job clusters; and checklists of performance responsibilities.

Communication of Position Information

Communication has been defined as the sharing of information between two or more people to achieve a common understanding about an object or situation. Problems in human resource management are not solved readily in the absence of effective communication. For this reason, four types of handbooks are needed in school systems to carry out the human resource function in a productive manner. These include a personnel handbook, a policy manual, a position manual, and an organization manual; a description of the organization manual follows.[8]

Position information in the school system organization manual that describes the job evaluation system can provide a framework for addressing matters relating to a variety of personnel processes; for example, position specifications help to ensure that persons performing the same job will receive the same salary. When properly designed, job evaluation systems help the school system to arrange a legal defense and a rationale for dealing with claims of system bias relating to age, sex, and race. Moreover, position information establishes the basis for managing personnel activities such as recruitment, selection, induction, compensation, career development, performance appraisal, grievance resolution, and reshaping the organization structure. Additional terminology relating to work analysis, developed by the Bureau of Intergovernmental Personnel Development Programs, can be found in the Glossary.[9]

Much importance is attached to the role of positions in the human resource function, because position information is vital for managing virtually all human resource activities.

A blueprint of tasks required to perform a job is referred to as *position* or *job design.* This aspect of human resource planning is a many-faceted undertaking involving consideration of such matters as job analysis, enlargement, enrichment, range, evaluation, and position and person satisfaction. Note that job design is a complex concept. Applying related principles and practices is not a simple task, but it is indispensable to the strategic planning needed to achieve effective and efficient management of the human resource function.

Employment Classification

Every organization, however large or small, has a number of tasks to be performed, as illustrated in Table 2.2. Such job categories or clusters can be further identified as full-time, part-time, temporary, salaried, hourly, tenured, probationary, nonadministrative, and administrative. This classification helps to sort out various issues relating to salaries, wages, benefits, over-time pay eligibility, and equity in job valuation. Information such as the foregoing is indispensable to bringing order, consistency, and fairness to employment practices.

Another approach to sorting out the relative value of system jobs is a job value hierarchy. A job complexity scale is designed to rank jobs from least to most complex. This practice permits establishment of job hierarchies for groups or job families. For example, the family of administrative jobs shown in Table 2.2 would be ranked from least to most complex. This information lays the foundation for establishing the economic value of positions and position holders.

Position Projection

Table 2.5 illustrates one of several methods that can be employed to transform planning information into professional positions that will be required in the future organization structure. Using the set of numerical transactions proposed, staffing assumptions can develop an idea of the kind of **organization structure** that should be established for a specific time span under a given set of conditions. The approach shown in Table 2.5 is not difficult to initiate; any school district can use it to undertake an analysis of staffing objectives and policies needed for their attainment. Advantages can be derived from the type of personnel projection illustrated in Table 2.5. These include:

- Extending the range of planning activities in a school administrative unit beyond a single year.
- Identifying future trends in enrollments on which to base personnel needs.
- Developing an inventory of present personnel components.
- Projecting the present numerical staff adequacy into the staff size ultimately desired in each of the system's operating units.
- Quantifying personnel needs for budgetary purposes.
- Translating planning assumptions into a future organizational structure.
- Linking personnel planning with other systemwide planning efforts.
- Determining the priority order of personnel needs.
- Identifying obstacles to realization of the total personnel plan and developing methods for surmounting them.

In preparing projections of professional positions, it is important to note that effective results depend on both accuracy of enrollment projections and proper representation of the desired ratio between pupils and professional personnel. There is no standard ratio applicable to all districts. Each district, through careful examination of relevant internal and external variables, must determine the ratio that will work most effectively for it. This involves consideration of the various economic, political, and social concerns that influence such a policy decision. Once established, this ratio is then used to methodically ascertain professional personnel requirements of the individual system.

It may well be that some systems facing a period of declining enrollments may not choose to permit the number of pupils per professional staff member to decline, but

TABLE 2.5
Projection of Professional Positions Required in the Future Organization Structure of the Cloudcroft School System

	Base Year	Base Year + 1	Base Year + 2	Base Year + 3	Base Year + 4	Base Year + 5
1. Enrollments						
K–6	6,819	7,153	7,228	7,195	7,083	6,829
7–9	2,583	2,983	3,208	3,457	3,630	3,861
10–12	2,308	2,337	2,449	2,485	2,634	2,839
Total	11,710	12,473	12,885	13,137	13,347	13,529
2. Personnel ratio objectives						
a. Pupil–teaching personnel	28:1	28:1	27:1	26:1	25:1	24:1
b. Pupil–instructional specialist personnel	213:1	211:1	211:1	190:1	178:1	169:1
c. Pupil–administrative personnel	532:1	480:1	460:1	438:1	417:1	423:1
d. Pupil–total professional personnel	24:1	24:1	23:1	22:1	21:1	20:1
e. Professional staff per 1,000 pupils	41	41	42	44	46	48
3. Ratio objectives expressed as staff size						
a. Teaching personnel	420	445	477	505	534	564
b. Instructional specialists	55	59	61	69	75	80
c. Administrative personnel	22	26	28	30	32	32
d. Total professional personnel	497	530	566	604	641	676
4. New positions						
a. Teaching personnel		25	32	28	29	30
b. Instructional specialists		4	2	8	6	5
c. Administrative personnel		4	2	2	2	0
d. Total professional personnel		33	36	38	37	35

Assumptions: Pupil–teacher ratio will be reduced from 28:1 in base year to 24:1 in base year + 5. Professional staff will increase from 41 per 1,000 pupils in base year to 48 per 1,000 pupils in base year + 5. Pupil–instructional specialist ratio and pupil–administrative personnel ratio will increase as shown above. *Note:* See Figure 2.9 for a method for computing the professional staff ratio (2e above).

rather to hold the ratio constant through staff attrition. Regardless of which decision is made about the desired staffing ratio, care must be taken to ensure that the intended change is gradual and attainable over the proposed period of time. In assessing the level of the overall professional staffing ratio, attention should also be focused on existing ratios among teaching, instructional, and administrative personnel. It may be that new ratio objectives would serve the educational mission more effectively.

The reader should recognize that the approach suggested in Table 2.5 is not offered as the ultimate solution to long-term human resource forecasting. For example, the technique employed to project professional personnel requirements could be broadened to include data on support personnel to make the planning more comprehensive. Moreover, techniques can be refined to quantify planning requirements for each school attendance unit prior to consolidating the data for systemwide forecasts. Planning tools for this purpose have been illustrated in the section on personnel information.

Structure Projection

Completing the forecast of the long-term human resource requirements for the system makes it possible to project the organizational structure in detail. The model of organization structure is projected in terms of redefined objectives, including the positions, functions, and reporting relationships best calculated to achieve them. Existing organizational functions, functionaries, and methods of operation are ignored in developing the model structure. Several types of planning tools that can be of assistance to school officials in redesigning the organization structure should be mentioned. These include the position guide, the organizational chart, and the organization manual.

The Position Guide

The **position guide,** an example of which is shown in Figure 2.7, can be used to specify the work or expectations of each position in the organization, relationships of the position, and qualifications needed to perform the work allocated to the position. It is also useful in the recruitment, compensation, development, position analysis, and control processes.

The Organization Chart

Although it is perfectly clear that an **organization chart,** such as the one shown in Figure 2.8, has limitations in portraying the realities of an organization structure, it is an extremely useful planning tool for establishing and appraising formal relationships. It helps to establish the organization's views of the functions, relationships, and levels of various positions in the administrative hierarchy. It provides a skeletal view of the total organization, its position composition, and a general picture of the relative importance and status of the several positions comprising the structure. It can also be used as a working hypothesis to test position guides and position responsibility charts.

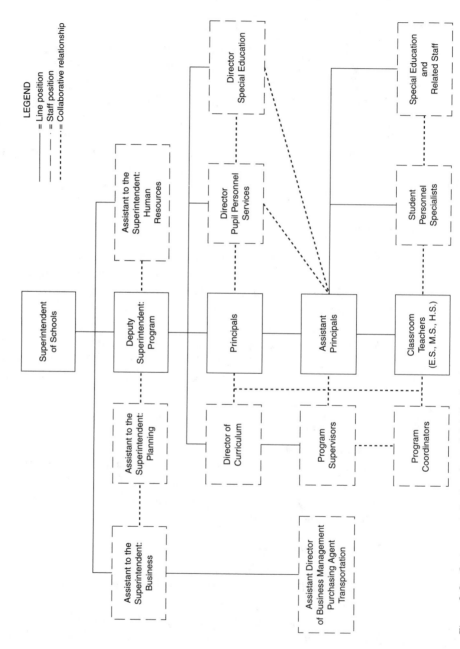

LEGEND

———— = Line position
— — — = Staff position
·········· = Collaborative relationship

Figure 2.8   System organization chart of the Cloudcroft School District.

The Organization Manual

An **organization manual,** as noted previously, is a document that describes the formal organization structure. It contains charts and statements relating to position authority and responsibility. The advantages of an organization manual are numerous. Most important, however, is that the manual represents a formal commitment by the organization to a structure. In addition, the manual helps to identify line and staff responsibilities, communicate to all members of the organization the nature of the structure, minimize overlapping of functions, enable the organization to allocate responsibilities, and improve the human resource function.

Planning activity involved in developing the foregoing tools is of considerable importance in that it can help to enhance personnel's role fulfillment, create better role understanding, lead to wiser use of the structural tools, and make a more effective organization.

External Environment Analysis

If a school system is to function well in contemporary society, it must understand and make plans to cope with dynamic temporal movements in the *external environment.* External factors, such as those identified in Figure 1.8, influence the organization as a whole, as well as its components and its effectiveness.

Assessment of external variables that affect the system's mission, as well as the informational inputs derived from such assessments as assumptions, forecasts, and projections, are important elements that must be integrated into the strategic planning process.

Because the number and types of variables in the external environment influencing the system and its functions are virtually limitless, one must decide which ones appear to be critical in planning the system's future. Examples of potentially relevant variables include:

- Extension of regulatory legislation and procedures generated by federal, state, county, and municipal agencies.
- School enrollment trends (short- and long-term).
- Educational reform movements (federal, state, county, and municipal).
- Extension or curtailment of state-mandated educational programs.
- Extension or curtailment of financial support for education.
- Community pressures for educational change.
- Personnel costs under varying economic conditions and contract negotiations.
- Personnel composition and skill-level demand under varying employment conditions.
- Trends in judicial rulings affecting the human resource function.
- Emerging educational technology and its potential for improving teaching and learning.
- Emerging technology for improving organization information systems and its application to strategic planning.

Variables selected for analysis and projection should be chosen on the basis of assumed relevance to achieving both system and human resource function aims. The preceding list of variables, as well as emerging issues pertinent to the human resource function, merit continuous monitoring in order to enhance more systematic approaches to strategic decision making.

Internal Environment Analysis

Internal as well as external forces, as noted in Chapter 1, affect the effectiveness of a school system. Interaction of multiple elements creates a variety of administrative concerns, especially the impact on individual and group behavior. Formal organization strategies are needed to cope with the inexorable tendencies of internal and external environmental change. Examination of Figure 1.8 brings into focus influential internal environmental factors that need to be considered in developing strategic plans.

Internal factors such as *formal organization, individual and group behavior, system culture,* and *work force diversity* in school systems are not readily measured. Although their influence on *strategic* plans is, for the most part, intangible, they are factors affecting organizational performance and must be considered in gaining an understanding of the causes of and ways to enhance individual, group, and system effectiveness. The following questions focus the analytic spotlight on the internal environment:

• What organizational characteristics promote or impede the system's ability to increase its responsiveness to current and future demands (policies, programs, processes, procedures, practices, rules, and regulations)?
• What is the quality of authority relationships as perceived by the system's individuals and groups?
• Is the system's division of labor efficiently structured?
• How satisfactory is the current approach to reward and punishment?
• Does our present leadership promote change and innovation?
• What are our strengths and weaknesses in each functional area (program, logistics, planning, human resources, and external relations)?
• Are the system's values, expectations, and attitudes being communicated effectively to the membership?
• How effective are the system's efforts to bring about in an ethnically diverse work force an understanding and appreciation of the values, norms, expected behaviors, abilities, and social knowledge needed to carry out position and performance standards, career development, and interpersonal relationships?

Stage Three: Development of a Strategic Plan

Stages One and Two of the human resource planning process include (a) identification of organizational and human resources objectives and (b) formation of data bases for use as tools in planning how to achieve future system goals. Stage Three involves drawing inferences, considering planning options, and making personnel decisions based on information derived from Stages One and Two.

Many factors are involved in and complicate decision making for human resource planning. For example:

- What are the planning implications of the pupil enrollment forecasts?
- Will there be a shortage or surplus of system personnel to meet future needs?
- To what extent do incumbents have the skills, abilities, and attitudes to fill projected positions?
- What assumptions should be made about professional staff size? Support staff size? (Staff size is the number of staff members per 1,000 students. See Figure 2.9 for a computation illustration.)
- To what extent should existing jobs be redesigned? New jobs designed?
- What decisions should be made about various kinds of staff balance (system; work unit; staff category; staff utilization; staff load; staff competency; and racial, ethnic, gender, age, and instructional balance)?
- How can the system redesign the organizational structure to clarify (a) the nature and location of each position, (b) the relationship of this position to other positions, (c) role specifications, (d) position level, (e) types of position interactions, (f) position authority and responsibility, (g) position status and importance, and (h) position expectations and rewards?
- How can the system make more effective and efficient use of its human resources?
- What changes should be made in personnel plans as a result of anticipated developments in the external environment?
- To what extent should existing instructional, administrative, support, specialist, and temporary positions be redesigned? New positions designed?

In brief, making the transition from an existing to a more desirable human resources condition requires systematic planning. The planning process described in this chapter should help to chart managerial direction, reduce uncertainty, and minimize random behavior in efforts to achieve the aims of both the school organization and its members.

Stage Four: Implementation of the Strategic Plan

Introducing changes in the human resource function involves a variety of activities to improve existing arrangements, as well as to develop new approaches and capabilities based on review of external–internal environmental conditions, threats, and opportunities. Stage Four of the human resources planning process presumes that there is organizational commitment to implement the design of the strategic development plan. As illustrated in Figure 2.10, implementation strategy takes into

A. Goodville School District has the following pupil membership:

Grades	Resident Membership	Nonresident Membership	Total Membership	Resident Pupils for Whom Tuition Is Paid in Another District	Staffing Pupil Units
K	939	1	940	0	470.0
1–6	4,065	39	4,104	0	4,104.0
7–12	3,397	25	3,422	1	3,764.2
Total	8,401	65	8,466	1	8,338.2

B. The district has 392 professional employees, including superintendent, principals, teachers, administrative assistants, special teachers, psychologists, nurses, teachers of special subjects (who are not counted as regular teachers), and librarians.

C. To compute the number of staffing units in the system, use the average daily membership, which includes pupils sent by other districts; exclude resident pupils sent to other districts.

   1. Divide total half-day kindergarten membership by 2 ($^{940}/_2$ = 470).

   2. Multiply total secondary membership by 1.1 to account for the difference in secondary over elementary school staffing (3,422 × 1.1 = 3,764.2).

   3. Compute total staff units 470.0 + 4,104.0 + 3,764.2 = 8,338.2).

D. Professional staff size:

$$\frac{\text{Professional employees} \times 1,000}{\text{Staffing pupil units}} = \frac{392 \times 1,000}{8,338.2}$$

$$= 47 \text{ professional staff members for every 1,000 pupils.}$$

Note: Staffing ratio is defined as the number of staff members per 1,000 students.

Figure 2.9   Method for computing professional staff ratio.

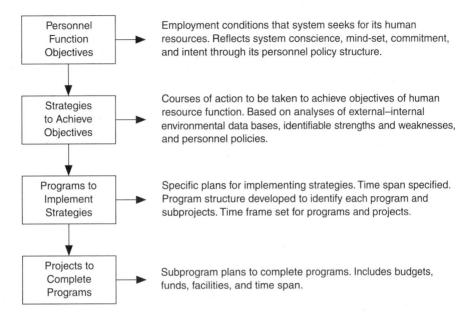

Personnel Function Objectives	Employment conditions that system seeks for its human resources. Reflects system conscience, mind-set, commitment, and intent through its personnel policy structure.
Strategies to Achieve Objectives	Courses of action to be taken to achieve objectives of human resource function. Based on analyses of external–internal environmental data bases, identifiable strengths and weaknesses, and personnel policies.
Programs to Implement Strategies	Specific plans for implementing strategies. Time span specified. Program structure developed to identify each program and subprojects. Time frame set for programs and projects.
Projects to Complete Programs	Subprogram plans to complete programs. Includes budgets, funds, facilities, and time span.

Figure 2.10   Sequential implementation of change strategies.

account objectives, strategies, programs, projects, timing of activities, delegation of responsibilities, and allocation of resources to undertake specified courses of action.

School systems differ in many ways, including size, location, leadership, resources, quality and quantity of personnel, instructional technology, complexity, stability, and internal and external environments. Each school system must determine how the process can be performed most effectively and efficiently. The planning process model shown in Figure 2.1 provides a framework for analyzing problems related to the function and the steps involved in developing approaches to achieve long-term objectives.

Table 2.6 illustrates a format employed in the Goodville school system to plan, manage, and monitor various activities associated with positions in the organizational structure. Worthy of note are (a) approaches employed to govern the creation, specifications, elimination, recruitment, selection, appraisal, forecasts, and relationships relevant to all positions in the budget; (b) allocation of authority and responsibility; (c) control guidelines; and (d) structural relationships.

Both internal and external organizational environments change and, in turn, generate system changes. Central and unit administrators are responsible for improving the function not only by resolving those problems inherent in existing plans but also by developing new policies and innovative ways of meeting old and new problems. New approaches to personnel motivation, new designs for feedback systems, application of emerging instructional technologies, and more effective use of personnel time are matters that are the responsibility of and should be of vital concern to those involved in administration of the function.

TABLE 2.6
Position Planning and Control Network of the Goodville School System

Position Network Elements	Professional Administrative Positions	Professional Teaching Positions	Professional Specialist Positions	Instructional Support Positions	Noninstructional Support Positions
Position location	C-A	A	C-A	A	C-A
Position reports to	5	5	5	5	5
New position route	5-3-2-1	5-3-2-1	5-3-2-1	5-3-2-1	5-3-2-1
Position abolition route	3-2-1	3-2-1	3-2-1	3-2-1	3-2-1
Request for new position route	5-3-2-1	5-3-2-1	5-3-2-1	5-3-2-1	5-3-2-1
Temporary replacement route	5-3-4	5-3-4	5-3-4	5-3-4	5-3-4
Permanent replacement route	5-3-4	5-3-4	5-3-4	5-3-4	5-3-4
Transfer route	5-3	5-3	5-3	5-3	5-3-4
Dismissal route	5-3-2-1	5-3-2-1	5-3-2-1	5-3-2-1	5-3-2-1
Position guide route	6-5-3-2-1	6-5-3-2-1	6-5-3-2-1	6-5-3-2-1	6-5-3-2-1
Performance appraisal process	5-R	5-R	5-R	5-R	5-R
Recruitment process	1-3-4-5	1-3-4-5	1-3-4-5	1-3-4-5	1-3-4-5
Internal	4-R	4-R	4-R	4-R	4-R
External	4-R	4-R	4-R	4-R	4-R
Selection process	4-R	4-R	4-R	4-R	4-R
Participation route	7	7	7	7	7
Recommendation route	7-3-2-1	7-3-2-1	7-3-2-1	7-3-2-1	7-3-2-1
Nomination responsibility	3	3	3	3	3
Appointment responsibility	1	1	1	1	1
Rejection resolution route	1-3-1	1-3-1	1-3-1	1-3-1	1-3-1
Position forecasts	6-3-2-1	6-3-2-1	6-3-2-1	6-3-2-1	6-3-2-1
Position relationship within organization structure	6-3-2-1	6-3-2-1	6-3-2-1	6-3-2-1	6-3-2-1

Guidelines elaborating position control concepts:
- Central recruitment, decentralized selection
- Position guides for each position, reviewed annually
- All positions open to internal application
- Unit heads (5) notify Asst. Supt., Human resources (4) of position vacancy (temporary or permanent)
- Selection committees have joint responsibility of (1) and (2)
- (4) Responsible for forms, documentation, processes in position, control plan
- Positions created or abolished in adoption of annual budgets; interim position replacement route specified above
- Chief Executive makes nomination to Board for each position
- If Board rejects nomination, Chief Executive nominates another candidate

Code
1 = Board as a whole
2 = Personnel committee
3 = Chief Executive
4 = Asst. Supt., Human Resources
5 = Unit head (see administrative almanac)
6 = Planning office
7 = Selection committee
C = Central administration
A = Attendance unit
R = Responsibility for administering

Stage Five: Monitoring, Assessing, and Adjusting the Strategic Plan

The final stage in the human resources planning process is to determine the appropriateness of plans to meet projected conditions and the extent to which performance conforms to plans. Inherent in the control function are three closely related steps that form the basis of this phase: (a) reviewing plans (including goals, objectives, programs, and standards); (b) checking results against expectations; and (c) adjusting to correct deviations from plans. Ideally, every plan that the school system puts into operation should have *built-in means* for judging its effectiveness. Viewed in this manner, monitoring and evaluating the effectiveness of plans is an omnipresent function of school administration, an aspect of the administrative process designed to keep means and ends in balance. Human resources planners need to know:

- How feasible are the planning assumptions on which the function is based?
- Is the current organizational structure conducive to system effectiveness?
- Are positions being filled according to position guides?
- What steps have been taken to implement systemwide development and career paths for personnel?
- Are the numbers and quality of personnel satisfactory?
- Are personnel deployed, balanced, and utilized effectively?
- What initiatives are needed to adjust differences between actual and expected planning outcomes?

Stage Six: Assessing Effectiveness of Strategic Initiatives

The ultimate test of any strategic initiative is **effectiveness,** meaning the realization of intended or expected results. Let us consider why effectiveness is an extraordinary aspect of organizational and human resource management. Interest groups and constituencies, both internal and external, have a stake in whether schools are effective. Taxpayers, boards of education, politicians, government bodies, home buyers, students, employers and employees, newspapers, colleges and universities, placement agencies, and factors such as antiorganization behavior, negative recruitment results, and needless absenteeism and lateness amount to more than a passing concern about school system quality. Consequently, school leadership has a strong obligation to define what effectiveness means and how it should be measured.

Figure 2.11 illustrates a procedure for putting Stage Six into operation. Two performance domains, defining and measuring school effectiveness, are incorporated in moving strategic initiatives from the drawing board to leadership action. These domains constitute the backbone of the transformation design. The five strategic initiatives listed in Figure 2.11 represent criteria for evaluating the effectiveness of the strategic plan. The broad intent of evaluating effectiveness on the

The following planning initiatives are intended to:
A. Direct all human resource processes of the school system to contribute to raising the student graduation rate from 68 percent to 90 percent.
B. Redirect recruitment-selection efforts away from past and present approaches toward realization of future strategic personnel requirements.
C. Develop the performance appraisal process to enhance personnel behavior consistent with meeting strategic personnel goals.
D. Redesign communication channels so that plans, facts, ideas, meanings, information, and understandings are effectively exchanged among system members.
E. Promote continuous improvement in the systematic control of school system records, assisted by information technology during their life span.

		Extent and Value of Progress Toward Realization of Planning Objectives					
Initiatives	Weight Assigned	None (0)	Some (1)	Satis-factory (2)	Superior (3)	Maximum (4)	Insert Score
A	5	0	5	10	15	(20)	(20)
B	4	(0)	4	8	12	16	(0)
C	3	0	(3)	6	9	12	(3)
D	2	0	2	4	(6)	8	(6)
E	1	0	1	(2)	3	4	(2)
						Total Score	(31)

Note:
Numbers in the columns under *Extent and Value of Progress* are the product of the value and, for each initiative, the weight selected.

To complete the profile:
• Under *Extent and Value of Progress* encircle for each initiative a number in the column that corresponds to the appropriate descriptor of progress.
• Then connect the selected numbers to obtain a graphic profile of the performance.
• The score for each initiative is the number encircled as representing the weighted degree of progress.

Figure 2.11   Strategic Planning Effectiveness Rating Scale (application of ratings, year 2 of 5).

basis of Initiatives A through E is to strengthen the planning process relative to needs that may be identified and to inform constituencies of progress toward those goals that have been selected.

A rating scale is provided in Figure 2.11 to measure the extent to which current performance is adequate to achieve each of the five strategic initiatives; the values range from 0 (representing no progress) to 5 (representing maximum progress).

Since the initiatives differ from each other in priority, a relative weight, to be used in deriving scores from the ratings, is assigned to each initiative. Scores are obtained by multiplying the numerical value of each rating on the scale of 0–5 by the appropriate weight assigned to each initiative. Should the ratings and derived scores appear in the middle or to the left of Figure 2.11, the question arises as to whether human resource practices reflect preservation of past conceptual underpinnings and whether there is lack of leadership vision, foresight, forethought, and energy devoted to system constituents on system results. Leaders are compelled to develop means by which information about school systems is collected, refined, and communicated to internal and external entities. Is there, for example, a superintendent of schools who dares to tell his constituents that we know nothing about the effectiveness of our appraisal process, our information system, our recruitment and selection processes, the quality of our internal and external communications, and the reasons our student graduation rate of 68 percent has not changed in recent years (see Figure 2.11, Initiative 1) because we are unable to define and measure these factors?

Human resource planning is a cyclical operation that probably will never attain perfection. Periodic revision of plans and the assumptions on which they are based will always be necessary. Nevertheless, if the planning process is carefully structured, implemented, and controlled, chances are good that the school system will have sufficient high-performing personnel to meet future staffing aims and will not have to endure constant organizational crises created by lack of qualified people to perform the variety of tasks essential to its purposes.

Careful consideration of the intent of Figure 2.11 brings into focus several points about defining and measuring strategic initiatives in public school systems.

• Variables involved in judging school system progress and its human resource function present complex defining and measuring tasks.
• Quantitative measures of effectiveness are but one of several evaluative approaches. Others include subjective evaluations and judgments, follow-up supervisory information, and periodic checkpoint indicators to determine how well the system is reacting to and coping with internal–external demands.
• Important as the foregoing points are, it should be apparent that leadership is always being judged by the intended future that strategic initiatives represent.

Review and Preview

The purpose of this chapter is to present a human resource planning process—the first of 11 processes that comprise the structure of this text. Six of the planning stages shown in Figure 2.1 include (a) establishing goals for the system's human resources, (b) assessing the present status of the human resource condition, (c) developing a strategic plan to project what the human resource function aims to accomplish in the long run, (d) stressing the importance of initiating courses of action to implement planning strategies, (e) monitoring and evaluating the strategic plan to check program performance against goals, and (f) assessing the effectiveness of strategic initiatives. Three planning concepts are highlighted as important components of the planning process: (a) viewing human resource planning as a framework for integrating all human resource activities; (b) developing relevant information to facilitate the planning process; and (c) monitoring and assessing the planning process to evaluate progress toward goals, identifying performance discrepancies, reexamining goals, and modifying courses of action where assessment indicates justifiable change.

Chapter 3 is devoted to three components—information, records, and communication—essential to the operation of the planning process and its linkage to internal and external environments.

Discussion Questions

1. The nature of any position in a school system creates specific expectations about *who does the work* (position holder), *how the work is to be done* (work methods), and *work performance* (position-holder behavior). What does strategic planning have to do with each of these position factors?

2. How does a school system go about determining how many employees are recruited, selected, inducted, developed, compensated, and evaluated, and how well, in terms of overall system strategy?

3. In developing a strategic plan for the school system's human resources, what roadblocks are likely to be encountered (union, external factors, internal factors, political factors, community factors, system culture factors)?

4. How should a school system go about assessing its strengths and weaknesses? What types of information are needed? What kinds of initiatives are necessary? Planning responsibility? Key areas to be assessed? Planning costs? Planning stages?

5. What is the role of a budget in enhancing strategic plans? Revenue forecasts? Personnel forecasts? Position redesign plans? Union–system contract? Internal–external environments?

Notes

1. Russell Ackoff, *A Concept of Planning* (New York: Wiley-Interscience, 1970), 2–4.

2. John I. Goodlad, *What Schools are For* (Bloomington, IN: Phi Delta Kappa Educational Foundation, 1994), 44.

3. Research on class size over three decades is summarized in William B. Castetter, *The Human Resource Function in Educational Administration*, 6th ed. (Englewood Cliffs, NJ: Prentice-Hall, Inc., 1996), 54–56, 78–79.

4. *Class size* refers to the number of pupils enrolled in a class or instructional group. Average class size is the average number of pupils enrolled in a school attendance unit or a school administrative unit (school

system). *Teacher–pupil ratio* is the number of pupils enrolled per full-time teacher. *Staff ratio* is the number of staff members per 1,000 pupils.

5. National School Boards Association, *Declining School Enrollments* (Alexandria, VA: The Association, 1976).

6. Phi Delta Kappa, *Enrollment Projections* (Bloomington, IN: Phi Delta Kappa, May 1989).

7. Joyce-King Stoops and Robert M. Slaby, "How Many Students Next Year?" *Phi Delta Kappan* 62, 9 (1981), 658.

8. Descriptive materials for developing human resource manuals are found in William B. Castetter, "The Personnel Manual and the Human Resource Function," *National Forum of Educational Administration and Supervision Journal* 13, 2 (1996), 3–23; Leo Lunine, *Personnel Policy Handbook* (New York: American Management Association, 1993); W. S. Hubbartt, *Personnel Policy Handbook* (New York: McGraw-Hill, Inc., 1993).

9. For information on jobs, job descriptions, and job analysis, see U.S. Department of Labor, *Dictionary of Occupational Titles* (Washington: U.S. Government Printing Office, Superintendent of Documents, 1991).

Supplementary Reading

Cascio, Wayne F. *Applied Psychology in Personnel Management,* 5th ed. Englewood Cliffs, NJ: Prentice-Hall, Inc., 1998.

Cascio, Wayne F. "Treats Using Human Resource Function Strategically," in *Managing Human Resources,* 5th ed. New York: McGraw-Hill, Inc., 1998, 24–27.

Duke, Daniel L. "Challenges of Designing the Next Generation of America's Schools." *Phi Delta Kappan* 80 (May 1998), 688.

Finn, Chester E., Jr.; and Herbert J. Walberg. "The World's Least Efficient Schools." *Wall Street Journal* (June 22, 1998), A22.

Garfinkel, Lynne; and Robert D. Campbell. "Strategies for Success in Measuring Performance." *HR Magazine* 41 (June 1996), 98–104.

Gubman, Edward L. *The Talent Solution: Aligning Strategy and People to Achieve Extraordinary Results.* New York: McGraw-Hill, Inc., 1998.

Lapointe, Joel; and Judy Parker-Matz. "People Make the System Go . . . or Not." *HR Magazine,* 43 (September 1998), 28–36.

Mornell, Pierre. 45 *Ways for Hiring Smart! How to Predict Winners and Losers in the Incredibly Expensive People Reading Game.* Berkeley, CA: Ten Speed Press (June 1998).

NEA Center for Educational Technology Brief. "Good Use of Technology Demands Staff Development." Harrisburg, PA: Published in the *Voice,* Pennsylvania State Education Association (April 1998), 7.

Rose, Lowell C. "Connecting with All Our Publics." *Phi Delta Kappan* 79 (September 1997), 2.

Schuler, Randall S. "Managing Organizational Change and Human Resource Planning." In *Managing Human Resources,* 6th ed. Cincinnati, OH: South-Western College Publishing (1998), Chapter 5.

Starkwether, Richard A.; and Cheryl L. Steinbacher. "Job Satisfaction Affects the Bottom Line." *HRMagazine* 43 (September, 1998), 111–112.

3

Information Technology and the Human Resource Function

CHAPTER OBJECTIVES

Furnish an overview of the architecture of the human resource information system.

Introduce the concept of an information system as a plan to acquire, refine, organize, store, maintain, retrieve, and transform knowledge into an organized body of information for the purpose of managing the school system and its functions.

Explain the communication process and its potential for integrating the system with its parts and with its internal and external environments.

Examine the relationship between information technology and the human resource function.

CHAPTER TERMS

Archives	Information process
Audit	Information system
Data	Privacy laws
Data base	Records
Data processing	Records center
Form information	Report
Information policy	Technology

Information and the Human Resource Function

Information is intimately and indelibly bound up with planning, organizing, directing, and controlling a school system. It plays a critical role not only in maintaining the daily life of an organization but also in providing for its survival and growth.

The school system can be viewed as an organized combination of elements, including mission, input, process, structure, and control, designed to form a unitary whole. Systems are also composed of subsystems (individual schools) and homogeneous functions (planning, curricula, logistics, human resources, and external relations). Each subsystem needs information unique to itself, but there is information common to all subsystems, some of which is needed between or among certain subsystems. Figure 3.1 illustrates the concept of unification of subsystems within an organization through information. Five major functions of a school system, shown in Figure 3.1, are linked to each other and to the system as a whole by means of an integrated information system.[1]

The concept of information integration, as shown in Figure 3.1, may be illustrated by reference to the human resource function and such subfunctions as human resources planning, recruitment, selection, compensation, and appraisal. Recruitment, selection, and induction activities cannot be performed effectively without information pertaining to personnel planning. Hence, there is an *interdependence* of personnel activities within the human resources function. The need for *integration*

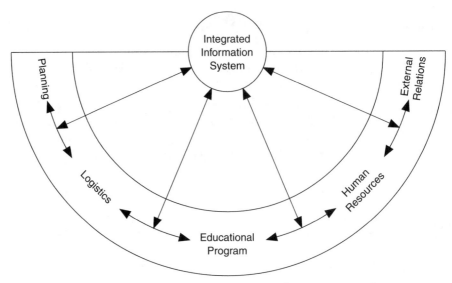

Figure 3.1   Human resource subsystem interactions with other organization subsystems.

among the major functions shown in Figure 3.1 becomes readily apparent when, for example, newly appointed personnel are put on the system payroll. In this case the human resource and logistics functions are linked through information provided by one function to another.

A school system, like other organizations, is composed of purposes, people, plans, tasks, technology, and a structure for fitting its parts together. The ability of the system to function depends on the *bonding* of these elements. Each element has an impact on other elements and, thus, on the whole. Interaction of the various parts to achieve broad system purposes is effected through an integrated *information system*. Information makes it possible to link individualized but coordinated action plans for positions, sections, departments, units, and schools into the overall mission of the system.

Architecture of the Human Resource Information System

Slowly and steadily, we have come to realize that of the three categories of management activity—authority, informational, and decisional—the performance of school system leadership depends most heavily on the effectiveness with which appropriate information skills are employed.[2]

Implicit in the administration of any organization is the realization that it is an entity in which people perform tasks in order to achieve established outcomes. The work to be done in school systems is structured into jobs (instruction); into groups (ele-

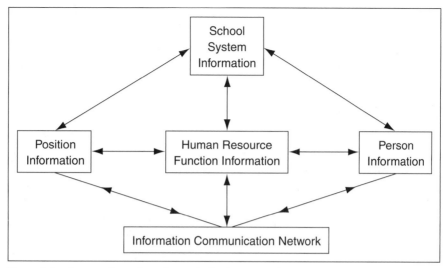

Figure 3.2   Types and interdependence of school system information.

mentary schools); and into specialized work such as accounting, clerical, maintenance, operation, and administration. Appropriate technology in the form of knowledge, tools, and work design is to be considered a planning aspect of any organization.

Information as a Planning Resource

Reference has been made above to the information-based role of leaders (superintendents, principals, supervisors, and department heads) responsible for carrying out
system expectations. Figure 3.2 illustrates common components of a data base structure for the human resource function. These components include system information,
position information, person information, human resource function information, and
communication information. These forms of information, when interconnected, provide the framework or structure of an information system. The data base structure
referred to above is employed through a variety of information channels to enlist
member support for making clear ideas about what results are expected and to identify ways and means by which outcomes are to be achieved. The components of a
human resource information system, as portrayed in Figure 3.2, are reviewed below.

System Information

The school system acquires, creates, and disseminates information to bring individuals, groups, and the system into congruence with its strategic direction and to enlist
the support of members to reach higher levels of achievement. Information is used
to create an institutional vision of expectations, as well as to establish purposes,
structures, plans, policies, programs, and projects for their realization. Information

is also directed toward shaping specific organizational guides such as codes of ethics, reporting relationships, performance standards, rules, regulations, responsibilities, and controls for internalizing this aspect of system culture and the behavioral boundaries involved.

Position Information

A *position* is defined as a collection of tasks constituting the total work assignment of a single worker. A position or job description prescribes its purpose and scope, major duties and functions, performance standards, authority, relationship to other positions, terms of employment, and position value (relative monetary worth and authority of the position in the organizational hierarchy). Positions are governed to some extent by applicable legislation and regulations. From the standpoint of the human resource function, a collection of job descriptions creates the foundation for virtually all human resource activities. A very useful tool in the human resource function is the job description manual, copies of which are given to members and employed for a wide variety of operational activities such as planning, recruitment, selection, compensation, and performance appraisal.[3]

Person Information

Person information is included in a document referred to as a *position specification.* Qualifications needed to occupy the position include factors such as legal require-ments (certificate, license, degree), experience, major area of study, health, disability, literacy, citizenship, aptitude, and such additions to the above as may be called for, such as residence within the community. Such qualifications provide exploratory information in the selection process. The higher the position in the organization structure, the more extensive the probing of the applicant's information. The selec-tion team may want information about the applicant's social and cultural expecta-tions, family life, behavioral background, professional standard of conduct, moral principles and values, and financial responsibility.

As will be pointed out subsequently in the discussion of records information, part of the data base includes information on currently employed personnel such as performance evaluations, work history, career path, recognition, and change in sta-tus or position.

Human Resource Function Information

To understand the kinds of information needed to administer the human resource function, a natural way to start is to identify the activities that are strongly related to the ultimate purpose of the function. Such activities are exemplified in the mod-ules of the information structure portrayed in Figure 3.3. The eleven processes

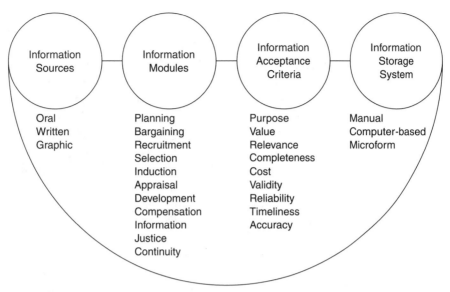

Figure 3.3   Model of the human resource information structure.

listed there are methods used to recruit, select, induct, develop, appraise, compensate, inform, and retain the personnel needed, in both quality and quantity, to achieve system and function purpose. Each of the processes listed in Figure 3.3 provides a basis for satisfying the needs of the system and its members.

Communication of Information

In any organization, information is provided by a communication system. Figure 3.2 emphasizes the principle that a communication system is the tie that binds the organization and operation of a school system. Communication of information allows interaction and interchange among system members. No school system could operate effectively, even for a short period of time, without acquiring and disseminating information about its human resources—those persons who enter, remain in, and leave. School systems are constantly confronted with information-communication problems centering on such matters as keeping abreast of the need for information, both in quantity and in quality, making information accessible to users as needed, and furnishing information to position holders that will help them achieve the position objectives for which they are employed. Isolating key communication system elements enables us to gain a better understanding of the sources of information and the course or flow of its direction. Facets of a communication system that are directly relevant to the school system and its operation are (a) channels of communication, (b) direction of communication, and (c) formal and informal communication.

Channels of Communication

Figure 3.3 indicates that there are three sources of personnel information—oral, written, and graphic. Oral information includes various kinds of personnel interviews, such as recruitment, appraisal, and exit interviews. Telephone reference checks, observations of a teacher's performance in the classroom, a personnel counseling session, conversations among administrators about personnel, and board discussion on personnel policy illustrate the nature and variety of oral sources of personnel information.

Written sources of information comprise the majority of the human resource data base in a school system. Basic to written sources of information are such elements as personnel handbooks, policy manuals, bulletins, memos, annual and periodic reports, circulars, computer printouts, and the well-known (and extremely useful) personnel forms, which cumulatively represent the written personnel record system.

Graphic sources of information are used less extensively than oral or written types, but they do exist in such forms as photographs, graphs, charts, tables, slides, transparencies, motion pictures, filmstrips, and televised information. On occasion, graphic sources of personnel information can be extremely valuable. For example, televising classroom teaching performances has proved to be useful in appraisal and development of classroom teachers.

Direction of Communication

The flow of information through communications can be considered in terms of four directions: (a) downward, (b) upward, (c) horizontal, and (d) diagonal.[4] Illustrations of downward communication within the organization structure include official statements or plans such as policies, procedures, personnel manuals, memoranda, bulletin boards, house organs, and various other types of written information, (e.g., a board of education's response to a teacher union contract proposal). Upward communication involves message senders rather than receivers and is commonly referred to as *feedback.* Its use provides the school administration with information about current problems and issues, as well as encouraging personnel participation and involvement (e.g., the teacher union's response to the board of education's proposal for sharing benefit costs). Horizontal, or peer-to-peer communication, might consist of an exchange of information between the system's athletic director and the coach. Diagonal communication is exemplified by a report from the high school's business manager to the principal regarding bids for the purchase of new field hockey uniforms. Diagonal communication may result in greater efficient use of time and effort.

Formal and Informal Communication

Formal devices for internal and external communication are generated by management to keep various interest groups informed about budgets, audits, strategic plans, employment contracts, school taxes, and occasionally legal issues confronting the system. Formal communications are usually downward and usually do not invite feedback. Informal communication, sometimes referred to as the *grapevine*, is a means of generating off-the-record information through peer relations. Informal channels of upward communication are considered useful ways to provide opportunities for expressing viewpoints, giving suggestions, challenging improper management actions, and allowing ideas to flow upward to draw official attention. Despite the array of modern communication technology available for use in school administration, an intractable organization communication problem is unilateral communication: downward (one-way) transmission of information without benefit of feedback. Experience indicates that both downward and upward flow of communication are essential for an effective information system.

Demand for and Supply of Human Resource Information

Information Demand

Information needed to conduct the human resources function can be thought of as a component of the total information system of the organization. It consists of a planned network of *forms, files, reports, records,* and *documents.* The nature and variety of information needed to conduct the human resources function can be inferred from the outline of information needs shown in Figure 3.4. More specifically, there is an insatiable demand from within and outside of the system for an extensive array of human resources information to (a) conduct day-to-day operations, (b) resolve short- and long-term personnel problems, (c) comply with external demands, (d) satisfy system needs for research and planning data, and (e) plan for and implement collective bargaining agreements.

As school administrative units become larger and more complex, demand for more and varied types of information increases. The necessity for creating, collecting, processing, storing, retrieving, disseminating, and integrating data to aid in the administration of an organization is hardly a matter for debate. It is becoming increasingly clear that sole dependence on the time-honored manual system of data processing is no longer appropriate to keep a modern educational institution abreast of informational requirements. As more school administrative units become large enough to offer comprehensive educational programs, it is inevitable that improved data processing methods will be employed to integrate information for major areas of the school system—*instruction, funds, facilities,* and *personnel.*

To sum up what has previously been discussed, the operation of a modern school system, with all the organizational, legal, political, governmental, and social ramifications entailed, has caused the volume of essential records and reports to soar. To cope with problems of record keeping and to make effective use of records

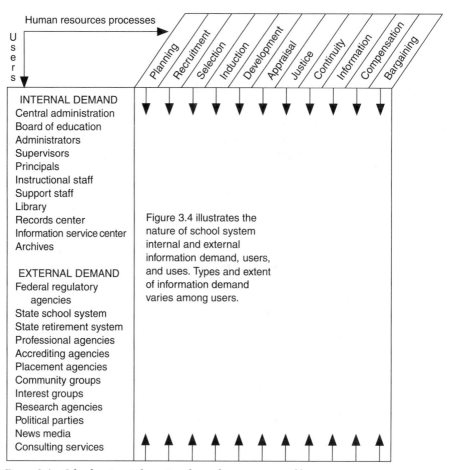

Figure 3.4 illustrates the nature of school system internal and external information demand, users, and uses. Types and extent of information demand varies among users.

Figure 3.4   School system information demand, users, uses, and human resource processes.

that are collected and stored, a new approach to records management is needed. This need can be met in part by making technological improvements in the information system. Innovation can and should be geared not only to improvement of the human resource function in general, but also to the welfare of each individual employed in the system. Considerable advances have been made in the use of electronic data processing equipment to facilitate collection of data and dissemination of information for decision making. These systems make possible storage and retrieval of highly detailed and organized personnel data that are useful in administering the human resource function. Although it is true that many personnel decisions cannot be programmed, it is reasonable to assume that personnel decision making can be improved by data that are better organized, more accurate, more complete, and more rapidly reported.

Information Supply

What is so rare as an organization that has an information system capable of providing, on demand, information on various personnel and related aspects such as employee data, contractual agreements, regulatory requirements, litigation, disclosure, decision fairness, discrimination, and personnel file access and records duplication?

Few systems can readily and fully meet information demands such as those noted above, as well as those listed in Figure 3.4. The gap between information supply and demand in many institutions can be due to a variety of problems, including absence of reliable records, outdated records, fragmentation of record creation and record keeping, needless files, record duplication, and inattention to transforming quantitative data into qualitative information. Moreover, and most important, the absence of a centrally directed and appropriately staffed records management program often leads to inability to resolve satisfactorily questions or disputes about discrimination, personnel performance, salary, wage, and benefit issues, disciplinary actions, and unauthorized disclosure of personnel data. Failure to modernize an information system is an open invitation to a host of human resource problems and charges because of a lack of appropriate information to resolve challenges such as those mentioned. Records and records management will be covered in greater detail in the section that follows.

Records and Records Management

Records and Their Purposes

The place of records and record keeping for both the school system and the human resource function is significant. Their importance as components of an information system is linked to meeting legal and contractual requirements, providing data resources, acting as a form of memory, and providing a foundation for carrying out both decision-making and operational activities. An initial understanding of the place of records, records management, and their employment in the human resource function involves an explanation of how certain attributes relating to records are defined.

Records

Records are any form of recorded information. The information may be recorded on paper, microfilm, audiotapes, computer generated, or other media. Records are fundamentally a means of storing facts or events in order to solve human resource problems. They represent vital activities relative to the human resource function and create essential information material. A **records center**

is defined as a storage area for *inactive records,* which can be located on site or off site. A *file* is a device (for example, a folder, case, or cabinet) where papers or publications (records) are arranged or classified in convenient order for storage, retrieval, reference, or preservation purposes. An **archive** is a place where public records or historical documents are preserved. Labeled folders in a metal or wooden filing cabinet located in school attendance units embody, for many school systems, the concept of an information system.

Data

Data consists of factual information (such as measurements or statistics) capable of being converted into information. A **data base** is a collection of organized data (such as employee personal data) especially for mass retrieval, usually computer arranged for rapid expansion, updating, or retrieval. **Data processing** involves the conversion of raw data into machine-readable form and its subsequent processing and refinement into information.

Information

Information is knowledge consisting of facts that have been analyzed in the context of school system management. An **information system** is a plan designed to acquire, refine, organize, store, maintain, retrieve, and communicate data in a valid and accurate form. Material from the human resource information system is used as a basis for discussing, reasoning, calculating, forecasting, and resolving problems related to the human resource function.

In the following sections, the connection among information, the human resources function, and the information revolution is given special focus.

Forms and Records

Forms and records are considered parts of a record system. A **form** used in the human resource function is defined as a document with blank spaces to be filled in with particular types of data. Examples include forms for employment application, personnel requisition, application identification, employment eligibility, job interest, employment interview, reference check, credit inquiry authorization, applicant flow, job descriptions, performance reports, and signature receipts of handbooks (job description, policy, information, personnel).[5] A **report** is a written account or statement describing in detail a relevant event as it pertains to the operation of the human resource function. An **audit** report of personnel records is illustrative. Both forms and reports become elements of an automated records system when properly designed, standardized, numbered, or identified appropriately for storage, retrieval, and automated processing purposes.

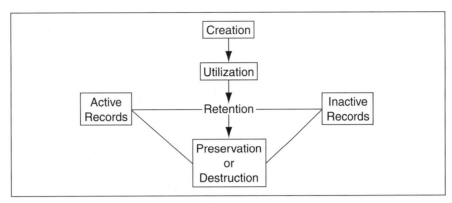

Figure 3.5   Life span attributes of records.

Life Span of Records

Figure 3.5 presents the sequence of activities in the life span of records. The sequence begins with records creation. Creation of data, which are later transformed into information, is exemplified by applications for employment, as well as files on current or former employees, medical records files, and computerized personnel files. Data from the sources noted above include facts transformed into information. Decisions on personnel selection, compensation, turnover, performance, termination, promotion, tenure, and benefits are transformed from raw data into information. Active records are those for current employees, inactive records are those stored, especially on former employees, and capable of ready retrieval. Records are retained or destroyed, depending on their legal, administrative, fiscal, historical, or archival significance. Organizational records, such as board of education minutes, contracts, property deeds, leases, and insurance policies are considered to be vital records and are included in the preservation category.[6]

Significance of the Records Policy

It is ironic that in the contemporary information age, more than a few educational institutions have been scored for the comatose or lethargic state of their information systems. At least four forces have contributed to this dilemma: (a) misunderstanding the importance of comprehensive personnel records; (b) proliferation of demand for school system information; (c) advances in electronic data processing; and (d) failure to staff the information system properly. One basic approach to improving records management is to establish records policy guidelines. The purpose of records management is to be able to retrieve from the computer or file drawer any item needed for operational and human resource function purposes.

Records Management Policy Guidelines

In the process of establishing, upgrading, enhancing, and formalizing a records management program, it is essential to develop policies for these purposes. A policy review of arrangements for systematizing school records is important because it aids in crystallizing issues and defining policy objectives such as the following:

• Appointing professional personnel such as an information system director and an office service manager, either full or part time, depending on the school system's size, to direct the records management program.
• Setting forth policy guidelines for record categories in areas of the human resource function (see Figure 3.6).
• Appointing record coordinators for work units such as attendance units (individual schools), central administration, and support services.
• Documenting personnel decisions as a basis for defending charges relating to termination, appraisal, layoff, and employment discrimination.
• Meeting statutory requirements.
• Utilizing electronic data processing technology when and where appropriate.
• Including school system record forms and reports as components of the records program.
• Setting aside space to accommodate a records center for storing and retrieving vital, inactive, and archival records.
• Issuing a records management manual containing policies, practices, and procedures for directing, controlling, and auditing the system's plan to make the program effective and efficient.

In closing this brief discussion of records and records management, it is worth noting that the sophistication of an information system depends on a number of factors affecting its design and operation. There is virtually no limit to the type of information that can be created, stored, used, and employed effectively. Some planning influences worthy of consideration are system size, complexity, strategic intent, cost, future employment need, internal and external information demands, and information specialists required. Wherever applicable, information technology will be treated as a concomitant of each of the later chapters in this book.

Information Technology and the Human Resource Function

As indicated in Chapter 1, **technology** refers to the totality of means employed to achieve the aims of the human resource function, as well as the broader mission of the school system. Included in information technology are member skills, knowledge, tools, mechanisms, techniques, and know-how to carry out the function's objectives. When a broad definition of technology is applied—namely, the applica-

It is the policy of the Riverpark school system to maintain an information system to facilitate the creation, refinement, reporting, utilization, storage, retrieval, and protection of recorded information. Key components include:

- *Purpose.* Establish a course of action to guide and determine present and future decisions concerning all aspects of the human resources information system. Improve individual, unit, and system effectiveness, decision making, and information processing efficiency. Establish paper-based and computer-based records to satisfy both internal and external information requirements.

- *Scope.* Create a uniform filing plan within the central information system to locate and retrieve any record readily, whether the file is centralized or decentralized. Institute guidelines governing the scope and boundaries of administrative decisions pertaining to the collection, storage, retrieval, retention, access, distribution, and disposition of human resources information.

- *Responsibility.* Set forth human resources information guidelines for administrative responsibilities in the central administration, attendance units, and support units relative to the scope of information described above. Place overall operational responsibility in one office, with a systemwide purview, to oversee the progress of human resources information through the several stages of its life cycle (*active, inactive,* and *archival*). A records center and or an information service center become the responsibility of the position (supervisor of records). Prepare a system records manual to communicate to employees the manner in which the information system operates at both the central and work unit levels (individual schools, departments, and offices). System members, as part of the information network, are instructed in standard uniform filing procedures.

- *Access.* Identify which classes of information are restricted, how access to restricted categories is granted, who has the authority to grant access or release which categories of information, and what controls will govern photocopying or other means of recorded reproduction.

- *Budget.* Include funding in the annual budget to maintain and improve the effectiveness of the information system.

- *Individual employee file.* The individual employee data base consists of three files (*basic file, evaluative file,* and *supervisory file*).

    Basic file: Objective material and no third-party evaluation or personal opinions. Employment profile, payroll, work data, etc., (see Table 10.1).

    Evaluative file: Performance data regarding employment retention tenure, probationary review, and position effectiveness. Destroyed within five years after decisions.

    Supervisory file: Confidential property of supervisor. Destroyed after supervisor's death, termination, or retirement.

- *Regulatory.* Adhere to regulatory provisions governing employee records and privacy safeguards.

Figure 3.6   Information policies, practices, and technology of the Riverpark school system.

tion of organized knowledge to the information process, as well as every form of recorded information, electronic and nonelectronic, programmed and nonprogrammed, computer hardware and software, *supported* and *supporting* activities, and information specialists—the meaning of information technology becomes more apparent. *Technology,* as the term is employed in the discussion that follows, refers to a wide range of administrative and instructional devices, including but not limited to computers and software, laser disc machine and programs, videocassette players and tapes, distance learning, cable, radio, microwave transmission, telephones for learning and data transmission, online services, and many combinations of these methods.

Technology has both internal and external aspects. Technological advances produced by the external environment, such as computer technology, models for developing instructional systems, research findings, and information processing, illustrate the importance of technology as a force that affects a school system and its operation. One of the many reasons school systems need to be continuously concerned about information technology is that prevailing knowledge, techniques, tools, and processes help to *extend individual, group,* and *system capabilities* to perform tasks more efficiently and effectively.

Part of an information system is a technology plan, especially as it applies to the human resource function. Assessment of the characteristics of existing technology regarding the human resource function includes what technology is currently in operation; how it is being used; what forms are being used in administration, instruction, and support services; how personnel are being trained or retrained; and responsibility for managing information technology. Assessment of current information technology includes methods for acquiring, installing, and using technology, the policy on accepting donations of used technology, and the maintenance cost of current and planned technology components.

Human Resource Information and the Computer

It has been said that information technology is the most revolutionary force in modern times. The list of changes being propelled by electronic technology is striking. In the corporate world, for example, the advent of the facsimile machine made Western Union obsolete in the field of overseas communication. In the public domain, manual preparation of a ranked salary analysis takes about half a day; electronically, it takes about five minutes. Tracking, accumulating, and summarizing employee attendance saves hours of manual labor. Applicant tracking, payroll preparation, position control, individual employment files, and résumé scanning can be added to the repertoire of human resources activities for which information can be compiled from various records, analyzed, and presented in a standard format.

While the debate in education over school reform, outcome-based education, and site-based decision making goes on, emerging and enhanced technologies and technological opportunities are revolutionizing the world. More extensive application of technology to school district information systems and human resources subsystems can play an essential part in the information revolution, which is bidding to change information creation from a paper to a paperless endeavor.

Computer Availability and Application

For a human resources information system to be effective and efficient, it must be capable of providing the kind of information required by those who use it in personnel practice. It should be designed to make available to all authorized personnel the quality and quantity of information when, where, and in what form it is needed. Computer availability helps the human resource function to develop the kind of information it requires to capture and process current data for meaningful analysis in the personal decision-making process.

In order to determine the manner and extent to which a computer should be linked to an information system, several factors must be considered. Among the more significant factors are (a) the kinds of information needed for the human resource function to operate effectively, (b) the strengths and limitations of a computer in providing desired information, (c) the role of a computer in the information system, (d) the people who will create the data designs and make the key decisions about their processing, and (e) the procedures and processes to be employed to optimize computer applications.

In developing computer inputs, one must first consider which questions are to be answered by the outputs. For example, in which processes and to what extent will the computer be applied to speed up the availability of data and the analytical capability of those in charge of the human resource function (recruitment, selection, collective bargaining, compensation, and/or planning)? What important personnel information can the computer provide in each of these areas that is not otherwise readily attainable? Is the computer's role to be limited to payroll, accounting, and personal information components? Will the computer be employed in forecasting enrollments, staff size, personnel budgets, and/or selection interviewing? How can the human resource function take full advantage of computer capabilities in such components as skills inventory, career interests, performance appraisal, and the analysis of historical interview responses to validate and predict the potential for tenure, absenteeism, and promotion? The information outputs, based on questions such as these, will influence the kinds of computer hardware and software to be purchased, who will do the programming, and who will be the data users.

The strengths and limitations of computer application in the human resources function should be taken into consideration. Computers are readily adaptable to provide selected types of information, save time, and relieve programmers of considerable effort in data processing. A computer can be viewed as a way to extend the human mind, enable it to identify personnel problem indicators, and take a wider view of data in decision making. For example, up-to-date information makes it possible to take corrective action, initiate investigative action, or take steps to resolve identified difficulties before they magnify. In effect, the capabilities of today's computer are numerous and far-reaching insofar as they enable the system to gather, process, and apply information that in years past was too expensive, too labor intensive, and in many respects beyond the power of existing information systems to obtain.

The *limitations* of computers should be considered in developing or expanding their use in the human resource function. Most important, the concept of an information system, as will be noted subsequently, *embraces more than computer application.* Moreover, usefulness of a computer depends on what program designers apply to its capabilities in the form of intelligence, vision, imagination, and creativity. The computer will not suffice to generate special kinds of information or to respond to certain on-the-job situations, such as those involving information in face-to-face exchanges, counseling, and establishing performance objectives. In brief, the computer is assuredly an important tool in performing the human resource function. However, this exceedingly valuable instrument cannot define personnel system information needs, nor can it make those personnel decisions that are a never-ending organizational responsibility.

Computerized Human Resource Information Systems

The increasing impact on school systems of data derived from both internal and external sources is compelling leadership to continually upgrade the systematization, utilization, and communication of information. Since human beings are the heart of an information system, this factor makes realization of personnel objectives a vital part of the information-communication axis. Decisions involved in improving an information system include two kinds of approaches—strategic and tactical. The strategic approach involves an information system that supports leadership action to achieve the system's mission. The tactical approach refers to the technology employed to achieve the system's strategic goals.[7] The discussion that follows deals with computer technology as a tactical component of the information system utilized to create, control, and communicate information in order to support school system actions that benefit the system, its personnel, and the children and youth for whom the system is educationally responsible.

It is generally recognized that human resources engage in every form of school system activity. One thing administrators must have in common is the desire to commit resources or marshal the technology, talent, and treasure to attract, retain, and develop their talent. One form of information system technology is the computer and its application in the form of software programs. Figure 3.7 presents a partial list of the many software programs and areas of the human resource function where they are applicable. One impression derived from viewing the software

Age Discrimination Law	Employee Absenteeism
Applicant Tracking	Employee Accident, Illness
Archival Records	Employee Appraisal
Attendance, Employee	Employee Communication
Benefit Administration	Employee References
Career Development	Human Resource Management
Compensation Administration	Human Resource Consulting
Computer-based Recruiting	Information Retrieval
Computer-based Testing	Job Descriptions
Computer-based Training	Medical Records
Data and Survey Analysis	Personnel Communication
Document Imaging	Position Control
Disabilities Act, American	Position Description

Figure 3.7   Types of computer software applications for the human resource function.

programs listed in this figure is that we have entered a new and entirely unprecedented age of emerging information system technology.

So many technical advances have occurred in computer hardware and software that school administrators, as well as human resource practitioners, are compelled to become computer literate. Information system literacy is essential in order to make sound decisions about what information technology is available for a given school system, how the technology should be used, and who will be responsible for its implementation and daily operation. The section that follows provides a structure for considering problems and issues about the extent to which the present information system should be modified or transformed electronically and managed to satisfy human resource needs relating to data gathering and processing, information management, instruction, staff development, communication, and decision support.

The Human Resource Information Process

Figure 3.8 is a general model with which to analyze the human resource **information process.** The model represents relationships within the process and will be used to examine these associations.

The design outlined in Figure 3.8 consists of five phases: (1) diagnosis, (2) preparation, (3) implementation, (4) evaluation, and (5) feedback. Each phase will be examined in the following discussion in terms of the total personnel information process, elements comprising the process, interrelationships among the elements, and integration of the information system into the total personnel function and the entire system. The design can be viewed as an organizational mechanism through which efforts are made to achieve a desired state relative to personnel information.

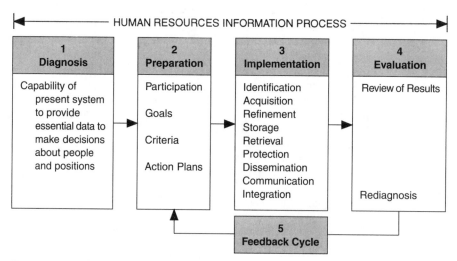

Figure 3.8   Model of the human resource information process.

Diagnosis

The first phase of the information process outlined in Figure 3.8 is *diagnosis,* meaning the fact-finding or data-collection activities designed to assess the extent to which the present information system is providing essential data to achieve the goals of the human resources function. Diagnostic efforts focus on questions relating to what information is now collected and utilized; the ability of the system to retrieve information easily and economically; the level of information accuracy and sophistication needed; the relationship of the information system to the size, structure, goals, organization style, nature of work, and composition of the work groups; and the quantity and quality of information needed at the operating and planning levels. The diagnostic phase of the information process should focus on these kinds of issues: Is the general system acceptable? Is the system operating as it should? Should the current system be revised? Is a new system needed? Should processing be centralized or decentralized?

Figure 3.9 illustrates some of the questions involved in determining which aspects of the human resources information system need improvement, as does the more detailed examination of the information process, which is the theme of the text that follows.

Preparation (Goals and Criteria)

Figure 3.8 indicates that *preparation* is the second major activity in the information process. This phase is concerned with translating the diagnoses of phase 1 (diagnosis) into decisions leading to a series of action plans to improve the personnel information system. Central to the preparation phase is a set of goals for the human resources information system along lines such as the following:

Human Information Inadequacies

- How adequate are the records in the information system regarding human problems in such areas as recruitment, selection, induction, appraisal, development, justice, compensation, continuity, and union relations?
- To what extent is information accessible regarding grievances, transfers, discharge, discrimination, communications, rewarding, discipline, tenure, promotions, resignations, level of technical competency, medical visits, strikes, alienation, job satisfaction, work stressors?
- Does the information system indicate which of the human resources problems are position-related? Nonposition-related (personal)?

Nonhuman Information Inadequacies

- *Technology Information Inadequacies*—Which of the following factors are considered to be obstacles to achieving desirable information system standards: money, materials, facilities, personnel, and equipment?
- *Record-keeping inadequacies*—To what extent are the following recordkeeping facilities adequate: records creation, processing, automation, retention and disposal, security, legal requirements, records management, forms management, records center, and archives?

Organization Information Inadequacies

- How effective are school system provisions regarding the design, implementation, maintenance, and evaluation of the human resources information system? Regarding interfacing with other system functions?
- To what extent does the system utilize tools of human resources research to gather information about the effectiveness of the information system? (Questionnaires, interviews, audits, reports, statistics, critical incidents, comparative studies, historical analysis, and individual and work unit responses to information communication.)

Organizational Impact of Information System Inadequacies

- What is the organizational impact of the information inadequacies on the well-being of the human resource function?

Organizational Implications for Action Planning

- What actions should the system take to remove inadequacies in the human resources information system?

Figure 3.9   Probing for inadequacies and issues in the human resource information system.

- Improvement and enhancement of the information system for collecting routine data, computerizing these transactions wherever possible.
- Elimination of information duplication.
- Elimination of useless information.
- Standardization, wherever possible, of methods for gathering information.
- Justification of information from the standpoints of efficiency and effectiveness.

- Improvement in availability, accuracy, flexibility, consistency, accessibility, and utility of information.
- Systematization of collection of nonroutine data.
- Involvement in the design of the information system of key people who will actually use both routine and nonroutine types of data.
- Development of criteria that will govern identification, acquisition, refinement, storage, protection, retrieval, dissemination, communication, and integration of information (see Figure 3.8).
- Organization and administration of the human resources information system in an effective and efficient manner. (The information system should be part of a master plan to use funds, facilities, people, technology, and machines to achieve system objectives. This means appointment of knowledgeable personnel with authority to manage the information system, update the plan annually, and focus on specific objectives for hardware, software, personnel, budgets, space, and applications.)

Figure 3.10 outlines areas of the human resource function and provides indicators of their application to an information system. Areas of the function shown in Figure 3.10 serve as grounds for reasonable inference about their potential for multiple applications. When the processes shown in Figure 3.10 are integrated so that data generated in one area can be accessed and used in another, the result is an extension of information system capabilities. For example, appraisal data can be accessed and used in development, compensation, and continuity processes. It is in this connection that information may be viewed as either programmed or nonprogrammed. Certain data can be computerized, as illustrated in Table 3.1, but information of a conceptual, hypothetical, or judgmental nature is not readily amenable to computer programming. Both types of information are shown in Table 3.1.

Implementation

Once the school system has defined the objectives of the personnel information system, determined what kind of information is needed, reviewed information sources and acceptance criteria as outlined in Figure 3.3, and allocated responsibilities for administering various activities related to the system, the next phase (implementation) of the personnel information process can be initiated. This phase, as outlined in Figure 3.10, consists of nine key activities: identification, acquisition, refinement, storage, retrieval, protection, dissemination, communication, and integration. In the following discussion, each of these activities will be examined in terms of its relationship to the personnel information process.

Identification of Information

The initial activity in the personnel information process, as depicted in Figure 3.10, is identification of information. Its primary focus is on implementing decisions by the central administration governing what information is needed to achieve the

Human Resources Areas		Illustrative Applications
• Planning	←——→	Strategic plans, structure projection, employee inventory, employee projections, assessment of impact of internal and external forces.
• Information	←——→	Position control, internal–external communication methods, information manuals (position descriptions, policy, personnel, compensation).
• Recruitment	←——→	Applicant tracking, positions and persons data, technology for assessing potential, recruitment policies, practices, procedures.
• Selection	←——→	Information technology for matching person qualifications and position requirements.
• Induction	←——→	Information, plans to assist inductees in adjusting readily to position, work unit, and system relationships, organization culture and ethics.
• Development	←——→	Information, plans, and activities designed to enhance or improve employee's current skills and performance; self-awareness and self-development feedback, career movement and counseling.
• Appraisal	←——→	Information technology relating to appraisee-appraiser performance reviews, critical incidents, behavioral checklists, narrative accounts, supervisory reports.
• Compensation	←——→	Information on how compensation is derived and distributed. Rules governing salary, wages, benefits, bonuses, incentives, rewards, position-person worth.
• Continuity	←——→	Information concerning tenure, disability, leaves, health and safety, employee assistance, transfer, reassignment, termination, promotion, demotion, absenteeism, substitution, retirement, death.
• Justice	←——→	Information on employment security, fair treatment, due process, grievances, academic freedom, justice system, ombuds practitioner, legal rights.
• Unionism	←——→	Information relative to bargaining process, scope, contract design, system-union rights and responsibilities, contract administration, arbitration.

Figure 3.10   Areas of the human resource function and their applications.

TABLE 3.1
Illustration of Programmed and Nonprogrammed Personnel Information

Programmed Information		Nonprogrammed Information
Payroll	Résumé	Personnel policies and procedures
Benefits	Certification	Performance appraisals
Attendance	Positions	Personnel motivation
Retirement	Master files	Personnel actions
Grievances	Tax reports	Organizational actions
Skills inventory	Turnover	Organizational structure
Personnel budget	Leaves	Personnel planning premises
	Compensation profile	Strategies and supporting plans
	Personnel statistics	

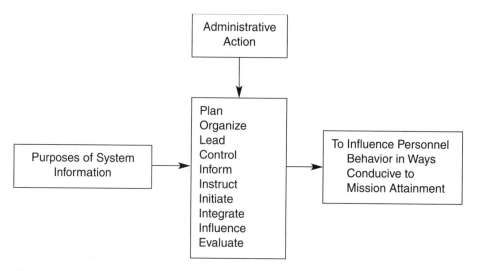

Figure 3.11   Goal-oriented purposes of information in educational administration.

goals of the system; purposes for which the information is needed; who will use the information; and what means shall be employed to gather, store, retrieve, and communicate it most effectively and efficiently. Consequently, the initial act in the information process is the central administration's conceptualization of the kind of personnel information system it plans to operate to influence personnel behavior in ways conducive to goal attainment. This perspective is outlined in Figure 3.11, which construes the purposes of all information to be mission oriented. Administration, as viewed in Figure 3.11, links information to action of various kinds. Some of the information will indicate what has happened (past), some will focus on what is happening (present), and some will be needed to plan what ought to happen in the system (future). All three types of information will be oriented toward influencing behavior of people to satisfy both individual and system needs.

Acquisition of Information

Acquisition of information, as noted in the personnel information process shown in Figure 3.10, follows plans for its identification and is defined by objectives of the system, as well as the user's needs, including the needs of administrators, staff, board, clients, and public. Acquisition of information includes identification, selection, development, and purchase of source material. Source material, as noted previously, includes many forms of oral, written, and graphic information. Acquisition of personnel information encompasses a network of forms, records, files, and reports. A *form* may be defined as a standardized method of recording data, as illustrated by a personnel application form. *Records* are the accumulation and organization of information regarded as of more than temporary significance. A personnel *file* (folder, case, or cabinet) is a collection of related information arranged in order for preservation or reference. Three kinds of personnel files are illustrative. The *basic* file contains objective material and no third-party evaluations or opinions. A *confidential* appraisal file contains supervisory reports, appraisals, and psychological and test assessments by third parties. The *career* file contains information regarding positions or assignment information within or outside of the organization, including career anchor, career ladder, and special talents, skills, and abilities. File control criteria points include purposes a file is to serve, file location and jurisdiction, access criteria, and disposal conditions. Finally, *reports* utilize records to communicate information. Other sources of personnel information include letters, profiles, studies, external and internal personnel data, and documents of various types.

As suggested in Figure 3.3, acquisition of information should be governed by criteria such as *purpose, value, relevance, completeness, cost, validity, reliability, timeliness,* and *accuracy.* Timeliness, or the currency of data, is an important criterion in determining whether information should be acquired. A personnel roster is of little use to the payroll department if it is not kept current. Information files on recruitable talent, promotable personnel, and position holders who have reached performance plateaus are useless if they have not been updated. Use of information on collateral benefits for administrative personnel in collective bargaining will be determined, for example, by its timeliness and by the aforementioned criteria. Up-to-date information is expensive to maintain. Although always desirable, it must be judged in terms of the cost/benefit concept. Certain kinds of information cost more money than other kinds of information to obtain, and their worth must be judged in terms of their benefit to the system.

Refinement

Most data acquired by the system need to be refined, some to a greater and some to a lesser degree, before they are stored for usage. Refinement includes checking data for accuracy. Information on paychecks, retirement contributions, and certification of personnel, for example, must be precise. Complete and accurate information concerning the skill of every staff member is essential to conduct the human resource planning process effectively. On the other hand, any collected data should include only those items the system really needs, inasmuch as the collecting and storing of information is relatively expensive. Other types of data refinement include editing all forms of information entering the system, eliminating redundant information or overlapping information-gathering efforts, and incorporating error checks into the information system in order to call attention to missing or erroneous data. In effect, the purpose of refining information is to ensure that it meets the acceptance criteria mentioned earlier. Refinement is conceived as a kind of screen to separate useful from useless information, to code and prepare acceptable information for entrance into the information system, to ensure that the information is valid and reliable, and to bring together one form of data with another that, when combined, will create new information and perhaps new perspectives that were not possible before the information elements were related.

The concept of information refinement includes many and varied activities aimed at acquiring and storing data in forms that enhance the work of the system. Refinement may include editing information inputs (such as payroll verification), combining quarterly performance appraisal reports for a performance profile, employing statistical techniques for meaningful summary descriptions of raw data, and drawing inferences from personnel data under conditions characterized by uncertainty. Refinement of information helps to make complex system phenomena more understandable and in some cases enables the system to achieve a new level of understanding about its human problems.

Storage

After information has been acquired and refined, arrangements must be made to store it for future use. As shown in Figure 3.3, information can be stored in manual, computer-based, or microform systems. Manual storage systems include direct files, inverted files, optical coincidence cards, edge-notched cards, and punched cards. Microform storage systems include rolls of film, microfilm jackets, aperture cards, microfiche, and opaque microcards. A computer-based storage system is one that processes data by electronic machines quickly, accurately, and automatically. Data processed by a computer are stored on memory devices, such as magnetic tapes, and must be programmed—that is, the computer must be instructed as to what operations are to be performed and in what sequence.

The decision as to which system or combination of systems will be used to store personnel information will depend on a variety of factors, including size of staff, uses to be made of the information, availability of fiscal resources, and whether there are competent staff personnel to design and operate the system. Because the primary function of a personnel information system is to provide information when it is needed, where it is needed, and in the form in which it is needed, the storage system should be designed to enhance this objective.

Generally speaking, manual and microfilm storage systems are used to record historical information; a mechanized system should deal with current information. Information on the current status of personnel may best be stored in a mechanized system; the performance history of each individual can be recorded in all three systems. The point to consider is that mechanized storage of certain kinds of information, such as the historical performance profile of an individual staff member, may be prohibitive from a cost standpoint.

Retrieval

Information retrieval, one of the activities in the implementation of the personnel information process outlined in Figure 3.8, refers to methods and procedures for recovering specific information from stored data. It goes without saying that information users should be able to retrieve stored information readily and in the form needed. Such is not always the case. Information stored manually, for example, is sometimes irretrievable because procedures employed in storing it were faulty. Information not properly classified, indexed, and coded will create problems when retrieval queries are posed. Consequently, one of the requirements for operating an effective information storage-retrieval system is training staff personnel in procedures for classifying, indexing, and coding all incoming material.

Retrieval begins with a *search strategy* designed to locate information to solve problems posed by the user. This search strategy includes evaluation of stored information to determine its relevance to such problems. The search is also conducted with consideration for the breadth and depth of information needed. The foregoing observation shows that there are various constraints affecting the search for personnel information, including time, funds, and personnel. Because information is the substance that holds an organization together and keeps it viable, designing the storage-retrieval system and training personnel to operate it efficiently and effectively are matters of importance to the administrative team.

Protection

Any organization that includes data about individuals in its personnel information system must concern itself with **privacy laws.** There are two federal laws that should be noted: the Freedom of Information Act of 1966 (Public Law 89-487; codified in 1967 by Public Law 90-23), amended in 1974, and the Privacy Act of 1974 (Public Law 93-579). The Freedom of Information Act requires government agencies to make available certain records that are requested. The Privacy Act is designed to resolve problems relating to disclosure, recording, inspection, and challenges to information about individuals in federal agency files.

The impact of the Privacy Act differs for various kinds of organizations, but its thrust is such that every organization needs to be knowledgeable about legal ramifications of personnel information and their implications for administering the information system. What records may be disclosed, by whom, and for what purposes; how disclosures are to be recorded; controls on individual inspection of records; and resolving disagreements about individual file information are among the problems involved in the protection of information.

General recommendations for establishing a fair information protection policy include the following:

- Set up policies and guidelines to protect information in the organization: types of data to be sought, methods of obtaining the data, retention and dissemination of information, employee or third-party access to information, release of information about former employees, and mishandling of information.
- Inform employees of these information-handling policies.
- Become thoroughly familiar with state and federal laws regarding privacy.
- Establish a policy that states specifically that employees and prospective employees cannot waive their right to privacy.
- Establish the policy that any manager or nonmanager who violates these privacy principles will be subject to discipline or termination.

• Avoid fraudulent, secretive, or unfair means of collecting data. When possible, collect data directly from the individual concerned.

• Do not maintain secret files on individuals. Inform them what information is stored on them, the purpose for which it was collected, how it will be used, and how long it will be kept.

• Collect only job-related information that is relevant for specific decisions.

• Maintain records of individuals or organizations that have regular access to or request information on a need-to-know basis.

• Periodically allow employees to inspect and update information stored on them.

• Gain assurance that any information released to outside parties will be used only for the purposes set forth prior to its release.[8]

Dissemination

Dissemination is defined as distribution of information (especially from a gathering or storage point, such as an information center) to individuals within and agencies outside of the system. Certain kinds of personnel information will be stored in each of the attendance units. Most will be stored in various offices of the central administration, especially those data vital to the operation of the human resource function. Some of the more important of these data are:

Personnel records	Position code
Personnel forms	Education of personnel
Payroll registers	Entrance-exit dates
Retirement plans	Appraisal reviews
Personnel rosters	Staffing policies and strategies
Personnel inventory	Personnel budget
Income tax computations	Personnel forecast
Salary schedules	Absenteeism
Worker's compensation	Turnover
Wage rates	Recruitment files
Leaves of absence	Selection data
Vacation eligibility	Personnel development
Insurance coverage	Collective bargaining
Hospital contract numbers	Tenure
Position classification	Separations

Communication

Observers of information systems generally state that there is a difference between information and communication. Peter F. Drucker has observed, for example, that "communication and information are different and indeed largely opposite—yet interdependent."[9] The subordinate may receive a periodic report on the appraisal of his or her performance, but if there is an absence of communication, the information may have no meaning for the subordinate whatsoever. This is true especially if there has been no prior communication between the subordinate and the supervisor

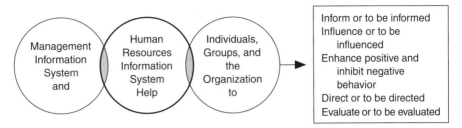

Figure 3.12   Linkage between information and management of the human resource function.

about the system's expectations for the position and its occupant, how the incumbent views the role, problems in performing it, and how it ought to be performed.

It has been noted that personnel performance and organizational communication are closely related. The individual's understanding of what the organization expects him or her to accomplish and how to accomplish it, how the organization plans to achieve its aims, and whether it considers the employee's work satisfactory all depend on the efficiency of the communication network.

It is generally agreed that within an organization there are many instances of failure to communicate, and these result in unsatisfactory individual performance, misunderstandings, resignations, lack of concern for systemwide goals, and general decline in coordinated behavior. In one sense, communication is an organization's peripheral nervous system; without it, organizational behavior is haphazard.

Integration

Earlier, it was stated that information links individuals, groups, and the organization. This concept is portrayed in Figure 3.12, the intent of which is to stress these points:

- One of the continuing and critical management tasks is to make effective personnel decisions.
- Personnel decisions cover the full spectrum of system activities (plans, funds, facilities, people, and structure), as well as internal and external environments.
- The key to personnel problem solving and decision making is a human resources information system.
- The need for a unified information system has been accentuated by an increase in the number and types of human problems in organizations, as well as by the need for more and quicker decisions to resolve these problems.
- One result of an integrated information system should be an increase in the ability of the organization, the units, and the individuals therein to perform effectively and efficiently because they are furnished with the quality and quantity of data essential to decision making and problem solving. In sum, contemporary changes in modern organizations are such that human resource decisions require an integrated information system that will enhance decision-making and problem-solving capabilities.

Evaluation and Feedback

The human resources information process outlined in Figure 3.8 includes *evaluation* and *feedback* as activities essential to its operation and improvement. Every organization needs to know how well the system as a whole and each of its parts are achieving assigned objectives. This is done through control procedures by which the outcomes achieved are compared to those desired. If deviations from plans are discovered, corrective action is taken. So it is with the personnel information system. The organization wants to know, for example, whether:

- The present system is effective.
- Parts of it need to be preserved or modified.
- The system is providing information to operate the human resource function effectively and efficiently.
- The system is capable of recording and reporting events daily as they occur.
- Information security tests meet the criteria emphasized in the Privacy Act (see Glossary).
- The information module interfaces properly with the total organization information system.

Securing answers to these questions involves various types of diagnoses, including determining what the major problems in the information system are, forces causing the problems, nature and timing of the changes needed to resolve the problems, goals to be brought about by the change, and how goal attainment will be measured. Through evaluation and feedback, needed improvements in the information system can be brought about so as to facilitate organizational decisions regarding personnel processes, policies, and the organization structure; provide information of higher quality to individuals and operating components; and generate improved knowledge and understanding of the human resources function.

Review and Preview

This chapter on information technology and the human resource function includes:

- Five major functions of a school system (planning, educational program, logistics, human resources, and external relations) are linked to each other and to the system as a whole by means of an integrated information system.

- The human resource function, as one of the modules of a total information system, consists of a planned network of forms, files, reports, records, and documents.
- In order to determine the manner and extent to which the computer should be linked to a personnel information system, factors that bear analysis include the kinds of information

needed to effectively contribute to personnel practice, the strengths and limitations of computers in providing essential information, the role of computers in the personnel information system, the people who will create the data designs and make the key decisions about their processing, and the procedures and processes needed to optimize computer applications.

• The personnel information process, as modeled in this chapter, consists of five phases: diagnosis, preparation, implementation, evaluation, and feedback.

• Policy points or protocols for bringing about order, method, and uniformity in the personnel information system include policy purpose, scope, responsibility, access, and active-inactive records.

• Information technology is viewed not as a cureall for the system's human resource problems, but as an investment in strategic advancement and as an enabling factor in extending the performance capabilities of the position holder, the work unit, and the system at large.

In the following chapter, the processes focus on strategic human resource requirements (numbers, skills, abilities, experience), followed by two stages—screening and selection. Both phases are viewed as being interconnected and interdependent.

Discussion Questions

1. Records management in any school system involves at least six essential administrative responsibilities. Can you identify these areas, their content, and their management accountability (chief executive, central administrators, supervisors, principals, department heads)?

2. Identify a records management policy to control (a) legally required records, (b) preemployment records, (c) employment records, (d) privacy records control, and (e) archival records retention.

3. Can you think of some communication attempts within the school system that are meaningful, efficient, and effective? Meaningless, inefficient, and ineffective?

4. What form of downward, upward, and horizontal communication do you send and receive in carrying out your position role?

5. In the role you are assigned, to what extent do you send or receive electronic information to improve your performance effectiveness?

Notes

1. William B. Castetter, *The Human Resource Function in Educational Administration,* 6th ed. (Englewood Cliffs, NJ: Prentice-Hall, Inc., 1996), 418.

2. Theodore T. Herbert, *Dimensions of Organizational Behavior,* 2nd ed. (New York: Macmillan Publishing Co., Inc., 1981), 38.

3. For examples, see National School Boards Association, *The School Personnel*

Management System, rev. ed. (Alexandria, VA., 1996), Chapter 7.

4. John M. Ivancevich and Michael Matteson, *Organizational Behavior and Management,* 3rd ed. (Homewood, IL: Richard D. Irwin, Inc., 1993), 638–639.

5. For example, see William B. Castetter, "The Personnel Manual and the Human Resource Function," in *National Forum of Educational Administration and Supervision,* 13, 2 (1996), 13–23; W. S. Hubbartt, *Personnel Policy Handbook: How to Develop a Manual That Works* (New York: McGraw-Hill, Inc., 1993).

6. The framework for this paragraph was drawn from Susan D. Diamond, *Records Management,* 3rd ed. (New York: American Management Association, 1995), 2–3.

7. Morton F. Meltzer, *The Information Imperative.* (New York: American Management Association, 1971), 2–3.

8. These recommendations have been drawn from Wayne F. Cascio, *Managing Human Resources,* 5th ed. (New York: McGraw-Hill, Inc., 1998), 548–549. Footnotes included in the following works: "A Model Employment Privacy Model," *Macworld* (July 1993), 121; and S. H. Cook, "Privacy Rights: Whose Life Is It Anyway?" 32, 4 "Personnel Administrator (1987), 58–65.

9. Peter F. Drucker, *Management, Tasks, Responsibilities* (New York: American Management Association, 1974), 483.

Supplementary Reading

Galvin, W. "Communications: The Lever of Effectiveness and Productivity." *Daedalus* 125 (Spring 1996), 137–147.

Hurst, Beth; Cindy Wilson; and Genny Cramer. "Professional Teaching Portfolios: Tools for Reflection, Growth, and Advancement." *Phi Delta Kappan* 79, 8 (April 1998), 578–583.

Lawson, Joseph W. R., Jr. *How to Develop an Employee Handbook,* 2nd ed. New York: American Management Association, 1997.

Pipho, Chris. "The Search for Better Education Information." *Phi Delta Kappan* 80, 3 (March 1998), 422.

Pitone, Louise. "Employee Records." In William R. Tracey, ed., *Human Resources Management and Development Handbook,* 2nd ed. New York: American Management Association, 1994, 467–477.

Roberts, Bill. "Software Selection Made Easier." *HRMagazine* 43, 7 (June 21, 1998), 44–47.

Schuler, Randall S. "Human Resource Data, Information, and Assessment Systems." In *Managing Human Resources,* 6th ed. Cincinnati, OH: South-Western College Publishing, 1998, Chapter 3.

Schuler, Randall S. "Understanding Internal and External Environments." In *Managing Human Resources,* Chapter 3.

Spencer, Lyme M.; and Randall C. Page. "Management Information Systems." In William R. Tracey, ed. *Human Resources Management and Development Handbook,* 2nd ed. New York: American Management Association, 1994, 467–477.

PART II

HUMAN RESOURCE PROCESSES: RECRUITMENT, SELECTION, INDUCTION, DEVELOPMENT, AND APPRAISAL

Part II examines six major human resources processes: recruitment, selection, induction, development, appraisal, and compensation. The intent of Part II is to expand our understanding of the key activities that make up organizational staffing. These activities include the following:

- Generating applicant pools
- Matching individual talents with present and future position requirements
- Adjustment and development of system members
- Assessing the performance of employees
- Establishing and maintaining a compensation system

4

Recruitment and Selection

CHAPTER OBJECTIVES

Develop and describe a model for recruitment of human resources.
Describe the relationship between public and system employment policies.
Provide information about applicant attraction strategies.
Develop an overview of the selection process.
Stress the importance of acquiring knowledge about selection technology.
Demonstrate the linkage between recruitment and selection processes.

CHAPTER TERMS

Adverse impact
Affirmative action
Application form
Base rate
Bona Fide Occupational
      Qualification (BFOQ)
Concentration statistic
Content validity
Criterion deficiency
Criterion-related validity analysis
Criterion relevance

Discrimination
Equal employment opportunity
Job analysis
Job content
Job critera
Job predictors
Job simulations
Objective theory
Placement
Practical significance
Protected class status

Recruitment	Stock statistic
Recruitment message	Subjective theory
Reference	Work itself theory
Selection	

School districts must identify, attract, acquire, and retain competent personnel to be effective. Unfortunately, acquiring competent personnel has become more difficult in recent years because of certain labor market changes. As one leading reform group has noted, no longer can school systems count on a captive market of bright, energetic minority members and women; these persons now have attractive alternatives in business, industry, and other professions.[1]

Activities associated with identifying, attracting, acquiring, and retaining personnel are part of separate but related administrative tasks of recruitment and selection. **Recruitment** refers to those activities designed to make available the number of applicants, the diversity of applicants, and the quality of personnel needed to carry on the work of the school system. **Selection** involves those activities concerned with reducing the initial pool of available applicants and choosing from among the final job candidates. "If educational leaders are not consistently competent in recruiting and selecting qualified and motivated individuals, efforts to improve the quality of education are bound to fail."[2]

Recruitment

Recruitment involves both short- and long-range planning activities. The short-range activities are those needed to meet current demands for personnel that exist in every organization; the long-term activities are designed to ensure a future supply of qualified professional and support personnel. Both short- and long-term activities are important because an extensive and aggressive program of recruitment is critical to the effectiveness of the organization.

The link between the human resource planning process (discussed in Chapter 2) and satisfaction of the demand for personnel through the implementation of that process is demonstrated in Figure 4.1. This figure indicates two key elements in human resource planning: *positions* and *individuals*. Both of these elements change because of changes in the internal and external environments of the school system and because of changes in the individual.

Because of position and individual changes, we shall first discuss coordination of public employment policy, system policy, and recruitment policy. The intent is to stress that modern recruitment does not take place in a social or organizational vac-

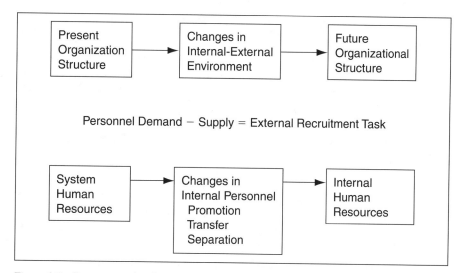

Figure 4.1   Perspective of multiyear human resource planning for an educational system.

uum. It is through the activities of the recruitment process that the system attracts candidates to fill anticipated position vacancies. Each of these activities is examined as an interdependent element, along with other components of the planning system. We emphasize that effective recruitment will minimize problems that usually follow the *selection* and *placement* of personnel.

There is a set of internal and external environmental circumstances, facts, and events—the recruitment contexture—that must be considered in developing recruitment strategies and the programs and the processes by which these strategies are implemented. Many of these factors must be determined long before the recruitment process reaches the individual applicant. Some of these factors involve administrative actions of employees; others require policy actions by boards of education.

Administrative actions are generally warranted in situations where decision makers require data on specific recruitment alternatives and in situations where procedures are needed to implement certain policies. Data are needed concerning immediate and long-range staffing needs, as illustrated in Chapter 2, and reflecting diversification of the present work force. Based on the information provided by administrators, school boards should formulate specific recruitment policies and practices.

Recruitment policies and practices are needed in situations where more than one acceptable alternative exists. The task of the school board is to evaluate the impact of various recruitment alternatives and to develop recruitment policies and practices. By approving certain recruitment policies and practices, boards of education set both the tone and the direction for recruitment activities.

Public Employment Policy and Recruitment

Various kinds of employment **discrimination** exist in our society. Because of documented past and potential future discrimination in employment, different types of legislation and regulations have been passed at the federal, state, and local levels. The purpose of these rulings is to prohibit future discrimination and, in some instances, to correct for past discrimination.

Many of these laws and regulations protect individuals or groups by forbidding discrimination in employment on the basis of **protected class status.** It is important to note that protected class status is defined only by specific legislation. Without the authority of that legislation, protected class status is an undefined term.

Major federal laws establishing protected class status are listed in Table 4.1. This list is not exhaustive. It is simply meant to illustrate some of the important acts affecting educational organizations.

By being included in a protected class by a specific legislative act, designated persons are protected from discrimination in employment. For example, the Civil Rights Act of 1964, as amended in 1991, prohibits discrimination on the basis of race, color, religion, national origin, and/or sex. The Age Discrimination in Employment Act of 1967, as amended in 1982, protects individuals older than 40 years of age.

In addition to the protected class groups, mentioned in Table 4.1, other groups of individuals can be given similar employment protection by state and local governments. For example, several states have recently used sexual preference to protect certain groups of individuals.

With respect to protected class individuals in recruitment and selection, school boards must establish certain employment policies. Foremost among these employment policies is the one that determines whether the school board is either an **equal employment opportunity** (EEO) employer or an **affirmative action** employer. The difference between these two perspectives is substantial and is generally a policy issue determined by a board of education.

The equal employment opportunity perspective is proactive and future oriented. "As applied to staffing, EEO refers to practices that are designated and used in a 'facially neutral' manner, meaning that all applicants and employees are treated similarly without regard to protected class characteristics such as race and sex."[3]

TABLE 4.1
Major Federal Laws Impacting Recruitment and Selection

Equal Pay Act of 1963
Title VII of the Civil Rights Act
Age Discrimination in Employment Act
Vocational Rehabilitation Act
Executive Order 11246
Vietnam Era Veterans Readjustment Assistance Act
Americans with Disabilities Act

This perspective implies that recruitment and selection practices, procedures, and policies will be based solely on the principle of merit, without regard to the protected class status of individuals.

The affirmative action perspective goes beyond the proactive stance of the equal employment opportunity perspective to consider the impact of past employment practices on protected class groups. That is, affirmative action seeks to correct past injustices in employment practices for these groups. To correct past employment injustices, a school board can adopt recruitment and selection policies that give preferential treatment to certain protected class groups using an affirmative action policy.

To illustrate the difference between the equal employment opportunity and affirmative action perspectives, consider the following examples. An equal employment opportunity policy would state that "all recruitment and selection decisions will be made without regard to any protected class status." An affirmative action policy would state that "if a protected class individual and a nonprotected class individual are deemed to be equally qualified for employment, preference will be given to the protected class individual."

Depending on the school board's choice between the equal employment opportunity perspective and the affirmative action perspective, a specific message is communicated and a specific legal responsibility is established. Problems, as well as legal difficulties, can occur when the actions and intentions of school boards and system employees are counter to the school board's formal employment policy. For example, if a school board adopts the equal employment opportunity perspective and then gives preferential treatment to individuals on the basis of protected class status, a violation has been committed. Likewise, if a school board adopts the affirmative action perspective and then fails to give preferential treatment to an equally qualified protected class person, a violation has been committed.

System Employment Policy and Recruitment

Recruitment is an essential part of a comprehensive plan to develop and maintain an excellent staff that will achieve the institution's purpose. The more today's school administrators consider the educational problems they are expected to solve, the more clearly they realize that they cannot succeed unless the organization is competently staffed. Effective solutions to many recruitment problems depend, to a large extent, on the employment policy of the board of education.

To be meaningful, personnel policies should be written, should inform every individual and agency of system standards, and should minimize uncertainties in the employment process. Without policy guidelines for decisions and actions on personnel matters, inconsistencies that develop will cause dissatisfaction and defeat the aims of the human resource function. Policy guidelines provide for continuity of the personnel process even when administrators and school board members come and go.

As noted previously in this chapter, policies related to recruitment and selection should not be formulated in a vacuum. Environmental factors that impact policy must be considered. At least two environmental factors should be assessed to guide employment policy formulation. One of these factors is external: the relevant labor market for the position; the other factor is internal: the characteristics of the current work force. Both of these factors should be assessed relative to the distribution of protected class persons.

The labor market is defined by the distance that an applicant could reasonably be expected to travel for employment consideration when seeking a position. It is important to note that distance, as used in defining a relevant labor market, is related to the employment consideration of an applicant for employment, not to the daily commute of an individual once employed. Because certain groups of applicants, like those seeking administrative positions, can be expected to travel much further for employment consideration than other groups of applicants, like those seeking support positions, the distance associated with a relevant labor market varies by position. For some positions the distance may be only a few miles (custodian), while for others it may be several hundred miles (teacher).

In additional to the external assessment of relevant labor markets for protected class persons, an internal assessment should be made that reflects the distribution of protected class persons employed by a school district. The latter assessment should be sensitive both to the number of protected class persons employed by the district and to the types of positions such persons hold. By obtaining data on the number of persons employed and the types of positions they hold, the school board can assess the organizational distribution of protected class persons within a district.

Data on the relative labor markets for different positions and for the distribution of protected class persons within a school district are captured by two different statistics: (1) a stock statistic and (2) a concentration statistic. A **stock statistic** provides information about the utilization of protected class persons in relation to the relevant labor market of these persons, and a **concentration statistic** provides information about the utilization of protected class persons at various organizational levels within the district hierarchy. Both statistics are illustrated in Table 4.2.

Stock statistics and concentration statistics should be calculated for each group of protected class persons. Without this information, it is unlikely that a school district can formulate adequate recruitment and selection policies. To illustrate stock and concentration statistics, we have used an aggregated group for all protected classes rather than addressing each specific group of protected class persons separately, as would be done in the field setting (see Table 4.2).

The stock statistics in Table 4.2 indicate a distinct difference in the distribution of protected class persons employed by the school district and available in the relevant labor market. The percentage of protected class persons employed by the school district is only 5% relative to the total work force, while the percentage of pro-

TABLE 4.2
Stock Statistics and Concentration Statistics of a Hypothetical School District

Applicant Stock Statistics			
Current Elementary Teachers		Available Elementary Teachers	
Nonprotected	Protected	Nonprotected	Protected
95%	5%	80%	20%

Applicant Concentration Statistics			
	Job Categories		
	Support	Instructional	Administrative
Females	90%	60%	10%
Males	10%	40%	90%

tected class persons relative to nonprotected class persons in the relevant labor market is 20%. This difference between those available and those employed indicates an underutilization of protected class persons relative to their availability.

To illustrate concentration statistics, only three broad categories of positions are used in Table 4.2. In actual practice, concentration statistics should also be compiled in a manner that reflects career progression. This involves dividing broad employee groupings. The administrator group should be divided according to line and staff positions, as well as according to organizational levels of employees. For example, elementary school principals differ from secondary school principals in some very important ways, and concentration statistics should reflect these ways. Elementary school principals tend to earn lower salaries, to be employed for fewer days during the contractual work year, and to have a different career progression (80 percent of superintendents have a secondary school background).

The concentration statistics in Table 4.2 provide additional insight into the internal staffing patterns of protected class persons employed by the hypothetical school district in question. Protected class persons are reasonably well represented in support positions but are underrepresented in administrator and teacher positions. Consequently, these data indicate some organizational segregation based on the protected class status of employees.

The data provided by stock and concentration statistics guide boards of education in formulating systemwide policies for recruitment and selection. This information should be used in determining whether the system will be an equal employment opportunity employer or an affirmative action employer. It can also be used to guide the development of other polices and procedures that impact recruitment and selection, such as those listed in Table 4.3.

TABLE 4.3
Policies and Procedures Related to Recruitment and Selection

Nondiscrimination (race, creed, religion, national background, age, gender, handicap, etc.)
Fairness in promotions, transfers, and separations
Position postings
Seniority preferences
Correction of staff imbalances within the system
Fairness in recruitment inquiries
Credential requirements
Skill inventories
Special persons (relatives, minors, part-time and temporary personnel, strikers, and rehires)
Position guides
Probationary employees
Proselytizing
Outside employment
Gifts and favors
Candidate information requirements
Testing

The Recruitment Process

As Figure 4.2 indicates, action plans and the structure for the recruitment process *are derived from the strategic plan.* In effect, the process model is based on the assumption that decisions have been made through strategic planning concerning the number of positions needed, requirements for the positions, and reallocation of people and positions. The *operational plan,* which derives from the strategic plan, identifies actions to be taken once the demand for and supply of human resources have been reconciled in the strategic plan.

Although the responsibility for several tasks involved in the recruitment process depends in part on the organizational structure of a school district, we can identify two features that characterize most successful recruitment efforts. These features are coordinating recruitment with the human resource plan and formalizing communication between the system and applicants.

Attracting Applicants

It has often been said that outstanding personnel are not necessarily seeking a change of position. Instead, they must be sought out and induced to change their place or position of employment. Clearly, the more intensive and extensive the system recruitment effort, the higher the cost and, it is hoped, the greater the return on expenditures.

Recruitment policies, established by boards of education with the advice of system employees, provide direction for the actual recruitment efforts of a school district. However, many school districts fail to consider the decisions of applicants, as individuals, when formulating and implementing recruitment polices and prac-

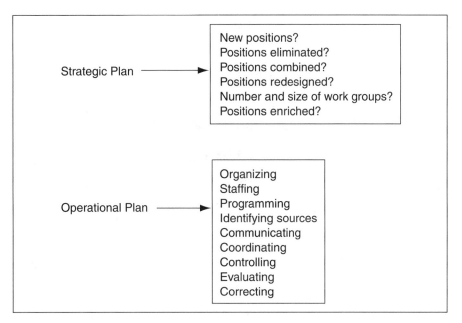

Figure 4.2   Model of the recruitment process.

tices. This omission on the part of employers can have an adverse impact on recruitment outcomes. If applicants fail to react favorably to recruitment efforts, school systems will have trouble taking advantage of the opportunities afforded by staffing needs and acquiring the best available talent in a competitive labor market.

Research on the reactions of applicants to recruitment efforts has just begun to be published in the professional literature. This research shows that job candidates make decisions about organizations in much the same manner as organizations make decisions about job candidates. Consequently, if school districts are to be competitive in the labor market, they must consider those factors that influence the decision of applicants to join an organization.

Applicants' decisions have been found to be influenced by several different recruitment and selection practices. Some of these practices include the orientation of individual applicants, the recruitment message, and the recruiter. Each of these sources of influence can play an important role in shaping successful recruitment practices in the school setting.

Orientation of Applicants

Several different theories exist about the orientation of applicants. These theories differ with respect to the basic motivation of applicants and the needs that applicants seek to fulfill when choosing among school districts as a place of employment. Because of the differences among these theories of recruitment attraction, each theory has distinct implications for the recruitment/selection process of a school district.

One recruitment attraction theory, often referred to as the **objective theory** of job choice, assumes that applicants are economic beings.[4] According to this theory, applicants view the job search process as a means of maximizing their economic return from the marketplace relative to their labor investment. To maximize their economic return, applicants are sensitive to the economic incentives offered by competing school districts.

Another recruitment attraction theory, the **subjective theory** of job choice, views applicants from a psychological perspective. This theory assumes that applicants have certain psychological needs and use the job search process as a means to fulfill these needs. Judge and Bretz noted that "individuals who match job or organizational values to their own are more satisfied and less likely to leave the organization."[5] From the subjective theory perspective, individuals are sensitive to issues relating to the organizational climate and the work environment when choosing among competing school districts.

Still another recruitment attraction theory, different from either the objective or the subjective theory of job choice, is the **work itself theory.** This theory views individuals as rational beings in the job search process who seek information about the tasks associated with potential employment opportunities. As such, information about the different job elements, job expectations, and actual tasks becomes important to applicants during the job search process.

Depending on the specific theory or theories of job choice favored by a school system, directions are provided for molding the recruitment process. Each theory provides information for writing recruitment messages and developing a recruitment strategy. The choice of one theory over another depends on its particular advantages for the school system.

Recruitment Message

Attracting applicants to fill positions involves considerable communication between the organization and the candidates. One type of communication directly controlled by the employer is the content of the recruitment message.[6] Research on this topic has shown that both the content of the recruitment message and the medium used to deliver it can have a decisive impact on the job choice of candidates.

The content of a **recruitment message** can vary in some very important ways. "There is a large number of potentially relevant attributes, and the attributes themselves may vary in numerous ways."[7] Recruitment messages can be constructed to reflect both positive and negative attributes of the employment opportunity, as suggested by *realistic job preview* (RJP) literature[8]; to reflect either general descriptions of attributes (competitive salary) or specific descriptions of attributes ($50,000 salary), as found in policy research[9]; or to reflect homogeneous groupings of attributes, as suggested by different theories of job choice.[10]

Recruitment messages are communicated to job candidates through several different media. Traditionally, these media have included job advertisements in newspapers and professional trade journals, video presentations at recruitment fairs, and interviews conducted by a system representative. More recently, some school districts have begun to use the Internet to reach potential job candidates.

Although little research exists on the use of the Internet, several studies are available to help school districts shape recruitment messages and determine the medium to be used to communicate them. Recruitment messages have been systematically manipulated experimentally and have been assessed with three types of candidates: inexperienced teachers seeking their first position, experienced teachers considering another position, and potential administrators for public school positions. Reactions to recruitment messages have been assessed for position postings and for recruitment interviews.

Certain position postings, such as those used for job announcements, are more effective than others. Effective position announcements identify a specific contact person, address candidates directly ("you should . . ."), and acknowledge applications by a telephone call. Ineffective position announcements identify an office to contact, use impersonal language ("applicant" rather than "you"), and fail to provide a means of acknowledging applications.[11]

Like position postings, certain recruitment messages are more effective than others when delivered by system representatives. Recruitment messages that present information about either the work environment of a school district or the work itself increase applicants' willingness to follow up and to accept employment offers. Interestingly, recruitment messages that emphasize economic incentives associated with a school district or a particular job have been found to be particularly ineffective.[12]

The Individual Recruiter

Regardless of how the recruitment effort is organized, it is likely that several persons will be assigned to make initial contacts and to negotiate with applicants. The significance of the recruiter to the success of the operation is not always understood or appreciated. Consequently, the school system must take several steps in selecting and training recruiters.

At some point in the recruitment process, decisions are made about which personnel will be assigned to represent the school district as recruiters. In larger school districts, this task is usually handled by the director of human resources. In smaller school districts, it is shifted among personnel so as not to overburden any particular individual. However, research on the impact of recruiters in attracting applicants suggests that recruiters should be chosen very carefully.

Well documented in the recruitment literature is the impact of the recruiter on the perceptions of job candidates.[13] Many job candidates have indicated that they chose to join a particular organization because of the personality of the organization's representative. An essential personality characteristic is personal warmth. This characteristic has been examined through the perceptions of applicants and by actual personality tests. Recruiters exhibiting personal warmth were much more effective organizational representatives than those exhibiting less warmth.[14]

Additional research has shown that recruitment effectiveness can be increased by considering the race and sex of recruiters, as well as the race and sex of applicants, when determining recruiter responsibilities and when writing recruitment messages. One study found that "Black applicants preferred female organizational representatives presenting recruitment messages emphasizing work environment attributes and work itself attributes. White applicants preferred male organizational representatives presenting recruitment messages stressing only work environment attributes."[15] Such recruitment studies provide support for different recruitment strategies for attracting educators.

In summary, every school system must carefully consider the selection and orientation of recruiters who have personal contact with applicants. Moreover, the organization should make sure that the recruiter is fully aware of what is expected. The system should:

- Identify those persons who will be responsible for contacting and discussing with applicants the vacancies to be filled.
- Make every effort to ensure that the recruiters have the knowledge, the interpersonal competence, and the verbal skills essential to the role.
- Standardize the role so that the recruiter will follow definite procedures, such as giving relevant information to each candidate about the organization.

Developing Sources of Applicants

A major objective of personnel recruitment is to improve the quality of the staff. This requires several kinds of analysis to identify imbalances in the makeup of total staff, in the ability to fill openings immediately, and in the number and types of openings available on both short- and long-term bases. Although the system will probably need to recruit some personnel from outside sources, it is also sound policy to promote and to transfer current staff members.

It should be clearly understood that certain types of positions provide no advancement and that certain individuals are satisfied to remain indefinitely in the same position. However, the general policy of promotion from within to better and more attractive positions is to be encouraged. Often overlooked is the fact that "current employees are potential candidates for whom the largest amount of job information is available."[16]

The manner in which positions are filled from the inside depends on the personnel procedures of the school system. Two methods are generally used: selection by the system and position posting. Under the first method, personnel within the system capable of advancing to better positions are identified and selected. Under the second method, personnel within the system are encouraged to apply for a better position using their own initiative.

Outside personnel sources are numerous and varied. The extent to which these sources can be used depends largely on the school system's recruitment policy and

TABLE 4.4
Sources for Recruiting Prospective External Candidates

Professional associations	Placement agencies	Unions
Walk-in candidates	Write-in candidates	Consulting firms
Advertising	Resumes on file	Government agencies
Referrals	High schools	Vocational schools
Technical schools	Conventions	Direct solicitation
Colleges	Specialized career centers	Military services

plans. If the recruitment effort is to succeed, it must produce a pool of applicants well in excess of the number of openings; otherwise, a selection process exists in name only. Major outside sources of supply are listed in Table 4.4; some of them pertain to professional personnel and others to support personnel.

If the system is to attract a pool of qualified candidates from the sources listed in Table 4.4, a plan for developing each source must be worked out. Schools with large numbers of vacancies will utilize different sources and employ techniques different from those preferred by small systems. Those employees who operate the recruitment program need to anticipate which sources will provide the greatest number of qualified applicants, how much time and money should be invested, and what methods should be used to attract competent individuals.

Coordinating the Search for Applicants

The recruitment activity moves from the planning stage to the goal realization stage when permission is given to spend recruitment funds. This step begins the applicant search and necessitates control. This process refers to activities involved in monitoring the progress of each candidate at various steps in the recruitment/selection process.

Two dimensions of recruitment are essential concerns. The first is *control,* which involves two steps: assessing how well the school system's recruitment plans are being achieved and developing courses of action to correct deficiencies. The second dimension is *effectiveness,* which involves checking recruitment performance against standards and linking strategic aims to the recruitment process. Recruitment control primarily involves an internal analysis of the recruitment process; recruitment effectiveness focuses on how well the recruitment process contributes to the strategic aims of the system for its human resources.

Careful accounting of recruitment expenses is essential for preparing the budget and for providing information about costs. In addition to recruitment expenses for personnel (professional and secretarial), there are operational expenses: advertising, communications (writing, telephone calls, and faxes), travel and living expenses, medical fees (physical examinations), printing supplies, and equipment. After total recruitment costs have been calculated, unit costs, such as cost per applicant employed, cost per applicant by source, cost by recruiter, cost per contact, and cost per professional versus cost of support employees hired are some of the indicators that may be analyzed to get a clear view of the cost of recruitment.

The costs associated with certain activities and certain sources reveal that some activities and sources are more productive than others. The system is interested in knowing what personnel sources yield the best-quality personnel and at what cost. It is understandable, for example, that the most satisfactory professionals might not be acquired from the nearest teacher education college. It is also conceivable that advertising might provide better secretarial personnel than an employment agency. Presumably, there is a maximum unit cost for each initial contact; beyond that cost, investment is not prudent.

The aim of controls is to make certain that recruitment results are in keeping with established goals. If goals are to be met, the collection, analysis, feedback, and use of relevant recruitment information are essential. Evaluation is useful to (a) extend information about and understanding of issues, problems, obstacles, and opportunities in human resources planning; (b) assess the strengths and weaknesses of the existing strategy; (c) identify new conditions in the internal and external environments and their potential impact on the human resources function; and (d) consider the interrelatedness of strategy, recruitment, work to be done, skilled personnel to do the work, environments, and fiscal resources.

As the process of securing competent personnel moves from recruitment to the selection phase, a number of formidable problems confront the human resources administration:

- Establishing role requirements.
- Determining what data are needed to select competent individuals from the pool of applicants.
- Deciding what devices and procedures are to be used in gathering the data.
- Securing staff participation in appraising the data and applicants.
- Relating qualifications of applicants to position requirements.
- Screening qualified from unqualified applicants.

In brief, one important facet of the human resources function is designing, initiating, and carrying out an effective selection process. Failure to recognize this fact will result in a less than effective recruitment process.

Selection: Purpose, Scope, and Challenges

The purpose of selection is to fill vacancies with personnel who meet the system's qualifications, appear likely to succeed, will remain in the system, will be effective contributors, and will be sufficiently motivated. A properly planned selection process has an additional benefit: The system is able to eliminate candidates who are unlikely to succeed.

"Many times, selection is equated with one event, namely, the interview. Nothing could be further from the truth if the best possible person/job match is to be made."[17] By definition, selection is a process in which one individual is chosen over another to fill a position, depending on how well the characteristics of the individual match the requirements of the position. Before we consider various steps in the selection process, the reader is cautioned against presuming that a model for human resources selection is enough to achieve selection strategies.

How to select the best-qualified candidate for an unfilled position is a perennial organizational problem. The selection process is fraught with possibilities for serious errors that can be costly to the school system, the community, the taxpayer, and the pupils. However, many of these potential errors can be minimized or eliminated by developing and applying an effective selection system.

The Selection Process

Whether a school system is small or large, it is easy to make a compelling case for valid selection procedures because a great deal of time, money, and effort is wasted when people selected for positions fail to meet the organization's expectations. Furthermore, the impact of poor teaching on children is so serious that the selection process in education is a critical issue. By increasing the quality of employees in our nation's schools, it is hoped that tomorrow's youth will be better prepared to function productively in society.[18]

Although the selection process should be varied to meet the special problems, needs, and characteristics of every school system, certain decisions within this process are universally applicable. As indicated in Figure 4.3, the first steps in

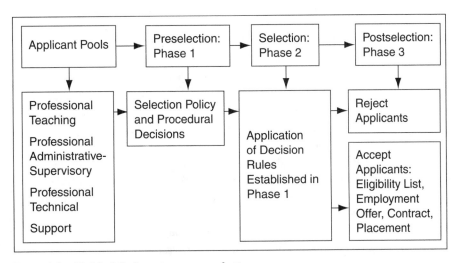

Figure 4.3   Model of the human resources selection process.

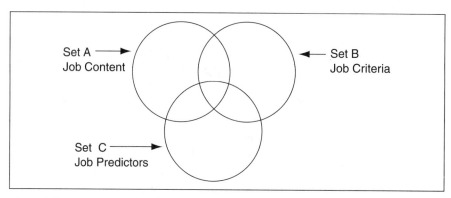

Figure 4.4   Venn diagram for selection components.

effective personnel selection are the recruitment of applicant pools and the development of employment policies. Because both of these topics are discussed in the section of this chapter on recruitment, here we focus on the other components of the selection process.

Process Model

A Venn diagram is used to illustrate other components of the selection process. This diagram, shown in Figure 4.4, is applicable to most, if not all, selection situations in school districts. The diagram contains three separate but related job sets to be considered either when developing an initial selection system or when evaluating an existing selection system: job content, job criteria, and job predictors.

The **job content** part of the diagram (Set A) consists of those job tasks performed by position holders. These tasks should reflect behaviors and processes germane to the effective performance of the job or jobs under consideration. To identify the important job tasks associated with particular position(s), a systematic job analysis (discussed below) is required.

Job criteria (Set B) are actual performance indicators that employees must have to perform the job. Performance indicators can reflect either an inferred process or an observed behavior. An inferred process involves a required knowledge base, while an observed behavior involves a specific skill.

Job predictors (Set C) measure those job criteria associated with knowledge and/or specific skills. They may include subjective data such as performance in an interview or objective data such as results from an analysis of transcripts. Job predictors are used to assess the qualifications of candidates relative to the job(s) to be performed.

Each of these separate but related sets helps to establish an effective selection process in the school setting. However, the selection process will be effective only to the extent that the job sets overlap or intersect when applied. Consequently, the goal of selection is to maximize the overlap among job content, job criteria, and job predictors.

Procedural Components

Unless there are clear-cut requirements for each position, it is difficult to select personnel in a systematic fashion. If the selection process is to focus on hiring people who can perform effectively, then work behaviors necessary for effective performance must be identified. The procedure used to identify these essential work behaviors is job analysis.

Job Analysis

Job analysis focuses on the position rather than the position holders. Positions, unlike position holders, are directly controlled by the organization and have certain unchanging properties. More specifically, job analysis should be directed to what tasks are performed, how, and why.

Job analysis should not be taken lightly by those responsible for developing a selection system. Acceptable techniques and standard procedures should be followed because several of the federal acts listed in Table 4.1 consider job analysis to be a crucial process. In fact, the outcome of many legal challenges has been decided on the basis of how well the job analysis was performed.[19]

A formal job analysis should be performed before any applicants are interviewed. Written records should be maintained to document the job analysis processes and procedures used by a school system. At a minimum, these records should describe the procedures used to identify job content, the qualifications of persons who conduct the job analysis, and the techniques used to assess the relevance of job content.

Several different procedures are used to identify job content for a job analysis. These include interviewing current employees, observing them performing their duties, reviewing written sources about the job, obtaining information from supervisors, administering job questionnaires, and consulting subject matter experts. In general, the more sources used to assess job content, the richer the information yield and the easier the defense of the job analysis when selection decisions are legally challenged.

Job content should be assessed according to two standards of practice: (a) how frequently each task is performed by a position holder and (b) how essential each task is for effective job performance. Answers to these questions have important implications for an effective selection process in the school setting.

Essential job tasks that are frequently performed are retained, while nonessential job tasks are eliminated. More difficult are essential job tasks that are performed infrequently. However, tasks in this category may not be used to exclude job candidates if other staff members can perform them without too much difficulty. In general, the job analysis should yield 15–25 different job task statements for most jobs.[20]

After important job tasks have been identified, the next step is to group different job tasks by common characteristics, or dimensions, such as instruction, supervision, communication, and so on. This requires a great deal of theorizing by those who are responsible for developing the selection system; "as a rule, there should be 4–8 dimensions, depending on the number of tasks statements."[21]

Job Criteria

Task dimensions are used to define actual **job criteria** used in the selection process (see Set B in Figure 4.4). These job criteria reflect the knowledge and skills required to perform the tasks associated with particular jobs. These requirements are defined by the Equal Employment Opportunity Commission (EEOC) guidelines on employee selection. The EEOC defines *knowledge* as "a body of information applied directly to the performance of a function" and *skill* as an "observable competence to perform a learned psychomotor act."[22]

An individual without the knowledge and skill requirements for a particular job would be an ineffective employee. For example, a common task dimension for elementary school principals is instruction, which requires both knowledge and skill. To be effective, elementary school principals need both knowledge of learning theory for early childhood and skill for demonstration teaching in the classroom setting.

As Figure 4.4 shows, actual job criteria do not completely overlap the required job tasks; instead, the overlap is only partial. This situation is similar to what would be encountered in the field setting. To use the previous example, only part of the knowledge of learning theory for early childhood helps elementary school principals perform effectively.

The overlap between actual job criteria and required job tasks is known as **criterion relevance.** The degree to which actual criteria and job tasks fail to overlap is referred to as **criterion deficiency.** Criterion relevance should be maximized and criterion deficiency minimized in an effective selection system.

To assess the relevance of actual criteria for the important tasks in the job(s) under consideration, a content validity analysis is required. **Content validity,** unlike other types of validity to be discussed, is determined analytically. Subject matter experts with in-depth knowledge about the position(s) under consideration are used to assess the relationship between actual criteria and required job tasks.

Actual criteria, the knowledge and skill required for effective performance, must be developed for each task dimension. The number of actual criteria will vary with the complexity of the task dimension. Some task dimensions may have several different knowledge and skill components, and each of these must be identified.

A comprehensive job analysis represents a considerable investment of time and energy. However, it is a wise investment given the importance of selection for the effective functioning of a school district. All too often, this important step in the selection process is omitted. Unless appropriate job criteria are identified, valid job predictors for an effective selection process are unobtainable, a topic we shall now address.

Job Predictors

After the validity of actual job criteria is established through a content validity analysis, the next step is to obtain or develop job predictors for these criteria. **Job predictors** are used to assess the competencies of applicants relative to actual job criteria and include "all selection procedures used as a basis for any employment decision."[23] Examples of job predictors used frequently by school systems are tests, interviews, references, and related experience.

The actual choice of job predictors is an extremely important decision for school districts and for applicants. Job predictors are used to determine which applicants will be given or denied a job offer. An effective selection process utilizes only those job predictors that are related to actual job criteria. However, the formal relationship between job predictors and job criteria is seldom assessed in the field setting. Far too many school systems choose predictors previously used within the district, untested practices used by other school districts, or promotional literature.

To assess the relationship between job predictors and job criteria, either a content validity analysis or a criterion-related validity analysis is necessary. Which validity analysis is used is determined by the type of job predictor under consideration. According to federal guidelines, "A selection procedure based upon inferences about mental processes cannot be supported solely or primarily on the basis of content validity. Thus, a content strategy is not appropriate for demonstrating the validity of selection procedures which purport to measure traits or constructs, such as intelligence, aptitude, personality, commonsense, judgement, leadership, and spatial ability."[24]

Because many predictors used by school districts seek to measure certain traits and characteristics of applicants as defined by the federal guidelines, a **criterion-related validity analysis** is required. A criterion-related validity analysis, unlike a content validity analysis, is assessed empirically by statistical techniques, most often a correlation.

A correlation provides a measure of overlap between job predictors and job criteria. This correlation can vary from zero, indicating no overlap, to unity, indicating perfect overlap. In practice, and as depicted in Figure 4.4, the assessed overlap will almost always be far less than unity for any particular predictor of job criteria. According to minimum federal requirements, "A selection procedure is considered related to the criterion, for purposes of these guidelines, when the relationship between performance on the predictor and performance on the criterion measure is statistically significant at the 0.05 level of significance."[25]

Although statistical significance is a minimum requirement for job predictors from a legal perspective, a truly effective selection system must exceed the minimum requirement. Here we can gain additional insight by looking at Figure 4.4. The area where Set B and Set C overlaps consists of two separate parts. One part involves only the overlap of job content, job criteria, and job predictors and is defined as *predictor relevance*. The other part involves only the overlap of job criteria and job predictors and is defined as *predictor contamination*.

Predictor relevance reflects that portion of the predictor that separates effective from ineffective applicants in terms of future job performance; it represents the practical significance of a predictor. In contrast, predictor contamination reflects that portion of the predictor that hinders effective selection because it contains elements unrelated to potential job performance. An effective selection system is one that uses predictors with high relevance and low contamination.

To obtain predictors with high relevance and low contamination is indeed a challenge for school systems. Unfortunately, most school systems choose predictors on the basis of face validity rather than assessed validity. As a result, many selection systems used by school districts are illegal, counterproductive, and unethical. However, existing selection systems can be improved and effective selection systems can be developed by adhering to this conceptual model, by using current research knowledge about predictors, and by performing additional analyses for predictors.

Actual Job Predictors

Job predictors are tools used by management to assess the potential job performance of applicants in specific positions. The number and type of predictors used varies both between and within school districts. Some districts use elaborate selection systems with many job predictors, while others use simple selection systems with few job predictors. Depending on the position under consideration, the number and type of job predictors may vary within a particular school system.

In this chapter, we focus on those job predictors that are used by almost all school systems and that provide insight into current knowledge about these popular predictors. By relying on current knowledge about popular predictors, school systems can increase the probability of obtaining statistical significance for job predictors, enhance the practical significance of job predictors, and reduce contamination. In this discussion, job predictors are classified according to information provided by applicants and information obtained by observing candidates.

Information Provided by Candidates

For purposes of selection, the number of candidates seeking a position must exceed the number of positions to be filled. To reduce the number of candidates seeking a vacant position, only those applicants who appear to be qualified are considered. The qualifications of job candidates relative to vacant positions are assessed initially on the basis of information provided by applicants.

Applicants provide information about themselves on either a placement file or an application form. These two information sources serve as job predictors within the selection process, and the choice between them is a policy decision made by the board of education. The application form is preferred, for reasons that will now be discussed.

Application Form

An **application form** has several advantages over a placement file. It allows the school system to dictate the type of information sought from applicants, and it yields comparable information about all applicants. Without comparable information, an adequate comparison among applicants is almost impossible.

Although school systems may have separate application forms for classified, certified, and administrative personnel, all application forms should have some common elements. They should all provide contact information about the candidate, information on experience relating to position requirements, and disclaimer statements for indemnifying school systems. School systems should be held harmless by applicants for actions related to employment verification, reference checks, and false information provided by applicants.

Items on the application form can be weighted and scored in a way that differentiates between ineffective and effective applicants. Certain items, such as those on related job experience, can be weighted more heavily than other items having less bearing on the positions under consideration.[26] When the items relating to knowledge and skill requirements for positions are weighted more heavily, the predictor relevance of the application form is increased.

Application forms that are scored can be developed. For example, many positions require a knowledge component to communicate clearly, part of which may involve written expression. Applicants' ability to write can be scored for grammar, syntax, and clarity based on their responses to open-ended questions on an application form.

Many application forms solicit information that is unrelated to job performance, that is a potential contaminant in the selection process, and that is prohibited by federal guidelines. Research has shown that screening decisions of school administrators are often influenced by factors unrelated to job performance, such as the age, the sex, and the handicap status of candidates.[27] To reduce these contaminants, school systems should carefully analyze all application forms, as well as all other types of information requested from job candidates.

Reference Information

"While it is not very difficult to verify the previous employment of an applicant, it can be rather difficult to verify the quality of his/her previous performance."[28] To assess the work quality of candidates in previous positions, school systems have used a variety of predictors to obtain **reference** information. The two predictors most frequently used are letters of recommendation and standardized reference forms.

Letters of recommendation can be provided by applicants on request, obtained from placement files, or requested by the school district. The information in these letters can be either confidential or nonconfidential, as designated by applicants. Although applicants may waive their right for access to letters of recommendation, employers are not allowed to differentiate among these letters on the basis of confidentiality status.

Research has shown that the screening decisions of school administrators are influenced by letters of recommendation. Of particular concern to administrators is the tone of a letter; anything less than a strongly positive letter has a negative effect.[29] In spite of popular perceptions, the length of letters of recommendation seems to have little influence on the screening decisions of school administrators.[30]

However, letters of recommendation often say more about the source (the author) than about the target (the applicant). That is, two letters written by the same author for two different job candidates are more consistent than two letters written by different authors for the same job candidate.[31] Thus, it should not be surprising that letters of recommendation account for less than 2% of the variance associated with job criteria.[32]

Using a standardized reference form to assess the qualifications of candidates can reduce many of the problems associated with letters of recommendation. A standardized reference form can be tailored to address specific knowledge and skill criteria associated with particular positions. As a predictor of future job performance, the standardized reference form provides comparable information about all candidates.

Information Obtained by Observing Applicants

Once an initial applicant pool has been created on the basis of information provided by job candidates, the remaining applicants are subjected to additional job predictors for further assessment. The initial pool of applicants is formed because these additional job predictors require a considerable investment of resources on the part of a school system. Job interviews and job simulations, when used as predictors of job performance by school systems, are very expensive.

Interviews

By far the most frequently used job predictor is the selection interview.[33] "What many employers fail to realize is that the interview is classified as a 'test' in the Uniform Guidelines and, as such, is subject to the same scrutiny as traditional pencil-and-paper employment tests."[34] In other words, selection interviews, like other job predictors, should be job related.

The selection interview provides information about job candidates beyond that obtainable with most other job predictors. However, the format of the interview can vary in several ways. Job interviews can be either unstructured or structured. Unstructured interviews are free-flowing, and topics are explored as they emerge during the interview session. Although unstructured interviews provide interviewers with the fewest restrictions and are used frequently as a job predictor, they have been found to be extremely poor predictors of future job performance because comparable information is not assessed with all applicants during interview sessions.[35]

A structured interview eliminates the problem of information comparability associated with an unstructured interview format. A structured interview uses a set of prescribed questions, and all candidates are assessed accordingly. These prescribed questions should be constructed to measure the knowledge and skill components associated with effective job performance of the positions under consideration.

In addition to their structure, interviews can be either dyadic or panel in design. In dyadic interviews, only one interviewer assesses all job candidates; in panel interviews, more than one interviewer is involved. Recently, many districts have begun to use panel interviews in schools experimenting with site-based management.

Although the choice between a dyadic and a panel interview is far less important than the choice between a structured and an unstructured interview, decisions made about job candidates have been shown to be a function of interview type. Because fewer candidates are recommended for employment when a dyadic interview is used than when a panel interview is used, selection policy should dictate the use of only one interview type when evaluating job candidates.[36] Otherwise, evaluation of candidates based on their interview performance may be more a function of the type of interview used than the actual job qualifications of candidates.

Job Simulations

Current research suggests that employee selection can be greatly improved by using predictors based on job simulations. **Job simulations** involve the use of predictors designed to measure actual job tasks performed by employees. Actual job tasks, when used in the selection process as predictors of future job performance, are referred to as *work samples.*

Work samples can be obtained from the job analysis process used to identify actual job criteria. For a teacher, a work sample might be teaching a demonstration unit of instruction appropriate for the position; for an administrator, a work sample might be completing an in-basket exercise. The use of work samples assumes that inferences associated with traditional job predictors are reduced because the selectors focus on the simulated job behaviors of candidates rather than on more distant proxy measures of potential job performance.

Although research on work samples in education is limited, some studies have been done. The validity of certain work samples for school administrators has been examined in assessment centers.[37] These initial results appear to be promising.

Predictor Assessment

Each predictor used by a school system to select employees should be assessed both for adverse impact and for practical significance. A job predictor is determined to have an adverse impact when the selection rate for protected class persons is less than 80% of the selection rate for nonprotected class persons as defined by federal guidelines. Practical significance concerns the degree to which a job predictor increases the effectiveness of the selection system.

Adverse Impact

To assess the potentially **adverse impact** of a predictor of job performance, flow statistics are calculated. These statistics reflect the number of protected and nonprotected class persons seeking employment, the number of protected and nonprotected class persons obtaining employment, and the selection ratios for these two groups of persons relative to their performance on the job predictor. An example of flow statistics for bus drivers, using sex of applicants as the protected class variable and a selection interview as the job predictor, is presented in Table 4.5. According to these data, the interview used by this system has an adverse impact on female job

TABLE 4.5
Hypothetical Example of Applicant Flow Statistics for School Bus Drivers

Classification	Applicant Numbers	Hires	Percentage
Female	100	5	5%
Male	100	30	30%

candidates because the selection rate for females is less than 80% of the selection rate for males.

When flow statistics indicate an adverse impact for protected class persons, school districts have two alternatives under federal guidelines. They can either discontinue using the predictor in or prove that the protected class characteristic, sex in this example, is a **bona fide occupational qualification (BFOQ).** However, within school systems, few if any BFOQs exist.

In fact, the assumption that a BFOQ exists has resulted in many lawsuits related to employment practices of school systems. For example, as shown by past hiring practices of school districts, it was assumed that sex was a BFOQ for a senior high school principal. Based on this assumption, women were excluded almost automatically from consideration for these positions. Although this happens less often today, as seen by the increased number of female senior high principals, all potential predictors of job performance used by school districts should be assessed for an adverse impact with each protected class group as defined by existing legislation.

Practical Significance

Each predictor of job performance used by a school district has a net effect on the effectiveness of a selection system. The net effect of a predictor for a selection system used by a school district concerns the advantage realized by using a particular predictor of job performance compared to not using that predictor. To measure the net effect of each predictor, the job success rates of applicants with and without the use of the predictor must be analyzed.

Success rates of applicants are illustrated in Figure 4.5 by four separate quadrants. These quadrants are determined by establishing the minimum criteria for effective job performance of a position holder (ordinate) and the minimum performance on a predictor required for an employment offer (axis). Because changing the standards of the expected job performance and/or the minimum predictor performance will alter the outcomes, policymakers must consider establishing acceptable levels of performance and cutoff scores.

Each quadrant in Figure 4.5 depicts a specific outcome associated with a particular predictor of job performance: Q1 contains those applicants who were predicted to do well and who did do well; QII contains those applicants who were not predicted to do well but who did do well; QIII contains those applicants who were

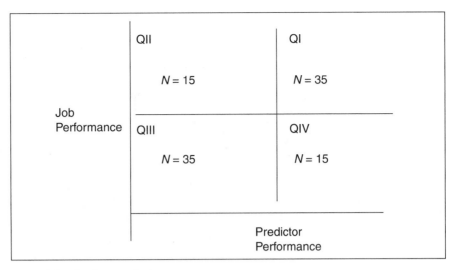

Figure 4.5   Quadrant analysis.

not predicted to do well and who did not do well; and QIV contains those applicants who were predicted to do well but who failed to do well. Quadrants I and III represent correct outcomes associated with a predictor, while quadrants II and IV represent incorrect outcomes associated with a predictor. Incorrect outcomes are labeled as *false negatives* (quadrant II) or as *false positives* (quadrant IV).

Quadrants I and II are used to calculate a **base rate.** The base rate indicates the percentage of persons employed by a district who are successful regardless of their performance on the predictor. Quadrants I and III indicate the number of correct employment decisions made by using a particular predictor to select employees for **placement** in vacant positions. By converting these different numbers to a percentage and by comparing these percentages, the **practical significance** of a predictor is assessed by the net difference. In this example, the school district could realize a net increase in effectiveness of 20% by using this particular predictor of job performance; this net difference provides a measure of practical significance associated with this predictor (see Table 4.6).

TABLE 4.6
Method Used to Calculate the Practical Significance of a Predictor

Practical Significance = Base Rate − Correct Decisions

Correct Decisions = QI + QIII / QI + QII + QIII + QIV = 70 / 100 = 70%

Base Rate = QI + QII / QI + QII + QIII + QIV = 50 / 100 = 50%

Practical Significance = 70% − 50% = 20%

Selection

The steps in the selection process (Phase 2 in Figure 4.3) examined so far have emphasized the development and assessment of potential predictors of job performance. The next step focuses on the question How good is the match? Stated another way, to what extent do the qualifications of applicants meet the requirements for the positions under consideration?

Rejection or acceptance of an applicant is a prediction based on information collected using particular predictors of job performance. The ideal practice is to place a numerical value on information from each of the several predictors in relation to various job criteria identified by the job analysis. Raw scores from predictors can be converted into percentile ranks or standard scores so as to be comparable with normative information. Graphic profiles may be used to portray the results of evaluation. By combining data from application blanks, interview guide sheets, reference and background check forms, tests, and other sources into a profile, the task of relating characteristics of applicants to actual job criteria for vacant positions can be accomplished more effectively.

When all information about a candidate is juxtaposed to the requirements of the position, the selector must compare the two sets of information and predict whether the applicant will perform according to expectations. In various school systems, one employment technique is to place those individuals judged to be qualified for a position on an eligibility list. Before this is done, it is customary to ask each candidate to prove that the certification or license requirements specified by law for a particular position have been met

Although eligibility is probably defined somewhat differently by various school districts, it generally means that the persons responsible for selecting personnel have designated as suitable for employment applicants who have met established qualifications. The eligibility list should adhere to the employment policy of the board of education (equal opportunity or affirmative action) and should provide a list of applicants, in rank order, who are eligible for appointment as vacancies occur.

In the selection process, it is not unusual to find that some applicants do not meet position requirements. When this happens, several alternatives (which can be explored before deciding to offer employment or to place the individual on the eligibility list) can be considered: (a) delay filling the position, (b) renew the search, (c) provide specific developmental experiences for persons considered to be good risks but who need to improve their skills to fill the position effectively, (d) fill the position temporarily, and (e) employ the applicant, but in a different position.

One difficulty in the selection process is the time factor. Many desirable candidates are lost to competing systems because of the time lag between initial interview and official appointment. Every effort should be made to keep the selection process as brief as possible; in particular, there should be no delay in notifying candidates of their official appointment.

Before the selection process is completed, the applicant and the organization must agree on the terms of employment. It is crucial that both parties completely understand the conditions of employment. Misunderstandings frequently occur about salaries, duties, authority, office or work space, secretarial assistance, collateral benefits, overtime, and extra pay for extra work.

Employment agreements made by telephone should be confirmed in writing. A contractual agreement is essential before hiring is completed. This practice has considerable merit, regardless of how the agreement is made.

Many people develop a negative attitude toward the organization when promises made during the selection period are not kept after the position has been accepted. Therefore, during the final stages of selection, it is good practice, to use a checklist containing the terms of employment. This checklist should be designed to ensure that the prospective employee knows the exact nature of the position and its responsibilities, moonlighting policy, compensation structure and its relationship to the applicant's paycheck, terms of the probationary period, collateral benefits, terms of any union or associational contracts in force, and provisions unique to a given position, such as status or status symbols.

Review and Preview

The theme of this chapter is that an extensive and aggressive program of recruitment and selection is necessary for placing and keeping qualified individuals in every position in the system. It was emphasized that recruitment and selection is both an individual and an organizational activity. Individuals must make decisions about organizations, and organizations must make decisions about individuals.

To guide the recruitment and selection process, certain policies and procedures were discussed. With respect to recruitment, a distinction was made between an equal opportunity employer and an affirmative action employer. Information was provided about orientation of applicants, recruitment messages, and organizational representatives.

A Venn diagram was used to illustrate the interrelationship among the different components and procedures comprising the selection process. Information concerning several types of job predictors was presented. Methodology was presented for assessing the statistical and practical significance of particular predictors, and attention was directed to assessing the disproportional impact of predictors.

Discussion Questions

1. Identify and describe briefly the internal and/or external circumstances that will expand or contract the future demand for human resources in a school system of your experience.

2. How should school officials go about determining the duties and responsibilities of *every* position on the payroll? The skills needed by *every* person on the payroll?

3. Define the term *demographic trends.* What is the relationship between demographic trends and strategic planning?

4. As a school principal, you have been notified of the impending retirement of one math teacher and one language arts teacher. You are requested to give the recruitment committee a document describing the position and person specifications that should be considered in hiring new teachers. Indicate your plan of action, including such details as the information for bridging the gap between the positions and the objectives of the school for which you are responsible.

5. What are the relative advantages and disadvantages of internal and external recruiting approaches?

6. Describe how recruitment policy is made in one organization you are familiar with by knowledge or personal experience (school system, city council, county government, state government, local housing authority).

7. Which of the following subjects should you consider or not consider in the recruitment search: age, previous experience, sex, race, references, religion, family, marital status, pregnancy, work experience, handicap, military background, arrests, association membership, credit status? Why are some of these items a matter of regulatory concern?

8. If you were directed to check the performance level of a superintendent of schools in another system, which of the following would you choose to interview: newspaper editors, school directors, union leaders, church officials, chamber of commerce president, PTA president, social groups concerned with school affairs? Defend your selection.

9. Develop a one-page response to each of the following statements:

a. The problem with traditional recruitment and selection methods is that they are past or present oriented.

b. Recruitment from within is touted as a means to improve morale and develop internal talent. It also tends to strengthen the status quo.

c. The use of past-oriented job descriptions is even more insidious than the inbreeding and resistance to change that may result from a promotion-from-within policy.

10. In a paragraph, describe the relationship between human resources strategy and recruitment.

11. What is the function of legal counsel with regard to recruitment?

12. Should school districts have an affirmative action program, whether or not they are government contractors or subcontractors? Whether they are large or small employers?

13. Give five examples of traditional recruitment practices that have been challenged by the courts (e.g., use of the application form).

14. You are a human resources director. Make a list of actions that you are prohibited from taking when recruiting new staff members.

15. Make a list of effectiveness criteria that should be applied in evaluating the recruitment program.

16. Different studies have produced different results regarding the efficiency of recruitment sources. What steps should a human resource director take in deciding which recruitment sources are most dependable for the school system in which he or she is employed?

17. One facet of contemporary life in the United States is the emergence of powerful forces that seek to influence public policy, especially public education policy. These interest groups include people who are black and white, rich and poor, native born and immigrants, old and young, and conservative and liberal. Following are two examples of these forces in the school system's external environment and their intent to influence school personnel decisions, as reported in newspaper articles. (Pair up class members to review and report discussion outcomes relative to the example questions.)

Example A—Four candidates for the superintendency of an urban school system (in which there were 58 different language groups) appeared before a community forum sponsored by the NAACP. The NAACP, it was reported, "intend[ed] to tell the Board the qualities the new superintendent should have. We would like to influence the characteristics of the person" (*Miami Herald*, March 4, 1990, 1B).

Example B—A public demonstration occurred in Selma, Alabama, on the grounds that the white-dominated school board refused to extend the contract of Selma's first black superintendent of schools (*Miami Herald*, March 5, 1990, 5A).

Example A questions—Would the employment criteria cited in Figure 3.4 be useful in setting forth board policy regarding recruitment and selection of candidates? How should the board go about informing the community about its employment policy? Would you advise the board to consider the option of inviting any and all special interest groups, including the teachers' union; political parties; and racial, national, tribal, linguistic, cultural origin, or background groups to sponsor community forums to assess candidates' qualities and to provide selection input? Should the board set forth its employment policies and procedures before initiation of the recruitment process?

Example B questions—What criteria should be employed to ascertain whether a school personnel decision is ethnically motivated? Of the 11 personnel processes discussed in this text, which would be most likely to yield sources of information to deal with the charge that personnel decisions are ethnically motivated? Is it possible for a board to establish a framework for dealing with the contention that the system's personnel decisions are ethnically motivated (see Figure 3.5)?

Notes

1. Holmes Group, *Tomorrow's Schools of Education* (East Lansing, MI: Holmes Group, 1995).

2. P. A. Winter, "Education Recruitment and Selection: A Review of Recent Studies and Recommendations for Best

Practice." In L. Wildman, ed., *Fifth NCPEA Yearbook* (Lancaster, PA: Technomic, 1997), 133–140.

3. H. G. Heneman and R. L. Heneman, *Staffing Organizations* (Middleton, WI: Mendota House, 1994), p. 57.

4. I. P. Young, J. S. Rinehart, and H. G. Heneman, "Effects of Job Attribute Categories, Applicant Job Experience, and Recruiter Sex on Applicant Job Attractiveness Ratings," *Journal of Personnel Evaluation in Education* 7 (1993), 55–66.

5. T. A. Judge and R. D. Bretz, "Effects of Work Values on Job Choice Decisions," *Journal of Applied Psychology* 77, 3 (1992), 261–271.

6. S. L. Rynes and A. E. Barber, "Applicant Attraction Strategies: An Organizational Perspective," *Academy of Management* 15 (1990), 286–310.

7. Young et al., "Effects of Job Attribute Categories," 56.

8. J. P. Wanous, *Organizational Entry*, 2nd ed. (Reading, MA: Addison-Wesley, 1992).

9. S. L. Rynes and J. Lawler, "A Policy Capturing Investigation of the Role of Expectancies in Decisions to Pursue Job Alternatives," *Journal of Applied Psychology* 68, 4 (1983), 620–631.

10. I. P. Young, A. W. Place, J. S. Rinehart, J. C. Jury, and D. F. Baits, "Teacher Recruitment: A Test of the Similarity-Attraction Hypothesis for Race and Sex," *Educational Administration Quarterly* 33, 1 (1997), 86–106.

11. P. A. Winter, "Applicant Evaluations of Formal Position Advertisements: The Influence of Sex, Job Message Content, and Information Order," *Journal of Personnel Evaluation in Education* 10 (1996), 105–116.

12. Young et al., "Teacher Recruitment."

13. S. L. Rynes, "Recruitment, Job Choice, and Post-hire Consequences: A Call for New Research Directions," in M. Dunnette and L. Hough, eds., *Handbook of Industrial and Organizational Psychology* (Palo Alto, CA: Consulting Psychologist Press, 1991), pp. 399–444.

14. I. P. Young and H. G. Heneman, "Predictors of Interviewee Reactions to the Selection Interview," *Journal of Research and Development in Education* 19 (1986), 29–36.

15. Young et al., "Teacher Recruitment," 86.

16. D. G. Pounder and I. P. Young, "Recruitment and Selection of Educational Administrators: Priorities for Today's Schools," in K. Leithwood, ed., *The International Handbook for Educational Leadership and Administration* (Amsterdam: Kluwer, 1996), pp. 279–308.

17. H. G. Heneman, R. L. Heneman, and T. A. Judge, *Staffing Organizations*, 2nd ed. (Middleton, WI: Mendota House, 1998), p. 362.

18. D. G. Pounder, "Improving the Predictive Validity of Teacher Selection Decisions: Lessons from Teacher Appraisal," *Journal of Personnel Evaluation in Education* 2 (1988), 141–150.

19. R. H. Faley, L. S. Kleiman, and M. L. Lengnick-Hall, "Age Discrimination and Personnel Psychology: A Review and Synthesis of Legal Literature with Implications for Future Research," *Personnel Psychology* 37, 2 (1984), 327–350.

20. Heneman et al., *Staffing Organizations*.

21. Ibid., 168.

22. Equal Employment Opportunity Commission, "Guidelines on Employee Selection Procedures," *Federal Register* 35 (1978), 12333–12336.

23. Ibid., Sect. 2B.

24. Ibid., Sect. C1.

25. Ibid., Sect. C5.

26. G. Dessler, *Personnel Management* (Upper Saddle River, NJ: Prentice-Hall, 1988).

27. I. P. Young, J. S. Rinehart, and D. M. Baits, "Age Discrimination: Impact of Chronological Age and Perceived Position Demands on Teacher Screening Decisions," *Journal of Research and Development in Education* 30, 2 (1997), 103–112; S. B. Reis, I. P. Young, and J. C. Jury, "Females Administrators: A Crack in the Glass Ceiling," paper presented at the American Educational Research Association annual meeting, San Diego, CA,

1998); I. P. Young and A. Prince, "Effects of Age and Handicap Status on Teacher Screening Decisions," paper presented at the American Educational Association Research Annual Meeting, Chicago, 1997.

28. M. G. Aamodt, D. A. Bryan, and A. J. Whitcomb, "Predicting Performance with Letters of Recommendation," *Public Personnel Management* 22 (1993), 81–91.

29. P. V. Bredeson, "The Effects of Letters of Recommendation on the Teacher Selection Process," unpublished doctoral dissertation, University of Wisconsin, 1992.

30. I. P. Young and B. R. McMurray, "Effects of Chronological Age, Focal Position, Quality of Information and Quantity of Information on Screening Decisions for Teacher Candidates," *Journal of Research and Development in Education* 19 (1986), 1–9.

31. J. C. Baxter, B. Brock, P. C. Hill, and R. M. Rozelle, "Letters of Recommendation: A Question of Value," *Journal of Applied Psychology* 66 (1981), 296–301.

32. R. R. Reilly and G. T. Chao, "Validity and Fairness of Some Alternative Employee Selection Procedures," *Personnel Psychology* 35 (1982), 1–62.

33. R. D. Arvey and R. H. Faley, *Fairness in Selecting Employees,"* 2nd ed. (Reading, MA: Addison-Wesley Publishing Company, 1992).

34. Ibid., 213.

35. R. I. Dipboye, *Selection Interviews: Process Perspectives* (Cincinnati: South-Western Publishing Company, 1992).

36. I. P. Young, "Administrators' Perceptions of Teacher Candidates in Dyad and Panel Interviews," *Educational Administration Quarterly* 13 (1983), 46–63.

37. N. Schmitt, R. Noe, R. Meritt, and M. Fitzgerald, "Validity of Assessment Center Ratings for the Prediction of Performance Ratings and School Climate of School Administrators," *Journal of Applied Psychology* 69, 2 (1984), 207–213.

Supplementary Reading

Arthur, Diane. *Recruiting, Interviewing, Selecting, and Orienting New Employees.* New York: American Management Association, 1986.

Bradley, J. "How to Interview for Information." *Training* 20, 4 (1983), 59–62.

Camden, Carl; and Bill Wallace. "Job Application Forms: A Hazardous Employment Practice." *Personnel Administrator* (March 1983), 31.

Candoli, I. E.; W. G. Hack; and J. R. Ray. *School Business Administration.* Boston: Allyn and Bacon, 1992.

Foulkes, F. "Organizing and Staffing the Personnel Function." In F. Foulkes, ed., *Strategic Human Resources Management: A Guide for Effective Practice.* Upper Saddle River, NJ: Prentice-Hall, Inc., 1986.

Fraser, Jill Andresky. "The Making of a Work Force." *Business Month* (September 1989), 58–62.

Glinow, Mary Ann Von. "Reward Strategies for Attracting, Evaluating, and Retaining Professionals." *Human Resource Management* 24, 2 (1985), 191–206.

Hallett, J. "Computers and the HR Professional." *Personnel Administrator* 31, 7 (1986), 16–20.

Johns, Horace E.; and H. Ronald Moser. "Where Has EEO Taken Personnel Policies?" *Personnel* (September 1989), 63–66.

Powell, Gary N. "Effects of Job Attributes and Recruiting Practices on Applicant Decisions: A Comparison." *Personnel Psychology* 37 (1984), 721–732.

U.S. Equal Employment Opportunity Commission. *Affirmative Action and Equal Employment: A Guidebook for Employees.* Vols. 1 and 2. Washington, DC: The Commission, 1974.

Wagner, I. D.; and S. M. Sniderman. *Budgeting School Dollars.* Washington, DC: National School Boards Association, 1984.

Wanous, J. *Organizational Entry: Recruiting, Selecting, and Socializing of Newcomers.* Reading, MA: Addison-Wesley Publishing Company, 1989.

Zippo, M.; and K. Greenberg. "Reference Checks: Myth and Facts." *Personnel* 59, 6 (1982), 52–53.

5

Induction

CHAPTER OBJECTIVES

Stress the importance of the induction process to socialization of inductees.
Present a working model of the induction process.
Focus on ways to help inductees achieve the highest level of performance in the shortest period of time.
Identify adjustments that are essential for inductees to perform effectively.
Link the induction process to individual career planning.

CHAPTER TERMS

Career planning
Induction

This chapter examines the induction process as a means of enhancing the organizational life of employees. Our discussion begins with an examination of the concept of induction as it relates to human performance within the organization. After discussing the behavioral foundations of induction, we present a model of the induction process, examining in detail the activities designed to achieve a long-range induction strategy.

Induction and Human Performance

Every year, most school districts must recruit, select, assign, reassign, and transfer personnel to maintain continuity of the educational enterprise. Employees who perform one of these human resource functions may confront new personal and environmental changes in their work lives. Some employees experience a vocational change. Probably at no other time of employment does the newly appointed or newly assigned employee need more consideration, guidance, and understanding.

Until these individuals become fully adjusted to the work they must perform, their new environment, and their new colleagues, they cannot be expected to give their best effort. Feelings triggered by new work assignments can harm employees as well as the organization if not properly managed by the school system. One method for helping new employees to manage their feelings and to master the new assignment is through a well-planned induction process.

A well planned **induction** process is a systematic organizational effort for helping personnel to adjust readily and effectively to new work assignments so that they can contribute maximally to organizational goals while achieving personal and work satisfaction. This definition of an effective induction process, it should be noted, goes beyond the conventional idea that induction is concerned only with new personnel. The induction process, as defined in this chapter, includes both personnel who accept new assignments because of forced or voluntary transfer or reassignment (see Figure 5.1) and personnel new to the system but not new to the profession.

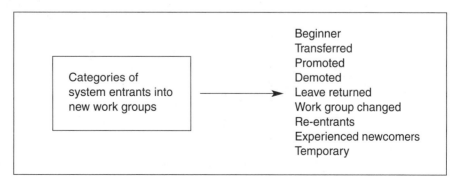

Figure 5.1   Entrants and re-entrants included in the induction program.

Most employees, whether new to the assignment or new to the system, seek an organizational environment in which they can find a reasonable degree of security and satisfaction in their work. The school employee beginning a new work assignment is no exception. In fact, for newcomers, the need for security and satisfaction is even greater than that of personnel continuing in their position.

New personnel may be apprehensive about many things, such as the community, their co-workers, or their ability to succeed. Generally, they are unaware of "the way we do things here." Most of them know nothing about the organization's objectives, their specific duties and responsibilities, school and community traditions and taboos, and personal and position standards to which members are expected to adhere.

Without this important knowledge about their new position, frustrated employees may withdraw from the new environment. This withdrawal takes several different forms. One form is frequent absence from work. This type of withdrawal almost always leads to voluntary resignation.

In school systems, many new employees resign voluntarily during their probation period. It has been noted, for example, that the number of first-year teachers who leave the profession is higher than it should be, and that the loss is higher than the profession should sustain. One study indicated that 20% of new teachers left prior to their second year of employment.[1]

Human resources managers know that absenteeism and voluntary turnover of new employees represent an economic loss to the system. Investment costs incurred when recruiting, selecting, inducting, and supervising new personnel are considered a financial loss when these persons are frequently absent or resign voluntarily. These costs can range from several hundred dollars for low-level positions to several thousand dollars for high-level administrative positions.

One presumed cause of absenteeism and voluntary turnover is the absence of well-planned induction practices. Newly assigned staff members must make so many adjustments before they are totally assimilated into the organization that a good induction program is important. One of the aims of such a program is to minimize the strain on the system's financial and human resources.

To say that educational systems have not been concerned with the problems of the inductee, either in the past or in the present, would be an understatement. Today, however, many excellent programs are in operation in a number of school districts. Some of these programs are based on recent educational reform and restructuring initiatives and include a variety of approaches. Depending on location, size, budgetary constraints, regulatory mandates, leadership, and proactive and reactive attitudes to institutional change, the activities within these programs vary. One way to characterize contemporary induction activity is in terms of four types of programs:

- University–school system collaboration
- Consortium programs for area school systems

- Districtwide programs
- School-based programs

Due in part to studies of new employees, the subject of induction has taken on a new and more crucial importance for reasons including the following:

- People change their behaviors when they become members of groups.[2]
- Formal induction programs tend to be better than unplanned activities.[3]
- Induction is crucial to both the organization and the inductee, enabling the newcomer to learn about the organization's culture, norms, and standards of behavior. The organization, through the induction process, can create programs designed to enhance the newcomer's quality of work.
- Entry problems such as a lack of organized induction activities, inappropriate first assignment, absence of feedback on early performance, and lack of relevant information needed by inductees can be minimized with carefully designed induction programs.[4]
- Induction studies have identified many types of induction problems experienced by newcomers, including the need for respect, liking, belonging, and a sense of competence; unknown expectations; and the need to plan and prepare for the new work assignment. Four common professional problems for beginners are affiliation problems, classroom control, relationships with parents, and time management.[5] With new state legislation on alternative certification,[6] as well as problems encountered by first-year employees, development of strategies for using the induction process to enhance professional competence has become an important aspect of the human resources function.

Behavior and the Induction Process

Current literature on the induction of new employees contains several synonyms for the process of acclimating new employees to their work environment. These synonyms include such terms as *induction, placement, organizational entry, assignment,* and *orientation.* Each of these terms has been used to define the process by which new personnel are assisted in meeting their need for security, belonging, status, information, and direction in both their new position and their new organization.

The induction process begins with the recruitment stage and ends when the newly assigned employee has made the personal, position, organizational, and social adaptations that enable him or her to function fully and effectively as a member of the school staff. This involves more than making new personnel feel at ease in an unfamiliar environment. In its broadest sense, the induction process is an extension of the recruitment and selection processes.

Few, if any, employees begin a new job assignment with all the skills necessary to perform all job tasks with maximum efficiency. In view of this situation, some investigators have categorized the skills of new employees, for both their position and their work environment, into separate categories. Luthans and Kreiter developed four categories to classify the behavioral skills of newcomers in relation to their position: (a) desirable performance-related job behavior, (b) potentially disruptive performance-related behavior, (c) behavior unrelated to performance, and (d) performance behavior deficiencies.[7]

By using these categories to classify the skills of newly assigned employees relative to all the different dimensions of job performance in their new position, certain identified behaviors can be reinforced, modified, and/or eliminated through what these authors refer to as a *shaping process.* Although the concept of shaping is employed in other human resources processes (and will be discussed subsequently in this and other chapters), the induction process is the starting point in employment for performance analysis and improvement of basic skills through shaping. Shaping for new employees begins when the system (a) gathers information about newcomers relative to desired behavior in their new position, (b) seeks to positively reinforce acceptable behaviors, (c) uses a management-by-objectives approach to correct deficiencies in performance, and (d) through day-by-day supervision, helps the individual to become part of the organization.

Nature and Scope of the Induction Process

A successful induction process for newly assigned employees should grow out of a formal plan of action developed and implemented by management. By relying on a formal plan of action for designing, implementing, and controlling the induction process, errors of omission are reduced and the induction process becomes more consistent. An action plan on the induction process for new employees should answer the following questions:

- What does the *system* expect to achieve through the induction process?
- What should happen to the *institution and the inductee* as a result of the induction process?
- What types of activities are needed to achieve the goals of the induction process?
- How will induction activities be divided into organizational units?
- Which induction activities will be assigned to the central administration?
- Which induction activities will be assigned to the attendance units?
- What actions should be taken prior to appointment, before the employee reports for work, and during the probationary period?
- Who does what during each phase of the induction process?
- What method should be used to make the induction process conform to the plan?
- What kinds of appraisals are necessary to determine the effectiveness of the induction process?

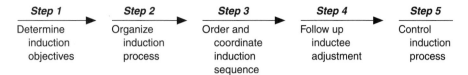

Figure 5.2   Model of the induction process.

A conceptual model for an effective induction process can answer these questions (see Figure 5.2). This model shows that the steps of the induction process include activities normally associated with any administrative task: planning, organizing, leading, and controlling. Worth noting is that the induction process is one of the components or subsystems of the human resources function; it is linked to other subsystems within the personnel domain and is an integral part of the total human resources system.

The induction model presented in Figure 5.2 illustrates the kinds of decisions that confront administrators when assimilating personnel into the system. The following sections consider in detail how a school system puts into practice the concepts suggested in the questions and steps reflected by this model.

Goals of the Induction Process

The purpose of the induction process is to help newly assigned personnel adjust to their new work environment. However, this purpose will have little significance for those who plan or implement the process unless it is translated into specific objectives (the first step in the induction process). Examples of specific objectives for an induction process gleaned from the professional literature are presented in Figure 5.3.

Underlying these objectives is knowledge about certain reactions that newly assigned employees exhibit or report. Such reactions indicate that (a) turnover occurs primarily during the early period of employment; (b) turnover often causes hostility and resistance within the system; (c) change within a social system generally tends to be viewed unfavorably; (d) haphazard induction procedures can precipitate anxiety, discouragement, disillusionment, or defensive behavior; (e) security, belonging, esteem, and information problems of inductees can be minimized during the induction period; and (f) frustration develops when new personnel discover inconsistencies between the realities of organizational life and their expectations at the beginning of their employment.

In addition to the objectives listed in Figure 5.3, other potential objectives of a successful induction process should be identified. Such potential objectives may be obtained by asking the opinions of designated personnel. Such personnel should include both newly assigned employees and those working closely with them.

The objectives presented in Figure 5.3 and revealed by assessment of designated personnel, will provide many alternatives to those responsible for designing and

- Assist members to appreciate the values, abilities, expected behaviors, and social knowledge essential to undertaking a system role and contributing to its mission.
- Provide inductees with complete and uniform information about the school system's mission, organization, structure, functions, policies, and work requirements.
- Develop loyal, effective, and productive workers.
- Reduce the likelihood of rule violation, discharges, resignations, and grievances.
- Address performance problems before they occur.
- Minimize the gap between employment expectancy and reality.
- Ease the transition from one institutional or work environment to another.
- Promote professional and personal well-being of inductees.
- Satisfy regulatory mandates.
- Develop a basic knowledge of the need for positive adjustment to external, internal, position, cultural, social, and personal aspects of system membership.
- Place inductees in positions so as to balance school system needs with individual competencies and aspirations.
- Reduce inductee anxiety.
- Reduce cost and supervisory time.

Figure 5.3   Induction objectives.

implementing an induction process for new personnel. For any given induction process to accomplish each of these objectives would indeed be an unrealistic expectation. Instead, the task for those who develop and implement a successful induction program is to determine the salience of each objective within their own school system.

For example, the induction process begins during the recruitment stage and continues into the selection stage. However, the individual or individuals responsible for recruitment and selection may have failed to explain to the recruit all the ramifications of a given position. Because of this failure, the induction process must provide the newly assigned employee with supplementary information.

The induction process should allow every inductee, from caretaker to chief executive, to be fully informed about the community; the duties, relationships, and responsibilities of the position; the characteristics of the system (purpose, policies, procedures, personnel, customs, and history); and the specific position to which the inductee is assigned. One major expectation of induction is that new personnel will be given whatever information is necessary to facilitate their adjustment.

When new personnel are given the information they need, they will be more likely to become self-directing and achieve job satisfaction. The process should enhance the employee's satisfaction and increase his or her ability to perform efficiently, reducing the need for supervision. For every new employee, a positive attitude toward the system should be developed, an attitude that will endure throughout his or her career.

The induction process, then, should focus on minimizing difficulties that changes in personnel pose for both existing and new employees. The system's interest in the newcomer should go well beyond the activities of the induction process. The organization also wishes the individual to remain in the system and become an effective employee, work independently, engage in self-development, and exceed role expectations through innovative and spontaneous behavior. These are long-term system objectives; the basis for these objectives can be laid during the induction process.

At the core of the induction process is a formal commitment by the board of education regarding induction policies and practices. One example of this official commitment, which serves as a keystone for the Riverpark school system's induction policies and practices, is presented in Figure 5.4. It is a formal declaration of the guiding principles concerning newly assigned personnel:

- It provides a vision for realizing short- and long-term induction objectives.
- It communicates the official induction intent of the board of education.
- It includes a formal proactive induction process, as well as an open forum that allows employees to participate in developing policies and practices that affect their lives and their world of work.

Organization of the Induction Process

One purpose of an induction program is to provide newly assigned employees with information they need to become assimilated into their new work environment. When this is done effectively, many adjustment problems can be prevented. Although the information needs of newcomers vary, depending on whether they are recent hires or newly assigned from within the system, certain problem areas common to all new employees have been identified in the literature.[8] These include:

- Problems in becoming acquainted with the *position.*
- Problems in *performing* the assignment.
- Problems in acquiring knowledge about the *system.*
- Problems in getting to know *personnel* in the system.
- Problems in becoming acquainted with the *community.*
- Problems in adjusting to a new *external environment.*

An analysis of these problem areas indicates that the induction process should be sensitive (see Step 2 of Figure 5.2) to three sources of information: those related

To create a stimulating environment for the investiture of inductees (initial hires, internal transfers, promotees, demotees, and temporaries) the Riverpark school system gives primacy to these courses of action:

- Envision inductee placement in the context of future system positions and human resources strategy.
- Embody state-of-the-art practices in the induction process.
- Establish lines of authority and responsibility for the conduct of the induction process.
- Ensure maintenance of ethical standards and integrity in the conduct of the induction process.
- Deal ethically and professionally with problems posed by special groups (disabled, inexperienced, underprivileged).
- Emphasize variation in work assignments such as team concept, work unit culture, and individual responsibility.
- Give consideration, when there is a diversity of positions available, by comparing an individual's aptitudes, abilities, interests, and temperament with requirements of various openings to determine inductee suitability.
- Design the induction process to enhance the ability of inductees to proceed from "newly appointed" to productive team members without loss or interval of time.
- Form cooperative and interdependent relationships in the system's social, work, and community environments.
- Shape the induction process through policies, programs, purposes, and procedures conducive to performance expectations, position expectations, and retentive power.
- Contribute to assimilation, socialization, security, personal development, and need satisfaction of position entrants.
- Gear the induction process to create a bonding among the three induction phases (preappointment, interim period, and probationary service).
- Update the human resources manual to provide for current information needs of appointees and members of the induction team.
- Utilize, during each of the induction stages, selected induction approaches for systemwide, departmental, work unit, and position application.

Figure 5.4   Form and structure of the Riverpark school system's induction process.

to position adjustment, system adjustment, and community adjustment. A discussion of each of these sources of information follows.

Position Information

Many of the adjustment problems of new employees could be prevented by proper selection and placement decisions. Often overlooked is that these decisions involve both the individual as a potential employee and the organization as a potential employer. Individuals must make decisions about joining the organization, and the organization must make decisions about selecting individuals.

Decisions required by individuals and by organizations during recruitment and selection can be improved by using information contained in position guides. These guides are valuable in helping new employees become acquainted with their assignments. They should not only prevent applicants from accepting positions for which they are unqualified, they should also provide information to those responsible for personnel selection and placement so that candidates and positions can be matched effectively.

Position guides can be used to help clarify new assignments. The inductee's immediate supervisor, with the aid of position guides, should be able to describe to a new employee the purposes of the position and the organization's expectations. The supervisor should also be able to appraise the employee's performance on the basis of the duties, responsibilities, and relationships specified in the position guide.

After the selection process is completed, the new employee is assigned to a work unit within the organization. When selecting and placing individuals in new assignments, certain contextual aspects of the assignment must be considered. These issues include the following:

- How well does the individual fit the leadership style of the work unit?
- How well will the individual fit into the work unit's environment?
- Will the newcomer be accepted by the work group?
- Will the assignment affect the types of staff balance (operating unit, competence, racial-ethnic-gender, program, load, utilization, and staff size) referred to in Chapter 2?

If those responsible for selecting and placing individuals in new assignments ignore these questions, it should not be surprising that the newly assigned employee has adjustment problems. These problems arise when the expectations, values, and goals of new employees are inconsistent with the realities of organizational life or when the work group believes that the employee's assignment is not based on merit. Unless the selection and placement decisions are sound, new employees will not be accepted.

The selection and placement processes frequently overlook these important elements: leadership and followership styles of the applicant, style of the persons the applicant will report to, styles of those reporting to the applicant (if the position is administrative), and the structure of the job situation.[9] In the discussion of the selection and placement processes, it was emphasized that *information* is the key to making judgments about placing an individual in a position. This includes learning as much as possible about the applicant and the position in question so that the compatibility between applicant and position can be judged carefully.

The adjustment problems of newly assigned employees can spill over to the work unit and cause major disruptions. Widespread dissatisfaction may occur when overqualified or under-qualified personnel become part of the work group. Serious problems may also develop when members of the work group perceive newcomers as sources of disruption.

It cannot be emphasized too strongly that improper selection and/or placement can be costly to both the employee and the system. Placing an incompetent individual in any position or a competent individual in the wrong position often leads to years of administrative grief, low productivity of the employee, and interference with attainment of system goals. Proactive rather than reactive selection and placement decisions are best for everyone involved in the employment process.

System Information

Newly assigned employees seek information about the system, as well as about their positions within the system. As noted earlier in this chapter, some of the adjustment problems of new employees are due to lack of information about the system. New employees need to know about the fringe benefits associated with the position, the support services available, and the relationship of the position to the organization as a whole.

Recent hires, as well as continuing employees with new assignments, must often make decisions about certain benefit options provided by the system and unique to their new assignment. Depending on whether the new position is administrative, instructional, or support, benefit packages may vary. Examples of benefit options that may vary by job classification include choosing an insurance carrier, claiming dependents, opting for a flexible spending account, using payroll deductions, and having direct deposit of pay checks.

The difficulty in choosing among benefit options is compounded for new personnel because these options often have a window of opportunity, which can be either irrevocable or penalty laden. Irrevocable windows require newly assigned employees to choose or to reject the benefit within a specified time, while penalty-laden windows penalize these employees for accepting a benefit at a later date in the employment cycle.

To make an informed choice among benefit options with windows of opportunity is difficult for many newly assigned employees. These employees are concerned about mastering the skills needed in their new position, understanding the expectations of their new supervisor, and blending with the organization. Some of the anxieties in choosing among fringe benefits with windows of opportunity can be reduced by providing appropriate and timely information in the induction process.

Most, if not all, newly assigned employees in schools have certain support functions, provided by the system, designed to help them perform effectively and efficiently. However, knowledge of these support systems is *assumed*, often at the expense of the individual and the system.

Many times newly assigned administrators are confronted with situations involving labor–management relations. In the absence of crystal clear contract language concerning the specific point of contention, these new administrators may be required to provide an interpretation. Any such interpretation should be tempered by past labor–management practices within the system. Information about these practices is obtainable through the support system provided by the district.

Teachers are often confronted with student-related issues. Some of these issues are academic, while others are nonacademic. In both cases, a satisfactory resolution of the problem may depend on the district's support system.

Classified employees also encounter problems requiring support systems. Equipment for processing information (clerical), preparing food (food service), cleaning buildings (custodians), transporting students (bus drivers), and facilitating instruction (instructional aids) may malfunction in the absence of an immediate supervisor. The support systems available to solve problems caused by malfunctions should be known by all classified personnel to prevent loss of time and effort by new employees.

Although a formal induction program for employees can provide information about available support services, sometimes services and service providers are not linked for newly assigned personnel. And unless a link is established, new employees may fail to recall what services are available to them when needed. This situation often results in underutilization of support systems by new employees. Seyfarth suggests that services and providers can be linked by having newly assigned employees interview the servers.[10] Such interviews, initiated by new employees, open channels of communication and allow the involved parties to establish rapport.

In addition to providing information about fringe benefits and support services, every organization must inform members of its purposes, policies, and procedures. Newly appointed staff members want to know, for example, about the operation of the system and about how their position fits into the total picture. They need to known not only the essential components of the system but also how the parts interact, contributing to the success (goal attainment) of the whole—in other words, the culture.

Every school system has a unique culture, that is, a set of interrelated values and priorities, norms and expectations, ideas and beliefs.[11] This culture, according to Smithers, serves a variety of useful functions for a system, including: (a) establishing standards and shared expectations that provide a range of acceptable behavior for group members, (b) providing guidelines that allow individuals to fit into the group, and (c) setting standards of behavior that facilitate interaction between members and provide a means of identifying with one's peers.[12]

Because each system has a unique culture, inductees often encounter difficulties in the adjustment that takes place between the individual and the organization during initial assignments in a new position. Schools may promote unique beliefs that conflict with those held by new employees.[13] Beliefs of new staff members on academic freedom, teaching controversial issues, the role of the teacher as a citizen, selection of reading matter, and student behavior, as well as their values, traditions, customs, beliefs, goals, appearance, and student discipline, may differ considerably from the system's official values and objectives.

To a certain extent, every system seeks to assimilate new personnel by orienting them to the culture of the system. Whether the new staff members will accept or reject the institution's culture, in whole or in part, is not certain. But awareness of the organizational culture is essential for effective adjustment during the period when the inductee is being considered for permanent employment.[14]

Cultural shaping and reinforcement are important aspects of the induction process for newly assigned personnel. Both at the time when these personnel enter the organization and later on, the system should develop and implement plans for cultural transmission and acquisition by helping inductees to understand what the organization expects of its members, as well as the various means by which the organizational culture is communicated. Thus, the induction process provides a timely opportunity to translate system philosophy into cultural reality by describing and interpreting the roles, relationships, and behaviors necessary for individual, unit, and organizational effectiveness.[15]

Cultural assimilation is most likely to be achieved in an effective induction process when certain socialization conditions are satisfied. These conditions have been outlined by Wanous in the following four-stage framework for the induction of newly assigned personnel:

• Newcomer learns the reality of the work environment.
• Newcomer identifies norms of co-workers and the boss.
• Newcomer makes accommodations between conflicts at the work setting and at home.
• Newcomer accepts norms and realizes that the organization is satisfied with job behavior.[16]

Community Information

The relationship between school systems and communities is complementary. The school system has a vested interest in the community, and the community has a vested interest in the school system. The success of both entities is closely linked. Although there are exceptions to any generality, there are few exceptions about the relationship between school systems and communities. Seldom does one find an excellent school system in an undesirable community or an excellent community with a below-average school system.

Because the success of one entity depends largely on the success of the other, school systems should make every effort to strengthen school–community relations. Research on this issue indicates that effective schools have more contact with parents and the community than less effective schools, and that effective schools usually have more positive parent-initiated contacts than less effective schools.[17] An interesting paradox with respect to research and practice, however, is that studies of induction consistently point out that the methods used to inform prospective or newly appointed personnel about the community or to help them adjust to it are generally unsatisfactory.

For personnel who are new to the community, personal problems encountered outside the school assignment itself merit attention. These relocation problems include finding suitable housing; arranging transportation; finding educational, religious, cultural, banking, and recreational facilities; and numerous other issues that must be attended to while adjusting to the new environment. The ability to cope with these problems is important to the administration because complete adjustment to the employee's new role will not occur until the anxieties involved in getting established are relieved.

Newly assigned employees, whether teachers, administrators, or support personnel moving into the community, need various kinds of information, not only to adjust to the community but also to become effective employees. Information on such matters as community geography, economy, housing, government, religious agencies, educational resources, law enforcement agencies, public safety, health conditions, medical resources, recreation facilities, child care, family welfare agencies, and community planning resources is needed to help these beginners better serve the school system, its clients, and the community.[18]

The school system has a responsibility to increase the public understanding of education. It also shares in the responsibility for community improvement. What the school staff contributes to these ends depends to a large extent on the staff's understanding of the community. The induction process gives the administration opportunities to help newcomers adjust to the community, showing them how they can achieve personal objectives and demonstrating how community resources can be used to improve the school system. If the relationship of the community to the school is really as strategic as it is believed to be, then the school system should develop induction programs to help the staff, especially new members, to understand the community and its effect on the school system.

Ordering and Coordinating the Induction Sequence

In the previous section we focused on the information needs of newly assigned employees. For clarity, these needs were classified according to position, organization, and community. Although these sources of information were treated separately, in reality much overlap exists among them with respect to the information needs of new personnel.

Because overlap exists, these sources of information should not be treated as independent components in an induction process. Instead, information across all sources should be integrated and ordered into a meaningful sequence for new employees. This process is noted in Step 3 of Figure 5.2.

The types of information to be included in an effective induction process should be determined by a number of factors, including past experience of personnel

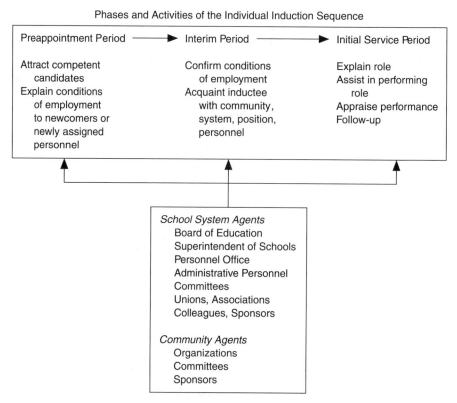

Figure 5.5   *Linkage of phases, agents, and activities of the induction sequence.*

replacements, anticipated need for new staff members, nature of the community, and size of the school district. Induction needs of new personnel vary from one system to another and from one year to the next. The type of program developed for a specific institution in any given year should be based on careful analysis of factors such as those just mentioned.

Even though information needs for new employees may vary among systems and across time, there are certain crucial periods within the employment cycle for all of these employees. We call these the *preappointment period*, the *interim period*, and the *initial service period* for purposes of discussion. A brief description of these periods (to be expanded in the following sections), along with some of the key agents for an effective induction process during each period, is presented in Figure 5.5.

Preappointment Period

The induction cycle actually begins before any initial contact is made between the institution and the applicant. Vacant positions to be filled must be identified and authorized, either through a long-range staffing plan, as described in Chapter 2, or by the exit of current personnel. In addition, regardless of whether vacant positions are newly created or previously established, certain types of information must be compiled.

For every vacancy, general information is needed about the school system and specific information is needed about the position. To provide information about the school system, many districts use or should use a recruitment brochure.[19] A well-prepared brochure informs applicants and employment agencies about the characteristics of the system and the community, the application process, and the names of contact persons within the system.

Specific information about the position is presented in a position guide. Sometimes a position guide must be developed; in other instances, an existing guide must be revisited and updated. Far too often, this is neglected and dated information is provided. As a result, neither the interests of the system nor those of the applicant are served if the position is described poorly or if the qualifications for the position are misrepresented.

The position guide should contain up-to-date information about the personal and experiential requirements for the position. This information is essential to several involved parties. It gives direction to those responsible for recruitment and selection; makes clear to the applicant the qualifications, duties, and responsibilities of the position; and enables placement agencies and recruiters to locate candidates who meet the requirements.

Information contained in recruitment brochures and position guides provides topics for exploration in the initial employment interview. In this interview, the recruiter can give the applicant various types of information likely to be needed in deciding whether to accept or reject the position. Moreover, during the interview, the applicant is able to ask questions about the position or to get information on a range of relevant issues.

If possible, the initial interview should be held at the work site for the vacant position. This enables the candidate to meet with additional administrative officials and school personnel and to visit the community. If the applicant is fully informed about the position, the conditions of employment, and the school and community environments in which the work is to be performed, an informed decision can be made. This is the primary goal of the first phase of the induction sequence.

Interim Induction Period

Formal appointment to a position poses problems for both the individual and the institution, problems different from those encountered earlier by either party. Plans of assistance, from the time of appointment until the first actual day on the job, will differ for various types of personnel. Induction activities for teachers, for example, should not be the same as those for secretaries or custodians.

However, although plans of assistance will vary, certain steps are common to all personnel in an effective induction process. The following list presents some of the preliminary steps planned and initiated by the human resources office to help all new employees adjust to the position, the system, and the community.

- Letters of welcome are sent by the board of education, superintendent of schools, and local employee associations.
- An experienced employee is assigned to serve as a sponsor to every newly assigned person.
- A brochure is prepared for sponsors that explains the aims of the induction program and the responsibilities of sponsors.
- A preliminary conference is held between sponsors and the immediate supervisor of the new employee.
- A conference between the immediate supervisor and the new appointee is held to discuss the work assignment. The supervisor should avoid giving the new appointee a heavy workload or unusual duties that make it difficult for the beginner to achieve a measure of success in the first year. Whenever possible assignments should be made on the basis of employee preference and the need to reduce the workload of the employee during the first year of service.
- Copies of handbooks, selected board policies, and relevant labor contacts are given to the new employee.
- Conditions of employment are confirmed. The organization makes certain that the newcomer understands the salary, collateral benefits, extra pay, merit pay, and other facets of the compensation structure.

These activities highlight the importance of the induction sequence for newly assigned employees. It is sound planning to begin this sequence before the individual arrives for the first full day of work. This eliminates some of the problems of new appointees and makes it easier for them to achieve their full service potential. Many of these activities can be handled in a pre-opening conference sponsored by the school system.

The pre-opening conference, which may assume a variety of forms, is employed by almost all school systems. It provides an opportunity to acquaint new personnel with members of the staff, as well as with the plans and procedures of the school. Some pre-opening conference activities involve the entire staff, others are restricted to the work unit, and still others are designed specifically for new personnel.

The immediate supervisor is responsible for helping the inductee to adjust readily to the new work assignment. This may include interpreting plans for the coming year, including those for appraising work performance and evaluating progress; acquainting the inductee with physical facilities, resources, and support services; and explaining the general policies and work routines of the unit.

Because the work of the unit and that of the individual employee are related to the life of the community, and because school personnel are members of the community because of their work, investing time and effort to ensure the new member's acceptance by the community is important. Group conferences with key members of the community, including parents, receptions by the board of education, and other social activities will ease the newcomer's transition into the new environment.

The previous list of induction activities is not exhaustive, and a given sequence of activities will not suffice in all situations. The wide range of induction problems in different institutions rules out a prescribed program applicable to all school systems. Each system can best achieve the goals of the induction process by developing and assessing the techniques and activities most effective for particular situations and conditions.

The forms presented in Figures 5.6 and 5.7 lend specificity to the foregoing suggestions. These forms illustrate a three-part induction plan for the time before the newcomer actually begins to work. The following outline is the substance of this plan:

- Sessions 1 and 2 cover *central administration* responsibilities. Their intent is to explain the organization and administration of systemwide personnel policies and procedures applicable to new members.
- Session 3 deals with *position* and *unit-oriented* responsibilities. Its intent is to acquaint individuals with their responsibilities and to introduce them to their new colleagues. This session is handled by the administrator of the new employee's unit.
- Copies of forms are given to inductees to acquaint them with the nature and scope of the conditions of employment, constraints that govern their work, and opportunities that will become available.
- The inductee and the administrator responsible for conducting the session sign the forms; these forms become a component of the new staff member's file.
- Instructional aids available for orientation sessions are virtually limitless, ranging from programmed materials to filmstrips, slides, films, tapes, cassettes, records, charts, transparencies, flip charts, videotapes, brochures, booklets, and mimeographed materials.

Our discussion in this section has addressed certain tasks, procedures, and concerns common to any effective induction process. We have focused primarily on the preappointment period and the interim period of the induction process (Figure 5.5). However, an effective induction process goes beyond these two periods to include the regular work cycle of new personnel throughout their probationary period (see Figures 5.2 and 5.5).

Follow-up of Inductee Adjustment

Induction responsibility for new personnel does not end with the opening of school, as noted in Figure 5.2. Although effective recruitment and selection can improve the quality of applicants and enhance the match between persons, positions, and work environments, both of these human resource functions signal the beginning rather

Foxcroft School System

Induction Checklist for New Personnel
(To Be Processed by Central Administration)

Directions—Form 100 has been designed to facilitate the induction of new staff members to the Foxcroft School System. The content of the three-phase induction program is outlined below, the intent of which is to provide newcomers with an information perspective so that they may readily become informed system members.

Name of new staff member _____ Starting date _____

Unit and position location _____ _____

Session 1: Human Resources Policies and Procedures

Date _____ Time _____ Place _____ Responsibility _____

   a. System mission and administrative structure _____ Policies _____

   b. Compensation

      Salary _____ Collateral benefits _____ Extra pay _____

   c. Performance appraisal _____ Probationary period _____

   d. Development _____

   e. Personnel inventory _____

   f. Leaves of absence _____ Holidays _____ Vacations _____

   g. Personnel services _____

   h. Community relationships _____

   i. Code of ethics _____

Session 2: Human Resources Policies and Procedures

Date _____ Time _____ Place _____ Responsibility _____

   a. Review and questions on Session 1 _____

   b. Union relations _____

   c. Tenure _____ Retirement _____ Social security _____

   d. Academic freedom and responsibility _____

   e. Payroll: Deductions __ Issuance __ Adjustments __ Responsibility __

   f. Transfers _____ Promotions _____

   g. Grievance procedures _____

All items checked have been discussed with inductee _____

Central administration representative _____ Date _____

Returned to personnel office for individual personnel file _____

Reviewed _____ Filed _____ by personnel office

Signature of inductee _____

Figure 5.6   *The three-phase induction plan of the Foxcroft school system (sessions 1 and 2).*

Foxcroft School System

Form 200

Position Orientation Checklist for New Personnel
(To Be Completed by Unit Administrators)

Directions—This checklist has been designed as a part of the induction program of the Foxcroft School System. Its primary intent is to acquaint new staff members with the position to which they have been assigned and the performance requirements that the roles involve. This step of the induction process is one of several planned to enable the individual to adjust quickly to the position, the school, the system, and the community. Directions for processing the checklist are included below.

Name of inductee _____

	Discussion Completed
Session 3: Position and Building Orientation	
1. Welcome and introduction to Foxcroft School System.	_____
2. Describe unit organization, objectives, functions, and relationships to system at large.	_____
3. Provide copy of position guide to inductee and explain contents.	_____
4. Explain the relationship the position inductee will hold to unit and system objectives.	_____
5. Explain position performance standards for continuance of employment.	_____
6. Explain performance appraisal process and its relationship to continuance of employment and promotion.	_____
7. Explain conditions of employment in unit, including:	_____

Hours of work   Provisions for lunch
Lunch hours   Parking
Building facilities   Transportation
Supplies and equipment   Services
Behavior   Other

8. Introduce to colleagues within unit and to other contact personnel.

Date _____

Signature of inductee _____

Signature of unit administrator _____

Returned to personnel office for individual personnel file   _____

Reviewed _____ Filed _____ by personnel office   _____

Figure 5.7   The three-phase induction plan of the Foxcroft school system (session 3).

than the end of the induction process.[20] Until the new employee has performed under actual conditions, and until the organization has had an opportunity to appraise the suitability of the newcomer for the position, induction is not complete.

The need for an induction process to continue after the pre-opening conference is based on two facts: (a) no inductee is ready to perform the new assignment flawlessly, and (b) even the best selection process is fallible. For these reasons, a probationary period for all new personnel is becoming increasingly a matter of institutional policy, and effective induction processes include this period.

The administration cannot ignore its responsibility for planning and administering a follow-up program (Step 4 in Figure 5.2) in an effective induction process. Whatever the nature of the new appointee's assignment, follow-up visits and interviews by the immediate supervisor are essential, especially during the first few weeks of employment. The timing of such assistance is important because the inductee may have trouble understanding the assignment or encounter difficulty on the job.

A well-developed induction process specifies such matters as the number, frequency, nature, and phasing of follow-up interviews. In addition, follow-up reports are submitted by the immediate supervisor to the central administration, which appraises such characteristics as quality of performance, difficulties encountered, and other factors deemed important to the effectiveness of the new employee.

Appraisal during the probationary period, as one phase of the total appraisal process, is designed not only to assist the competent probationer but to spot the potentially incompetent, marginal, or undesirable one as well. Those individuals who cannot perform satisfactorily in one position may be reassigned, given more personal supervision, or provided with intensified training to overcome their deficiencies. Prompt rehabilitation or elimination of unsuitable appointees will save money, time, and effort for the system.

To monitor the job behaviors of newly assigned employees during the probationary period, it is necessary to assess the perceptions both of the employee and of the immediate supervisor. Figure 5.8 is an example of a self-appraisal form to be completed by the inductee. It is designed to provide feedback to the immediate supervisor on position problems and on progress toward effective role performance as perceived by the new employee.

Complementing the self-assessment form is a form to be completed by the immediate supervisor, an example of which is given in Figure 5.9. This form contains impression of both parties and is used to inform the central administration about the progress of employees during the probationary period.

Analysis and synthesis of the information obtained from both forms provides the basis for counseling and coaching discussions during follow-up sessions between the inductee and the immediate supervisor. Formalizing the methods of collecting information about new employees at the probationary stage communicates an important message: that the system has a continuing interest in their welfare, their adjustment to the assigned position, and their contribution to the organization.

Position Design

Do you have a clear understanding of the expectations your immediate supervisor has for you in your present position?

Do you have a clear understanding of the goals of the work unit to which you are assigned?

Does your immediate supervisor give you specific help in improving your position performance?

Do you feel you are well-placed in your present assignment?

Performance Appraisal

Does your immediate supervisor give you the necessary information to enable you to know how you are getting on with your role?

How worthwhile was your last performance appraisal in helping you to improve your performance?

Summarize the overall strengths and weaknesses you have demonstrated in performing your present assignment.

Development

How much assistance have you been given by your supervisor in planning your career development?

How do you feel about the progress you have made thus far in performing your role?

How confident are you that your career aspirations can be met by remaining in this organization?

Do you feel you have potential beyond your present assignment?

How have you demonstrated this potential?

Communication

Do you receive sufficient information to perform your role effectively?

Do you receive sufficient information to understand the relationships among your role, the unit to which you are assigned, and the mission of the school system?

Is your supervisor well-informed about your requirements for performing the role effectively?

Role Satisfaction

How do you feel about the kind of work you are doing in your present position?

Are there significant observations that you think should be noted about the dimensions of your position that affect your performance and should be brought to the attention of your unit, such as unit objectives, position design, organization structure, supervisory process, and results achieved?

How effectively do you feel you have met the responsibilities of your position?

Signature of inductee _____ Date _____

Figure 5.8   Self-appraisal form for inductees.

Adjustment Progress and Problems	Analysis by Unit Administrator	Analysis by Inductee

What progress has been made by the inductee during the review period in making the following adjustments:
  a. Community adjustment?
  b. Position adjustment?
  c. System adjustment?
  d. Individual and group adjustment?
  e. Personal adjustment?		

What are the obstacles to achieving adjustment expectations in the areas listed above?		
What comments should be made on the results achieved for each of the adjustments listed above?		
In what areas has the inductee made the most progress in adjustment? The least progress?		
Do the adjustment expectations need to be revised?		
What are the plans and priorities for achieving adjustment expectations?		

Name of inductee _____ Organization unit _____ Position _____

Signature of inductee _____

Signature of unit administrator _____

Date of review _____ Next review period _____

Figure 5.9   Form for performance review of new personnel by the unit administrator.

Controlling the Induction Process

Assessments of new personnel are essential to an effective induction program. The financial and human capital investments associated with recruiting, selecting, and inducting new personnel are considerable for most school systems. The loss suffered by the system when the inductee's service is terminated or when he or she leaves the organization voluntarily warrants the attention of management.

In theory, recruitment, selection, and induction processes should result in the attraction and retention of the number, kinds, and quality of personnel needed by the system for an effective education program. Periodic assessments of the actual outcomes (Step 5 of Figure 5.2) of these three human resource processes should provide information to minimize turnover costs due to faulty recruitment, selection, and placement. Such assessments provide information on personnel need satisfaction; position compatibility; immediate supervisor's opinion of the new employee's effectiveness; and validity of the recruitment, selection, and induction processes. If and when these processes do not lead to the desired results, the system can take corrective action.

Assessments of the induction process should focus on several different outcome measures. The most important one is whether the new personnel performed effectively. Because most work assignments have a proficiency curve in which job performance improves over time, the effectiveness of new personnel should be assessed at different times during the probationary period.

It is imperative to determine if the predictions of performance made before selection agree with actual job performance. The ultimate purpose of analyzing the recruitment, selection, and induction processes is to determine how well the system is succeeding in attracting and holding a competent staff. The evaluation should reveal what adjustments must be made to achieve these goals.

Because individuals as well as organizations must commit to the employment process, it is important to give special attention to those employees who performed effectively but resigned during the probationary period. Voluntary resignations of effective probationers may or may not be related to their experiences in the recruitment, selection, assignment, or induction processes. Exit interviews with these employees can be extremely enlightening to those responsible for monitoring the induction process.

Although it is true that much time, money, and talent are invested in recruitment, selection, and induction, it is also true that person–position mismatches are costly, time-consuming, and counterproductive. To minimize such potential mismatches, ongoing assessment of the induction process is essential.

Induction and Human Resource Strategy

Throughout this book, the various functions of a school system (presented in Figure 1.2) and of the human resource processes (shown in Figure 2.1) have been implicitly viewed as interdependent. For instance, recruitment, selection, appraisal, and development are considered to be intertwined. This interdependence among personnel processes should be taken into account in shaping the overall human resources strategy. Thus viewed, induction, as one of the processes of the personnel function, has considerable potential for achieving the aims of the system, especially the right to be informed, coached, mentored, and assisted in various ways to achieve specific goals.

School systems use many methods to help new employees achieve relative independence as mature staff members with personal sets of behavioral determiners.

This assistance includes various forms of support designated in the literature by labels such as *peer coaching, buddy system, master teacher support, mentor–protégé relationship,* and *clinical teacher support.* The types of staff assistance provided to inductees focus on enhancing their development, depending on the individual's personality and willingness to adjust and adapt to the internal and external aspects of the workplace.

This chapter has emphasized that an effective induction process serves a number of purposes, including socialization; reduction of personnel anxieties, turnover, and supervisory time; helping individuals to understand themselves; and helping the system to understand new employees. Recent educational reform efforts in the United States, however, have caused more and more school systems to reconsider the induction process. Today an effective induction process requires systems to use a career development model that will enable employees to realize their full potential, achieve personal and position satisfaction, and enhance the effectiveness of the system.

Career Modeling

When considering a change from traditional induction to induction involving **career planning,** a model is very helpful. The career planning model for new personnel, outlined in the following discussion, includes three phases: Phase I—individual career planning; Phase II—human resource (system) planning; and Phase III—career development planning. This model provides a guide for redesigning personal growth programs, identifying individuals' key competencies and system development needs, and developing human resource strategies that help individuals to recognize their present and potential strengths as they move through their careers. Figure 5.10 defines the terms generally associated with career planning.

Phase I—Individual Career Planning

As defined in Figure 5.10, career planning is the personal process of establishing career goals and approaches and determining how they can be attained. Career planning, it should be emphasized, is primarily an individual responsibility. In planning their careers, employees make assessments and initiate plans to acquire

- *Self-knowledge*—knowledge or understanding of one's own character, education, experience, capabilities, motivations, career orientation, special talents, work preferences, career anchor, strengths, and weaknesses.
- *Position knowledge*—knowledge or understanding of career opportunities within the school system, career paths (functional, horizontal, and geographic), position requirements, position openings, potential assignments, reassignment, transfer, and promotion policies.
- *Career knowledge*—knowledge or understanding of the system's commitment, policies, and procedures to assist individuals in self-analysis so that they can deter-

mine career opportunities and choices, career objectives, and performance improvement plans.

In an enriched induction period, the school system can use various personnel processes (recruitment, selection, placement, appraisal, counseling) not only to meet staffing needs but also to design programs that encourage individual career planning activities and to make challenging initial assignments possible. Induction is a time when individuals should have opportunities and encouragement to understand their potential and to shape their short- and long-term aspirations accordingly.

Phase II—Human Resource Planning

Human resource planning refers to the school system's role in creating, supporting, and encouraging career perspectives for employees. It is the system's responsibility to shape its human resources into effective conduits through which an organizational climate is established that enhances individual career planning. Unless the system contains a set of values that places a premium on activities to achieve desired

---

Career. (a). An ongoing sequence of work-related activities; (b) a field for or pursuit of progressive achievement over the span of one's work life.

Career anchor. A preferred career path based on an individual's abilities, motives, goals, attitudes, organizational security, creativity, and competence.

Career cycle. Stages or periods through which a person's career takes shape.

Career development. The process of obtaining the necessary experience, skills, motivation, and attitudes for career progression. Includes counseling, staff development, career information systems, career pathing, performance appraisal, position enrichment, and position previews.

Career goals. Personalized immediate, intermediate, and long-term objectives toward which an individual's strategic aims are directed.

Career information. Programs designed to make available information about position openings and qualifications needed to fill them. Includes opportunities for career dialogues between personnel and counselors, assistance in reviewing career goals, and procedures by which members may apply for these opportunities.

Career instruction. A process employed to inform personnel about career paths through workshops, seminars, group study, and self-study activities.

Career ladder. A promotion path involving a hierarchy of specialized assignments. Teaching, for example, becomes the career anchor, while opportunities are provided to engage in other teaching-related activities such as being a master teacher, mentor, consultant, and director of induction or special instructional projects. Career ladder teachers are sometimes referred to as stage I, II, or III career ladder teachers.

(continued)

Figure 5.10   Terms commonly employed in career planning and development.

Career lattice. A network of positions that permits individuals to move across job families. Establishes the movement of members among grade levels, departments, divisions, and programs.

Career life stages. Early adulthood, mature adult, midlife, and old age. Often compared with career stages such as establishment, advancement, maintenance, and withdrawal.

Career management. Choices an individual makes in deciding which occupational opportunities will enhance attainment of career objectives.

Career path. A sequence of specific positions that enables members to match aspirations with system needs and opportunities.

Career planning. The process of establishing individual career goals and the manner in which they can be achieved.

Career stages. Phases individuals pass through during their careers, such as prework, establishment, advancement, maintenance, and retirement.

Career strategy. Consideration by system members of their vocational strengths and weaknesses, opportunities for advancement, skills needed, and means of giving long-term direction to their careers.

Career strengths and weaknesses. Analysis of individual competitive advantages and disadvantages in developing a career strategy. Includes education, experiences, abilities, aptitudes, special talents, career inventory, and sponsorship.

Career transition. Change in positions along a career path.

Figure 5.10   continued.

individual performance, there is little chance that individual career planning will result in positive outcomes.

Organizational strategies to make the entry-level stage a period when career development begins to take shape include consideration of three variables: the *individual, positions,* and the *organizational climate.* Courses of action to link these components include:

•   Establishing policies, programs, and procedures on which to base operational activities involved in career planning.
•   Providing orientation, counseling, and mentoring services to assist persons with problems relating to entry-level adjustment, self-evaluation, and career planning.
•   Designing appraisal systems that provide performance feedback linked to career planning.
•   Initiating a plan for analyzing and specifying job requirements, from which essential information can be gleaned for describing the content of positions and the characteristics of persons who might perform in these positions successfully.

- Shaping challenging first jobs and enriching job assignments.
- Making career planning workshops, seminars, career path information, job previews, and psychological and aptitude test services available to newcomers.
- Establishing programs and practices to integrate career development with present and future staffing needs.

System involvement in career planning is now necessary and will become even more necessary as the kinds of skills needed to cope with social and technological developments change; as organizational environments (both internal and external) evolve; and as ways are sought to adjust to the shortage of skilled personnel and the variety of personnel demands stemming from the push for reforms.

Phase III—Career Development Planning

Phase III of the career planning model acknowledges that contemporary school systems are facing the demands of a changing culture and will continue to do so. This phase of the model is viewed as a sharing of responsibility between the individual and the organization in which a comprehensive career development program is fostered to meet the career growth needs of a diverse work force. Questions that should be asked and answered in career development planning during the induction process include the following:

- Is there a performance appraisal process in place designed to encourage career growth? Does the process stress the importance of performance diagnosis and behavioral objectives? Does the performance appraisal model fit the system's human resources strategies?
- To what extent is the supervisory staff committed to the belief that entry-level personnel need assistance and encouragement in job performance and career planning? That the sink-or-swim induction model is a strategy whose time is over?
- Which of the following mechanisms are in place to assist newcomers in planning performance improvement and career moves: formal and informal counseling, career information, position posting, talent profiles, skills inventories, position previews, role exploration, and position rotation?
- Are there mentoring programs for guiding, developing, and help individuals to achieve self-actualization, performance effectiveness, peer acceptance, and career mobility?

Although the foregoing discussion has centered on individualized plans for new hires and reassigned personnel, personnel development also includes new tasks for present personnel and for those employees preparing for new positions. These aspects of personnel development are treated in Chapter 6 in terms of plans featuring elements such as types of learning needed to achieve individual and group objectives, environments for optimum learning, cost-effective programming, and delivery systems compatible with staff development needs.

Review and Preview

In this chapter, analysis of induction problems suggests that an effective induction process is one way that the system can help new members to assimilate, as well as to enhance their personal development, security, and need satisfaction. A school system can recruit and select personnel, but until new employees become fully aware of and adjusted to the work to be performed, the work environment, and their new colleagues, they cannot be expected to contribute efficiently and effectively to the organization's goals. An induction process is needed to help new personnel to resolve community, system, position, and development problems by creating plans to enhance their position knowledge, skills, and behavior. Use of this process indicates a recognition of and an attempt to do something about the fact that human maladjustment is expensive, detrimental to individual and organizational goal achievement, and harmful to the socialization process involving the individual and the system. The induction process also assumes that the main determinant of motivation is the attraction the position holds for the individual, and that induction activities designed to enhance the potential for motivated action will result in better performance on the job.

Chapter 6 is concerned with methods used to achieve individual, unit, and system goals.

Discussion Questions

1. Define organizational culture and explain its importance in relation to the induction process.

2. Form two groups of five members each. Each group member is to describe the culture of an organization (e.g., school, church, local community, government, hospital, commercial corporation, or political entity). Each group will identify and report to the entire class the shared values, beliefs, cultural reinforcement, and group behavioral patterns that influence individual behavior; then the class will debate whether the culture is positive or negative.

3. Define socialization and its importance in the induction process.

4. Respond to this statement: "Socialization begins with the selection process; applicants should be rigorously screened in order to discourage those who may not fit into the culture."

5. How should a school system go about communicating its culture to inductees? Outline your plan.

6. List the strategic aims of socialization.

7. Describe the major steps you would take to increase the likelihood that an induction process will lead to desired and permanent changes in behavior.

8. What should school systems do about deviant inductees who reject group norms and behave independently (e.g., eating lunch alone, violating the dress code, and disregarding the performance culture)? Should they be punished, ostracized, closely supervised, terminated, or treated tolerantly?

9. What aspects of contemporary induction programs appear to be most neglected? For what reasons?

10. To what extent should school systems develop induction programs for support personnel? Temporary personnel? What should be the form and content of such programs?

11. What would you consider to be your visionary career plan? What work experiences have you had that would contribute to your ideal career plan? What types of satisfaction do you anticipate from a career plan? What obstacles do you envision in achieving a career plan? What course of action should you take to achieve your career goals?

12. Respond to the following statement: "The induction process is the least suitable method to use in career planning."

13. Consider the following statements regarding organizational culture and indicate the extent to which you agree or disagree with each:
- "A school system's culture is reflected in the pattern of signals the administration sends to its personnel indicating how they are expected to behave."
- "The culture of a school system can be positive or negative."
- "The leadership style of a school principal tends to define the culture of the school."
- "The organizational culture of some school systems rewards ineffective performance."

14. Some persons believe that a well-designed, carefully implemented recruitment and selection program eliminates the need for an induction program. Refute or defend this statement.

15. What unique induction considerations might arise in a rural school? A suburban school? A large city school?

16. Should a teachers' union participate in the induction process? If so, define its role.

17. Develop a one-page description of the components of a plan to evaluate the effectiveness of a school induction process in a suburban school system.

Notes

1. M. D. Chester and B. Q. Beaudin, "Efficacy Beliefs of Newly Hired Teachers in Urban Schools," *American Educational Research Journal* 33, 1 (Spring 1996), 233–257.

2. Robert D. Smithers, *The Psychology of Work and Human Performance* (New York: Harper & Row, 1988), 361.

3. Wendell L. French, *The Personnel Management Process,* 6th ed. (Boston: Houghton Mifflin Company, 1987), 297.

4. Ibid.

5. T. Bienenstok and W. R. Sayres, *Problems in Job Satisfaction among Junior High School Teachers* (Albany: New York State Education Department, n.d.); B. Dell Felder, Loye Y. Hollis, Martha K. Piper, and Robert W. Houston, *Problems and Perspectives of Beginning Teachers: A Follow-Up Study* (Houston, TX: University of Houston Central Campus, 1980); Frances F. Fuller and Oliver H. Brown, "Becoming a Teacher," in *Teacher Education, 74th Yearbook of the National Society for the Study of Education* (Chicago: NSSE, 1975); Nathalie Gehrke and Kaoru Yamamoto, "A Grounded Theory Study of the Role Personalization of Beginning Secondary Teachers," paper presented at the annual meeting of the American Educational Research Association,

Toronto, Canada, March 1978; Robert W. Houston and B. Dell Felder, "Break Horses, Not Teachers," *Phi Delta Kappan* 64, 7 (March 1982), 457–460; Joseph Liguna, *What Happens to the Attitudes of Beginning Teachers?* (Danville, IL: Interstate Printers & Publishers, Inc., 1970); Dan C. Lortie, *Schoolteacher* (Chicago: University of Chicago Press, 1975); Kevin Ryan et al., *Biting the Apple: Accounts of First-Year Teachers* (New York: Longman, Inc., 1980); John P. Cotter, "Managing the Joining-Up Process," *Personnel* 49 (July–August 1972), 46–56; Donald C. Feldman, "A Socialization Process That Helps New Recruits Succeed," *Personnel* 57 (March–April 1980), 11–23; and Donald R. Cruikshank, "Five Areas of Teacher Concern," *Phi Delta Kappan* 64, 7 (March 1982), 460.

6. J. Shen, "Has the Alternative Certification Policy Materialized Its Promise? A Comparison Between Traditionally and Alternatively Certified Teachers in Public Schools," *Educational Evaluation and Policy Analysis* 19, 3 (Fall 1997), 276–283.

7. Fred Luthans and Robert Kreitner, *Organizational Behavior Modification* (Glenview, IL: Scott, Foresman & Co., 1975), 97.

8. J. A. LeGore and L. Parker, "First Year Principal Succession: A Study of Leadership, Role, and Change," *Journal of School Leadership* 7, 4 (1997), 369–385.

9. For a detailed discussion of the interaction of leadership and followership styles in the placement aspects of induction, see Daniel A. Tagliere, *People, Power, and Organization* (New York: American Management Association, 1973).

10. J. T. Seyfarth, *Personnel Management for Effective Schools* (Needham Heights, MA: Allyn & Bacon, 1996).

11. W. K. Hoy and D. J. Sabo, *Quality Middle Schools: Open and Healthy.* (Thousand Oaks, CA: Corwin Press, 1980).

12. Smithers, *Psychology of Work,* 368–369.

13. P. M. Short and J. T. Greer, *Leadership in Empowered Schools* (Upper Saddle River, NJ: Merrill, 1997).

14. P. A. Winter, R. M. Newton, and R. L. Kirkpatrick, "The Influence of Work Values on Teacher Selection Decisions: The Effects of Principal Values, Teacher Values, and Principal–Teacher Value Interactions," in *Teaching and Teacher Education* 14, 4 (1998), 385–400.

15. Useful information on organizational culture is contained in Michael Albert and Murray Silverman, "Making Management Philosophy a Cultural Reality, Part II: Design Human Resources Programs Accordingly," *Personnel* 61, 2 (March–April 1984), 28–35; Edwin L. Baker, "Managing Organizational Culture," *Management Review* 69, 7 (July 1980), 8–17; and Fred Luthans, Richard M. Hodgetts, and Kenneth R. Thompson, *Social Issues in Business,* 4th ed. (New York: Macmillan Publishing Company, 1984), Chapter 4.

16. J. P. Wanous, *Organizational Entry,* 2nd ed. (Reading, MA: Addison Wesley Publishing Company, 1992).

17. W. Brookover et al., "Elementary School Social Climate and School Achievement," *American Educational Research Journal* 15, 2 (1978), 301–18.

18. G. White and J. Wehlage, "Community Collaboration: It Is Such A Good Idea, Why Is It So Hard?" *Educational Evaluation and Policy Analyses* 17, 4 (1995), 23–38.

19. P. A. Winter, "Educational Recruitment and Selection: A Review of Recent Studies and Recommendations for Best Practice," in L. Wildman, ed., *Fifth NCPEA Yearbook* (Lancaster, PA: Technomic, 1997), 133–140.

20. Ibid.

Supplementary Reading

Arends, R. I. "Beginning Teachers as Learners." *Journal of Educational Research* 7, 4 (1983), 236–242.

Bradley, Leo; and Stephen P. Gordon. "Comparing the Ideal to the Real in State-Mandated Teacher Induction Programs."

Journal of Staff Development 15, 3 (Summer 1994), 44–50.

Brooks, D. M. *Teacher Induction: A New Beginning.* Reston, VA: Association of Teacher Education, 1987.

Driscoll, A., et al. "Designing a Mentor Program for Beginning Teachers." *Journal of Staff Development* 6, 2 (October 1985).

Egbert, Richard T. *The Employee Handbook.* Upper Saddle River, NJ: Prentice Hall, 1990.

Evan, William M. "Peer Group Interaction and Organizational Socialization: A Study of Employee Turnover." *American Sociological Review* 28 (1963), 436–440.

Griffin, G. A. "Crossing the Bridge: The First Years of Teaching." *National Commission on Excellence in Teacher Education* (1984), 250–292.

Haines, R. C.; and K. F. Mitchell. "Teacher Career Development in Charlotte-Mecklenburg." *Educational Leadership* 433 (November 1985), 11–13.

Hartzell, G. "Induction of Experienced Assistant Principals." *NASSP Bulletin* 75, 533 (1991), 75–84.

Heckman, Paul. "Understanding School Culture," in John I. Goodlad, ed., *The Ecology of School Renewal: 86th NSSE Yearbook, Part 1.* Chicago: National Society for the Study of Education, University of Chicago Press, 1987.

Hoffman, G.; and S. Link. "Beginning Teacher's Perceptions of Mentors." *Journal of Teacher Education* 37, 1 (January–February 1986), 22–25.

Jacoby, David. "Rewards Make the Mentor." *Personnel* 66, 12 (December 1989), 10–14.

Josefowitz, Natasha; and Herman Gordon. *How to Get a Good Start in Your New Job.* Reading, MA: Addison-Wesley, 1988.

Lasley, T. J., ed. "Teacher Induction." *Journal of Teacher Education* (Special Issue) 37, 1 (1989).

Mardenfeld, S. "The Best Way to Get a New Employee Up to Speed." *Working Woman* 4 (November 1989), 34.

Moran, Sheila W. "Schools and the Beginning Teacher." *Phi Delta Kappan* 72, 3 (November 1990), 210–214.

National Staff Development Council. *The Journal of Staff Development* 11, 4 (Fall 1990), 2–50. This issue contains a wealth of information on teacher induction, including these articles: Stephanie A. Hirsh, "New Teacher Induction: An Interview with Leslie Huling Austin"; Ardra L. Cole, "Helping Teachers Become 'Real': Opportunities in Teacher Induction"; Sandra J. Odell, "A Collaborative Approach to Teacher Induction That Works"; Louis M. Thies-Sprinthall and Edwin R. Gerler, Jr., "Support Groups for Novice Teachers"; Stephanie A. Hirsh, "Designing Induction Programs with the Beginning Teacher in Mind"; Gary N. Hartzell, "Induction of Experienced Teachers into a New School Site"; Joellen P. Killion, "The Benefits of an Induction Program for Experienced Teachers"; Victoria L. Bernhardt and Geraldine M. Flaherty, "Assisting New Teachers in Isolated, Rural School Districts"; Mary M. Harris and Michelle P. Collay, "Teacher Induction in Rural Schools"; and Harriet P. Feldlaufer, Joan M. Hoffman, and Larry Schaefer, "Support Teachers in the Connecticut Induction Program."

Newcombe, E., ed. *Perspectives on Teacher Induction: A Review of the Literature and Promising Program Models.* Baltimore, MD: Maryland State Department of Education, 1987.

Reinhartz. *Teacher Induction.* Washington, DC: National Education Association, 1989.

Shuman, Baird R. *Classroom Encounters, Problems, Case Studies, Solutions.* Washington, DC: National Education Association, 1989.

Sikula, J., ed. "Teacher Induction." *Action in Teacher Education* (Special Issue) 8, 4 (1987).

Steffy, B. *Career Stages of Classroom Teachers.* Lancaster, PA: Technomic Publishing Company, 1989.

Veenam, V. S. "Perceived Problems of Beginning Teachers." *Review of Educational Research* 54, 2 (1984), 143–178.

Yeager, Neal. *Career Map: Deciding What You Want, Getting It, and Keeping It.* New York: John Wiley and Sons, 1988.

6 *Development*

CHAPTER OBJECTIVES

Develop an awareness of the importance and extensive implications of staff development for achieving system goals for human resources.
Consider internal and external conditions that influence staff development programs.
Illuminate key elements in the staff development process.
Stress the importance of organizational development policies and procedures that enhance attainment of individual, unit, and system aims.

CHAPTER TERMS

Career stages
Development process

In-service education
Staff development

172

Human resource administration is a function that must be performed day in and day out, year in and year out, if the school system is to work effectively. More specifically, human resources activities do not end when vacancies have been filled; they must be concerned with the destiny, productivity, and need satisfaction of people after they are employed. This involves activities relating to staff development, health, tenure, leaves of absence, substitute service, employee associations, grievances, and retirement. This chapter emphasizes the administrative process by which plans for development of human resources are conceived, implemented, and controlled. A model is used to guide the discussion of the process by which plans for *organizational, group,* and *individual development* are planned, implemented, and evaluated.

Staff Development by Design

The previous chapter addressed the development needs of a special group of employees at a particular time in their employment cycle: those new to the system and those new to the assignment. For both types of employees, the previous chapter focused on facilitating their assimilation into the community, the system, the work unit, and the position during their probationary period.

In this chapter, we consider development activities designed for all employees throughout the entire employment cycle. All individuals affiliated with a school district can benefit from a focused program of appropriate development activities for an assigned role or for an anticipated new role. Included in this group are members of the board of education, as well as line and staff administrators, teachers, and classified staff.

Including all individuals in a formal development program designed to enhance the performance of their current role or their anticipated new role sends a distinct message to employees: that development is an important organizational activity and that it is expected of all individuals, not specific groups. Through leading by example in the development process, board members provide one of the most influential means of endorsement for professional development programs in a school system.

While working for a school system, all employees witness many environmental changes that impact its operation. These changes may originate outside the system, within the system, or from an interaction of both sources. External changes can stem from research findings, international comparisons, federal agendas, state mandates, and community expectations. Internal changes can come from priorities of the board of education, desires of the central administration, and needs of individual employees.

Development of employees should be an ongoing process and should consider their immediate as well as their advanced career stages. To maintain the momentum necessary for an effective development process focusing on both types of career stages, certain tasks must be addressed continuously by those charged with development responsibilities. The tasks include:

- Assessing how effectively current staff development programs are improving individual, unit, and system performance.
- Highlighting ineffective and inefficient development activities for *improvement* or *elimination.*
- Designing and shaping development programs to attain strategic human resources goals and objectives.
- Linking subprocesses of the human resource functions such as recruitment, selection, induction, and performance appraisal to the staff development process.
- Viewing staff development as an important vehicle for *career development* plans.
- Considering the strategic importance of *changes in the internal and external environments.*
- Establishing a planning scheme that anticipates rather than reacts to development needs.
- Basing staff development programs on the assumption that the needs of the individual school system (avoiding the temptation to clone other development programs) are paramount and critical to any development endeavor.
- Upgrading the investment in staff development activities in areas found to have the *greatest impact on performance improvement.*
- Creating a master plan that identifies high-impact development activities, anticipates outcomes, and achieves optimal results.

Staff Development Problems

Staff development, one of the major processes within the human resources function, has not escaped criticism. Commission reports, reform initiatives, and the media have criticized staff development efforts in school systems. These criticisms are based on international comparisons, state-mandated proficiency test results, and escalating district operating budgets.

For many school systems, these criticisms of staff development efforts have merit. Indeed, staff development efforts in some school systems have been and continue to be a series of haphazard, isolated events unrelated to system goals that represent inefficient use of public funds. Some of the most common factors in ineffective staff development are listed in Figure 6.1.

Awareness of the most common problems can greatly benefit those responsible for staff development activities. The problems listed in Figure 6.1 can be used to assess the current operation of staff development programs and activities in one's own school system. Once problems within the school system have been identified, corrective measures can be taken.

Underlying many of the problems in Figure 6.1 is the absence of any systematic attempt to link staff development efforts to the strategic plans of the school system.

- Allocating staff development resources without knowing what, if anything, has been derived from the expenditure.
- Spurning the concept of staff development as a tool for leveraging human resources strategy.
- Viewing staff development as an end in itself rather than as a means to an end.
- Initiating unguided and unorganized staff development programs.
- Disregarding the need for professionalization of internal change agents.
- Giving individual development precedence instead of linking individual, group, and system development.
- Taking for granted that there is a close fit between programs and individual and group needs.
- Failing to apply recruiting, selection, and induction strategies to find, attract, and retain the right candidates.
- Minimizing the importance of validating job-relatedness of staff development programs.
- Offering tuition reimbursement programs without linkage to position requirements.
- Disregarding needs assessment when granting funds for self-nomination development plans.
- Assuming that correcting staff development problems will solve major organizational problems.
- Lacking models to analyze whether programs produce changes; whether they were desired ones; and whether changes in performance met targeted need.
- Viewing staff development conventions as vacation time, as rest and recreation, as a position perquisite, as a hiatus in position demands.
- Failing to aim the staff development process at specific behavioral objectives in advance of program initiation.
- Emphasizing program activities rather than facilitation of learning and resultant behaviors.
- Extending benefit provisions of system–union negotiated contracts without serious review of objectives, costs, outcomes, or linkage to aims of strategic human resources planning.
- Precluding greater centralized control over the cost effectiveness of staff development programs.

Figure 6.1   Illustration of contemporary staff development problems.

This problem can be attributed, at least in part, to the tendency to view staff development as a series of isolated events. The problem can be solved by using a systems approach to staff development.

A systems approach for linking staff development efforts to the strategic plans of the district has been suggested by Asayesh.[1] This approach uses the concept of *system*

- Each individual is a part of a whole—every individual action has consequences for the system as a whole.
- To change the outcomes of an organization, one must change the system—not just its parts.
- Organizations must focus on the root causes of problems and long-term goals and consequences, not the symptoms.
- Effective change occurs by understanding the system and its behaviors, and working with the flow of the system, not against it.

Effective staff development for a systems approach includes:

- Training in the concepts, values, and specific tools of systems thinking.
- Ongoing processes that involve all segments of the organization in a dialogue so that there is collective rather than individual staff development.
- A focus on the application of the beliefs and tools of the system in the context of day-to-day workings of schools and the school system.
- Questioning and examining underlying assumptions and beliefs.

Figure 6.2   Key principles of systems thinking.
Source: Gelareh Asayesh, "Using Systems Thinking to Change Systems," *Journal of Staff Development* 14, 4 (Fall 1993), 8–140.

thinking (see Figure 6.2), which is a tool for dealing with various organizational problems that are difficult to resolve by the temporary application of isolated practices.

A major benefit of applying systems theory to staff development is that it enables planners to consider both the internal and external dimensions of organizational behavior. School systems acquire substantial resources from external sources, are regulated externally, must satisfy a host of external interests, and are subject to various forces over which they have little control. Thus, systems theory embraces the view that organizational effectiveness depends on the ability to adapt to the demands of the external environment and to shape the culture of the internal environment to meet external demands.

Staff Development Domain

Providing systematic means for the continuous development of skills, knowledge, problem-solving abilities, and attitudes of system personnel has been a cardinal professional tenet for centuries. Education has been no exception. Considerable efforts and numerous resources have been and continue to be directed to the improvement of educators as professional employees.

For example, many states have passed laws requiring development activities for certificated personnel. Some states require these individuals to obtain a master's degree within a specified time period following initial certification by the state department of education. Failure to do so renders an individual ineligible for future certification in these states.

Almost without exception, states have codified **in-service education** expectations for employees by designating a minimum number of days that must be devoted to in-service activities each year. Initially, in-service education was restricted to teachers and other certificated personnel; later on, it was expanded to cover all employees in the school system. According to most state codes, failure to perform in-service activities is grounds for employee termination.

Accompanying state-mandated requirements for development activities have been certain general trends. Political action in the late 1970s resulted in the creation of federally supported teacher centers as a means of upgrading staff development programs.[2] In the 1980s, state legislators and local school administrators viewed staff development as a key aspect of school improvement efforts.[3] A 1991 report advocated expansion of the staff development process to include educational organizations as a single entity.[4]

When staff development for educational organizations is viewed as an integrated activity from a systems perspective, it can be linked to those processes designed by the system to attract, retain, and improve the quality and quantity of staff members needed to achieve desired goals. Staff development is vitally linked to human resources planning because, as will be recalled, a sound human resources plan calls for

- Improving the job performance of all employees.
- Developing key skills of selected personnel to fill anticipated vacancies.
- Promoting the self-development of all employees to facilitate need satisfaction.
- Identifying and developing individuals in each employee group who have the potential to be promoted.

Staff development, as considered here, includes both informal and formal approaches to the improvement of employee effectiveness. As illustrated in Figure 6.3, this involves both short- and long-range activities; each activity has different

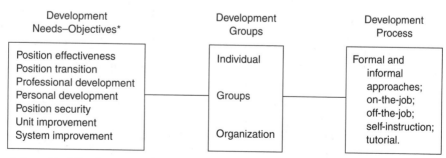

* A need is defined as a discrepancy between an actual and desired state. Objectives are the counterpart of needs and are employed to translate problems into programs.

Figure 6.3   A typology of personnel development.

objectives, involves different levels of personnel, and addresses a variety of ways for conceptualizing and organizing the staff improvement function. In effect, staff development is the process of staff improvement through approaches that emphasize self-realization, self-growth, and self-development. Development includes those activities aimed at the improvement and growth of abilities, attitudes, skills, and knowledge of system members for both current and anticipated assignments.

Figure 6.3 indicates that staff development includes various situations in every work organization that call for some form of individual or group development. The following statements are illustrative:

- Development requires interrelationships among system, unit, and individual goals and has implications for the design and implementation of development programs.
- Development includes all school personnel. Although emphasis on the professional staff is proper, the discussion that follows applies to the development of all employees.
- Development entails meeting two kinds of expectations: the contribution of the individual to the school system and the rewards anticipated by the individual in return.
- Development involves all activities designed to increase an individual's ability to work effectively, whatever the role and whatever the level of performance.
- Development is focused on two kinds of activities: (a) those specifically planned and administered by the school system (formal approaches) and (b) those initiated by personnel (informal approaches).
- Development is concerned with values, norms, and behaviors of individuals and groups.
- Development is designed to serve the following purposes: personal growth, professional development, problem solving, remedial action, motivation, upward mobility, and member security.
- Development programs initiated by the system are aimed at educating individuals above and beyond the immediate technical requirements of their position.
- Development programs sanction activities related to immediately practical and position-oriented needs, as well as to longer-range purposes focused on full development of the individual.
- Development encourages career-long staff development for all personnel as an organizational necessity.
- Development activity has generally been evaluated judgmentally rather than experimentally.
- Development has failed to capitalize fully on existing knowledge and theory regarding staff development.
- Development programs have been subjected to an array of fads and fashions that have not been based on a sound process development model (such as human resource objectives) or carefully designed, administered, and tested experiences.

•   Development is a powerful tool for effecting individual, unit, and system change.

Improvement of employee performance calls for a variety of approaches to modify the behavior patterns of individuals and of groups to maximize organizational effectiveness. A framework by which efforts are systematized to deal with the many development problems that arise continually in school systems, both individual and group, is referred to as a *process model.* The section that follows presents a comprehensive development process model consisting of sequential and interrelated phases.

Staff Development Process

Staff development activities in educational organizations have changed substantially over the last two decades. Beginning as a group of unconnected, isolated events, staff development has become one of the key human resource functions in a school system. Some of these changes in staff development that have evolved over time are presented in Figure 6.4.

Many of these changes associated with staff development stem from certain inferences about labor markets and certain views about **career stages.** From a labor market perspective, boards of education are beginning to view staff development as an ongoing process rather than as a periodic event and have taken note of the emerging reality for human resource planning. This emerging reality reflects a dramatic shift taking place in the work force of this country, a shift that affects every employer in America, not just educational systems.

No longer are traditional labor pools available for recruitment and selection. Growth of the pool of workers is slowing, and the work force is diversifying. Because of these changes, recruiting and retaining knowledgeable personnel has become extremely difficult for all organizations.

The U.S. Department of Labor predicts that only 15% of new employees between 1987 and the year 2000 will be native white males compared with 47% in 1987. Nearly one-third of all new entrants will come from minority groups.[5] Among the broad initiatives that should be considered as school systems prepare to cope with these changes in the modern work force are identifying and maximizing the talents of employees capable of making teaching and learning more effective, emphasizing ongoing development programs for all members at all levels, creating a culture that attracts the kind of talent essential to achieve system goals, and designing compensation programs that encourage and reward contributions to the school system.

One way of identifying and maximizing the talents of employees is by viewing development activities from a career perspective. In the professional literature and in the work world, increasing attention is being devoted to the relationship between career stages and staff development programs. Three descriptions of career stages for employees are presented in Figure 6.5.

Away from.	Toward. . . . . .
Top-down approach	Bottom-up approach
Narrow approach to staff development	Comprehensive approach to staff development
Isolated projects	Interactive and interdependent programs
Control	Empowerment
Off-the-shelf projects	Customized programs
System-initiated changes	System and staff initiated changes
Inattention to school culture	Collaboration to change school culture
Centralized plans	Site-based plans
Solving problems for staff members	Building staff capacity to solve own problems
Individual emphasis	Individual and team emphasis
Preparation and experience emphasis	Performance emphasis
Indifference to development outcomes	Emphasis on staff development outcomes
Development of teaching staff	Development of all classes of personnel
Sole emphasis on self-fulfillment	Individual, unit, and system goals
Development as an event	Development as a continuous process
Sporadic and disorganized programs	Systematic strategies and well-defined objectives
Limited financial support	Local, state, and federal support
Focus on remediation	Focus on remediation and growth
Administrative initiative	Administration–individual initiatives
Formal approaches	Formal and informal approaches
Programs preplanned	Staff participates in planning
Reliance on external agents/ agencies	Inside or outside support as appropriate
Assuming positive program impact	Evaluating actual impact
Intuition and prior experience	Theoretical exploration
Role development	Role and career development
Random-based planning	Systems-based planning
System evaluation	System and self-evaluation
Uncoordinated, ad hoc, and fragmented projects	Staff development models
Limited use of electronic technology	Emerging emphasis on use of electronic technology
Limited methods and types of delivery	Unlimited methods and types of delivery
Lack of application of systems thinking	Using systems thinking to change systems

Figure 6.4   Value trends in staff development.

• Early Stage
  Tenured Stage
  Retirement Stage
  All Stages[a]
	• Pre-work Stage
	  Initial Work Stage
	  Stable Work Stage
	  Retirement Stage[b]
		• Establishment Stage
		  (early adulthood)
		  Advancement Stage
		  (mature adulthood)
		  Maintenance Stage
		  (midlife)
		  Withdrawal (old age)[c]

Figure 6.5   Three descriptions of career stages.
Sources: [a]University of Pennsylvania, *Almanac Supplement* (February 28, 1989), IX–XII. [b]John M. Ivancevich and William F. Glueck, *Foundations of Personnel/Human Resource Management*, 3rd ed. (Plano, TX: Business Publications, Inc., 1983), 523. [c]L. Baird and K. Kram, "Career Dynamics: Managing the Superior–Subordinate Relationship," *Organizational Dynamics* 11 (1983), 209–216.

It is important to stress that staff development occurs over time, goes through several stages, cuts across a wide range of development issues, and includes changing tasks and personal needs. Traditionally, some organizations have viewed these career stages only from a vertical perspective. From this perspective, individuals enter the organization and move up the hierarchy through a series of promotions during their term of employment.

However, career stages involving only vertical movement may have little appeal today for many employees in school systems. For some positions requiring certification (e.g., teacher, psychologist, librarian), incumbents have invested several years in specialized training and have established an identity with a professional group. To move vertically within the school system would require further study in a different subject matter area and professional affiliation with a different group.

Unions representing certain employees have made substantial economic gains through collective bargaining with boards of education. These economic gains have often exceeded those of entry-level management and supervisory personnel. For midcareer employees to use vertical movement for career progression would often result in lesser economic benefits than those enjoyed by employees at the top of the career ladder in their current bargaining unit position.

Management and supervisory personnel have career needs. Although some of these individuals may have successfully cleared some of the hurdles associated with vertical movement confronting their subordinates, many of them may be relegated to the same position or to the same level within the organization for many years. These employees, like all others, have career plateaus and career needs.

In most communities, the single largest employer is the school system. School systems are pyramidal, and the number of opportunities near the top is small relative to the number of employees. Therefore, even if most employees sought vertical movement as a means of career progression, only a few could be accommodated within their current school system.

To protect their initial investments in recruitment and selection, as well as to keep effective employees in their current position or in similar positions at the same organizational level, innovative school systems have changed their ideas about career stages within the staff development process. These farsighted school systems now view career stages from a horizontal as well as a vertical perspective. Effective staff development programs include ways to enrich and revitalize the work life of all employees, including those seeking vertical as well as horizontal advancement.

Research and practice addressing career stages from both vertical and horizontal perspectives suggest several implications and raise several questions, including the following:

- When staff development becomes an organizational policy commitment, it signals that the system is willing to provide continuing improvement opportunities for personnel. These opportunities may relate to career goals, career counseling, and career paths; information about position openings; and various forms of development programs, some of which address special needs such as problems relating to outplacement, retirement and preretirement, induction, and choices confronting midcareer staff members and those who have developed physical disabilities.
- Administrative responsibility for career development is both a central function and a matter for individual work groups. Responsibilities include leading the way, developing policy, providing financial and opportunity initiatives, and influencing units that lag behind to pursue activities pioneered by other work groups.
- Many types of opportunities exist for enhancing career development. The development process model should include decisions to develop programs most suited to specific work group needs.
- Recognizing that the pool of skilled help is decreasing, organizations throughout the nation are broadening their roles regarding staff development and retention. (This is especially true in the cases of women and minorities.)
- Emerging issues relating to the design of career development programs include the following: What are the system's ambitions for the career stages of its employees? Does the system have sufficient mechanisms in place to support career development? In an era of increased competition for personnel, what career plans are best calculated to retain and improve current and future staff members?
- Are there particular development incentives, such as sabbaticals, tuition grants, research accounts, or flexible teaching loads, that have the potential to enhance the pursuit of careers within the system?
- Have proactive steps been taken to ensure the future availability of personnel at all levels of the system?

A process model provides a framework to facilitate the systemization of development activities and to resolve some of the issues concerning staff development activities. An example of a process model for developmental activities that could be used by school systems is presented in Figure 6.6. This model contains four steps, each of which requires certain decisions and actions by those responsible for establishing and implementing development activities at the local level.

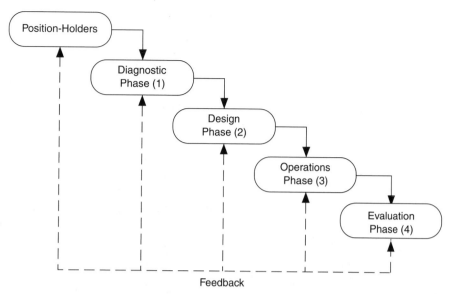

Figure 6.6   Model of the personnel development process.

Phase 1: Diagnosing Development Needs

The initial step in the process model in Figure 6.6 is diagnosing development needs. *Development needs* are defined as a discrepancy between the actual level of functioning and the desired level. The purpose of a **development process** is to reduce this discrepancy.

Considering development needs from two separate but related perspectives facilitates the diagnosis of these needs. One perspective concerns the source of the development needs; the other perspective involves the content.

Development needs vary according to the source; these sources include the individual, the group, and the organization. McGehee and Thayer identified these potential sources of development needs almost 40 years ago.[6] Since that time, according to Scarpello, Ledvinka, and Bergman, these sources of development needs have become an accepted standard for most development processes and models used today by most organizations.[7]

Development needs of the individual focus on the person as an employee. These needs may be attributed to skill deficiency, skill obsolescence, and/or motivation problems. Skill deficiencies occur when individuals lack knowledge or basic skill necessary to work in a satisfactory manner. Without this knowledge and/or skill, these individuals do not know how to achieve satisfactory performance.

Skill obsolescence occurs when the individual's skills and knowledge become outdated. New developments may alter the way work should now be performed. These individuals know what work to do but do not know the best way to do it.

In some cases, the individual may know what to do, as well as the best way to do it, yet may still fail to perform at an optimal level, as defined by organizational standards. In this situation, the employee may have a motivational need. A major cause of motivational problems in employees who fail to perform optimally is believed to be burnout.[8]

In addition to variation in sources of development needs (individual, group, and organization), development needs vary by content. Seyfarth identified two content areas for development needs: technological and structural.[9] However, this classification of content omitted consideration of the affective needs of employees in educational organizations.

Technological needs stem from technological advances that can enhance the way work is performed. Today, more than ever, technological advances have changed the way educational organizations conduct business. Efficient school systems have incorporated many of these advances into their operation. This requires extensive development activity on the part of an organization to change the attitudes and skills of employees.

Structural needs address the manner in which the work is performed. Many school districts have begun to experiment with alternative management strategies involving decentralized decision making such as site-based management. These strategies alter substantially the way work is performed and require considerable development efforts to succeed.

Affective needs pertain to employees' attitudes toward and perceptions about the work and the workplace. Often overlooked as appropriate content for a development program by school districts, affective needs have long attracted the interest of the private sector. Many times, affective needs of individuals are the causes of dysfunctional behaviors such as absenteeism, tardiness, and grievances. Development efforts have focused erroneously only on the symptoms of dysfunctional behavior rather than on its causes.

In keeping with the systems view of development, potential needs diagnosed in this phase of the development model may have internal or external origins. Internal development needs may be due to program initiatives, performance assessments, or opinion polls. External causes include current events, government agencies, and research and development outcomes.

Development needs (technological, structural, or affective) may surface at various levels (organization, unit, or individual), at different times, and for various reasons (internal or external). Personnel shortages may occur, legislation may be passed requiring new programs, or information may be compiled that indicates certain types of skill deficiencies. Consequently, every development need is likely to be subjected to some form of priority analysis to determine if it should be included in the staff development plan currently in operation.

Before development needs are translated into program designs, several planning issues need to be examined. Among these are the following:

- Is there a consensus that a general need exists?
- How important is the need in terms of system development priorities and resources?
- Can the need be met through system action?
- What is the probability that satisfaction of the need will be cost effective?

It is important to achieve a consensus on whether a need should become part of the system's development program. Although need identification is an *analytic* process, need satisfaction is a *political process.* This means that for a need to achieve program status, persons, powers, and parties must be clearly aligned.[10]

Underlying this discussion is the premise that ongoing diagnosis of system development is an essential management task. These diagnoses identify which needs are important to individual, group, and organizational effectiveness, and which ones are faddish and unnecessary.

Phase 2: Designing Development Plans

After development needs have been diagnosed, and prioritized, a plan of action must be constructed. Without an adequate plan, programming of developed needs will likely be haphazard, unrelated to strategic goals, and not cost effective. At minimum, the action plan should include the following:

- A statement of reasons for undertaking the development problem or the need.
- A description of the specific goal(s) and objectives selected as outcomes.
- A detailing of the participants to be served and how or why they (groups or individuals) are related to goals and objectives.
- A plan for identifying and developing successors for critically important positions.
- A calendar of major events showing their relationship to objectives and participants.
- A designation of the responsible person or group assigned to each major event.
- A list of resource requirements for each major event and one for overall coordination.
- A description of procedures for evaluating the plan and for providing timely feedback.
- A schedule and list of procedures for monitoring the total operation.[11]

In the design phase of the planning process, considerable effort is devoted to issues related to format. *Format* refers to the way program elements such as development needs are translated into program specifics. Format components include program methodology, content setting, resources, and explication.

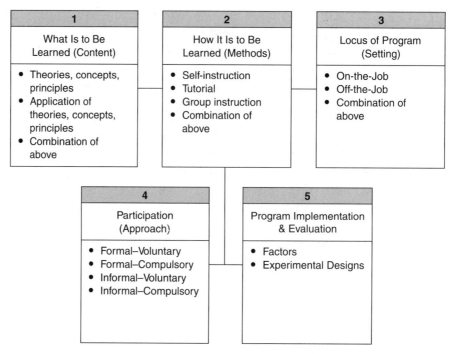

Figure 6.7   Framework for designing personnel development program formats.

Figure 6.7 presents a framework for designing personnel development program formats. This framework identifies five major elements: *content, methods, setting, participation,* and *implementation and evaluation.* Each of these elements will be discussed in the following sections. The purpose of these sections is to tie together the discussion of program formats so that the reader can understand the variables involved and the connections among them.

Program Content

Block 1 in Figure 6.7 indicates that there are two types of learning to consider in designing a program format for development activities: (a) theories, concepts, and principles and (b) learning their application. The two types of learning are complementary. Both types are necessary to transfer content from the development program to the actual work setting.

Firestone and Pennell suggested that these types of learning involve acquiring both procedural knowledge and conceptual knowledge about program content.[12] Procedural knowledge is acquired by mastering the content of a development program. Content acquisition, however, is only part of the learning process that employees need for application on the job.

On-the-job application of the content of a development program requires conceptual as well as procedural knowledge. Conceptual knowledge represents a higher level of learning than procedural knowledge. To acquire conceptual knowledge, individuals must be able to internalize the information presented in a development program and apply it in the work setting.

Far too often, development programs and activities in school systems have focused on procedural knowledge and have neglected conceptual knowledge. Participants are treated as passive learners and are given content but little contextual information. Because conceptual knowledge is often ignored in the design phase of the development program, the most common criticism offered by program participants is that the content is not relevant.

Although procedural knowledge may be all that is necessary for certain development activities or certain elements within a development activity, most development efforts require both types of knowledge. The key task of program designers is to decide which type of knowledge is needed to achieve the particular program objective and how all elements of a planned development activity can best be learned by participants. This decision has important implications for other components of the framework in Figure 6.7.

Program Methods

Block 2 in Figure 6.7 addresses the method used to present the content of development activities to participants. The method to be used in a particular program format or in a particular element of a program will depend on a number of factors. These factors include the objectives of the program, number of personnel involved, cost per participant, availability of personnel to conduct the program, availability of learning aids, and learning ability of program participants.

All methods can be effective in certain situations. Effectiveness will depend on the learning conditions, including what is to be learned and the type of knowledge to be acquired. Especially important, according to research, is the relevance of a particular method for attaining a specific organizational goal.

Many teaching methods can be used when designing development programs and activities. The most effective ones rely on a variety of methods. Some of these methods are passive; others are active.

Passive teaching methods rely heavily on individuals as self-directed learners. The content of development programs and activities is communicated largely by a single method. Passive learning techniques commonly used by school systems include conferences, academic classes, and independent study.

Conferences have been and continue to be a mainstay for development programs and activities involving personnel at all levels of the school system. Most conferences focus on a single topic and are of short duration. In communicating the content of development programs and activities, conferences are particularly effective in increasing the employee's procedural knowledge about certain topics or issues.

With the recent emphasis on distance learning in colleges and universities, academic classes are becoming a viable development option for many school districts. Academic classes can cover a broad range of topics and can take many weeks to complete. Class assignments can be designed to enhance both the procedural and the conceptual knowledge that employees need to transfer development programs and activities to the work setting.

Independent study, as a passive teaching technique, has an advantage over conferences and classes. The content can be tailored to the specific needs of the individual. Selected readings and programmed instruction can often reduce the difference between actual and desired levels of performance.

Active teaching methods in development programs and activities require behavioral as well as cognitive responses from participants. With active methods, participants are given opportunities to apply the skills, knowledge, and/or behaviors they have learned. Common examples of active methods for teaching development programs and activities are role playing, simulation, and coaching.

Role playing allows individuals to act out certain skills or behaviors in a protective environment. Using this method, program participants often act out the counterpart to their role in the organization. By assuming the role of their counterpart, individuals will supposedly gain a better understanding of their own organizational role by viewing it from the perspective of the other person.

Simulations, like role playing, are removed from the actual job setting. With this development technique, employees are required to perform or exhibit the actual skills and behaviors required by their current position or by an anticipated position. This technique gives them an opportunity to develop and refine certain job skills and behaviors in a protective setting.

Coaching involves acquiring and developing job skills and behaviors in an actual job situation. With this technique, individuals practice the skills and behaviors under the tutelage of an accomplished mentor in the work setting. Mentors provide modeling behavior, performance assessments, and critical feedback designed to promote the development of employees in their current or anticipated position.

As previously noted, the choice of a passive or an active teaching method in development programs or activities depends on many variables. One method of presentation is not necessarily superior to others, and each method must be evaluated within the constraints of the development program. Again, it must be emphasized that effective development programs and activities utilize more than one of these techniques in teaching employees within a school system.

Location of the Program

The program setting, as indicated in Block 3 of Figure 6.7, can be located on the job, off the job, or both. The choice depends largely on the resources of the school system. Resources for development programs include instructors, facilities, funds, time, and materials.

One key question usually asked in preparing a program format is, Where can the most competent instructor be found? The search for a good instructor may lead to colleges or universities, regional education agencies, commercial enterprises, private consultants, and personnel within the system. Since the school system's funds and facilities are usually limited, some organizations share instructors, facilities, and materials.

Another problem associated with development programs and activities is the need to free personnel for participation in development programs and activities. The organization must subsidize the time of these personnel in the form of paid leaves of absence, time off with pay, or time off during the school day without extra pay. Lack of funding for release time has been a major deterrent to the improvement of development programs for employees at all levels within the school system.

Still another issue involves the administration of development programs and activities. Each program format, if it is to succeed, involves an administrative process that includes planning, organizing, directing, coordinating, and controlling. These processes call for a combination of data, competence, and participation, which must be provided by the system.

Answers to many of the format issues require alternative ways of viewing development programs and activities that involve a combination of locations. This suggests that staff development programs and activities must be diversified. Diversification can provide new and exciting alternatives to traditional staff development activities for all educational employees.

One relatively new teaching method involves using computers to establish professional networks. Professional networks connect a number of individuals, both inside and outside the school system, who have a common interest and a common identity. Professional networks focus on a single topic (reform movement, subject area, etc.), support a number of activities (workshops, conferences, etc.), provide ongoing discussion, and give participants opportunities to lead.[13]

Another new method of development programs involves collaboration between school systems and outside agencies. Partnerships are formed in which development activities and resources are shared by the organizations. Initially conceived as university–school agreements focusing on instructional issues involving teachers, collaborative efforts have been expanded to include other types of organizations and all categories of personnel.

Participation

Approaches to staff participation in development programs are listed in Block 4 of Figure 6.7 and are classified as voluntary or compulsory. Both types of programs may be either formal or informal, depending on the program's objective. Examples of each type of program and each type of participation are as follows:

- *Formal-voluntary*—System conducts a problem-centered seminar for new teachers; attendance is voluntary.
- *Informal-voluntary*—Teachers are awarded a budgetary allowance for personal and professional development.
- *Formal-compulsory*—System conducts a seminar on force-field analysis for supervisory personnel.

- *Informal-compulsory*—System establishes a deadline for personnel to meet certification requirements. Individuals are free to choose among various approaches to meet the requirements.

Examination of these forms of participation leads to two inferences about approaches to personnel participation. The first is that uniformity in the design of development programs and activities is neither feasible nor desirable. The second inference is that program format planning calls for great flexibility in meeting the development needs of various types of personnel. Moreover, the extent, flexibility, and planning involved in choosing programs and formats require careful and constant coordination among system personnel.

Before we discuss Phase 3, which involves implementing development programs and activities, certain issues should be recapitulated. The specifics of each program format for staff development, as discussed in Phase 2, need to be summarized and disseminated for review, formalization, and implementation. A form for linking program formats to development objectives is shown in Figure 6.8. This form emphasizes that, prior to implementation, each development program should be reviewed for links between program format, program objectives, and strategic goals of the organization.

By analyzing the elements of the form in Figure 6.8, planners can determine whether development objectives have been translated into specific operations and whether the program format is capable of achieving the objectives of the program and the strategic goals of the system. The analysis should reveal gaps to be filled and revisions needed before plans are implemented in the work setting.

Phase 3: Implementing Development Programs

Reexamination of the model in Figure 6.6 indicates that completion of Phase 2 (program design) leads to Phase 3 (implementation of development activities). Phase 3 occurs when the design of the program is shaped into an operational structure and when the planning activities are put into operation. At this time, Phases 1 and 2 are meshed to link together individual, unit, and organization goals.

In the implementation phase of the development process, several types of decisions are required. The persons responsible for developing and implementing the process must determine the timing and sequencing of development activities. These decisions are incorporated into an operational structure known as the *experimental design.*

The experimental design of development programs or activities determines the protocol for program administration. The experimental design dictates who gets certain program components and activities, as well as when these program components and activities are administered. The answers to these questions have profound implications for Phase 4 (evaluation) of the development process.

Form D-10

DEVELOPMENT PROGRAM PLANNING FORMAT

1. Title of program: _____

2. Program purpose:
   ___ Personal development   ___ Professional development
   ___ Position effectiveness   ___ Position transition   ___ Position security
   ___ School unit improvement   ___ School system improvement

3. Specific program objective:
   ___ Dissemination of knowledge   ___ Developing skills
   ___ Acquisition of knowledge   ___ Creating organizational climate
   ___ Interpersonal skills   ___ Changing attitudes
   ___ Problem-solving skills   ___ General development of personnel

4. Organized for: ___ Administrative and Supervisory Personnel
                    ___ Instructional Personnel   ___ Support Personnel

5. System level: ___ Elementary   ___ Intermediate   ___ Other

6. Level of learning: ___ Simple   ___ Complex   ___ Highly complex

7. Content: Theories, concepts, and principles: application of theories and concepts

8. Program scope: ___ Systemwide   ___ Building   ___ Individual

9. Duration: _____ to _____

10. Number of participants: _____

11. Funds allocated: ___ Amount   Source of funds: ___ Internal ___ External

12. Program/methods: ___ Self-instruction ___Tutorial ___ Group instruction

13. Program setting: ___ On the job   ___ Off the job

14. Participation: ___ Voluntary   ___ Compulsory

15. Linked to performance appraisal: ___ Yes   ___ No

16. Program resources needed:
    ___ Funds   ___ Facilities   ___ Materials   ___ Personnel
    ___ Management   ___ Information

17. Program leadership: _____

18. Program evaluation responsibility: _____

19. Evaluation criteria: ___ Participant reaction   ___ Learning behavior
                          ___ Results

20. Outcome intent: In what way will system, unit, or individual change as a result of the program?

Figure 6.8   Development program planning format for the Cloudcroft school system.

Far too often, little thought is devoted to the implementation phase, and no experimental design is created. In the absence of an experimental design, the outcomes of development efforts may be difficult, if not impossible, to evaluate precisely. Thus, the outcomes supposedly due to development programs and activities may actually be a result of other factors. Such outside factors that may influence the outcomes of development efforts have been identified by Campbell and Stanley.[14] Because these factors have important implications for development programs and activities in the work setting, they will now be discussed. Afterward, we will focus on choosing an experimental design to guide the implementation process.

Factors

The factors identified by Campbell and Stanley that may erroneously influence the assessment of outcomes attributable to development efforts should be controlled in the implementation phase. Although these factors will be treated independently in this discussion, in practice they may interact and may have a combined influence on the assessment of outcomes associated with development programs or activities. These factors include history, maturation, testing, instrumentation, regression, selection, and mortality.

History includes external events or factors outside of the staff development activity that influence the desired knowledge, skills, and/or attitudes of participants beyond the content of the program. This factor is of particular concern when development activities address topical issues such as substance abuse or violence control, which are often covered in the popular press. Because this coverage is outside the development program, the effects attributed to the program may be overestimated by ignoring this external influence when assessing the impact of a specific development program or activity.

Maturation concerns developmental changes experienced by employees due to the normal developmental process. Employees new to the organization or new to their assignment will become somewhat acclimated over time, regardless of any development programs or activities. Programs and activities designed to acclimate new employees may appear to be effective when in fact a certain level of adjustment should be expected to occur normally.

Testing involves the preassessment of the knowledge, skills, and/or attitudes of participants in regard to development activities before actually involving them in development programs or activities by using a pretest. Initial deficiencies in content knowledge, as detected by pretesting, may sensitize participants to certain content areas that might go unnoticed during a training program in the absence of pretesting. Because of information gaps detected by pretesting, certain content areas may become important for employees taking part in development programs or activities.

Instrumentation pertains to changes in the measuring instrument during the development process. For many staff development activities, the measuring instrument is the immediate supervisor. If the proficiency of this supervisor improves through practice during the staff development process, changes in employee performance may be attributable to the improvement in the supervisor rather than to the content of the development activity.

Regression occurs when employees are selected for development programs or activities because of their extremely poor performance on certain measures (job performance, absenteeism, etc.). Because their current performance is well below average, it can only improve (rise toward the mean) if they are to remain employed. As a result of regression, remedial programs often appear to be more effective than development programs and activities.

Selection relates to the choice of participants and to the motivation of these employees. Participation in development programs and activities can be either voluntary or compulsory (see Block 4 of Figure 6.7). Development programs and activities that appear to be highly successful with voluntary participants may be disastrous with compulsory participants even when the content and methods are the same.

Mortality focuses on the number of individuals who complete development programs and activities. Some of these programs and activities require a great deal of time and effort on the part of participants. If participants are allowed to drop out, an assessment of the knowledge, skills, and attitudes of only those who remain in the program may provide a distorted view of the program's effectiveness. Assessments should include both those who drop out and those who complete the program.

These factors may influence assessments of development programs and activities and may provide misleading information to those responsible for developing, implementing, and evaluating these programs and activities. Although not all of these factors may be pertinent to all development programs and activities, some of them can influence every program and activity. To control for or to assess the impact of these factors, an experimental design must be carefully selected in the implementation phase.

Experimental Design

The experimental design provides the framework within which development programs and activities are carried out. School systems use several types of experimental designs. These designs vary both in complexity and in sensitivity to those factors that can potentially confound the assessment of development programs and activities (history, maturation, etc.). Choosing among experimental designs is a major task in Phase 3 of the implementation process (see Figure 6.6).

Three of the most frequently used experimental designs for development programs and activities are shown in Figure 6.9.[15] In these designs, two symbols are used to denote the implementation and assessment of program activities. "X" represents the actual development program or activity, as executed in the work setting, and "O" represents an outcome assessment associated with that particular program or activity.

Design A in Figure 6.9 is by far the most frequently used design for development activities in the educational setting. This design is called a *one-shot case study.* In

Design A	Design B	Design C
X O	*O X O*	*X O$_1$* O$_2$
One Shot	Pre-Post	Post-Control
Note: *X* denotes training: *O* denotes assessment.		

Figure 6.9　*Experimental designs.*

such a study, participants take part in a development program or activity. Afterward, the program or activity is assessed with the participants.

Although educational organizations often use the one-shot case study in implementing development activities, this design is an extremely poor choice for the implementation phase of the development process. With a one-shot case study, it is impossible to determine what effects are attributable to the development program or activity and what effects are attributable to outside factors (history, maturation, etc.). Even when participants perform exceptionally well on the assessment, their work may well reflect a prior level of performance rather than performance enhanced by the development efforts.

To provide information about the prior level of performance of participants in development programs or activities, design B in Figure 6.9 is often used in implementing development activities. This design (is called a *pre-posttest design.* With this design, participants are assessed prior to the development program or activity and again after they complete it. When the two assessments are compared, a measure of program or activity effectiveness is obtained.

The pre-posttest design is slightly superior to the one-shot case study because it provides baseline data on participants. However, the pre-posttest design may sometimes pose a problem because of pretesting, and it has some of the same problems as the one-shot case study with respect to controlling for history, maturation, testing, regression, instrumentation, and mortality.

Substantial improvements over the one-shot case study and the pre-posttest design can be achieved by using design C in Figure 6.9 in implementing development activities. Design C is a posttest control group design. In this design, some participants receive the development program or activity and others do not (at least not at the time of assessment). Both groups are assessed at the same time.

The posttest control group design, when properly constructed, provides an extremely effective framework for implementing development programs and activities in the work setting. By using a proper control group for comparison, many potential factors other than those attributable to the development effort can be addressed. Specifically, the posttest control group design either assesses or controls for such factors as testing, selection, regression, history, instrumentation, and mortality.

The designs presented in Figure 6.9 are only some of the designs frequently used to implement a development program in the work setting. Other designs and other options exist, and those responsible for implementing development efforts must make an informed choice based on the potential factors in a given situation.[16] The design chosen influences not only the implementation phase of the development process but the evaluation phase as well.

Phase 4: Evaluating Staff Development Programs

Development efforts have often been criticized for not focusing on significant individual or organizational needs, attacking the wrong problems, or attempting to solve valid problems with inappropriate instructional techniques. It should be noted that (a) in some school systems, evaluation does not take place at all and that (b) evaluation frequently occurs to planners as an afterthought. The development process introduced in Figure 6.6 includes Phase 4 (evaluation) as the last step in the development model.

If the evaluation phase is omitted, there is no feedback to identify and correct program defects, little useful information to enhance decision making, and no sound foundation for improving the total development effort. There are many constraints and many obstacles to overcome in evaluating staff development programs. In addition, there are varying viewpoints regarding the necessity for, approaches to, effects of, and values derived from evaluation.

Nevertheless, it is generally believed that staff development improvement requires evaluation. There is also considerable agreement that awareness of important factors in the evaluation phase makes it possible to avoid useless evaluations and to derive information that will be helpful in directing development planning. In this connection, key considerations in the evaluation of staff development programs are outlined in Figure 6.10.

It is worth emphasizing that program content (what to teach) and program methods (how it should be taught) are critical decisions in the design and evaluation of staff development programs. The learning process by which new behaviors (skills, knowledge, abilities, and attitudes) are acquired involves practicing those behaviors so that they result in relatively permanent change. The types of questions used to determine whether a development project has succeeded include the following:

- *Participant impact*—What has the project done to change the behavior of the participant?
- *Position impact*—Did the participant's performance in the work setting improve?
- *Organizational impact*—In what ways and to what extent did the development efforts contribute to attainment of organizational goals?

These questions bring into focus the need to carefully specify the objectives of a development program and to identify criteria by which to measure the objectives. If the objectives are not clear, it will be difficult to choose or develop appropriate measuring techniques or to judge whether the intended results were achieved.

Factors	Illustrative Questions
Purposes of evaluation	What is to be evaluated? (Program objectives? Methods? Program? People? Processes? Products?)
Principles of evaluation	Will the evaluation be based on principles? (Systematic? Objectivity? Relevance? Verification of results? Quantification? Feasibility? Specificity? Cost effectiveness?)
Types of evaluation	Evaluation of a specific program? Specific technique? Total program effort? (Formative? Summative?)
Criteria	Reaction criteria? Learning criteria? Behavioral criteria? Results criteria? Combinations of the above?
Criterion measures	What criterion measures will be employed? (Observational techniques? Tests? Ratings? System performance records? Interviews?)
Evaluation data	How will the data be recorded? Analyzed? Interpreted? Valued?
Outcomes	What types of outcomes will be evaluated? (Professional competence? Learner gain? Program involvement? Training validity? Performance validity? Intraorganizational validity? Interorganizational validity?

Figure 6.10   Major considerations in the evaluation of staff development programs.

Rational decisions can be made with greater conviction if there is some basis for determining whether improvement programs have been or will be effective and efficient. There are many questions relating to the extent to which knowledge, skills, attitudes, work behavior, and organizational impact have changed. In addition, some persons want to know whether changes in these variables are due to the staff development program or to some of the extraneous factors previously discussed.

Analysis of Figure 6.10 leads to these observations:

• The evaluation process is complex and extensive. Sophisticated knowledge is needed to initiate, implement, and coordinate all of its facets.

• The evaluation phase requires knowledge, skills, attitudes, and position behaviors to improve the system's evaluation capabilities.

• The purposes of evaluation constitute the "engine" that pulls the evaluation train. Evaluation methods, criteria, criterion measures, and collection and refinement of data derived from evaluation inform future development efforts.

We summarize this section on the evaluation phase of staff development by suggesting that nurturing an organization's human resources is a primary leadership responsibility. This requires an organizational investment of considerable time, money, and talent to solve major evaluation problems. These problems—either by design or by default—have been seriously neglected and will become even more critical in light of social change, technological developments, and public concern about the quality and effectiveness of the nation's schools.

Review and Preview

This chapter has stated that the school system that embraces the policy of continual development has important strategic advantages. Key ideas of this thesis include the following:

• School improvement through personnel development is best accomplished within individual schools and school systems. Traditional practices do not generate effective staff development programs.
• The staff development process includes identifying needs, establishing program objectives, creating plans to achieve the objectives (including teaching methods), and evaluating program outcomes.
• Staff development includes individual, group, system, and board member development.
• Major factors to be considered in the assessment of personnel needs are the external and internal environments, the school system, positions, position holders, position–person matches, position context, and work groups.
• Cues for designing programs can be derived from system policy, research and practice, value trends, career stages, and the external environment.
• Formal development program design includes program content, methods, setting, participation, and resources.
• Criteria for evaluating staff development programs include the participant, position, work group, and organizational impact.

In Chapter 7, appraisal will be treated as a process that is closely intertwined with the staff development process, and one that can provide meaningful information to help decision makers answer questions about the selection, implementation, and evaluation of development methods and the entire development effort.

Discussion Questions

1. Would you defend or refute each of the following statements?

• A school system's culture is set by the board of education.
• Culture is the prevailing attitudes and values that characterize its employees.
• A school system's culture is set by its union culture.
• When personnel do not perform up to par, it is because they do not know what par is.
• The most popular development technique in school systems is coaching by superiors.
• The primary purpose of team building is to help a work group solve major school system problems.
• Learning cannot be observed; only its results can be measured.
• The primary criteria for developing a staff development program are trainee preferences and capabilities.

- Needs assessment reveals shortcomings that can be traced directly to the human resources function.
- Each position in a career path should be specified in terms of educational credentials, age, and work experience.
- Recruitment, selection, and orientation processes may minimize or eliminate the need for staff development.
- No school system endeavor has been so neglected as staff development.
- Evidence suggests that group processes improve through team-building development programs.
- Experienced teachers as prospective mentors generally have effective training and coaching abilities to develop successful mentoring relationships.
- Change must be introduced gradually because you can never go back to the way things were before the change.
- Staff turnover data are good indicators of the effectiveness of staff development programs.
- The most important outcome a staff member wants from a job is the opportunity to advance.
- Self-development is a paper strategy that rarely becomes a reality.
- Evidence suggests that staff development conventions, university courses, and lectures produce measurable payoffs.
- Assessing outcomes on the basis of objectives is believed to be almost impossible.
- Restructuring and staff development programs have the same purposes.

2. Why is knowledge of how people learn important in designing development programs?

3. Three theories of learning (behavioral, social, and cognitive) are considered important in designing development programs. What are the implications of each theory for deciding how and what to teach?

4. List 10 reasons why staff development is crucial to individual, group, and system effectiveness.

5. What are the implications of career planning for staff development? For administrative personnel? Supervisory personnel? Support personnel?

6. What is the organizational motivation for linking career planning to staff development?

7. Do individuals have the responsibility to manage their own careers?

8. Develop a model for determining the development needs of a school system with an enrollment of 10,000 pupils.

9. Critique this statement: "There is no hard evidence to support the contention that sabbaticals improve performance effectiveness."

10. What are some of the problems in evaluating the effectiveness of staff development programs?

11. For the system in which you are employed, answer the following questions: To what extent have staff development programs been initiated in the past five years? For administrative personnel? Supervisory personnel? Teaching personnel? Support personnel?

12. Which of the development programs mentioned in question 11 have been evaluated in terms of systemwide outcomes? Participant outcomes? Instructional outcomes? Administrative outcomes?

13. As you view the staff development needs of your institution, what are the most crucial development needs

at the management level? Supervisory level? Teaching level? Support level?

14. Review the staff development models and study the format in Table 6.1. Then respond to the following:

- Study Table 6.1 and indicate, in your judgment, which staff development models (vertical columns) are most suitable for meeting the various staff development needs (horizontal columns).
- Study Table 6.1. Which staff development models in the table are appropriate for meeting staff development needs in order to implement the type of videodisc curriculum proposed by the Texas State Textbook Committee? Explain the rationale underlying your decision.
- What steps would you advise your superiors to take in implementing any one of the five models in Table 6.1? Justify your answer.
- What are the major steps in implementing the training model? The inquiry model?

15. Examine Tables 6.2, 6.3, and 6.4. The data, which are the results of a survey, provide a profile on staff development and staff developers in North America. After examing the data, respond to these questions:

TABLE 6.1

Staff Development Matrix Linking Staff Development Needs to Staff Development Models

	Staff Development Models (Types of Personnel)				
	Individually Guided Staff Development	Observation/ Assessment	Involvement in Development/ Improvement Process	Training	Inquiry
Teaching personnel					
Beginning					
Experienced					
Marginal performer					
Meets position requirements					
Exceeds position requirements					
Administrative—supervisory personnel					
Beginning					
Experienced					
Marginal performer					
Meets position requirements					
Exceeds position requirements					
Support personnel					
Marginal performer					
Meets position requirements					
Exceeds position requirements					
Board of education					
Beginning					
Continuing education					

Note: See Table 6.3 for details of staff development models.

- Do the data in Tables 6.2, 6.3, and 6.4 represent current practice *norms* (averages) or *standards* to be adopted by school systems?
- What do the standard deviation figures in Tables 6.3 and 6.4 mean?
- What is the meaning of organizational development as presented in Table 6.4?
- To what do you attribute the minimal use of computer technology, as reported in Table 6.2?
- How do your views on staff development differ from those presented in Tables 6.2, 6.3, and 6.4?

- To what extent does the staff development profile presented in Tables 6.2, 6.3, and 6.4 differ from the profiles in school systems of your acquaintance?
- Give your opinion of the following two statements: (a) Higher education is not meeting the needs of staff developers, (b) Formal course work is the least likely source for continuing education in staff development.
- Does the profile presented in Tables 6.2, 6.3, and 6.4 reflect the diversity of school systems in North America (cultural, geographic, student, suburban, urban, rural, community, and faculty diversity)?

TABLE 6.2
Instructional Methods and Types of Delivery

Workshops	85.8%
Meetings	61.9%
Cooperative learning	60.2%
Videotapes	59.0%
Seminars	54.4%
Lectures	46.2%
One-on-one instruction	23.8%
Laboratory learning (human interaction, etc.)	21.2%
Games and/or simulation	18.5%
Role plays	16.6%
Case studies	13.2%
Computerized instruction (videodiscs, etc.)	10.5%
Films	10.2%
Audiotapes	9.6%
Slides	7.9%
Self-testing instruments	6.1%
Visualization/visioning	6.0%
Video teleconferencing	5.9%
Teleconferencing	3.8%
Non-computerized self study (distance education, etc.)	3.2%
Computer conferencing	1.5%

Source: Neil Davidson, Jim Henkelman, and Helen Stasinowski, "Findings from and NSDC Status Survey of Staff Development and Staff Developers," *Journal of Staff Development* 14, 4 (Fall 1993), 58–64.

TABLE 6.3
Views of an Ideal Staff Development Program in Terms of External and Internal Consultants

View	Mean*	Standard Deviation
1. Staff development programs should make use of both external and internal expertise.	1.2	0.4
2. Staff development programs should be planned and overseen by an advisory committee with representation of, and accountability to, all affected groups and individuals in the organization.	1.5	0.7
3. Staff development programs should make use of internal consultants only.	3.6	0.6
4. Staff development programs should make use of external consultants only.	3.8	0.5

*(1 strongly agree, 4 strongly disagree)

Source: Neil Davidson, Jim Henkelman, and Helen Stasinowski, "Findings from and NSDC Status Survey of Staff Development and Staff Developers," Journal of Staff Development 14, 4 (Fall 1993), 58–64.

TABLE 6.4
Views of Individual/Organization Development

View	Mean*	Standard Deviation
1. Individuals and the organization should be developed concurrently.	1.4	0.6
2. Organizations/schools are realizing more and more the value of their human resources.	1.9	0.7
3. Organizations/schools value curriculum development over human resource development.	2.5	0.9
4. Development of the whole organization should take precedence over individual development.	2.8	0.9
5. Individual development should take precedence over the development of the organization.	3.1	0.7

*(1 strongly agree, 4 strongly disagree)

Source: Neil Davidson, Jim Henkelman, and Helen Stasinowski, "Findings from and NSDC Status Survey of Staff Development and Staff Developers," Journal of Staff Development 14, 4 (Fall 1993), 58–64.

Notes

1. Gelareh Asayesh, "Using Systems Thinking to Change Systems," *Journal of Staff Development* 14, 4 (Fall 1993), 8–140.

2. Joseph R. DeLuca, "The Evolution of Staff Development for Teachers," *Journal of Staff Development* 12, 3 (Summer 1991), 45.

3. Ibid.

4. Ibid.

5. Thomas R. Horton, "The Workforce of the Year 2000," *Management Review* 78 (August 1989), 5.

6. W. McGehee and P. Thayer, *Training in Business and Industry* (New York: John Wiley & Sons, 1961).

7. V. G. Scarpello, J. Ledvinka, and T. J. Bergman, *Human Resource Management:*

Environments and Functions (Cincinnati: South-Western Publishing Company, 1995).

8. R. W. Mondy and R. M. Noe, *Human Resource Management* (Upper Saddle River, NJ: Prentice-Hall, Inc., 1996).

9. J. T. Seyfarth, *Personnel Management for Effective Schools* (Boston: Allyn & Bacon, 1996).

10. Leslie J. Bishop, *Staff Development and Instructional Improvement* (Boston: Allyn & Bacon, 1976), 34.

11. Ben M. Harris, *Improving Staff Performance through In-Service Education* (Boston: Allyn & Bacon, 1980), 108–109.

12. W. A. Firestone and J. R. Pennell, "Designing State-Sponsored Networks: A Comparison of Two Cases," *American Educational Research Journal* 34, 2 (1997), 237–266.

13. A. Lieberman and M. W. McLaughlin, "Network for Educational Change: Powerful and Problematic," *Kappan* 73 (1992), 673–677.

14. Donald T. Campbell and Julian C. Stanley, *Experimental and Quasi-Experimental Designs* (Chicago: Rand McNally, 1963).

15. Ibid.

16. Ibid.

Supplementary Reading

Andreson, Kathleen M.; and Omar Durant. "Training Managers of Classified Personnel." *Journal of Staff Development* 12, 1 (Winter 1991), 56–60.

Berry, Barnett; and Rick Ginsberg. "Creating Lead Teachers: From Policy to Implementation." *Phi Delta Kappan* 71, 8 (April 1990), 616–662.

Bird, Tom; and Judith W. Little. *From Teacher to Leader: Training and Support for Instructional Leadership by Teachers.* San Francisco: Far West Research Laboratory for Educational Research and Development, 1985.

Brown, Brenda. "Designing Staff/Curriculum Content for Cultural Diversity: The Staff Developer's Role." *Journal of Staff Development* 13, 2 (Spring 1992), 16–22.

Burke, Peter J.; Judith C. Christensen; and Ralph Fessler. *Teacher Career Stages: Implications for Staff Development.* Bloomington, IN: Phi Delta Kappa, 1984.

Caldwell, S., ed. *Staff Development: A Handbook of Effective Practices.* Oxford, OH: National Staff Development Council, 1989.

Christensen, Judith C.; John H. McDonnel; and Jay R. Price. *Personalizing Staff Development: The Career Lattice Model.* Bloomington, IN: Phi Delta Kappa, 1988.

DeMoulin, D. F. "Staff Development and Teacher Effectiveness: Administrative Concerns." *Focus* (1988), 8+.

DeMoulin, Donald F.; and John W. Guyton. "An Analysis of Career Development to Enhance Individualized Staff Development." National Forum of Educational Administration and Supervision Journal 7, 3 (1990–91), 301+.

Fitch, Margaret E.; and O. W. Kopp. *Staff Development: A Practical Guide for the Practitioner.* Springfield, IL: Charles C Thomas, 1990.

Gilley, Jerry W.; and Steven A. Eggland. *Principles of Human Resource Development.* Reading, MA: Addison-Wesley, 1989.

Gross, James A. *Teachers on Trial: Values, Standards, and Equity in Judging Conduct and Competency.* Ithaca, NY: ILR Press, 1988.

Houston, Robert W., ed. *Handbook of Research on Teacher Education.* New York: Macmillan Publishing Company, 1990.

Jandura, Ronald M.; and Peter J. Burke. *Differentiated Career Opportunities for Teachers.* Bloomington, IN: Phi Delta Kappa, 1989.

Joyce, Bruce; and B. Showers. *Student Achievement through Staff Development.* New York: Longman Inc., 1988.

Katzenmeyer, Marilyn H.; and George A. Reid, Jr. "Compelling Views of Staff Development for the 1990s." *Journal of Staff Development* 12, 3 (Summer 1991), 30–34.

Lambert, Linda. "Staff Development Redesigned." *Phi Delta Kappan* 69, 9 (May 1988), 665–669.

Lee, J. F.; and K. W. Pruitt. "Staff Development: An Individualized Staff Development Model." *Record* (1983), 51–54.

McKay, Ian. *Thirty-Five Checklists for Human Resource Development*. Brookfield, VT: Gower Publishing Company Ltd., 1989.

Mecklenburger, James A. "What the Ostrich Sees: Technology and the Mission of American Education." *Phi Delta Kappan* 70, 1 (September 1988), 18–20.

Miller, Leslie M.; William A. Thompson; and Robert E. Rousch. "Mentorships and Perceived Educational Payoff." *Phi Delta Kappan* 69, 9 (February 1989), 465–468.

National Staff Development Council. "Nine Perspectives on the Future of Staff Development." *Journal of Staff Development* 12, 1 (Winter 1991), 2–12.

Neubert, Gloria A. *Improving Teaching Through Coaching*. Bloomington, IN: Phi Delta Kappa, 1988.

Owen, Jim Mirman. "Three Roles of Staff Development in Restructuring Schools." *Journal of Staff Development* 12, 3 (Summer 1991), 10–16.

Perelman, Lewis J. *Technology and Transformation of Schools*. Alexandria, VA: National School Boards Association, 1987.

Quinn, Michael J. "Staff Development: A Process of Growth." *The Education Digest* LV 7 (March 1990), 43–47.

Showers, B.; B. Joyce; and B. Bennett. "Synthesis of Research on Staff Development." *Educational Leadership* 45, 3 (1987), 77–87.

Sousa, David A. "Ten Questions for Rating Your Staff Development Program." *Journal of Staff Development* 13, 2 (1992), 34–38.

Thompson, Jay C.; and Van E. Cooley. "National Study of Outstanding Staff Development Programs." *Educational Horizons* 86, 1 (1986), 94.

Wood, Fred H.; and Sarah D. Caldwell. "Planning and Training to Implement Site-Based Management." *Journal of Staff Development* 12, 3 (Summer 1991), 25–30.

Wood, F.; S. Thompson; and F. Russell. "Designing Effective Staff Programs." In B. Dillon-Peterson, ed., *Staff Development/Organizational Development*. Alexandria, VA: Association for Supervision and Curriculum Development, 1981.

Wood, Fred H.; and Steven R. Thompson. "Assumptions About Staff Development Based on Research and Best Practice." *National Staff Development Council* 14, 4 (Fall 1993), 58–63.

7

Performance Appraisal

CHAPTER OBJECTIVES

Understand what performance appraisal is expected to accomplish.
Describe the organizational context of performance appraisal.
Identify the purposes of performance appraisal.
Develop a model of the performance appraisal process.
Discuss the ethical aspects of performance appraisal.
Examine the interaction between the performance appraisal process and the
      human resources function.

CHAPTER TERMS

Compensatory model	Norm-referenced
Criterion-referenced	Performance appraisal system
Eclectic model	Ranking systems
Management by objectives (MBO)	Rating system
Multiple-cutoff model	Self-referenced
Narrative systems	Standard of comparison

This chapter draws together several streams of thought about performance appraisal in the educational setting. Most notably, performance appraisals are not based on one approach considered to be successful in all situations and under all circumstances. Instead, several approaches of performance appraisal exist. Their success depends on the purpose for which they are used and on certain operative decisions made about the components of the appraisal system.

The Context of Performance Appraisal

Performance appraisal may be defined as the process of making judgments about individuals. It has long been accepted that appraisal of human performance is essential. In fact, performance appraisal is common; few people escape it. A baseball player's ability is judged by the batting average; a quarterback's skill is evaluated by the number of pass completions; and a salesperson's success is judged by the number of products or services sold.

Interestingly, people seldom question the need for performance appraisal. The problem is to develop and improve valid and reliable appraisal procedures, and to create a better understanding of the purposes and limitations of performance appraisals so that the results derived from the process will not be misused.

Growth of formal organizations, and recognition of their importance to our complex society, have led to the need for systematic approaches to performance appraisal. In the first several decades of the twentieth century, criticism of casual, haphazard, unsystematic, highly personal, and esoteric plans for evaluating employees brought about many efforts to reform performance appraisal plans. These included federal and state civil service legislation governing the *rating* of personnel, such as the Federal Civil Service Classification Act of 1923, the Taft-Hartley Labor Act of 1947, the Fair Labor Standards Act of 1963, the Civil Rights Act of 1964, and the equal employment opportunity legislation during the 1970s[1] (see Table 3.2). Between 1962 and the 1990s, several significant events and advances combined to influence all of the human resources functions shown in Figure 1.2, including performance appraisal. These events and advances included

- The Civil Rights Act of 1964.
- Computer technology.
- Court decisions affecting workers and the workplace.
- Legal and political activism in the teaching profession.
- Education reform movements in the 1980s and 1990s.

Numerous assertions from congressional committees, politicians, the media, think tanks, federal and state education agencies, and educators about the shortcomings of and proposed remedies for education in the United States have made the appraisal process a focus of public attention. Examples of reactions from the preceding sources, as well as from court cases and judicial decisions, include:

- Condemnation of the negative stance of teachers' unions.
- Negative feelings about the nature and ambiguity of performance reviews.
- Mishandling of personnel terminations.
- Inability of personnel administrators to manage costs due to litigation.
- Reluctance to link rewards to performance.
- Failure to link practice to educational program objectives.
- Unwillingness to rid the system of its incompetents.
- Lack of progress in moving from traits to learning outcomes.
- Public opinion polls favoring teacher pay based on performance.
- System inertia in creating an organizational performance culture.

Among the developments relating to performance appraisal that have contributed to performance improvement are

- Changes in the way performance appraisal is viewed and administered.
- Greater sensitivity of school officials to the treatment of employees.
- Increasing demands for *equity* and *ethics* from appraisers.
- Vulnerability of those charged with making personnel decisions.
- Growing awareness of the need to modernize the traditional performance appraisal process.

Traditional Appraisal Systems

The quest in the last half-century for ways of eliminating favoritism, seniority, and inequitable treatment in compensation plans has led to a multitude of rating programs both inside and outside of government organizations. These plans are referred to as *traditional approaches.*[2] These approaches, for the most part, are psychometrically oriented and consist of appraisals of personality traits or preconceived characteristics deemed essential to the work an individual performs in the organization.

Traditional appraisal systems include a variety of approaches, including ranking, person-to-person comparison, grading, graphic scales, checklists, forced-choice methods, and critical incident techniques. In the field of education, many traditional techniques have been and still are employed to appraise the performance of school personnel. These include self-rating as well as ratings by pupils, school administrators, supervisors, colleagues, special committees, outside professionals, and laypersons. Some plans base appraisal on the type of instruction, personal characteristics, cumulative personnel record information, pupil behavior, classroom social climate, and written responses (on questionnaires and examinations).

After nearly a half-century of use, the weaknesses of traditional appraisal systems appear to be legion. Criticisms include the following:

- Appraisals focus on an individual's personality.
- Most administrators are not qualified to assess the personality of an individual.
- Appraisal tools lack validity.
- Raters display biases.
- Ratings and raters are subject to influence by the organization.
- The appraisal system does not apply to all personnel.
- Results of appraisal are not used to promote individual development.
- Appraisal devices do not provide administrators with effective counseling tools.
- Most plans fail to establish organizational expectations for individuals.
- Appraisals used for discipline, salary, promotion, or dismissal are arbitrary.
- Personnel do not understand the criteria on which performance is appraised.
- Performance is unrelated to the goals of the organization.
- Appraisal procedures hamper communication between appraiser and appraisee.
- Appraisal methods fails to change individual behavior.
- Appraisal methods do not encourage the satisfaction of higher-level needs.
- Appraisal models do not complement appraisal purposes.

Most traditional performance appraisal plans used in the first half of the twentieth century were devoted to *nonadministrative* personnel. Apparently, a primary purpose of these plans was to link the organization's assessment to the employee's salary. A review of the history of performance appraisal both inside and outside of school systems leads to the following observations:[3]

- For the better part of a century, organizations have been experimenting with various types of performance appraisal. However, about the only consensus is that performance appraisal is an essential and continuing activity. The methods used to appraise performance remain a controversial issue.
- Increasingly, performance appraisal is being viewed as a means of *personnel development*. Appraisal is not something done *to* personnel; it is something done *for* personnel.
- Many appraisal systems are ineffective because they are not linked to organizational purposes, unit objectives, and personnel goals. As a result, employees are extremely dissatisfied with the results of performance appraisal.
- The fact of organization is as old as human existence; the theory of organization is modern. Formal appraisal of personnel performance, as well as the theory on which it is based are contemporary. The second half of the twentieth century witnessed a resurgence of interest in performance appraisal, especially in developing total appraisal systems that include *all personnel,* so as to integrate the

objectives of individuals with those of the organization. Some of the forces behind this renewed interest are discussed later in this chapter.
•   Accountability, cost-benefit, and quality-assurance concepts have filtered down from federal and state governments and the media to the local level, forcing school officials and boards of education to reconsider the purposes, designs, and methods of implementing appraisal systems.

Performance appraisal is a school system's most serious problem, yet it remains the key to achieving a satisfactory level of individual, group, and organizational performance. Of the 11 processes identified in Figure 1.2, performance appraisal is probably the most difficult to design, implement, monitor, and evaluate effectively in school systems.

Impediments to Performance Appraisal

Effective, dynamic performance appraisal is the exception rather than the rule in educational institutions. Why has so little progress been made in improving performance appraisal systems in education? The reasons include the following:

•   *Administrative irrationality*—Examples include adherence to obsolete concepts such as these: performance appraisal is unnecessary; performance is not tied to results; performance is not linked to behavior; performance appraisal always means rating; administrators should not be involved in performance appraisal; performance appraisal never involves confrontation; performance has little to do with individual, group, and system objectives; and teaching does not lend itself to adequate measurement of performance.
•   *Technical irrationality*—This refers to poor use of the many techniques, operations, materials, and growing knowledge that can be applied in a performance appraisal system. As noted throughout this chapter, absence or abuse of available technology can block the development of effective appraisal systems.
•   *State legislation*—State-generated performance appraisal systems use only a numerical system to *rate* personnel performance.
•   *Administrative board of education*—The school board participates in the formal and informal evaluation of school employees, rather than restricting its role to policy making.
•   *Administrative–supervision dichotomy*—In this point of view, there is a clear dividing line between administration and supervision.
•   *Environmental impediments*—These include the influence of unions, courts, the regulatory environment, boards of education, political organizations, community groups, and power groups that impede effective use of performance appraisal systems.

Purposes of Performance Appraisal

Both informal and formal performance appraisal systems exist in every organization. In the informal appraisal system, personnel are judged without the benefit of an organized evaluation system. In contrast, a formal performance appraisal system is one established by an educational institution, endorsed by the governing board, and operated systematically by designated administrators.

Formal performance appraisal systems have been used for many purposes, as noted in Figure 7.1. Many authors have tried to simplify these purposes by using terms such as *formative* or *summative* classifications to classify appraisal systems.[4] *Formative evaluations* occur during the initial and intermediate stages of employment and are aimed at personal development. *Summative evaluations* focus on actions concerning employees such as compensation, tenure, dismissal, promotion, and reemployment. However, most of the purposes of evaluation can be grouped into three categories: (a) compensation decisions, (b) employment decisions, and

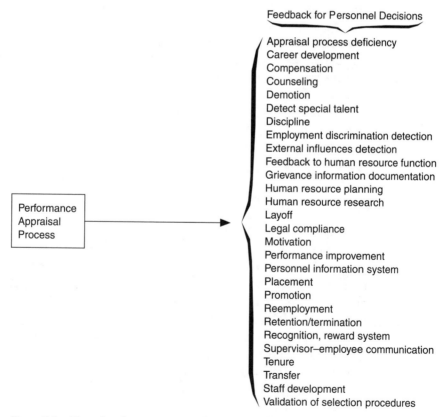

Feedback for Personnel Decisions

Appraisal process deficiency
Career development
Compensation
Counseling
Demotion
Detect special talent
Discipline
Employment discrimination detection
External influences detection
Feedback to human resource function
Grievance information documentation
Human resource planning
Human resource research
Layoff
Legal compliance
Motivation
Performance improvement
Personnel information system
Placement
Promotion
Reemployment
Retention/termination
Recognition, reward system
Supervisor–employee communication
Tenure
Transfer
Staff development
Validation of selection procedures

Performance Appraisal Process

Figure 7.1   Uses of performance appraisal in the human resource function.

(c) performance enhancement decisions. Many federal laws have influenced these decisions and have played a prominent role in shaping performance appraisal systems.

Contemporary Modifying Forces

Figure 7.2 presents some of the forces that are now changing the traditional performance appraisal system for school personnel. *Social changes* have convinced many employees that there is great discrepancy between what appraisal systems are and what they should be. To many employees, the traditional appraisal system is dehumanizing—an organizational barrier to self-realization and to the development of a career in which experiences on the job are meaningful and satisfying.

Legal changes have caused many modifications in performance appraisal systems. These include Title VII of the Civil Rights Act of 1964, state legislation governing teacher evaluation, court decisions, and an increasing amount of litigation challenging current performance appraisal systems. A variety of employment decisions, including those on compensation, employment continuation, and performance enhancement, fall within the legal purview of performance appraisal.

Organizational changes have created awareness of the inadequacy of appraisal plans that are divorced from organizational purposes. Educational organizations became more complex and positions more specialized in the 1990s. Decentralization and site-based management practices reflect new organizational trends in education.

Economic changes have increased salaries to a level more in keeping with the responsibilities of educational personnel. Salary improvement has also brought demands from the community that school personnel perform effectively. For some school districts, "pay for performance" has become a reality.[5]

Client reactions to school systems have been heard across the nation, expressed by the term *accountability*. Although this word means different things to different people, one implication is that schools today are not functioning effectively to achieve their major purposes. Clients are demanding better schools, and school officials are seeking better appraisal systems to motivate personnel to perform at higher levels.

Theorist reactions to the traditional appraisal system have led to a variety of ideas from behavioral scientists, resulting in a deemphasis on quantitative approaches to appraisal. Educational systems planning, management by objectives, competency-based teacher education, behavioral objectives, performance contracting, mutual goal setting, counseling, peer review, integration of individual and organizational goals, and need satisfaction of staff members are only a few of the contributions of theorists to performance appraisal.

Personnel reactions to traditional performance appraisal systems are negative; a variety of administrative barbarities have been perpetrated in the name of appraisal. The list is long, ranging from failure to identify job expectations for employees to a total failure to apply appraisal results on the job.

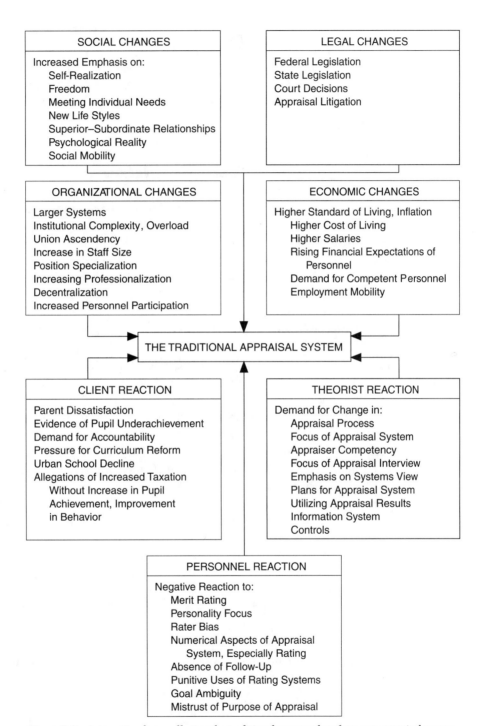

Figure 7.2   Interacting forces affecting the traditional personnel performance appraisal system.

Because of these impacts of contemporary forces, much attention has been redirected to understanding performance appraisal as an integral part of the human resources function. As a result, several important components of the performance appraisal process have been identified. These components play a key role in designing and implementing an effective performance appraisal system in the school system.

Design of the Performance Appraisal System

A properly designed, professionally implemented **performance appraisal system** is an invaluable tool for a school district. The more precisely it is constructed, the more effective the appraisal system is. Consequently, the purposes of a performance appraisal process must be carefully analyzed to determine the components of the system.

A performance appraisal system can have one focus and one purpose or multiple foci with several purposes. However, as the number of purposes increases, the precision of the appraisal process decreases.

Three broad purposes of a performance appraisal system were noted earlier in this chapter: compensation, employment, and development. Although these purposes may at first seem complementary, each of them contains meaningful differences for development and implementation of an effective performance appraisal process in the school setting.

For example, compensation decisions based on performance appraisal can be made for either merit purposes or award purposes. Although these two types of decisions may seem quite similar, important differences exist. For example, the number of employees eligible for merit pay is unlimited and is based solely on job performance, while the number of employees eligible for an award is restricted and is based on available resources. Merit decisions require an employee's job performance to be compared to established standards defining meritorious performance, whereas in award decisions, the employee's performance is compared to the performances of other employees competing for limited funds.

A performance appraisal process can be designed to provide information for employment decisions. These decisions can focus on probationary employees, continuing employees, and/or at will employees. All of these employee categories can exist simultaneously within a given work group and impose different operational demands on the appraisal process.

Development purposes associated with performance appraisal can focus on either individuals or groups. To help individuals improve their job performance, a plan of action for each employee must be developed based on relative performance standards. Enhancing the job performance of a group usually involves staff development plans based on absolute performance standards across employees.

The three broad purposes of a performance appraisal system are central to every aspect of the human resources function, are used in a range of personnel decisions, and have far-reaching implications for both appraisers and appraisees. Consequently, in designing the appraisal system, it is very important to specify the purpose of the system and to direct coordinated actions to this purpose. Coordinated actions must include both operational and behavioral concerns if the appraisal process is to operate effectively.

Operational Concerns for Performance Appraisal Systems

Every purpose of a performance appraisal system requires a specific set of decisions by those responsible for developing and implementing the system in the school setting. These decisions determine, to a great extent, the success of a performance appraisal process on the job.

A framework for considering some of the decision elements in an appraisal system is presented in Figure 7.3. These choices include: (a) a standard of comparison, (b) a model for combining job dimensions, (c) a method for weighting criteria, and (d) a choice among appraisers.

Standard of Comparison

In job appraisal, a **standard of comparison** for employees involves the referent source(s) against which the actual job performance of employees is compared. Depending on the purpose(s) of a performance appraisal system, different standards of comparison are required. A standard of comparison may be norm referenced, criterion referenced, or self-referenced.

Norm-referenced systems of performance appraisal use the job performance of other employees as a standard of comparison. The results of norm-referenced systems are particularly useful in differentiating relative levels of job performance among employees but cannot be used to determine the absolute level of job performance for any given employee. That is, one employee can be better than another, but the job performance of both employees can be either satisfactory or unsatisfactory.

The absolute job performance level of any given employee is assessed by performance appraisal systems utilizing criterion-referenced standards. **Criterion-referenced** systems compare the job performance of the employee to an external standard that is established independently of the job performance of other employees. The results obtained from criterion-referenced comparison systems reflect the degree to which the employee's job performance meets this external standard.

Self-referenced comparison systems focus on the job performance of an individual employee rather than on the job performance of other employees (norm referenced) or on job performance as defined by external standards (criterion

• Standards of Comparison	• Models for Combining Dimensions
• Methods for Weighting Criteria	• Choices among Appraisers

Figure 7.3   Decision elements in a performance appraisal system.

referenced). The purpose of self-referenced comparison systems is to identify the area(s) of relative job performance for a specific employee. When this is accomplished, an individualized enhancement plan can be developed and implemented for that employee.

Combining Job Dimensions

The literature on job performance evaluation indicates that all jobs have many dimensions. For example, in school systems, three broad dimensions of job performance are student concerns, district responsibilities, and community relations. These dimensions pertain to all employees, from custodians to administrators.

Regardless of its purpose, any adequate performance appraisal system must capture these different job dimensions. To do so, the appraisal system must measure each dimension of job performance. The method used to combine these different job dimensions in an appraisal system will vary, depending on the purpose of the system.

At least three different models have been used to combine job dimensions for assessment by a multidimensional performance appraisal system: the multiple-cutoff model, the compensatory model, and the eclectic model. Each of these models has a different implication for the performance appraisal system adopted by a school system.

In the **multiple-cutoff model,** job performance on each dimension is examined separately for every employee. That is, for every employee, performance on each dimension is viewed in either a relative or an absolute sense. This method is particularly appropriate when specific diagnostic information about employees is needed.

With a **compensatory model,** information about an employee's performance on all job dimensions is combined to form a composite measure of job performance. Low performance on one dimension can be balanced by high performance on another dimension. However, when job performances across all dimensions are combined, certain strengths and weakness on individual performance dimensions may be masked.

The **eclectic model** as the name implies, combines certain processes of the multiple-cutoff and compensatory models. In the eclectic model, an initial level of minimum competence is required on each dimension of a multidimensional performance appraisal system. Once this minimum level has been achieved, appraisal focuses on the employee's performance across all dimensions, rather than on performance on each dimension.

Criteria Weighting

To measure the complexity of the different dimensions in a multidimensional performance appraisal system, each dimension is assessed according to multiple criteria. These criteria may vary in importance, depending on the purpose of the appraisal system. The importance of various criteria can be captured in several different ways by applying specific weighting schemes.

The use of weighting schemes in performance appraisal systems is by no means new to educators. For example, students often take tests composed of different types of items (true-false, multiple choice, essay, fill in the blank, etc.). Seldom, if ever, are all test items given the same weight (value) by the teacher when scoring the test. Some items are given more weight than others.

In performance appraisal, several different methods are used to assign weights to the criteria for a multidimensional appraisal system. The outcomes of a performance appraisal process will vary substantially, depending on the weighting scheme chosen. These weighting systems, which range from simple to complex, include weighting criteria by equality, by variability, by stability, and by subjectivity.

Equal weighting of the criteria in a multidimensional performance appraisal system implies that all criteria are equally important. This scheme is the one used most frequently. Its popularity may be due, at least in part, to unfamiliarity with other types of weighting schemes.

Sometimes a performance appraisal process requires maximum differentiation among the employees being evaluated, such as in an award system. This can be achieved by weighting each criterion according to its variability. The *variability* associated with a particular criterion is generally assessed by calculating the standard deviation for that criterion and weighting the criterion accordingly. The distribution of job performance obtained with the use of variability as the weighting scheme will reflect maximum differentiation among employees.

Criteria defining the different dimensions of job performance in an appraisal system differ in stability of measurement. Job performance assessed by certain criteria remains relatively stable across time, while job performance assessed by other criteria fluctuates over time. The *stability* associated with each criterion can be assessed by test-retest reliability procedures, and more stable job behaviors can be given greater weight in the performance appraisal process.

The *subjective* weighting scheme gives policy makers and administrators considerable latitude in shaping the direction of a school system. When certain criteria are considered more important than others in the performance appraisal process, organizational priorities are communicated to employees. In the subjective scheme, weights are determined on a priority basis reflecting the goals and linked to the strategic plan of the organization.

Appraiser Designation

Every performance appraisal system should have a designated appraiser. This person is responsible for implementing the appraisal process, ensuring the accuracy of the process, and communicating its results to the parties of concern. Because the outcomes of an appraisal process may have profound implications for employees, and because employees enjoy certain implied as well as vested rights in their positions, the designated appraiser should have a contract with the school district.

However, this contractual relationship does not preclude the use of inputs from other sources. Depending on the purpose of the performance appraisal process, certain outside sources can provide valuable information about the employee's job performance. Such sources include students, parents, and other external constituencies such as state departments of education and university personnel.

A designated appraiser can be either an individual or a committee. Individuals who may serve as designated assessors include a supervisor, a peer, or, in some instances, the employee. Committees may consist of peers, an administrative team, or a combination of these personnel.

Behavioral Concerns for Performance Appraisal Systems

Just as important as operational concerns to an effective performance appraisal system are certain behavioral concerns. To develop a set of behavioral concerns about an appraisal system is to state the organization's beliefs about appraisal. These behavioral concerns form a basis for *integrating individual and organizational interests,* to the benefit of all concerned parties.

Not to be overlooked when considering behavioral concerns is that the basic mission of educational systems is to deliver effective services to clients that satisfy the needs of both the individual and society. Personnel employed in educational systems expect certain things of the organization. These expectations include a given amount of pay for a given amount of work, participation in decisions affecting work conditions, a method for settling grievances, strong leadership, opportunity for self-realization, position and personal security, the right to be heard, fair treatment, and the use of up-to-date administrative practices.

The organization expects personnel to accept the hierarchy of authority, the concept of appraiser–appraisee relationships, and the rules, regulations, procedures, controls, and rituals comprising the culture of the organization. This is considered essential if the organization is to accomplish its mission. Frequently, the expectations of the individual and those of the organization conflict if the concerns of one or both parties are overlooked when formulating the performance appraisal system.

The performance appraisal system, with its human relations potential, is a powerful mechanism for integrating the interests of the employee and the organization. The concepts it embraces, including mutual goal setting, flexibility in position performance, occupational mobility, self-development, and work creativity, are conducive to development of personal attachment to the organization and to voluntary cooperation in achieving the goals of both the employee and the system.

Advancing the self-development of personnel is one of several aims of the performance appraisal system. Development refers to activities undertaken by both the individual and the organization to improve the performance of personnel from the time they are hired to retirement. Its aim is to satisfy two kinds of expectations: (a) the contribution required of the individual by the school system and (b) the material and emotional rewards anticipated in return by the individual.

The past several decades have seen a profound conceptual shift concerning the function of an appraisal system. The trend toward *management by results* has shifted the focus of the system from its traditional role of determining the size of an employee's paycheck to facilitating the employee's on-the-job performance. However, this change in the values and outlook of organizations regarding the central concern of the appraisal system should not be interpreted to mean that performance appraisal and compensation are unrelated. Rather, this new development in performance appraisal involves a deliberate attempt to stretch the potential use of the appraisal system beyond compensation concerns and to improve the relationship between the individual and the organization in their quest to satisfy mutual expectations. Today rewards based on performance appraisal are given either to work groups in a gainsharing strategy or to individual employees.[6,7]

The quality of the appraiser–appraisee relationship considerably influences the effectiveness of the performance appraisal process. The basic act of performance appraisal occurs between two people: the appraisee and the appraiser. Although information about the performance of an appraisee may be derived from several sources, the appraisal process is a continuing experience involving both of these parties. This experience is intensely personal and emotional for both participants. In it, two people are attempting to establish an individual–organizational fit. These individuals need to develop and maintain an emotional climate in which to identify (a) what the appraisee wants and (b) what the appraiser wants to achieve for the organization.

Clearly, the quality of the relationship between appraiser and appraisee determines whether an organization functions effectively. Without a relationship that is emotionally attractive and psychologically and occupationally gratifying, the support plans described earlier as essential to the performance appraisal system will be useless.

Today there is increasing awareness of the necessity for change in performance appraisal systems. Employees of educational institutions, with all their intelligence, education, and organizational knowledge, will not tolerate a performance appraisal system that inhibits personal freedom, self-development, creativity, and organizational democracy. The organization, on the other hand, to become effective in the twenty-first century, must make adaptations that will enable personnel to help achieve the purposes of the organization. These reflections lead to a more detailed consideration of the ethics underlying a performance appraisal system.

Every appraisal system needs a set of values to guide the conduct of appraisers who make judgments about the appraisees they supervise, judgments that may affect either positively or negatively the short- and long-run interests and destinies of subordinates. These ethical values are established and reinforced at the system level and set forth the standards of behavior expected of those responsible for appraising personnel. The most desirable form of morality prevails in the appraisal process when there are system standards and a climate that enhances human dignity, status, career growth, equitable compensation, competent leadership, and maximum use of human potential.

In brief, the central administration establishes the system's moral tone and ethical expectations for appraisers and consistently enforces behavioral standards relevant to performance appraisal. Consistent application of appraisal ethics is the best insurance that the security interests of the individual will be protected as an integral part of the appraisal process.

Methods of Performance Appraisal

Appraisal methods are used to assess the job performance of employees, and the constant search for new and better methods has led to the development of various appraisal systems and techniques. By and large, these systems and techniques fall into three basic categories: (a) ranking systems, (b) rating systems, and (c) narrative systems.

Within each of these different methods of appraisal, several procedural variations exist. Because no particular system or derivation within a particular system is superior to any other, the choice of one system over another depends entirely on the purpose(s) of the performance appraisal process and on the institutional history of the district. To make an informed choice, a basic understanding of each system is required.

Ranking Systems

All **ranking systems** are norm referenced. As previously noted, in norm-referenced systems, the overall job performance of each employee is compared to the overall job performance of a defined group of other employees. This comparison can be made by using one of three formats: (a) forced distribution, (b) alternate ranking, and (c) paired comparison.

The *forced distribution* technique has been suggested to be analogous to grading on a curve, a practice well known to all educators.[8] Preestablished categories of job performance are defined (exceptional, above average, average, etc.) prior to evaluating the job performance of employees, and each employee is slotted into one of these categories based on the employee's relative performance. Using this technique, all employees in a given preestablished category are assumed to have similar levels of job performance, and all employees in other categories are assumed to have different levels of job performance.

The *alternate ranking* technique provides relative job performance assessments for each employee rather than relative job assessments between preestablished categories of job performance. This technique consists of first selecting the employee with the highest relative level of job performance and then selecting the employee with the lowest relative level of job performance. This process of choosing the next highest employee and, alternately, the next lowest employee continues until a relative job performance ranking is obtained for all employees.

The *paired comparison* technique provides even greater differentiation among employees than the forced distribution or alternate ranking technique. In the paired comparison technique, the relative level of job performance for each employee is compared to the relative level of job performance for all other employees on an individual-by-individual basis. For each dyadic comparison, a decision is made about which employee exhibits better job performance (ties not permitted). An employee's overall ranking of relative job performance is determined by calculating the number of times the employee was chosen as superior to the other employee in each dyadic pairing.

Rating Systems

By far the most frequently used method of appraisal in the work setting is a **rating system.** Rating systems use a criterion reference standard for assessing job performance and provide information about an individual's absolute level of job performance in relation to established standards. Popular rating systems are the critical incident checklist, the graphic rating scale, and the behavioral anchored rating scale.

The *critical incident checklist* contains descriptors of potential behaviors that could be performed by an employee. Some descriptors reflect incidents indicative of effective job performance; other descriptors reflect incidents signaling ineffective job performance. Both positive and negative incidents are assessed, and the employee's level of job performance is determined by the net difference between the two types of incidents.

In contrast to rating the presence or absence of specific job behaviors, as checklists do, *graphic rating scales* try to measure the degree to which an employee's actual job performance conforms to certain standards. This technique uses either numbers (1, 2, 3, etc.) or words (*always, frequently, sometimes,* etc.) to rate degrees of job performance. The degrees of job performance should be between 4 and 11 points. Degree levels of less than 4 points make it hard for the appraiser to differentiate among levels of job performance, and levels of more than 11 points are too complex to be useful. Research suggests that each graphic rating scale should measure only one dimension of job performance and that all graphic rating scales should move in the same direction (either from positive to negative or from negative to positive in presentation).

Behavioral anchored rating scales (BARS) are considered by most authorities to be the best technique for assessing job performance. Anchor points for scale values in a BARS system are defined by examples of actual job performance rather than by numerical values or descriptive words. Because actual behavioral descriptors are used, the accuracy of the appraiser is increased and the information provided to the appraisee is enhanced.

Narrative Systems

Most self-referenced appraisal systems rely on **narrative systems.** Narrative systems focus on relative levels of performance as perceived by the employee across the different job dimensions. Examples of narrative methods include work diaries, management by objectives, and portfolios.

Work diaries are compiled by employees in narrative format at scheduled times during the work cycle to provide a sampling of the actual tasks performed by an employee. Specific incidents of on-the-job behavior are cataloged, enriched with contextual information, and analyzed by the employee in a reflective summary. The work diary is shared with the appraiser, and a developmental plan is tailored for the employee based on the information in the diary.

Management by objectives (MBO) involves the preestablishment of work goals or objectives for an employee through mutual agreement between the employee and the appraiser. Ideally, these goals or objectives are linked to the strategic plans of the school district, but this technique does not preclude remedial goals or objectives for the employee. The assessment of job performance is based on the degree to which the employee meets the preestablished goals or objectives in a specified time period.

Portfolios are perhaps the most recent appraisal method to emerge within the educational setting. Compiled by the employee, portfolios contain samples of actual work performed, supporting materials used, and products produced on the job. To assess job performance using portfolios requires content analysis of these tasks, materials, and products.

A wide variety of appraisal tools is available for assessing the job performance of employees. Research and practice indicate that there are limitations to any instrument, any observation system, or any criterion. Different methods are most applicable to different purposes and different kinds of positions. On the other hand, some assessment approaches are better in a relative sense given the circumstances in a particular school system. There are problems, situations, and conditions in every school system that may limit or enhance the use and effectiveness of certain appraisal methods.

In addition, when policy makers become familiar with the variety of appraisal techniques available, they will gain a repertory of approaches to be used for different purposes with personnel at various levels of the organization.[9] The performance evaluation systems generally used in education today are regarded as unsatisfactory; testing and developing existing and new appraisal techniques is essential to both the system and its members. The solution is not to eliminate performance appraisal altogether, but rather to make effective use of knowledge now available and to experiment continuously with techniques that promise to yield positive results.

The section that follows proposes a model for appraising the performance of school personnel. This model will (a) address several phases of the process; (b) note some of the organizational and human obstacles to be encountered in establishing the process; and (c) examine the sequential, interrelated steps in its implementation. Again, it is worth noting that there is no ideal performance appraisal process. The effectiveness of any appraisal process is determined by various factors, including (a) whether the process is to be *developmental, remedial,* or *maintenance* in purpose and (b) the extent to which collective external and internal conditions contribute to the formation, operation, and maintenance of its desired mode of existence.

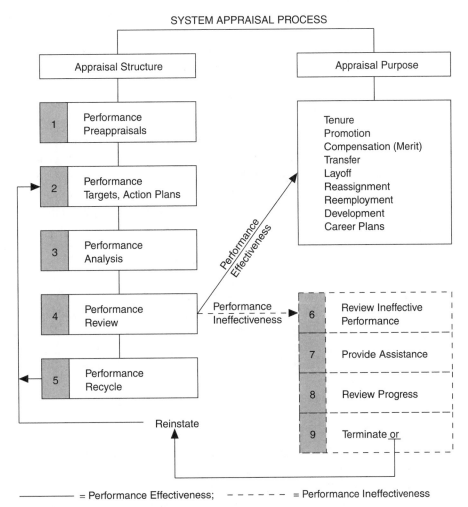

Figure 7.4   Performance appraisal goal-focused model.

The Performance Appraisal Process

A general model for a performance appraisal process of personnel is presented in Figure 7.4. The model portrays performance appraisal as a process rather than as an event, incorporating several interrelated phases into its design.

Phase 1: Appraisee–Appraiser Planning Conference

Phase 1 consists of a series of steps or activities designed to acquaint or to reacquaint the appraiser and appraisee with the scope, intent, procedures, and expectations of the appraisal process. In the preappraisal planning conference, appraiser and appraisee exchange information about the process. Generally speaking, the conference is designed to perform several functions: (a) enable the appraiser and the appraisee to inform and to become informed about the appraisal process, (b) clarify for the appraisee the organization's expectations for the position, (c) elucidate any differences between present and desired levels of job performance, (d) establish future performance expectations, and (e) allow the appraiser and the appraisee to influence each other in planning the appraisal process.

The major task in Phase 1 of the performance appraisal process is communication. It is in this conference that the organization communicates to the employee the relationship of the performance appraisal system to the position.

There are several steps involved in the planning conference. The appraiser and the appraisee review organizational purposes, unit objectives, position goals, performance standards, and appraisal procedures. The organization can facilitate this process by preparing a performance appraisal manual.

At this point, it is useful to highlight important assumptions about what takes place in a *preappraisal planning conference.*

• Performance appraisal is considered to be a systematized organizational activity that takes place primarily between two people: appraiser and appraisee.
• One purpose of a planning conference is to discuss the organization's view of the position and the manner in which it expects the work to be performed.
• The first and focal point of the planning conference should be to improve the appraisee's performance.
• The planning conference also focuses on development and self-realization of the appraisee.
• The planning conference should help to inform the employee about desired behavior or performance, how the organization will help the employee to achieve the desired level of behavior, and how it will measure job performance. In addition, the session should be used to analyze the duties of the position and the work behavior necessary to perform effectively, as well as to discover difficulties the employee may have in performing according to plan.
• *Four major position concepts* associated with the performance appraisal process are reviewed by the appraiser and the appraisee in Phase 1: *performance effectiveness, performance effectiveness areas, performance standards,* and *performance targets.* These concepts are outlined in Figure 7.5.

Although *appraisee self-evaluation* is considered an important element in Phase 4 (appraisal review), this process is also important in Phase 1. It is generally agreed that self-evaluation by the employee should *precede* the appraiser's evaluation. This gives the appraiser perceptions and other information to review and helps to minimize the possibility that the appraisee's performance will be judged solely be the perceptions of the appraiser.

As we move from *preappraisal to the actual appraisal phases* of the model outlined in Figure 7.4, concern focuses on two key ingredients of performance appraisal:

Performance Effectiveness	Performance Effectiveness Areas	Performance Standards	Performance Targets
Performance effectiveness is the extent to which an individual administrator achieves the general and specific objectives of the position to which he/she is assigned. Effectiveness is construed as results actually achieved rather than what activities the position holder engages in to achieve the results.	Key functional areas associated with a position constitute performance effectiveness areas.	Position standards are statements of conditions that will exist when the responsibilities assigned to the position are being carried out effectively. Standards are desired end results the individual is being paid to accomplish; they specify the conditions that exist when the role is being performed satisfactorily.	Position performance targets are specific statements agreed on by appraiser and appraisee that indicate what is to be accomplished to meet a specific position objective. Position performance targets are time bounded, measurable, and focus on what a position holder should achieve (results) rather than on the means by which it is to be accomplished.

Figure 7.5   Major concepts involved in appraising and documenting the performance of school personnel.

(a) collaborative setting of performance targets and (b) the behavior used by the appraiser to improve the performance of units and employees. One of the hard lessons organizations have been learning about the appraisal process is that its success depends largely on changes appraisers make in their own behavior.

Phase 2: Setting Performance Targets

The previous section demonstrated that when the appraiser understands what the appraisee's performance behavior means and what the performance needs of the appraisee are in relation to performance, the next phases of the appraisal process can be implemented. These phases include setting performance targets, measuring behavior change and performance improvement, and establishing a program of individual development based on the outcome of the appraisal review.

As discussed previously, appraiser and appraisee are concerned both with targets and with the process of setting targets. Moreover, targets are set collaboratively. Neither the appraiser nor the appraisee can set targets effectively without the advice and counsel of the other. The following questions should be answered when judging performance targets: Do the targets have priorities? Are they limited in number? Are they doable? Have time limits been set? Are the targets measurable? Are they specific? Are they understandable?

Several other points in setting performance targets should be noted, including types of performance targets to be set, target derivation, the target-setting process, and the target documentation procedure. These factors will now be considered.

Types of Performance Targets

There are two major types of performance targets: position targets and behavioral targets. A *position target* is an outcome to be achieved in one of the key areas established for the position. The purpose of this target is to translate a functional activity of a position into desired outcomes or results using specific operational terms.

For example, one responsibility of the principal of a middle school is to manage information about the pupils. This responsibility can be converted into a performance target as follows:

- By the beginning of the school year, improve the efficiency and systematic maintenance of necessary and desirable individual pupil records.
- By the beginning of the school year, provide for the maintenance and use of special-purpose short-term records.
- By the beginning of the school year, initiate a plan for managing the confidentiality of student records.

A *behavioral target* is the behavior an individual must use to achieve a performance target. The improvement, acquisition, or modification of human, technical, or conceptual skills, and the work habits needed to achieve position goals, indicate the general nature of behavioral targets. Acquiring skills in a summer seminar, reviewing the pupil management procedures used by other districts, and designing a computerized program for managing pupil records are some of the behavioral targets that may be needed to achieve given performance targets.

Target Derivation

Performance targets will be derived *initially* from a variety of sources, such as observations of the appraiser and appraisee about common problems in key results areas that need attention; indicators from surveys, management audits, and assessments; and complaints about unsatisfactory aspects of performance. *After* the performance appraisal plan has been initiated, the performance targets will emerge (Phases 3 and 4) from the appraisee's self-evaluation and from analyses of the appraisee's performance by the appraiser during periodic performance reviews throughout the appraisee's work cycle.

Target-Setting Process

Earlier, it was stated that in setting performance targets, neither the appraiser nor the appraisee can or should act independently. Targets must fit into and link with desired results of the position and with other positions within the unit, as well as with system goals and unit objectives. There are both internal and external constraints that need to be considered. Union contracts governing conditions of work, the leadership style of the appraiser's superior, and the personality and length of service of the appraisee, as well as pressures for system, unit, and individual change, are forces the appraiser must contend with in setting targets.

Target Documentation

The target-setting process is brought full circle by means of a written record of the events occurring in Phase 2 of the appraisal process. Essential features of a form for recording performance targets and the results achieved are illustrated in Figure 7.6. This form includes a record of specific targets the appraisee will work toward and serves as a primary source of documentation. This form can also be used to develop an action plan and to review the extent to which performance targets have been met. The items to be documented include effectiveness areas, objectives, priorities, appraisal methods, performance results, and signatories of the form.

Phase 3: Performance Analysis

The model in Figure 7.4 shows that Phase 3 is the core of the appraisal process. It calls for *self-appraisal* by the appraisee on the extent to which the goals are being achieved. In addition, the appraiser makes an independent judgment of the results achieved in relation to performance targets that have been established jointly. As will be discussed later, the results of both appraisals are recorded separately because both inputs are essential to the appraisal process.

1. *Appraisee*
   Title of position _____
   Position location _____ Central administration _____ Attendance unit _____
   Reports to (give position to which this position reports) _____
   Nature of
       responsibility: Line ____ Staff ____ Professional experience
   No. of professional staff   Years of professional exp.   19__ to 19__
       reporting to position _____
   No. of supportive staff   Years of teaching exp.   19__ to 19__
       reporting to position _____
   Incumbent _____ Age _____   Years of administrative exp. 19__ to 19__

   Education   Previous administrative positions
   B.A. from _____ Year _____   _____ 19__ to 19__
   M.A. from _____ Year _____   _____ 19__ to 19__
   Doctorate from _____ Year _____   _____ 19__ to 19__

2. *Appraiser*
   Title of position _____   Position location _____
   Name of incumbent _____   Dates of quarterly reviews _____

3. *Position*
   If position is in central administration, indicate with which of the following major
   organization functions is chiefly concerned:

   Ed. program ____ Logistics ____ Personnel____ External relations ____ Planning __

   If position is at attendance unit (building) level, indicate the following:
   Pupil-teacher ratio _____   Faculty experience _____
   Pupil-professional staff ratio____   % non-English speaking pupils_____
   Client composition _____   Types of special programs (nonsystemwide)
   Pupil mobility _____   _____
   Socioeconomic level _____   _____
   Faculty preparation _____   _____

Figure 7.6   Administrative position review form from the Camelot school system (items 1–3: position record sheet; items 4–8: performance target record form).

Appraisee Makes Self-Appraisal and Records Problems and Progress

One of the essential activities in Phase 3 (performance analysis) is self-appraisal by the employee. To a considerable extent, the appraisee goes through the same analytical process as the appraiser to determine if the position requirements are being met. The self-appraisal process has at least three purposes: (a) to assist the employee in analyzing present performance; (b) to provide information for a progress review conference with the appraiser; and (c) to help the employee identify strengths, weaknesses, and potential, as well as to help make plans for improving performance. Figure 7.7 lists the kinds of questions that can be addressed in Phase 3.

Appraiser Observes the Performance of the Appraisee

Let us now examine in detail how the appraiser goes about basing a performance evaluation on the dimensions noted in Figure 7.4. It is helpful to note that the appraiser must appraise the performance of the appraisee from two standpoints:

4. Common position dimensions	With which of the following common position dimensions is the performance target primarily associated? Systems dimension _____ Leadership dimension _____ Human resources dimension _____
5. Performance target	a. What specific performance condition needs to be improved to achieve the performance target? Priority no. __ b. Is this performance target focused on: Routine objective _____ Problem-solving objective ___ Innovative objective _____
6. Appraisal method	How will the appraiser judge when the performance target has been reached? By what means?

7. Performance target action plan (What is the plan of action? What steps are to be taken to achieve the performance target?)	Performance target activity serial number / Performance target activity / Planned date of completion / Date actually completed
	
	1.0 What does
	1.1 appraisee do to
	1.2 move from the
	1.3 present condition
	1.4 to the future
	1.5 condition (target)?
	1.6 What specific
	       steps must be
	       taken and in
	       what order?

8. Performance results	To what extent was the performance target (not the program of activities) actually achieved? Appraiser _____ Appraisee _____ Date _____

Figure 7.6   continued.

•   Are the goals of the position being achieved? Here we are talking about the long-range goals of the position, especially those established by the organization in the position guide. The appraiser is constantly interested in determining the extent to which the appraisee's performance meets the performance standards indicating how the work should be done.

•   To what extent are the short-term goals or performance targets being achieved? The relationship between performance targets and long-range results examined by the appraiser is illustrated in Figure 7.8. The performance targets are relatively short term, decided on jointly by appraiser and appraisee in order to give day-by-day direction to the latter. These targets suggest priority actions to be taken by the appraisee, as well as the skills, habits, and attitudes needed to improve total performance.

1. Summarize the overall strengths that you have demonstrated in performing your present assignment.

2. Do you feel that you are well placed in your present assignment? If not, please explain.

3. In what areas of your present assignment or in the way you perform your present assignment do you think you can improve your performance?

4. Do you feel that you have potential beyond your present assignment? How have you demonstrated this potential? What can you suggest as your next assignment?

5. Are there significant facts that you think should be noted about the dimensions of your position that affect your performance and that you think should be brought to the attention of your superior, such as:

    Unit objectives
    Position design
    Human, technical, and conceptual skills
    Social setting
    Situational factors
    Results achieved

6. How effectively do you feel you have met the responsibilities of your position?

Signature of appraisee _____ Date _____

Figure 7.7   A self-appraisal form.

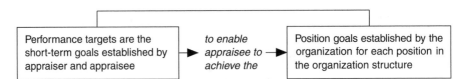

Figure 7.8   Relationship of performance targets to position goals.

Appraiser Records Observations

For a variety of reasons, the appraiser needs to record observations concerning the performance of employees. These reasons include recording information for the follow-up conference with the appraiser, for performance analysis, for the action program to be developed, and *for the performance history of the employee.* Essential features of forms for recording observations on the performance of an *administrator* are shown in Figure 7.6.

Phase 4: Performance Progress Review

Once performance appraisals are completed by the appraiser and appraisee, the next step in the appraisal process, as shown in Figure 7.4, is the performance *progress review conference,* sometimes referred to as the *postappraisal interview.*

One purpose of the progress review conference is to exchange information between the appraiser and appraisee about the latter's performance. The appraiser prepares for the conference by reviewing the results of completed appraisals. The appraisee, who receives a copy of the report, also reviews it in preparation for the discussion.

A second purpose of the progress review conference is to clarify viewpoints about the appraisee's performance. Differing perceptions of the position's goals, responsibilities, authority, and relationships can be identified, examined, and clarified. The appraisee's feelings toward achieving performance targets can be studied. Obstacles to progress, whether individual or organizational, are also topics for discussion.

The self-development of the appraisee is a third purpose of the progress review conference. As noted earlier, performance appraisal is designed not only to achieve organizational goals but also to help the individual attain personal objectives, one of which should be performance improvement. It is at this stage of the conference that the appraiser attempts to counsel or coach the appraisee in order to solve any problems affecting performance.

Illustrated in Figure 7.9 are means by which the appraiser can compare his or her judgments with those of the appraisee on the latter's performance. The information in this form provides the basis for the progress review conference and the individual development program.

Another aspect of Phase 4 in the appraisal process is the joint development of an action program for the appraisee based on the progress review conference. The essence of the individual development program may be summarized as follows:

• Performance appraisal reports should indicate to both the appraiser and the appraisee how well the latter has done in reaching previously established performance and behavior targets.
• On the basis of the progress review conference (which should make clear both the results achieved and those to be achieved), the appraiser and appraisee come to a common understanding on what performance targets should be reestablished for the next review period.
• During the period set for the individual development program, the appraiser has great responsibility for guiding and motivating the behavior of the appraisee to achieve performance targets.

Name of appraisee _____   Organization unit _____

Position _____

1. What progress does the   What progress does the *appraisee*
    appraiser think the *appraisee*   think he/she has made in closing
    made during the review period in   the gap between actual and
    closing the gap between actual   desired performance?
    and desired performance?

2. In what areas does the   In what respects does the *appraisee*
    appraiser think the *appraisee*   think he/she can improve?
    can improve?

3. Since the last appraisal, in what   Since the last appraisal, in what ways
    ways does the *appraiser* think   does the *appraisee* think his/her
    the performance of the   performance has improved?
    appraisee has improved?

4. What specifically does the   What are the *appraisee's* plans for
    appraiser plan to do to improve   helping himself/herself?
    the performance of the
    appraisee?

5. What follow-up action will be   What appears to be the general reac-
    taken by the *appraiser* on the   tion of the *appraisee* to (a) the
    basis of this review?   performance appraisal and (b)
                                          the ways by which performance
                                          can be improved?

Signature of appraiser _____

Date of review _____

Figure 7.9   Performance progress review form.

Figure 7.10 is part of a questionnaire used to evaluate the appraisee's perceptions of a performance appraisal interview. It enables collection of data on particular characteristics of interest (i.e., equity, accuracy, and clarity). The 7-point scales
measure a person's perceptions of the characteristics of performance appraisal
interviews.[10] The questionnaire can also be used to obtain feedback for the
appraiser, system evaluation of the appraisal process, documentation of the
appraisee's assessment of the appraisal process, and an individual performance profile for the system's data base.

Directions: Circle the number that best describes your opinion of the most recent appraisal interview.

	Very False					Very True

1. The appraisal interview covered my entire job.   1 2 3 4 5 6 7
2. The discussion of my performance during the appraisal interview was covered equitably.   1 2 3 4 5 6 7
3. The appraisal interview was accurately conducted.   1 2 3 4 5 6 7
4. I didn't have to ask for any clarification.   1 2 3 4 5 6 7
5. The interview was fair in every respect.   1 2 3 4 5 6 7
6. The interview really raised my anxiety level.   1 2 3 4 5 6 7
7. The interview's purpose was simply not clear to me.   1 2 3 4 5 6 7
8. The appraisal interview really made me think about working smarter on the job.   1 2 3 4 5 6 7
9. The interview was encouraging to me personally.   1 2 3 4 5 6 7
10. I dreaded the actual interview itself.   1 2 3 4 5 6 7
11. The boss was totally aboveboard in all phases of the interview.   1 2 3 4 5 6 7
12. The interview gave me some direction and purpose.   1 2 3 4 5 6 7
13. The interview really pinpointed areas for improvement.   1 2 3 4 5 6 7
14. The interview was disorganized and frustrating.   1 2 3 4 5 6 7
15. I disliked the interview because the intent was not clear.   1 2 3 4 5 6 7
16. The appraisal interviewer (boss) was not well trained.   1 2 3 4 5 6 7
17. The interview has been my guide for correcting weaknesses.   1 2 3 4 5 6 7
18. I understood the meaning of each performance area better after the interview.   1 2 3 4 5 6 7
19. The interview time was too rushed.   1 2 3 4 5 6 7
20. I received no advanced notice about the interview.   1 2 3 4 5 6 7
21. The interview analyzed my performance fairly.   1 2 3 4 5 6 7
22. I was often upset because the interview data were not accurate.   1 2 3 4 5 6 7
23. My record as it was introduced in the interview contained no errors.   1 2 3 4 5 6 7

Figure 7.10 Appraisal interview questionnaire.
Source: John M. Ivancevich and Michael T. Matteson, Organizational Behavior and Management, Third Edition (Homewood, IL: Richard D. Irwin, Inc. 1993), 69–70.

Phase 5: Performance Diagnosis and Recycling

As Figure 7.4 indicates, Phase 5 of the appraisal model is the time for diagnosis of performance results and for recycling of the appraisal process. This phase of the process is designed to check the results of the individual development program and to establish new or modified performance targets for the next review period. In effect, the appraisal process is being recycled.

As performance standards are reached, the appraisal process is redirected to other areas of performance where improvement is needed. The purpose of diagnosis is to establish continuity and stability in the individual's development program. Concrete plans should emerge for extending the program in areas where it has been good. Kindall and Gatza make several interesting points with regard to checking results:

- Here is a key point in the understanding of this appraisal program: hitting the target is not the measure of success. It is expected that some targets will be surpassed, some never even approached. The person who sets meager targets and always hits them is certainly of no greater value to the company than the person who sets unreachable targets, falls short consistently, yet in doing so makes substantial improvements in work performance.

  If one's "score" in hitting the bull's-eye is not the important thing, then what is the important thing? Simply this: the results achieved by the total process of establishing targets, striving to attain targets, and analyzing what intervenes between planned and actual performance. When a judgment must be made, the individual is evaluated on ability to set targets as well as on ability to attain targets.

- In checking results, the superior should do all possible to emphasize success—to build on successful accomplishment, the superior should help the subordinate. This help takes many forms: coaching, training, work assignments, allowing the subordinate to substitute for the superior, and so on.

- There is nothing in the recommended appraisal procedure that suggests that a superior should abdicate managerial responsibility. Suppose that after coaching, training, and other help, a subordinate fails to set and reach targets deemed realistic by his superior. At this point the boss should act, even though it might mean demotion, transfer, or release of the subordinate.[11]

Another important aspect of Phase 5 is that in addition to diagnosing individual development, the unit administrator includes in the periodic review the progress being made by the unit toward its objectives and system goals. Diagnosis and recycling of unit objectives and performance are designed to promote coordination and integration of plans and results of plans within the work unit and across the system.

Review and Preview

This chapter has provided an overview of the performance appraisal process. Forces were identified that impact traditional appraisal systems and will continue to influence the appraisal systems used today. Specific suggestions were offered for designing and implementing a performance appraisal system in the educational setting.

The most important thing is to focus on the purpose(s) of the appraisal system. Certain operational and behavioral concerns that demand specific choices by those who develop an appraisal system were identified. It was shown how the specific purpose(s) of the system require different implications for operational and behavior concerns.

Because no universal system for effective performance appraisal exists, several different appraisal methods were reviewed. In each of these methods, at least three different evaluation formats were discussed. Each format was linked to certain appraisal purposes, operational concerns, and behavioral concerns.

A five-phase model for implementing a performance appraisal process was presented. Each phase of the model focused on specific responsibilities and tasks to be accomplished.

Finally, it was emphasized that performance appraisal should be part of the ongoing life of an employee rather than an isolated yearly event. As a process, every aspect of this important managerial tool must be continually revisited to ensure that the goals of students, parents, employees, boards of education, and taxpayers are being met.

In Chapter 8 the topic of employee compensation will be addressed. Special attention will be given to criteria used to assess current compensation practices within a school district. Procedures will be presented for establishing new compensation methods.

Discussion Questions

1. Using the list of personnel decisions in Figure 7.1, examine the way these decisions are made in a selected school system. How is the decision system organized? Which school officials are involved? To what extent?

2. Respond to these statements derived from the literature on performance appraisal:

• In recent years, the most significant trend in teacher evaluation has been the heavy emphasis on the use of research on teaching for appraisal criteria.

• Evaluation should be conducted very early in the employment cycle so that the activities undertaken later in the cycle can be addressed.

• Much that is right and wrong in current organizations can be explained in terms of the evaluation process.

• Measure excellent people on a different scale; expect more from them; when they deliver, be prepared to offer commensurate rewards.

• A mediocre appraisal program designed by system members is better than an ideal program designed by management.

3. Why is there so much criticism of performance rating scales?

4. Develop a directive to school principals on how to conduct an appraisal interview.

5. Make a list of 10 things to do and 10 things to avoid in appraising performance.

6. Why is timely performance feedback important? List five criteria that should be established for performance feedback.

7. Develop a procedure to minimize a school system's vulnerability to litigation caused by the appraisal process.

8. What are some organizational determinants of performance? Individual determinants?

9. Read the following and compare the findings with your experience in or knowledge about performance appraisal in the public sector. A performance appraisal survey including more than 3,500 participants in the private sector indicated that:

• Managers tolerate poor performance too long.

• Supervisors do a poor job of solving "people problems."

• Supervisors fail to give performance feedback regularly.

• Supervisors tolerate poor employee performance.

• Responsible employees are tired of picking up the slack.

10. If you were to choose an evaluation technique to be applied to your position, which one would you select? Why? Under what circumstances is each of the following kinds of appraisal appropriate: appraisal by supervisor, peers, self-appraisal, group or committee, parents, and pupils?

11. Should individual pupil characteristics be considered in judging teacher effectiveness?

Notes

1. See Dena B. Schneir, "The Impact of EEO Legislation on Performance Appraisal," *Personnel* 55, 4 (July–August 1978), 24–35.

2. Terms used to describe traditional appraisal plans include *merit rating, efficiency rating,* and *employee rating.*

3. Information on the history of personnel evaluation in the twentieth century is contained in William B. Castetter, *The Per-sonnel Function in Educational Administration,* 5th ed. (New York: Macmillan Publishing Company, 1992), 256.

4. B. M. Harris and B. J. Monk, *Personnel Administration in Education: Leadership for Instructional Improvement,* 3rd ed. (Boston: Allyn & Bacon, 1992).

5. R. L. Heneman and G. E. Ledford, "Competency Pay for Professionals and

Managers in Business: A Review and Implication for Teachers," *Journal of Personnel Evaluation in Education* 12, 2 (1998), 103–121.

6. C. Kelley and J. Protsik, "Risk and Reward: Perspectives on the Implementation of Kentucky's School-Based Performance Award Program," *Educational Administration Quarterly* (in press).

7. H. G. Heneman, "Assessment of the Motivational Reactions of Teachers to a School-Based Performance Award Program," *Journal of Personnel Evaluation in Education* 12, 1 (1998), 43–59.

8. G. Dessler, *Personnel Management* (Englewood, NJ: Simmon, 1988).

9. Various techniques listed in Table 7.4 are described in Richard A. Fear, *The Evaluation Interview* (New York: McGraw-Hill Book Company, 1984); Wendell French, *Personnel Management Process*, 6th ed. (Boston: Houghton Mifflin Company, 1978); John M.

Ivancevich and William F. Glueck, *Foundations of Personnel/Human Resource Management*, 3rd ed. (Plano, TX: Business Publications, Inc., 1986); and Robert L. Mathis and John Jackson, *Human Resources Management*, 5th ed. (St. Paul, MN: West Publishing Company, 1988).

10. John M. Ivancevich and Michael T. Matteson, *Organizational Behavior and Management*, 3rd ed. (Homewood, IL: Richard D. Irwin, Inc., 1993), 69–70.

11. Reprinted by permission of Harvard Business Review. An excerpt from "Positive Program for Performance Appraisal" by Alva F. Kindall and James Gatza, 41 (November/December 1963). © 1963 by the President and Fellows of Harvard College; All rights reserved. Developmental and counseling assistance is treated extensively in Edward Roseman, *Confronting Nonpromotability* (New York: American Management Associations, 1977).

Supplementary Reading

Bridges, E. *The Incompetent Teacher: The Challenge and the Response.* Philadelphia: Taylor and Francis, 1988.

Cook, Mary F., editor. *The Human Resources Yearbook, 1993/1994 Edition.* Upper Saddle River, NJ: Prentice-Hall, Inc., 1993.

Educational Leadership. "Progress in Evaluating Teaching." *Educational Leadership* 44, 7 (April), entire issue.

Harris, B. *Developmental Teacher Evaluation.* Rockleigh, NJ: Allyn & Bacon, 1986.

Jenkins, George H. *Data Processing: Policies and Procedures Manual.* Upper Saddle River, NJ: Prentice-Hall, Inc., 1994.

Klein, Theodore J. "Performance Reviews That Rate an A." *Personnel* 67, 5 (May 1990), 38–41.

Langlois, D. E.; and M. Colarusso. "Improving Teacher Evaluation." *The Education Digest* 54 (November 1988), 13–15.

Milman, J., editor. *Handbook of Teacher Evaluation.* Beverly Hills, CA: Sage Publications, 1981.

Mohrman, Allan M., Jr.; Susan M. Resnick-West; and Edward E. Lawler III. *Designing Performance Appraisal Systems and Organizational Realities.* San Francisco: Jossey-Bass, 1989.

Phi Delta Kappa. *Teacher Evaluation: The Formative Process.* Bloomington, IN: Phi Delta Kappa, 1985.

Plachy, Roger J.; and Sandra J. Plachy. *Performance Management.* New York: American Management Association, 1988.

Popham, W. James. *Educational Evaluation*, 3rd ed. Rockleigh, NJ: Allyn & Bacon, 1992.

Popham, W. James. "The Merits of Measurements-Driven Instruction." *Phi Delta Kappan* 68, 9 (May 1987), 679–683.

Schuler, Randall S.; and Vandra L. Huber. *Personnel and Human Resources Management*, 5th ed. St. Paul, MN: West Publishing Company, 1993.

Schuler, Randall S.; and James Walker, editors. *Managing Human Resources in the*

Information Age. Washington, D.C.: Bureau of National Affairs, 1991.

Szilagi, Andrew, Jr. *Management and Performance.* Glenview, IL: Scott Foresman, 1988.

Thomas, M. Donald. *Performance Evaluation of Educational Personnel.* Bloomington, IN: Phi Delta Kappa, 1979.

Werther, William B., Jr. *Human Resources and Personnel Management.* New York: McGraw-Hill, Inc., 1993.

Wittrock, M. C., editor. *Handbook of Research on Teaching,* 3rd ed. New York: MacMillan Publishing Company, 1986.

8 *Compensation*

CHAPTER OBJECTIVES

Develop an understanding of current compensation practices and problems.
Provide a model or blueprint for designing the compensation process.
Analyze the compensable factors that comprise the pay structure.
Identify external and internal factors that influence pay policies and levels.
Describe approaches to developing the economic worth of positions.
Stress the importance of assessing compensation process outcomes.

CHAPTER TERMS

Appropriate labor market
Base pay
Benefits
Compensation policy
Compression
Elasticity

Internal consistency
Learning curve
Rationality
Salary
Wage

Human Resources Compensation: Perennial Challenge

For the better part of the twentieth century, school personnel, school boards, and special interests groups have debated the matter of fair and adequate compensation for school system employees, offering views about the merits and demerits of the single salary schedule, benefits, merit pay, comparable worth, pay for performance, pay equity, pay levels, pay structure, pay form, rewards, incentives, and union influence on compensation. Yet the problems involved in developing and executing a compensation plan so that both the school system and its employees achieve their goals remain unsettled.

This chapter views compensation as unfinished business. It provides a perspective on compensation decision making, the goal of which is to solve, effectively and efficiently, pay problems affecting the community, the school system, and its employees. This perspective includes the components of the compensation process, leading the reader through the steps by which the economic worth of positions and persons is determined, as well as the environmental influences on this issue.

Compensation Strategy

Designing a school system compensation plan starts by considering the link between organizational purpose and compensation strategy. Organizational purpose focuses on the outcomes to be achieved by the system; strategies are the methods used. This perspective, the connection between outcomes and strategy, is illustrated in Figure 8.1 and provides the basis for designing a compensation strategy.

Central to the compensation strategy is the mission of the school system. This mission, as noted in Chapter 1, should be based on the purposes of the school district.

As Figure 8.1 shows, organizational strategy is anticipatory, future oriented, concerned with emerging environmental conditions, and designed to make education a meaningful experience for employees. Organizational strategy is a set of plans for moving the school system from an existing state to a desired state in order to achieve its mission more effectively and efficiently. Its purpose is to establish mission-oriented guidelines.

Mission-oriented guidelines are driven by the interaction between human resources strategy and compensation policy. Human resources strategy addresses the number and kinds of positions needed (see Chapter 2) and the skills and abilities required for position holders (see Chapter 3). Compensation policy indicates the system's intent with regard to compensation obligations and responsibilities. This complex web of human resources and **compensation policy,** when integrated into a strategic planning framework, can be used to guide the many administrative judgments involved in creating and implementing a compensation strategy.

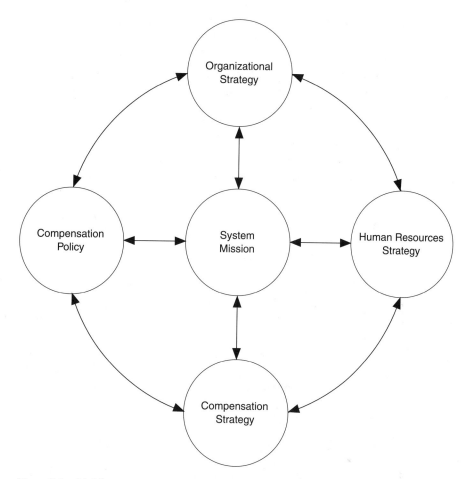

Figure 8.1   Link between system mission and organizational strategies.

A compensation strategy may be viewed as a set of interrelated decisions that allocate fiscal resources to change the system's current compensation status to one that will contribute more effectively to the organizational strategy. This includes plans that direct attention and resources to present and emerging pay problems such as direct and indirect compensation, incentives, benefits, market conditions, performance-dependent pay, marginal performance, and rewarding outstanding performance.

In developing compensation strategies, one central task of educational administrators is to devise plans for allocating funds to employees for services rendered. This should be done through a formal compensation system. Such a system, properly conceived and fairly administered, helps to promote the organization's objectives and the satisfaction of its members. The goals of compensation planning include:

- Attracting and retaining competent career personnel.
- Motivating personnel to perform well.
- Creating incentives to improve performance.
- Maximizing the return in service relative to the economic investment.
- Making the plan internally consistent and externally competitive.
- Providing salaries commensurate with the kinds of personnel the organization requires.
- Establishing a compensation structure conducive to personal satisfaction.
- Minimizing union and individual grievances.
- Controlling an item that accounts for four-fifths of the system's budget.
- Ensuring continuity of funds needed for an effective salary, wage, and benefits program.

These goals highlight the problems involved in designing the compensation process. In a school system, a good compensation plan is the basic element in employee satisfaction. Without an effective compensation plan, all other system plans, programs, and processes lose their force.

However, compensation plans, like all human resource plans, are subject to external and internal influences, as shown in Figure 8.2. External forces have a cumulative effect and play a large part in determining the characteristics of a compensation system. Internal variables (human and organizational) are frequently changing, and require direction and coordination to align the organization with the outside environment.

Components of Total Compensation Systems

Most school systems administer three different compensation systems: those for administrators, teachers, and support personnel. Some of these compensation systems are directly controlled by the school system, which alone is responsible for establishing and implementing them. Other compensation systems are only partially controlled by the school system and require bilateral actions by the school system in the collective bargaining process. Collective bargaining, by definition, requires that the school system and the unions representing different groups of employees agree on all aspects of the compensation system.

However, regardless of the need for mutual agreement, all compensation systems have several components, each of which is influenced by external and internal factors impacting the school district (see Figure 8.2). One component concerns direct payments to employees; another component is indirect payments. Both consist of several subcomponents, all of which must be considered within the total compensation process.

Direct compensation is the actual dollars paid to employees. The major source of direct payments is the salary or the wage received for services rendered to a school system. Whether an employee receives a salary or a wage depends both on the

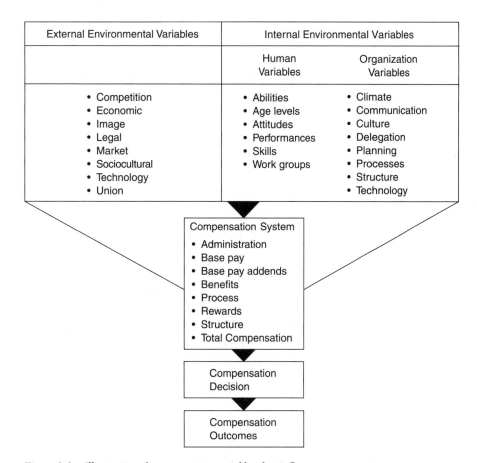

Figure 8.2   Illustration of compensation variables that influence compensation outcomes.

method used to calculate the source of the direct payment and on the employee's job characteristics, as defined by the Fair Labor Standards Act of 1938. In general, a **salary** is paid to employees who are exempt from this act; their compensation is related to the job rather than to the amount of time worked. A **wage,** on the other hand, is paid to employees who are covered by this act and who are paid on an hourly basis. In the school setting, administrators, supervisors, and teachers receive salaries, while custodians, aides, and clerical personnel receive wages.

A minimum salary or wage associated with a particular position is referred to as the **base pay.** This rate may be supplemented through additional effort on the part of an employee. For salaried employees, additional effort usually involves taking on an extra assignment, such as coaching performed by a teacher. For employees receiving a wage, it involves working overtime.

Indirect compensation refers to certain economic advantages received by an employee beyond salaries or wages and known as **benefits.** These benefits include sick leave, medical insurance, and pensions and represent a substantial cost for a school district. In fact, benefits usually cost a school district an additional 40% beyond the salary or wage paid to an employee.

Benefits play a very important role in the employment process. For school districts, they serve as an incentive to attract potential employees and to retain current ones. Often, it is this form of indirect compensation, rather than the salary or wage, that gives a school district a competitive edge in the labor market. Because compensation includes both direct and indirect costs, we focus on both types in this chapter.

Direct Cost

The primary direct cost in a compensation system is the base salary or base wage paid to an employee. This base salary or base wage can generally be ascertained from a salary schedule. Salary schedules vary in several ways both between and within school systems. They can be simple or complex, and can have fixed or variable dollar amounts associated with a particular position or with different persons holding the same position. The use of any particular type of salary schedule is based on certain assumptions about the position and the employees. These assumptions are often overlooked by school districts, resulting far too often in rigid compliance with past compensation practices. When this happens, many attempted improvements are stymied and the status quo is maintained.

Single Rate Wage Schedule

An example of a single rate wage schedule is found in Table 8.1. This type of wage schedule is frequently used for support personnel paid an hourly wage. This schedule contains different hourly rates for employees at different levels (I through V).

Each level of a single rate wage schedule pertains either to a single position or to multiple positions. All positions at a particular level are assumed to have the same worth to a school system, and positions at separate levels are assumed to have different worth. Because the worth assigned to a position by a school system determines the base rate of pay, an employee must change levels/jobs to increase the base rate.

Table 8.1 shows that a single rate wage schedule fails to provide any growth incentive or to reward experience on the job. All employees at the same level receive the same base wage, regardless of their education and experience. Thus, this type of wage structure assumes a similar organizational worth and an equal base rate pay for all job holders at a particular salary level.

TABLE 8.1
Example of a Single Rate Wage Schedule (Hourly Rate)

Level I	$12.50
Level II	$13.00
Level III	$13.50
Level IV	$14.00
Level V	$14.50

Teacher Salary Schedule

In contrast to the single rate wage schedule is the teacher salary schedule (see Table 8.2). Almost all teacher salary schedules provide for a growth incentive and reward experience. Although the organizational worth of the growth incentive and of employment experience varies considerably among school districts within the same state, this type of teacher salary schedule exists throughout the United States.

The growth incentives associated with teacher salary schedules are defined by education and represent a weak form of competency-based pay.[1] Education includes formal course work, continuing educational units, and/or other approved plans for professional development. Underlying the use of growth incentives to raise the base salary of a teacher is the assumption that additional education increases the teacher's competence on the job. However, "in practice, teachers are often rewarded for taking courses that may have little or nothing to do with the knowledge and skill set needed by the school organization."[2]

Employment experience is another compensable factor common to teacher salary schedules. The use of employment experience in determining compensation should be based on the learning curve associated with the job. In some jobs, proficiency increases with experience, and salary schedules should reflect this situation by awarding increases reflecting the slope of the **learning curve.**

Interestingly, little disagreement exists about what counts for appropriate employment experience of teachers. However, there is considerable controversy over the organizational worth of such experience. Depending on whether the teacher is

TABLE 8.2
A Hypothetical Teacher Salary Schedule

Experience (years)	Education						
	BA	BA+15	BA+25	MA	MA+15	MA+30	MA+45
1	$28,500	$28,550	$28,600	$28,650	$29,000	$29,500	$30,000
2	28,550	28,600	28,650	28,700	29,050	29,550	30,050
3	28,600	28,650	28,700	28,750	29,100	29,600	30,100
4	28,650	28,700	28,750	28,800	29,150	29,650	30,150
5	28,700	28,750	28,800	28,850	29,200	29,700	30,200
6	28,750	28,800	28,850	28,900	29,250	29,750	30,250
7	28,800	28,850	28,900	28,950	29,300	29,800	30,300
8	28,850	28,900	28,950	29,000	29,350	29,850	30,350
9	28,900	28,950	29,000	29,050	29,400	29,900	30,400
10	28,950	29,000	29,050	29,100	29,450	29,950	30,450
11	29,000	29,050	29,100	29,150	29,500	30,000	30,500
12	29,050	29,100	29,150	29,200	29,550	30,050	30,550
13	29,100	29,150	29,200	29,250	29,600	30,100	30,600
14	29,150	29,200	29,250	29,300	29,650	30,150	30,650
15	29,200	29,250	29,300	29,350	29,700	30,200	30,700
20	29,250	29,300	29,350	29,400	29,750	30,250	30,750

new to the system or an incumbent, the organizational worth of experience may vary within a particular school district.

The organizational worth of employment experience should be based on the learning curve associated with the job rather than on seniority. Nevertheless, some school districts cap employment experience when placing potential job candidates on the teacher salary schedule. This practice has limited economic value to a school system and restricts its ability to compete in the labor market when recruiting teachers.

Although many school systems use the traditional salary structure for compensating teachers, some systems are beginning to develop new strategies. Many of these changes involve gainsharing procedures, especially in systems experimenting with site-based management.

Gainsharing is a compensation strategy in which money is awarded to work units (school buildings) for their performance. This money is separate from the base rates of individual unit members (teachers). However, unit members have discretion in spending the money as long as the expenditure has educational implications for the work unit.[3]

Administrator Salary Schedules

Many school systems have no formal administrator salary schedule to establish base rates of direct compensation for administrators. Within these school systems, administrators, unlike all teachers and most support personnel, have their base rate of compensation set in lieu of a formal administrator salary schedule. Base rates for direct compensation within districts lacking an administrator salary schedule are a function of the salary awarded to an individual on initial appointment to an administrative position rather than as specified by a formal salary schedule. Following initial appointment, administrators receive, as an increase to base rates of compensation, a salary that reflects the increases received by other employee groups within the school system.

School systems using an administrator salary schedule to establish the base rate usually model this schedule on the teacher salary schedule. Although administrator and teacher salary schedules may contain provisions for growth incentives and employment experience, these factors have less worth in the administrator salary than in the teacher salary schedule. Administrator salary schedules adhere more closely than teacher salary schedules to the basic assumptions of competency-based pay and learning curves for job experience (see Table 8.3).

Although many administrator salary schedules are structurally similar to teacher salary schedules, some administrator salary schedules may be operationally different. Unlike teacher salary schedules with automatic advances for experience, some administrator salary schedules award advances on the basis of performance. These types of systems are called *pay for performance* or *merit pay* systems.

Pay for performance salary schedules fail to recognize a learning curve. These compensation systems assume that all administrators have the skills necessary to perform their jobs. Consequently, pay for performance focuses on the actions of the employee rather than on a learning curve or seniority.

TABLE 8.3
Administrator Salary Schedule Reflecting Daily Rates

Classification		Step 1	Step 2	Step 3	Step 4	Step 5	Step 6	Step 7	Step 8	Step 9	Step 10
I	Doctorate	369	278	388	397	406	414	422	430	438	447
	Masters	361	370	379	388	397	405	413	421	429	437
II	Doctorate	313	321	328	336	344	351	358	365	372	378
	Masters	305	313	321	328	336	343	349	356	363	370
III	Doctorate	285	292	299	306	313	319	326	332	338	344
	Masters	277	284	291	298	305	311	317	323	329	336
IV	Doctorate	271	278	284	291	298	304	310	316	322	328
	Masters	265	271	278	284	291	297	303	308	314	320
V	Doctorate	258	265	271	278	284	290	295	301	307	312
	Masters	252	258	264	271	277	283	288	294	299	305

TABLE 8.4
Typical Benefits Received by Employees

Medical insurance	Dental insurance	Vision insurance
Long-term disability insurance	Life insurance	Annuity
Retirement pickup	Flexible spending account	Sick leave
Personal leave	Vacation	Holiday pay
Tuition reimbursement	Sabbaticals	Conferences

Indirect Cost

Another source of economic concern for a school system is the indirect cost of benefits. A benefit is a form of indirect compensation that does not require additional services beyond those required by the contract, as noted in Table 8.4, and may be categorized as either uniform or variable. Uniform benefits provide the same coverage to all personnel. By contrast, with variable benefits, each employee receives the amount of money the system allocates for benefit purposes and may then spend that money any way he or she chooses.

It is assumed that benefits enhance the position and personal satisfaction of employees, creating an environment that nourishes personal development and to engender satisfaction associated with a position. Benefits extend compensation beyond base pay and incentives. They are intended to be dollar free and to focus on a variety of protective arrangements in addition to monetary components.

Criticism is mounting and changes are being initiated in the design and administration of benefits. The following points are illustrative:

- Benefit demands are insatiable.
- Benefit costs are often almost half of all personnel costs.
- Benefits do not depend on performance.
- Benefits are not congruent in two-career households.
- Benefits are not designed to motivate high performance.

Exploding expenditures for health care benefits (20–30% a year) and the increasing demand for and cost of most other personnel benefits have:

- Created an interest in cafeteria-style benefit plans.
- Forced school systems to implement benefit cost-containment controls.
- Brought about efforts to balance benefit costs in the total compensation structure.
- Stimulated calls for reexamination of benefit plans.

Consequently, the design of compensation plans should involve careful evaluation of existing or proposed benefits in terms of their impact on base salary, incentive compensation, and performance.[4]

Audit of Compensation Structures

The direct cost associated with salaries and wages and the indirect cost associated with collateral benefits are influenced by both external and internal factors (see Figure 8.2). Because of these influences, direct and indirect costs can become misaligned with the total compensation system. These misalignments fall into three categories: (a) those attributable to the formal structure of salary schedules, (b) those due to the compensation practices of compensation system administrators, and (c) those related to insensitivity to labor market conditions.

To identify potential misalignments of compensation outcomes with the total compensation system, an audit of the system's compensation structure is required. An audit will reveal potential problem areas, indicate remedial actions, and identify sources of inequity. At minimum, an audit should focus on four factors: elasticity, compression, rationality, and market sensitivity.

Elasticity

Elasticity refers to the theoretical earning potential associated with salary schedules. The theoretical earning potential is defined by the minimum and maximum base rates that define a particular salary range or pay grade within a salary schedule. Because these minimum and maximum base rates may not reflect the actual base rate received by a specific employee, the term *theoretical* rather than *actual* is used in the definition of elasticity.

To calculate the theoretical earning potential associated with a particular salary range or pay grade, some simple computations are required. For each level (salary range or pay grade) of the compensation structure, the maximum allowable salary is divided by the minimum beginning salary (maximum salary / minimum salary). The result is then converted to a percentage; this percentage is the theoretical earning potential for a particular level of the salary schedule.

An example involving the elasticity criterion for a group of elementary school principals is provided in Table 8.5. These data reflect a minimum salary rate of $255 per day and a maximum salary rate of $308 per day. The minimum salary is the smallest amount that can be awarded, and the maximum salary is the largest amount that can be paid.

The theoretical earning potential associated with this pay grade for elementary principals is derived by dividing the maximum rate ($308) by the minimum rate ($255), subtracting 1 from the result, and converting the final number to a percentage. If the same computations are used for all salary levels within a compensation structure, the theoretical earning potential can be assessed for an entire compensation structure involving administrators and supervisors in a public school district.

Table 8.6 presents four potential outcomes relative to elasticity. These outcomes are shown for lack of elasticity (Example A), for elasticity varying according to pay grades (Example B), for elasticity varying inversely with pay grades (Example C), and for elasticity varying unsystematically among pay grades (Example D). Each example has certain implications for the current and future compensation practices of a school district.

If the theoretical earning potential among pay levels within a school district varies substantially, then the compensation structure is elastic because some pay grades have greater earning potential than others. Whether elasticity has a positive or negative effect on compensation practices depends largely on the relationship between the organizational level of pay grades and the size of earning potentials associated with pay grades. Positive effects on compensation practices are most likely to occur either when elasticity does not exist or when it increases according to the organizational level of pay grades.

TABLE 8.5
Computational Procedures for Calculating a Theoretical Earning Potential

Minimum ← ── → *Maximum*

| 255 | 261 | 267 | 274 | 280 | 286 | 291 | 297 | 301 | 308 |

$= \text{(maximum rate / minimum rate)} - 1 \times 100$
$= (308 / 255) - 1 \times 100$
$= 20.78\%$

TABLE 8.6
Examples of Elasticity

	Example A	*Example B*	*Example C*	*Example D*
Level I	25%	25%	10%	25%
Level II	25%	20%	15%	10%
Level III	25%	15%	20%	15%
Level IV	25%	10%	25%	20%

Lack of elasticity suggests that the theoretical earning potential for employees is a constant percentage throughout the compensation structure (see Table 8.6, Example A). Lower-level employees have the same earning potential as their superiors. Earning potential that is equal or constant across all organizational levels (lacking elasticity) generally has strong appeal to employees and reflects sound compensation practices of the school system.

Elasticity can also have a positive effect when earning potential increases systematically according to the level within the hierarchy (see Table 8.6, Example B). With this type of elasticity, higher-level employees have greater earning potential than lower-level employees. Underlying this type of elasticity is the assumption that higher-level positions are more difficult to obtain through promotion and require employees to remain within a grade for a longer period of time. To compensate for these limitations, earning potentials increase according to the level within the hierarchy.

The negative effects of elasticity often occur when earning potentials vary unsystematically among organizational levels or vary inversely with levels. Earning potentials that vary unsystematically among levels are a problem often found during an internal audit. Because unsystematic variations usually have no logical explanation, they lead to accusations of favoritism benefiting certain employee groups and reflect poor compensation practices by the school system.

The accusation of favoritism is also made by higher-level employees when earning potentials vary inversely with level. In this situation, lower-level employees have greater earning potential than those higher up in the hierarchy. At best, this arrangement creates a competitive rather than a cooperative work environment; at worst, it results in a work environment perceived as inequitable.

The negative effects of elasticity can usually be traced to certain compensation decisions made in the past. With unsystematic variation, barring any actions intended to create a privileged group, market competition for certain groups may have required selective adjustments to attract good employees. If some employee groups receive an adjustment for market fluctuations and other groups do not, the former will have a greater earning potential than the latter.

Elasticity characterized by an inverse relationship between earning potential and organizational level can result from techniques used to update compensation systems. To update compensation systems, school boards can use either a proportional rate technique based on a fixed percentage or a constant rate technique involving a fixed dollar amount. The former technique will maintain the status quo with respect to earning potential, while the latter technique will increase the earning potential for lower-level employees.

Compression

Another criterion for evaluating the compensation structures and practices of a school district is **compression,** which addresses the functional as opposed to the theoretical growth potential for employees within a given pay grade. Compression considers the actual distribution of salaries within a salary grade rather than the theoretical earning potential defined by elasticity.

To assess the actual growth potential for a group of employees, again, some simple calculations are required. For each salary level or pay grade, the base rate of the lowest-paid employee is divided by the maximum allowable base rate associated with the targeted pay grade. The result of this division is then converted to a percentage; the percentage is the actual growth potential within the pay grade.

Table 8.7 shows the computations used to assess the compression for a particular pay grade. The table shows the salaries of a group of elementary school principals. In addition to the specific salaries, the anchor points or salary ranges associated with the pay grade are presented.

Rather than using the minimum theoretical base rate, as for elasticity, compression analysis utilizes the minimum actual base rate received by the lowest-paid principal ($297); this is the divisor. The maximum allowable theoretical base rate specified by the schedule ($308) serves as the dividend. After performing the division (maximum theoretical base rate / minimum actual base rate) and subtracting 1 from the finding, the result is converted to a percentage and the actual growth potential is obtained.

The same calculations for assessing compression should be used for each salary range or pay grade (see Table 8.8) within a compensation structure. These calculations reveal the absolute degree of compression for any particular pay grade. The smaller the number, the greater the compression.

TABLE 8.7
Computational Procedure for Calculating Compression for Elementary School Principles

Minimum ←								→ Maximum
255	261	267	280	286	291	297	302	308

Rebecca's rate $297
Jeff's rate $302
Julie's rate $302
Susan's rate $302
= (maximum schedule rate / minimum actual rate) − 1 × 100
= (308 / 297) − 1 × 100
= 3.7%

TABLE 8.8
Illustration of Variations in Compression Across Positions

Position	Compression
Assistant superintendent	15%
Secondary school principal	12%
Elementary school principal	4%
Supervisor	18%

Compression, like elasticity, can vary among salary grades. Within a school district, it is not uncommon to find that some salary grades exhibit very little compression, while others exhibit a great deal. An example of variations in compression is presented in Table 8.8.

In Table 8.8, the salary grade for supervisors shows very little compression, as noted by the actual growth potential of 18%. By contrast, the salary grade for elementary school principals exhibits extreme compression, as noted by the actual growth potential of 4%. Because the principals in this compensation system have little room for advancement other than through adjustments to their base salaries, they are likely to be less satisfied with the compensation system than the supervisors.

Compression can be caused by several factors. If the compensation system used with the principals in Table 8.8 awards salary advances based on experience within the district, and if all these principals have been with the district for a long time, then compression may result because of a lack of turnover. If this is the case, and if the compensation structure has been maintained appropriately, compression will be reduced in time by turnover within this group of principals. Replacements for existing employees should have beginning salaries lower than those of continuing employees. Thus, compression will be reduced.

However, a more common cause of compression than work force stability is failure to update the compensation system relative to market values. When this happens, beginning salaries will be too low to attract quality applicants. To solve this problem, the school district may offer starting salaries that fall in the upper levels of the pay grade or salary range of existing employees.

If new hires have high salaries in the pay range, these salaries encroach on those of long-term employees. This results in compression and produces dissatisfaction among existing employees. As a result of this type of compression, existing employees are likely to question the school board's appreciation for continuous employment in the system and to complain about a lack of economic incentives for advancement.

Rationality

Another criterion for evaluating compensation structures and practices is **rationality,** which addresses the relationship between the salaries of superiors and their subordinates. Underlying the rationality criterion is the assumption that superiors should receive higher salaries.

Although compensation specialists generally agree that rationality assessments should be limited to situations involving direct reporting relationships between superiors and subordinates, two definitions exist for subordinates in education. One definition favors the superior and uses the highest-paid subordinate to assess rationality. The other definition favors the employer and uses a subordinate with like type qualifications relative to the superior.

To illustrate the difference between these two definitions, consider the superior–subordinate relationship involving an elementary school principal and a teacher. For the liberal definition favoring the superior, the subordinate chosen to assess rationality would be the highest-paid teacher in the school. In contrast, for the conservative definition favoring the employer, the subordinate chosen for rationality assessment would be a teacher with the same education and the same experience as the elementary school principal.

Choosing whether to use the liberal rather than the conservative definition is largely a policy issue. However, the choice usually has a substantial impact on the outcome of the rationality assessment. Consequently, a choice should be made about the definition of a subordinate before rationality is assessed.

After the definition of a subordinate is selected, the length of the work year must be considered. In the present example involving an elementary school principal and a teacher, the principal's work year will almost always be longer. In many public school systems the principal's work year is 220 days, while that of the teacher is approximately 180 days.

To control for a work year of varying length, each salary must be converted to a common unit of analysis for rationality assessment. This usually involves using a daily rate of pay. For each position used in rationality assessments, the daily rate is obtained by dividing the base annual salary by the number of days comprising the employee's work year.

An example of a rationality assessment using actual field data is presented in Table 8.9. These data, obtained from a public school district, involve rationality assessments between line administrators who directly supervise teachers in this district. The assessments are based on the conservative definition of a subordinate using a teacher with like type credentials for each line administrator.

As Table 8.9 shows, the rationality assessment reveals an inverse relationship between the salaries of administrators and those of like-type teachers. In this district, administrators responsible for the direct supervision of teachers would earn higher salaries if they were paid like teachers. On any given day during the academic school year when both administrators and teachers report to work, administrators earn less money per day than teachers with similar credentials.

TABLE 8.9
An Illustration of Rationality Using Daily Rates of Pay for Line Administrators and Teachers (1997–98 data)

	Administrator Salary	Teacher Schedule	Actual Difference	Rational Difference	Rational Adjustment
Superintendent	382	376	6	38	32
High school principal	355	346	7	35	28
Middle school principal	290	284	6	28	22
Elementary 2–4	308	358	−50	36	86
Elementary K–1	284	328	−44	33	77
Assistant high school principal	289	280	9	28	19

The inverse economic relationship between line administrators and teachers shown in this example is not unique. In fact, a survey of over 50 public school districts in a typical Midwestern state revealed that the vast majority of those districts had the same problem with respect to rationality assessments involving administrators and teachers. As a result, many of these districts reported problems attracting talented teachers from within the district to fill vacant administrator positions.

Violation of the rationality principle often has several interrelated causes. For rationality assessments involving administrators and teachers, these causes often stem from issues relating to representation of employees by unions and to salary adjustment procedures used to update schedules for different groups of employees.

In many states, unions represent teachers and negotiate their salaries with the school board. Negotiations require an agreement by both sides and have greatly enhanced the economic situation of teachers. However, administrators, unlike teachers, are seldom represented by a union; instead, their salaries are determined solely by the school board.

When establishing salaries for administrators, school boards have used often the percentage increase awarded to teachers through negotiations as a guideline for making adjustments to base salaries. This percentage is usually calculated on increases in the base salary of teachers and fails to consider step increases within the teacher compensation system. Because of this omission of step increases in calculating the adjustment factor for administrators, any preexisting salary difference between administrators and teachers (rationality) is reduced with each budget year.

Assessments of rationality should not be limited to comparisons between line administrators and teachers. These assessments should be expanded to include the economic relationship for all administrators and superior–subordinate reporting relationships within the district. When assessments of administrator–administrator and other superior–subordinate relationships are included, the rationality of a compensation structure can be examined from a between-group as well as a within-group perspective.

Appropriate Labor Market

Market Sensitivity

School systems must compete with other organizations to acquire and retain quality personnel. Success in this endeavor depends, at least in part, on the reward structure of a particular school system relative to the reward structures of competing school systems. To assess the reward structures of other school systems, a market analysis should be performed.

A market analysis requires the identification of an **appropriate labor market.** In reality, many different potential labor markets exist, and each will yield unique results for a market analysis. Defining an appropriate labor market, as opposed to the most appropriate labor market, is a policy decision.

TABLE 8.10
Different Criteria That May Be Used to Identify an Appropriate Labor Market

Geographical area
Student enrollment
District wealth
Athletic conference
Academic performance

To identify an appropriate labor market for a market analysis, several different factors can be used. Some of the more common factors believed to inform decision making about an appropriate labor market are found in Table 8.10. Underlying each factor are certain basic assumptions about what constitutes an appropriate labor market.

Geographical location, when used to define a labor market, includes the school systems in the immediate area. By being in the immediate area of the target district, potential and current employees, it is assumed, can seek employment in these competing districts without changing their place of residence. With very few exceptions, potential and current employees can always improve their economic position if they are willing to relocate.

Student enrollments are used to define a labor market that contains districts of similar size. Similar-size districts are assumed to have organizational structures and positions comparable to those in the target district. Comparable organizational structures and positions require comparable skills and knowledge on the part of employees.

District wealth has been defined by factors either for acquiring resources (assessed property value) or for distributing resources (per pupil expenditures). Depending on the definition of wealth used, this factor assumes a labor market defined by fiscal responsibility. Fiscal responsibility implies that similar resources dictate a similar economic effort on the part of school systems.

In defining a competitive labor market, the district's athletic conference is often used. This factor is somewhat sensitive to geographical area and district size and has general public appeal. If residents of a school district are asked to identify comparable school districts, generally some of the districts in the athletic conference of the target school district are mentioned.

School districts have recently begun to use academic performance to define an appropriate labor market. With many states legislating standardized proficiency tests, the results of these tests have been used to select school districts for a market analysis. The underlying assumption here is that similar academic performance should yield similar compensation packages for employees.

Any single factor or any combination of factors will define a unique external labor market for a particular school district. As such, the results of a market analysis are market specific. For this reason, the choice of factors used to define an appropriate labor market for a school system is a policy decision rather than an administrative decision.

After an appropriate labor market has been determined, the direct and indirect costs of employee compensation within this labor market are analyzed. At minimum, this analysis should focus on the base rates of the positions under consideration, the contractual work year for each position, qualifications of employees occupying these positions, and the amount of money spent for different types of collateral. When information about base rates and the dollar value of collateral benefits is combined, a reasonable assessment of total compensation can be obtained. In addition, the relative worth of education and experience can be factored into the total compensation costs of the school districts within the appropriate market.[5]

Internal Consistency of Compensation Structures

Compensation practices and structures can be assessed according to several different criteria. In the previous section, four criteria were addressed: elasticity, compression, rationality, and market sensitivity. Each criterion provides a standard for gaining important baseline information about certain aspects of compensation systems.

However, these criteria are insensitive to another important compensation principle: **internal consistency,** the relative relationship among all positions within a particular compensation structure. Although the rationality criterion addresses the superior–subordinate relationship, it fails to consider the relationships among other pairs of positions.

For example, in most school districts there is usually some disagreement between elementary school principals and assistant high school principals concerning base rates of compensation. Elementary school principals tend to believe that they should be paid more than assistant high school principals; the latter take the opposite position. To resolve this disagreement, as well as similar disagreements involving other positions, school boards have two options.

One option is to consider all positions to be of equal value and to pay all personnel within the compensation system the same base rate, regardless of their position. With this option, elementary school principals would be paid the same as assistant high school principals. However, this option is seldom used and would probably be unsatisfactory both for boards of education and for school district employees. The other option is to differentiate among personnel within the compensation system in terms of organizational value and base salary. That is, some positions would command higher pay than others. This is the option generally used.

Salary differentiation within the compensation system should be based, however, on the following principle: Positions of similar organizational value should be compensated at a similar rate, while positions of different organizational value should be compensated at a different rate. To determine the organizational value of various positions is difficult but not impossible.

Some school boards might decide to differentiate among positions with respect to base rates of compensation on the basis of budgetary responsibilities. Because most elementary school principals are responsible for administering a building-level budget, whereas few assistant high school principals are involved in budget administration, the disagreement is resolved. Using the budgetary criterion, elementary school principals would be entitled to a higher base rate of compensation than assistant high school principals.

In contrast, other school boards might decide to differentiate among positions with respect to time spent performing work for the district that extends beyond the regular workday. Because most assistant high school principals are involved extensively in extracurricular activities after the regular workday, whereas most elementary school principals are not, again, the disagreement is resolved. Using the extended workday criterion, assistant high school principals would be entitled to higher pay than elementary school principals.

These examples serve both to illustrate a point and to raise an important question. The point is that the solution to the disagreement concerning the base pay of elementary school principals and assistant high school principals depends on the criterion chosen to evaluate the organizational worth of the positions. When the criterion changes, the solution to the disagreement changes.

The important question raised by these examples concerns the choice of criterion (budgetary or extended day) to be used for evaluating the positions. Either criterion is a reasonable choice for a school board. Therefore, the choice is a policy decision rather than an administrative decision.

Policy decisions are required in situations where more than one potential outcome exists and where all potential outcomes are equally appropriate. In these cases, policy decisions depend on the preference of the designated policy group. And in turn, the preference for a particular criterion or criteria for assessing the organizational worth of positions depends on the method used to evaluate these positions.

Position Evaluation

Several methods exist for establishing internal consistency relative to organizational worth among positions within a compensation structure. All methods have some common features while varying in very important ways. Common to all methods used to establish internal consistency is a focus on positions rather than on position holders.

Positions serve as the unit of analysis for several reasons. First, positions are established to perform certain tasks within the organization, and these tasks determine the relative organizational value of the positions. Second, the organizational worth of these tasks is independent of their actual performance. Tasks can be performed well or poorly, but their worth to the school system remains the same. Third, positions are part of the organizational structure and can be changed only by the organization.

The methods used to evaluate positions differ in complexity. Some methods use only a single global criterion, while others use several different criteria. Although the compensation literature is replete with methods that can be employed to establish internal consistency among positions relative to organizational worth, almost all of them are variants of one of four basic systems: ranking, job classification, factor comparison, and point.[6]

Each of these systems has been used in education and has been applied to districts with as few as four administrators and as many as several hundred. However, since the systems used most frequently are the ranking and point methods, we limit our discussion to these two types.

The ranking method is both the simplest and the oldest method used to evaluate the organizational worth of positions. It uses only one global criterion. The criterion is discretionary and should be chosen by a designated policy group.

Some examples of a single criterion are overall organizational worth, impact on children, extended workday responsibilities, and fiscal responsibilities. Because any criterion for evaluating positions has advantages as well as disadvantages, the choice should be made only after these advantages and disadvantages have been thoroughly discussed. This discussion should focus on organizational implications, rather than on particular positions or position holders, in order to reach a consensus about the single global criterion to be chosen.

If a consensus on a single global criterion has been achieved, the next task is to establish the relative worth of all positions in the compensation system. Relative worth, as defined by the ranking method, involves comparing positions with respect to the single global criterion. The comparison process can use one of the following methods: simple ranking, alternative ranking, or paired comparison. Each method uses a different decisional strategy.

To use any of these methods for assessing organizational worth and internal consistency among positions, a set of 5×8 cards is needed. On each card, the title of a single position is recorded. In a particular set of cards, the number of cards should equal the number of positions.

Each person in the designated policy group should receive a single set of cards listing all positions under consideration. Members of the policy group are instructed to work independently and to rank their set of cards according to the global criterion. These ranks should be in descending order, with the one position exceeding all other positions on the global criterion being ranked as 1.

After each member of the designated policy group has ranked independently all the positions in the compensation study, the ranks across members should be compiled. Initial results of the rankings will almost always reveal disagreements among policy group members; these disagreements should be discussed in a forum. The members of the designated policy group should explain their rankings and question those of other group members. Afterward, the group should once again rank independently all positions under consideration.

Several iterations of independent rankings, followed by discussions, should be performed to obtain a consensus. However, in many situations, no consensus will emerge. If this happens, the simple ranking method should be abandoned and another method used.

Another derivation of the simple ranking technique is the alternative ranking procedure. This procedure uses the same materials as the simple ranking technique but requires a different decisional strategy. With alternative ranking, group members first select the most important position relative to the single global criterion; next, they select the least important position relative to that criterion. This strategy is used with all positions in the compensation study.

The alternative ranking procedure forces maximum differentiation among the positions in a compensation system. Disagreements on internal consistency are most likely to occur with midrange positions. When these positions lead to problems in establishing internal consistency, one other comparison process may be used. This is the paired-comparison process, and it involves still a different decisional strategy.

In the paired-comparison process, each position (target position) is compared to all other positions (object positions) in the compensation study. Target positions considered more important than the object position are awarded a plus, and target positions considered less important than the object position are awarded a minus. The organizational worth of any particular target position is determined by assessed net worth reflecting the difference between the pluses and minuses assigned a particular position.

Norm-based systems are often used by school systems to establish the internal consistency of positions in a compensation system. These systems have been used to determine the relative ordering of support personnel in a single wage rate salary schedule and the relative ordering of supplementary assignments for teachers involving extracurricular pay increments to base salary.

In general, norm-based ranking systems are easy to implement, simple to understand, and equitable in application. Thus, employees tend to endorse these systems as a means of establishing the internal consistency of a compensation system. However, the strengths of norm-based ranking systems can be weaknesses when these systems are applied to complex jobs such as those held by administrators and supervisors.

To capture the complexities of administrator and supervisor positions in a compensation system, a criterion-based reference system is generally employed. This system requires a different decisional strategy than a norm-based system. In a criterion-based system, positions are evaluated relative to different criteria rather than relative to other positions, as is the case with norm-based systems.

The criterion-based strategy used most frequently to establish internal consistency is the point method. This method assumes that all positions in a compensation structure have certain underlying factors or common denominators, such as supervision responsibilities, judgement/discretion, fiscal management, community relations, and involvement with parents.

Factors used in the point method can vary both in degree and in weight. For example, supervision could vary in degree by including direct supervision, indirect supervision, and/or the number of work groups supervised. Degrees of judgement/discretion could be analyzed from either a policy involvement perspective or an organizational impact perspective. In some positions, the organizational impact may exist only for the immediate work site (assistant principal); in other positions, it may span several work sites (middle school principal); and in still other positions, it may extend across the entire school system (chief financial officer).

The outcomes obtained with the point method are related to the factors selected, the degrees used, and the weight given to each factor. If any alteration is made in factor, degree, or weight, then a different picture of the relative worth of specific positions will be produced. For this reason, the choice of factors, degrees, and weightings is a policy decision rather than an administrative decision.

Once the factors, degrees, and weights have been chosen, each position in the compensation study is evaluated accordingly. Results of the evaluation of positions for one school district using the point method are presented in Table 8.11. The policy group in this example was the board of education, which chose four factors and assigned a different weight to each one.

As Table 8.11 shows, some ratings have a plus sign and others have a minus sign because all ratings are standardized to a normal curve equivalence (z-score transformation) within each criterion. Within any particular criterion, the average performance of all combined position ratings is zero, and the specific rating of any particular

TABLE 8.11
Results of Position Ratings Across Five Criteria

	Judgment Discretion	Parental Involvement	Instruction Leadership	Personnel Evaluation	Extended Day
Department of Psychological Services	−0.23441	−0.06830	−0.42078	−0.38396	−0.10108
Assistant supt.	+0.52663	+0.36054	+0.67013	+0.10964	+0.14499
Department of finance	+0.52663	−0.12391	−0.49870	−0.01122	+0.16873
Supervisor Building and Grounds	−0.10502	−0.17952	−0.49870	−0.17683	−0.10108
Public relations	−0.23441	−0.06830	−1.27792	−0.38396	−0.09229
Transportation	−0.20016	−0.16839	−0.49870	−0.19205	−0.07910
Assistant middle school principal	−0.10274	−0.02359	−0.49870	+0.11343	−0.05712
Food services	−0.23441	−0.17952	−0.49870	−0.17683	−0.10108
Elementary principal	+0.00343	+0.06307	+0.67013	+0.13880	−0.03014
Senior high principal	+0.17465	+0.09098	+0.67013	+0.28218	+0.08300
Elementary principal	+0.00343	+0.06307	+0.67013	+0.13880	−0.03014
Sutton	−0.06315	−0.04147	+0.08571	+0.07297	−0.05712
Director of athletics	+0.03198	+0.18040	−0.49870	+0.05775	+0.14027
Assistant senior high principal	−0.12024	−0.02359	−0.34286	+0.13880	+0.03082
Supervisor of curriculum	+0.03198	+0.06307	+0.67013	+0.26696	+0.05780

position is given in standard units from the average. To illustrate, positions with large plus ratings (high school principal) involve far more supervision than does the average position in this particular district, while positions with large minus ratings (food service) involve much less supervision than does the average position in the district.

Standardization of ratings allows direct comparison of all positions within any criterion and direct comparison of all positions across all criteria. If certain positions are considered undervalued or overvalued, as reflected by standardized ratings, then ratings within any criterion can be used to help redesign positions. For example, the food service position is rated low in supervision; this rating could be increased by shifting supervisory responsibility for cooks and servers from principals to food service.

The overall value of positions using the point method is calculated by summing the weighted ratings across all criteria for each position. The overall value of positions, as calculated on the basis of weighted ratings, are used to order the positions in a classification system, and the classification system reflects the internal consistency among the positions relative to the factors, degrees, and weights selected by the policy group. Once established, a classification system should be linked to a total compensation system containing direct and indirect costs.

The Total Compensation Perspective

The ideal compensation system will be sensitive to both external and internal factors influencing compensation (see Figure 8.2), address the elasticity associated with theoretical earning potentials across pay levels (see Table 8.1), eliminate compression between positions within the same pay level (see Table 8.2), establish rationality for superior–subordinate pairings both within and between compensation systems (see Table 8.9), be sensitive to external market parameters assessed with comparable districts (see Table 8.10), and reflect internal consistency among all positions (see Table 8.11). However, a perfect compensation system exists more in theory than in practice. In practice, the best compensation system that can be obtained by most school systems is a reasonable system.

A reasonable compensation system is derived from informed decisions based on different sources of information. Beyond the different data sources described in this chapter, a reasonable compensation system must be sensitive both to the fiscal constraints of the school district and to the perceptions of employees in the compensation system.

In most cases, the fiscal constraints of a school district are fixed assets. Regardless of the best intentions of those who develop and administer a compensation system, most school districts have fixed economic resources for a compensation system. Consequently, certain choices or compromises must be made when developing and administering a compensation system for a particular group of employees.

Perceptions of particular groups of employees about a compensation system vary on two dimensions: procedural and distributive.[7] Procedural perceptions pertain to the methods used to establish the compensation system; distributive perceptions concern the actual economic incentives provided by the compensation system. Both types of perceptions influence the satisfaction of employees in the public school setting.[8]

When considering all sources of data, a balance between system restraints and employee concerns requires certain compromises. For example, it might be determined that rationality can be established and maintained for employees within the same compensation structure (administrator–supervisor pairings) but not for employees in different compensation structures (administrator–teacher pairings). Likewise, it might be determined that internal consistency can be established and maintained among positions within the same compensation structure at the expense of external market sensitivity, as assessed with comparable school districts.

Compromises based on informed decisions will yield a reasonable compensation system for a particular group of employees. Such a compensation system could involve direct costs associated with a fixed rate salary schedule, with advancement governed by determined factors (education and experience); direct costs associated with a mixed rate salary schedule, with advancement governed by determined and variable factors (job performance); or direct costs associated with a variable rate salary schedule, with advancement governed by job performance alone. Depending on the type of salary schedule (fixed, mixed, or variable rate), the economic value of advancements reflected by a salary schedule must be established.

Indirect costs, involving the collateral benefits of a reasonable compensation system, can be either uniform or variable. Uniform benefit plans fail to consider the needs of specific employees but provide a larger return for a fixed dollar amount due to mass purchasing power. On the other hand, variable benefit plans consider the needs of specific employees while suffering from economy of scale.

Because direct and indirect costs interact to influence the total compensation costs of a compensation system, several different compensation models should be developed. These models should be used to conduct economic forecasts, and these forecasts should provide information about each model relative to total implementation costs and total projected costs in subsequent years. Based on the outcomes of the forecasts, a specific compensation system should be adopted.

The resulting compensation system will be less than perfect. In addition, a reasonable compensation system in one district will not necessarily be reasonable in another district. Consequently, the compensation system adopted by any school system should depend on the unique situation of that school system at a given point in time.

Compensation Control and Adjustment

A reasonable compensation system has a short life expectancy. Major components of a compensation system, such as those involving internal consistency, have a life expectancy of about five years. Other components, such as those involving base rates and collateral benefits, become dated with each budgetary cycle.

To maintain a reasonable compensation system requires continuous monitoring by those who develop and administer it. At minimum, monitoring involves realigning the compensation structure with the mission of the school district (see Figure 8.1), keeping abreast of external and internal factors impacting the compensation structure (see Figure 8.2), and assessing changes associated with the direct and indirect costs of an appropriate labor market (see Table 8.12).

In assessing how well the actual operation of a reasonable compensation plan conforms to standards, goals and audit measures suggested earlier may be used as standards. The ultimate success of a reasonable compensation plan can be judged by the extent to which it attracts competent personnel; motivates them to cooperate voluntarily in achieving the goals of the system; maintains external and internal equity under existing legal constraints and collective bargaining agreements; and results in improved conditions for teaching and learning.

Because the ramifications of any reasonable compensation system are so extensive, checks are required to determine how well compensation plans are reinforcing other plans in contributing to organizational purposes. For example, compensation practices play a key role in determining long-range and operating plans for (a) recruitment and selection of personnel, (b) appraisal and improvement of performance, (c) design of the organizational structure, and (d) budgeting of expenditures.

The first strategic point considered here is the selection of personnel before assigning them to positions. Every organization, regardless of the nature of its compensation system, should design a selection plan to screen all applicants for system positions. With the help of position guides, qualifications of applicants can be checked against position requirements to determine how well they are fitted to perform the function and to estimate their potential for advancement. At this point, it should be determined whether the base salaries at each level of the compensation structure are adequate to attract qualified personnel. One test of adequacy is how closely compensation at each level conforms to the appropriate labor market. The question to be asked is, How much would it cost to replace a current employee with someone else who has the desired qualifications?

The second strategic point concerns performance appraisal after the individual has been assigned. Results of the appraisal, aside from yielding information necessary for making judgments about salary increases, should contribute to plans for the development of employees and for determining whether each employee should be retained in the position, transferred to another position, promoted, or dismissed. Here the test of effectiveness of the compensation plan is whether it provides for systematic appraisal of personnel performance.

The third strategic point concerns the organizational structure. This area is constantly in need of review and, occasionally, revision. As positions are added, eliminated, or modified, these changes should be reflected in the organizational structure and ultimately in the compensation system and the employee's salary. The criterion for this test of the compensation structure is its congruency with the organizational structure. Clearly, a sound organizational structure is indispensable to both the integrity of the compensation plan and to the workability of the appraisal process.

The final point to be considered, control of expenditures for the compensation plan, is essential. One check on the compensation plan is information relating to its impact on the annual and long-term budgets, such as anticipated salary changes by adoption of the compensation plan, annual cost of the plan, and impact of the plan on the community's tax structure.

In a very real sense, then, controlling the compensation plan is as vital to its success as the design of the structure on which it rests. Information yielded by checking the foregoing points, as well as others not mentioned, can be collected, analyzed, and presented periodically to the board of education so that the final step in the control processes—corrective action—can be taken to make certain that the goals of the plan are constantly being achieved.

Review and Preview

In this chapter, we have examined the compensation process and its relationship to the human resources function. Although satisfying the monetary needs of school system employees is not the only responsibility of the administration, absence of a sound compensation plan creates human problems that defy easy resolution. Because the size of the employee's paycheck is related to the satisfaction of both economic and noneconomic needs, the process by which compensation in a school system is determined is crucial to the system's ability to implement an effective human resources plan.

The compensation process presented in this chapter contains various subprocesses, including developing compensation policies, negotiating with unions, establishing the position structure, determining the economic value of positions and position holders, making provisions in the compensation structure for administrative and support personnel, formalizing the compensation plan, and keeping the plan current.

A number of interrelated factors affect an employee's paycheck. These factors include compensation legislation, prevailing salaries, collective bargaining, supply and demand, ability to pay, standard and cost of living, and collateral considerations. Although all of these factors enter into compensation levels established in an organization, one factor or combination of factors may be more important at a given time than others, depending on the circumstances.

Employment may be viewed as an exchange transaction between the individual and the organization in which each gets something in return for giving something. The employment exchanges between the individual and the system are perceived differently by both parties. One of the major problems in compensation planning is to reach agreements between parties by reconciling the nature of the input–output relationship.

Discussion Questions

1. Explain why the following aspects of pay structures have not been widely introduced in school systems: incentive rewards, flexible benefit plans, performance-dependent remuneration, and market-sensitive salaries.

2. Two criticisms of many educational compensation programs are that they are inequitable and that the salaries do not compare favorably with those of other school systems or other professions. Do these criticisms have any basis in fact?

3. Develop the elements of a pay structure that would provide the kinds of rewards that are important to you.

4. Is there any truth to the assertion that pay based on merit rating is only one of many kinds of incentive options? Do incentives have to be based on a *performance appraisal rating?*

5. How do unions influence pay practices directly? Indirectly? How do boards of education influence compensation practices?

6. In what ways are the compensation practices of public school systems influenced by state governments? The federal government?

7. Many states have passed comparable worth legislation for the public sector (ensuring that women and minorities receive payment commensurate with the value of their jobs). Does compensation discrimination exist in female-dominated occupations (clerical, teaching, nursing)? Have teacher unions pursued the comparable worth issue in negotiations? To what extent?

8. Many salary plans include three methods of compensation: (a) automatic increases, (b) pay for performance, and (c) a combination of (a) and (b). What are the strengths and weaknesses of each method? Why is method (b) the least popular? What values are lost by strict adherence to a method?

9. Why is the cost of contemporary benefit plans being subjected to stricter controls?

10. Develop a set of guidelines for improving incentive plans.

11. Examine the hypothetical salary schedule in Table 8.2. Respond to each of these questions:

- What are the strengths and weaknesses of the salary schedule?
- Do you agree that experience should be used as a measure of performance effectiveness?
- Does the schedule provide incentives?
- Does the schedule address criticisms of the single-salary schedule generated by the education reform movement?
- Will the average pay raise over five years benefit more-experienced or less-experienced teachers?
- If collateral benefits in this school system amount to 35% of total salaries for teachers, what would be the compensation costs for a teacher in 1999 with 16 years of experience? (Assume that all benefits are uniform for all teachers.)

12. Name three comparison sources by which personnel can assess a system's compensation fairness.

Notes

1. C. Kelley, "Teacher Compensation and Organization," *Educational Evaluation and Policy Analysis* 19, 1 (1997) 15–28.

2. Ibid., p. 17.

3. H. G. Heneman, "Assessment of the Motivational Reactions of Teachers to School-Based Performance Award Program," *Journal of Personnel Evaluation in Education* 12, 1 (1998), 43–59.

4. Benefits are treated extensively in Jerry Rosenbloom, *The Handbook of Employee Benefits* (Homewood, IL: Dow-Jones/Irwin, 1988).

5. I. P. Young, "Dimensions of Employee Compensation: Practical and Theoretical Implications for Superintendents," *Educational Administration Quarterly* 33, 4 (1997) 506–525.

6. G. T. Milkovich and J. M. Newman, *Compensation* (Boston: Irwin, 1996).

7. J. Greenberg, "Reactions to Procedural Injustice in Payment Distributions: Do the Ends Justify the Means?", *Journal of Applied Psychology*, 72 (1987), 55–61.

8. Young, "Dimensions of Employee Compensation."

Supplementary Reading

Berry, Barnett; and Rick Ginsberg. "Creating Lead Teaches: From Policy to Implementation." *Phi Delta Kappa* 71, 8 (April 1990), 616–622.

Cook, Mary F., editor. *The Human Resources Yearbook: 1993/1994 Edition.* Upper Saddle River, NJ: Prentice-Hall, Inc., 1993, Chapters 5 and 6.

Giblin, Edward J.; Geoffrey A. Wiegman; and Frank Sanfillippo. "Bringing Pay Up to Date." *Personnel* 67, 11 (November 1990), 17–18.

Heneman, R. L.; and G. E. Ledford. "Competency Pay for Professionals and Managers in Business: A Review and Implications for Teachers." *Journal of Personnel Evaluation in Education* 12, 2 (1998), 103–121.

Iseri, Billy A.; and Robert Cangemi. "Flexible Benefits: A Growing Option." *Personnel* 67, 3 (March 1990), 30–34.

Lawler, Edward A., III. *Strategic Pay.* San Francisco: Jossey-Bass, 1990.

Milkovich, G. T.; and J. M., Newman, *Compensation.* Boston: Irwin, 1996.

Rock, Milton L.; and Lance A. Berger, editors. *The Compensation Handbook: A State-of-the-Art Guide to Compensation Strategy and Design,* 3rd ed. New York: McGraw-Hill, Inc., 1991.

Shanker, Albert. "The End of the Traditional Model of Schooling and a Proposal for Using Incentives to Restructure Our Public Schools." *Phi Delta Kappan* 71, 5 (January 1990).

Young, I. P.; and J. A. Brown, "Sex Bias in Compensation: An Examination of Compensation Differentials for Female and Male Administrators." *Educational Administration Quarterly* 32, 1 (1996), 142–159.

PART III

EMPLOYMENT CONTINUITY, JUSTICE, AND UNIONISM

Chapter 9
Employment Continuity

Chapter 10
Employment Justice

Chapter 11
Unionism and the Human Resource Function

Part III is designed to:

- Present an approach for designing, implementing, and assessing the content and process of employment continuity.
- Portray the importance of a sound disciplinary system as the basis for procedural justice in public school systems.
- Increase understanding of three aspects of the collective bargaining system in public education: (a) components of the collective bargaining process; (b) the contemporary collective bargaining condition; and (c) strategic school system opportunities inherent in the collective bargaining process and its managerial implications.

9 *Employment Continuity*

CHAPTER OBJECTIVES

Portray the relevance of school system culture and system equilibrium to employment continuity and its strategic implications.
Identify factors that affect employment continuity and discontinuity.
Present an approach for designing the process and content of employment continuity.
Stress the potential impact on employment continuity of turnover, absenteeism, lateness, layoffs, severance, retirement, and death.

Americans with Disabilities Act
Continuity process
Culture
Disability

Family and Medical Leave Act
Pregnancy Disability Act
Severance
Turnover

School System Culture and Employment Continuity

Understanding the process of employment continuity involves considering the importance of the influence of the school system's cultural environment. Regardless of its size or nature, the basic building block of a school system is its people and the culture they establish in order to perform the system's work. In order for the school system to render the services for which it exists, members must not only perform their assigned tasks, but also behave in certain ways so that the system can fulfill its primary purposes of teaching and learning.

The **culture** of the school includes such elements as attitudes, routines, habitual ways of doing things, behavioral norms, rules of conduct, position requirements, and the network of social relationships within which people work. One role of leadership is to generate social and operational practices designed to reconcile human and organizational employment needs.

The school system culture has two strategic implications: (a) it is necessary to develop a cultural environment that will convince applicants that the school system is a good place to work and develop a career and (b) people are not likely to remain in the system where cultural conditions induce loss of meaning in work, social isolation, disloyalty, lack of commitment to system goals, insubordination, rule breaking, and failure to adhere to system policy. In consequence, attracting the kinds of people willing and able to achieve work goals and appropriate standards of behavior, and creating a cultural environment conducive to their retention and career advancement, depends largely on the leadership's understanding of the power of workplace culture and acculturation of its human resources.

Effective educational programs, community support, class size, organizational structure, funds and facilities—all are essential components of system efficiency, effectiveness, motivation of a diverse work force, and fulfillment of individual needs. But unless there is a positive human resource culture to shape these elements into effective strategic and tactical actions, the condition of the system will be unsatisfactory.

Human Problems in School Systems

We have examined various processes of the human resource function essential to attracting competent people into the system, including human resources planning, compensation, recruitment, selection, and induction. In addition, we have looked at ways of helping personnel to develop abilities and to integrate individual and group interests with those of the organization. In brief, these processes seek to transform inexperienced outsiders into qualified insiders.

In this chapter, we will look at organizational provisions designed to retain personnel and foster continuity in personnel service. We will focus on detailed plans for improving continuity of service, as well as on the process by which such plans are designed, implemented, and controlled. In so doing, we will see what organizations can do to maintain the health and occupational mobility of members, provide for their well-being, arrange for their separation from the system, and have replacements available when, for any reason, they are unable to perform their work.

Even in institutions where the system's concepts are subscribed to and implemented, things do not always run smoothly. A sustained effort must be made to keep any organization operating effectively on a day-to-day basis. Human beings have a way of interfering with plans, violating rules, and behaving in other ways inimical to the interests of the organization. So long as individuals fill positions in organizations, there will be problems. Some will become physically or mentally ill, others obsolescent. Some will need to be absent from work. Some will have work-connected accidents. Some will be affected by the physical conditions of employment, such as the amount of light, heat, ventilation, or noise, as well as sanitation conditions and safety hazards. Some will have stresses connected with work, home, or interpersonal relationships that will require counseling. Some may become unproductive if they do not have leaves of absence for self-renewal. Some will be dismissed, promoted, or reassigned. Some will be separated because of external conditions over which they or the system have no control.

The system must deal with these personnel problems primarily because they affect two of its strategic goals: stability and development. The system needs healthy, productive people continuously on the job who are physically and mentally able to contribute maximally to the work of the enterprise and who maintain a favorable attitude toward their roles and the environment in which they function.

The nature and scope of provisions for maintaining continuity of personnel service are determined by the system. It decides to what extent provisions should be made for enhancing continuity of service, what types of programs are needed, and how they will be organized and administered. Next, we will examine the process by which plans for continuing employment are designed and implemented.

The Employment Continuity Process

Keeping the system continually staffed with competent personnel involves consideration of and action on problems related to leaves of absence, substitute service, health, safety, promotion, reassignment, separation, resignation, termination, and retirement. The employment **continuity process** by which the foregoing problems are dealt with varies from but has much in common with arrangements for making and carrying out other organizational decisions. Operations relating to some phases

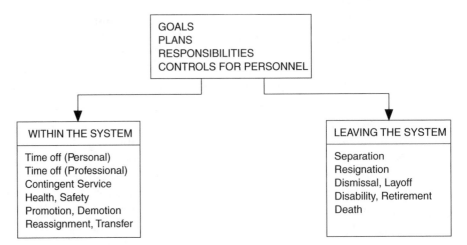

Figure 9.1   Framework of the employment continuity process.

of personnel service recur frequently; leaves of absence, health, substitute service, and safety are aspects of personnel administration that confront administrators daily. One important use of the process outlined in Figure 9.1 is to help planners isolate the recurring elements of these problems and to standardize the manner in which they are treated. If, for example, a relative of one of the system's teachers dies, the procedures employed in handling requests by teachers for such leaves of absence to attend funerals should be routinized well in advance of such events.

It is not suggested that the activities listed in Figure 9.1 occur sequentially; rather, the intent of the process outlined is to show that if the system is to be staffed properly and continuously, a course of action must be projected. In this case, it consists of making a series of decisions about continuity of service, including (a) what the plans are expected to achieve, (b) types of plans needed to realize expectations, (c) who will be responsible for what phases of the program, (d) the specifics of each type of program, and (e) how the results of the process will be determined. In sum, plans are developed for each of the subprocesses listed in Figure 9.1. This includes selecting activities to implement each subprocess, having the human and physical resources available when and where they are needed, and linking these plans to other plans and subplans relating to personnel administration.

Analysis of activities involved in the personnel continuity process outlined in Figure 9.1 indicates that there are two clusters of activities. One group is concerned with the health, safety, and mobility of continuing personnel; the second is focused on members who are voluntarily or involuntarily leaving the system. Expectations or results that the system intends to achieve from plans for service continuity are both long- and short-range and include:

- Improve the ability of the system to perform its function.
- Improve the system's physical, psychological, and organizational environment.

- Prevent and control occupational stress.
- Control personnel costs.
- Provide position security for personnel.
- Control avoidable absenteeism and lateness.
- Furnish financial protection against risks such as illness and accidents.
- Reduce personnel turnover.
- Facilitate change within the system.
- Improve individual and system effectiveness.
- Prevent accidents.
- Maintain position and system performance standards.
- Comply with statutory requirements.
- Provide opportunities for personnel self-development and self-renewal.
- Establish program limits.
- Attend to preretirement problems of personnel adjustment.

Once the goals for maintaining continuity of personnel service have been set forth, implementation by school officials follows. Early in the planning stages, at least two types of action are necessary. One of these is the preparation of a series of policy statements to guide members in designing and implementing specific programs. The other is a set of specific plans needed to carry out the intent of the policy, such as the manner in which personnel continuity programs will be organized and administered, as well as controls essential to resolution of personnel problems associated with their health and safety, internal mobility, and employment termination. Thus, we find the Riverpark school system defining its policies as illustrated in Figure 9.2.

The employment continuity policy presented in Figure 9.2 illustrates an approach to reducing desired outcomes through the continuity process. The policy's intent is to (a) exercise continuous direction, guiding action and control over planning and implementing the process; (b) influence action and conduct of system members regarding employment continuity; and (c) serve as a precedent or guiding principle for the growth of the work force and its organizational entity. The following supporting statements are employed to interpret and translate the Riverpark school system's continuity policy into more specific operational plans and procedures.

Provisions Conducive to Employment Continuity

Provisions essential to employment continuity described in this chapter are defined as certain direct or indirect forms of compensation that do not require additional services to be performed beyond those required under the basic compensation structure or union contract. Employee benefits have been classified as (a) entitlements; (b) privileges; (c) conveniences earned or granted at no cost to the employee; (d) conveniences with costs shared between the employer and the employee; and (e) conveniences

It is the policy of the Riverpark school system to:

- Provide continuity of personnel employment insofar as this is economically feasible.
- Control reduction in force on the basis of performance, ability, and length of service. When these factors are approximately equal, length of service with the system will govern.
- Grant leaves of absence for acceptable reasons.
- Provide assistance to individual staff members in maintaining and improving physical and mental health.
- Provide an attractive and efficient environment by maintaining good physical working conditions.
- Install every practical safety device, take every measure to prevent accidents, guard against mechanical failure, and provide adequate equipment for accident and fire prevention.
- Make available adequate substitutes for absentees.
- Fill vacancies by upgrading or promotion from within whenever present employees are qualified.
- Encourage reassignment when it is in the interest of the individual and the system.
- Protect personnel against unfair separation from the system.
- Assist personnel to plan for retirement.

Figure 9.2   Illustration of an employment continuity policy.

funded wholly by the employee. These benefits can be categorized as statutory, protection, equity benefits, and entitlements.[1]

Time-Related Benefits

Of the two clusters of personnel activities shown in Figure 9.1, one focuses generally on personnel health and development and the other on personnel separation. In the following text we will consider activities in the first cluster and their relationship to continuity of personnel service. First, we will examine time-off provisions in the context of the continuity process.

As indicated in Figure 9.1, time off may be categorized as (a) personal or (b) professional. Time-off policies express the system's attitude toward permitting personnel to take time off from work without severing the employment relationship and the extent to which the individual will be paid for time lost. Table 9.1 lists types of absences grouped under personal and professional time off.

Personnel time off may be defined as time away from employment by permission, with or without compensation, for a stated period of time without severing the

TABLE 9.1
Types of Personal and Professional Time-Off Provisions

Personal Time Off	Professional Time Off
Illness	Exchange teaching
Maternity, paternity	Research
Family and bereavement	Serving professional organizations
Marriage	Professional improvement
Voting	Grievances and negotiations
Civic duty	Conferences
Jury and trial witness duty	Receiving degrees
Military duty	
Social services	
Religious holidays	

Note: Authorization of time-off provisions may derive from *statutes, negotiated contracts,* or *board of education policy.* Such provisions are generally considered to be intrinsic forms of pay that extend coverage of the benefit program.

employment relationship. Regardless of system size, time-off policies and procedures are essential, as may be seen from the many reasons listed in Table 9.1. Increasingly, school systems throughout the nation are initiating or improving provisions governing personnel time off.

Although a time-off plan serves many purposes, its primary focus is on the satisfaction of individual needs. In safeguarding employees' mental and physical well-being, maintaining employment security, and fostering professional growth and morale, these benefits are not considered to be gratuitous or a generous gesture of the board of education. The investment is made on the assumption that it will provide conditions of employment conducive to personnel productivity and work satisfaction. Time off with pay accounts for a significant amount of the total costs of collateral benefits, and the trend is toward expansion in both number and kind.

Characteristics of Time-Off Provisions

It is customary, and frequently mandatory, to establish provisions governing absence of personnel because of illness and other reasons. *Illness plans* can be classified as either limited or unlimited. The limited plan, frequently, established by statute, generally contains provisions governing:

- Extent of compensation for time lost.
- Number of days allowed each year for authorized absences.
- Number of days for which authorized absence is granted with full or partial salary.
- Verification of illness.
- Board regulations extending the period of absence with pay in excess of statutory provisions.

- Waiver of sick-leave provisions in the event that absence is the result of injury when personnel are engaged in remunerative work unrelated to school duties.

Some states have statutory regulations that determine the amount of sick leave on the basis of length of service, others specify how many days of sick leave are mandatory at full pay, and still others leave this matter to the discretion of the board of education.

Extended absences because of physical disability are governed by provisions for salary continuation or health and accident insurance policies. Allowances are designed to pay less than regular salary as an incentive for personnel to return to work.

The unlimited sick-leave plan, in effect in relatively few school districts, places no limit on the number of days personnel may be absent because of illness. This type of leave may provide for full or partial pay or for a combination in which full pay is granted for a limited number of days, after which time partial pay is granted without time limitations.

Organizational experience with sick-leave programs provides little support for the assumption that such programs increase job satisfaction or member motivation. Experience indicates also that (a) the potential for abuse of the sick-leave privilege exists in any organization; (b) illness has a significant impact on instructional continuity; (c) the cost of sick leave and other benefits has risen so dramatically in recent years that school systems are struggling to prevent imbalance among salaries, wages, benefits, and nonsalary performance incentives; (d) changing social attitudes and public school economics are placing greater emphasis on maintaining *wellness* and rewarding good health than on extended illness provisions; and (e) the concept of a sick-leave bank plan provides an alternative to traditional sick-leave practices. This approach includes development of a pool of sick-leave days by system members in order to protect those physically unable to perform their duties for an extended period of time. Alternative means of stressing the wellness concept are included in comprehensive health maintenance programs, a subject discussed later in this chapter.

Leaves of absence for purposes *other than illness* are less often prescribed by statute. These include leaves for professional development, professional service, civic duties, and personal matters. Death in the family, professional study, exchange teaching, maternity, paternity, and attendance at educational meetings account for a majority of leaves granted for reasons other than illness. By and large, these provisions for time off are usually the subject of union–system negotiations.

Guidelines for Administering Time-Off Programs

A comprehensive personnel time-off program, which increasingly appears to be an organizational necessity as well as a national tendency, calls for resolution of many varied issues, including:

- Reasons for which a school district should grant personnel time off.
- Limits on the amount of personal or nonillness time off.

- Conditions for each type of absence, type of application required, salary on return to service, service required after return from leave, assignment on return to service, termination of absence, and notice of the intention to return to service.
- Plans for minimizing abuse of the time-off privilege.
- Arrangements necessary for safeguarding the education of pupils.
- Priorities of the time-off program (nonmandatory features) set forth in the negotiated contract.
- Plans for keeping personnel informed of current practices and recent changes.
- Records and reports needed to administer time-off programs effectively.

Although it is inappropriate to suggest here what the authorized time-off program for an individual system should be, certain suggestions can be made as a guide to planning. Analysis of the system's experience with time-off provisions over a period of years is a useful starting point. One of the purposes of such an audit would be to determine the nature and scope of time-off requests, frequency of occurrence, budgetary requirements, priorities, privileges subject to abuse, and suitability of existing administrative controls.

Personnel absence is the subject of statutory law and is frequently litigated in the courts, especially legal rights relative to sabbatical leave. The matter of mandatory maternity leaves, for example, has received consideration in government and in the courts. In precedent-setting decrees, courts and federal and state authorities have branded compulsory maternity leaves either unconstitutional or illegal. Increasingly, disabilities or illnesses caused or contributed to by pregnancy, miscarriage, abortion, childbirth, and recovery therefrom must be treated like any other **disability** or illness by the employing school system. Personnel disabled because of pregnancy or childbirth are entitled to the same leaves of absence, sick leaves, and job rights as any other temporarily disabled personnel.

The unpaid leave of absence, although infrequently employed, is a provision needed for dealing with personnel situations that arise occasionally. Most school systems, either through policy or contractual agreement, permit unpaid leaves of absence for a variety of reasons, including graduate study, child care, teacher burnout, pursuit of other interests or other forms of employment, health restoration, and political or social action. (Leaves for political or social action are gradually being incorporated into general personnel policy.)

Regulatory Influence on Leaves of Absence

Leaves of absence are influenced in various ways by the regulatory environment. Federal, state, and local lawmakers pass laws that empower these agencies to take various forms of regulatory action; and the court oversees this process by resolving disputes among the school system and its employees. The following federal regulatory provisions illustrate the direct and indirect impact of leave-related provisions.

- **Pregnancy Disability Act** (PDA) of 1978—-Amends Title VII of the Civil Rights Act of 1964. Prohibits discrimination on the basis of pregnancy, childbirth, or related medical conditions.
- **Americans with Disabilities Act** (ADA) of 1990—Designed to change the attitudes of employers and to give people with disabilities an equal chance in the workplace.
- **Family and Medical Leave Act** of 1993—Guarantees employees up to 12 weeks a year off, unpaid, for births, adoptions, or the care of sick children, spouses, or parents.

Examination of these governmental mandates indicates that the United States has been witness in recent years to an unrelenting succession of legislation affecting the human resource function in a variety of ways. These comprehensive pieces of legislation have created the foundation for change and conflict in employee–employer relationships and the need for reconsideration of ways of adhering to statutory requirements regarding employee health, leave conditions, and fair treatment for persons with disabilities.

School systems are not out of the range of the regulatory environment concerning human resources legislation. In one way or another, school systems as well as other organizations are on the brink of a radical shakeup in the way they provide and manage leave provisions, health care, and disability statutes, each of which is linked directly and indirectly to the human resource function and its various processes.

Conditions of Leave

From an administrative perspective, there are five key components of time-related benefits: (a) application procedures, (b) eligibility requirements, (c) conditions of absence, (d) termination procedures, and (e) compensation provisions. The most important factor is the manner in which the conditions of leave are specified. A personnel benefits manual is an important method used to explain conditions of time-off provisions, as well as the operational aspects of the five components mentioned above. The utmost attention must be given to the array of leave-related elements, not only because of litigation, as well as regulatory, fiscal, and employee continuity implications, but also because of the changing range of benefit choices to be considered and how the benefits structure should be designed to cope with current employment market conditions. The arrangement of leave-related elements now provided for personnel requires a comprehensive, coordinated, and integrated structure that contains controls for resolving disputes, employee concerns, and potential legal liabilities. This includes actions such as:

- Using a task force to review and reconsider existing leave policies and procedures for each type of leave.
- Including in the conditions of leaves those defined by regulatory agencies.

• Updating and communicating policies and procedures in the human resources handbook regarding leave provisions.
• Defining eligibility for employee benefits while employees take leaves of absence.
• Specifying employment rights governing acceptance of employment while on leave.
• Training administrative personnel in the leave of absence process and how it is administered.

The previous discussion addressed the *supply side* of leaves of absence—arrangements the school system provides for its employees when personal and professional need arises for such situations as illness, maternity, bereavement, mental and physical stress, and jury duty. Because of the rising cost of leave provisions, as well as the increasing demand for such benefits, there is mounting evidence that both public and private employers are initiating moves to control the *demand side* of the health care equation. Thus, health system promotion initiatives, designed to improve the overall health of its human resources, as well as to engender positive effects on health care costs, are the subject of the section that follows.

Health Maintenance Programs

School systems in contemporary society are confronted with resolution of a variety of issues related to the health and safety of personnel, such as:

• Selecting applicants significantly free of health problems.
• Maintaining and improving the health of the entire school staff.
• Making professional advice available to unit leaders to assist them in dealing with performers who are ineffective because of health or emotional problems, prolonged illness, absenteeism and substance abuse, stress, and infectious diseases.
• Identifying and removing health hazards.
• Planning for health-related emergencies.
• Maintaining confidentiality of medical records.
• Initiating plans for emergency treatment.
• Promoting good health (e.g., by way of blood banks, food services, and exercise programs).
• Developing plans for special health problems (e.g., alcoholism, drug abuse, absenteeism, contagious diseases, maternity, body odors, smoking abstention, stress management, cancer detection, hypertension screening, and diet/weight control).
• Hiring, placement, and health maintenance of people with disabilities.
• Providing a clean and aesthetically appealing work environment.
• Addressing the health education of personnel from foreign countries where health is neglected and health services are not readily available.
• Preventing exposure to hazardous materials.

•   Providing adequate health insurance (dealing effectively with such issues as rising costs, adequate coverage, selecting from available coverage options, and handling the conflicting and shifting health-care needs of personnel).
•   Helping employees promote healthy lifestyles in light of the fact that 8 of the 10 leading causes of death are largely preventable.[2]

A desirable feature of any plan for maintaining continuity of personnel service is a comprehensive physical and mental *health maintenance program.* This is a responsibility every educational institution must assume, if for no other reason than the need to ensure the welfare of the school child. The purpose of the health program for school personnel is to maintain an optimum environment for children; reduce personnel absence; secure maximum personnel performance; and place personnel in positions compatible with their physical, mental, and emotional qualifications. Basic elements of a health program for school personnel include:

•   A selection process designed to eliminate from employment those applicants with chronic health problems.
•   Placement of handicapped personnel in positions suitable to their performance level.
•   A counseling program designed to assist unit administrators in dealing with personnel who have mental or physical problems that interfere seriously with their day-to-day performance.
•   Periodic examinations to ensure the physical and emotional fitness of personnel.
•   Arrangements to care for personnel involved in accidents or medical emergencies.
•   Provisions for evaluating the physical fitness of personnel employed for or transferred to work entailing physical stress, such as transportation or gymnastics, and of personnel returning to work after extended absence owing to illness or injury.

Employer Involvement in Employee Health Maintenance

There has never been a serious challenge to the proposition that one of the school system's fundamental responsibilities is to establish and maintain plans for a healthy work force. Contemporary employer initiatives to encourage wellness and to promote healthy lifestyles have led to various forms of health-related incentives and disincentives. Underlying greater system involvement in health care maintenance is the general intent to achieve improved employee health and system medical cost containment. Examples of both health incentives and disincentives are noted below.

Health-Related Incentives

Health-related incentives represent one approach to encourage employees to improve and maintain physical fitness. These incentives include on- and off-site classes, workshops, newsletters, educational and training materials, health risk appraisals and assessments, and preventive care accounts.

Health-Related Disincentives

Disincentive plans are designed to link employee health to medical plan coverage. Certain types of health insurance plans provide less favorable coverage for high-risk individuals in the form of higher insurance contributions and higher deductibles. Risk factors include tobacco use, obesity, failure to use a seat belt, poor physical condition, high cholesterol level, chemical dependency, and alcohol abuse.

Employee Assistance Programs

Special kinds of health problems noted previously that have emerged in the latter half of the twentieth century have become so widespread that many organizations, including school systems, have taken steps to develop *employee assistance programs.* Underlying the need for such support systems is the fact that more employees than ever before are showing signs of performance dysfunction. Sources of deterioration in work performance stem from both internal and external environmental factors, such as changes in work load or work relationships, discrimination, marital adjustment, stressful superior–subordinate conditions, and various forms of substance abuse.

Organizational consequences flowing from disruptions to an employee's mental or physical functions are numerous and far-reaching. These include personal disorganization, absenteeism, tardiness, increased costs for health insurance, grievance filing, litigation, and, most important, erosion of the relationship of the school system to personnel well-being.

There are three important reasons underlying the formation of personnel support systems: (a) humanitarian considerations basic to assisting members to deal with problems affecting performance, (b) cost containment, and (c) maintenance of performance continuity and strengthening of the link between individual and system effectiveness.

With the cost of health insurance premiums rising annually, controlling health-related expenditures has become a key factor in collective bargaining. This involves focusing on reducing insurance claims while increasing the system's ability to develop a viable support system for its members.

Regardless of system size, member behavior problems of various kinds are inevitable and warrant carefully designed plans to meet the objectives of the human resource function. Employee assistance programs include these options: (a) *wellness* programs, which stress preventive health maintenance; (b) programs focusing on personnel behavior problems that stem from *work assignments* or *work relationships;* (c) programs designed to treat *personal problems* that affect member performance; and (d) any combination of these options.

The kinds and extent of programs offered depend on a variety of factors, including program objectives, system size and resources, problem prevalence, and organizational recognition of the existence of a problem and commitment to its resolution.

In general, there is a positive relationship between system size and program breadth: the larger the system, the greater the likelihood that the program services will be more extensive.

In order to design, implement, and monitor an employee assistance program properly, certain issues must be addressed. These issues are brought into focus through questions such as:

- To what extent have personnel problems been identified that warrant initiation of a support program (e.g., absenteeism, tardiness, gambling, stressful work-related conditions, personal problems affecting individual performance, and substance abuse)?
- Of the four options regarding employee assistance programs described previously, which is most suitable as a planning strategy? This issue involves enlisting employee participation in decisions concerning courses of action designed to maintain their well-being as well as that of the system.

Some of the factors considered important to the success of health-related programs include:

- *Policy*—A policy statement forms the bedrock on which to establish both wellness and assistance programs. Policy is intended to make clear program objectives; board of education commitment; the scope, nature, and extent of assistance eligibility (e.g., salaried, nonsalaried, or contingent personnel); and internal and or external provisions for referral, counseling, and treatment stipulations.
- *Procedures*—Programs that center on dysfunctional behavior require established procedures. These include such steps as problem identification, referral (system or self), diagnosis, treatment, and follow-up.
- *Sponsorship*—Costs of assistance programs remain a disturbing issue; the extent to which expenses should be borne by the employer, the union, the individual, or a combination of these must be considered. Because expenditures for all forms of benefits are reaching new heights, and because more personnel seek or are urged to seek various forms of treatment, cost considerations enter into policy and program decisions. System trends in health maintenance costs and forecasts of health risks are among the kinds of information that should become part of the system's personnel data base.
- *Education*—Educating all supervisory personnel about procedures for dealing with both wellness and assistance programs is deemed an integral component of program implementation. Program objectives, procedures, confidentiality of information, and forms of treatment and care are examples of program elements about which personnel need to be informed and educated.
- *Flexibility*—Due to the size range of school systems in the United States, both wellness and assistance programs must be modeled to fit the experiences, conditions, trends, and needs of individual systems and individuals within the systems.

Need identification is diagnosed through such sources as insurance claims, medical records, surveys, performance appraisal information, and budgetary indicators.

In sum, examination of the contemporary social scene, changing member expectations, and stressful conditions in both internal and external environments lead to the realization that wellness and assistance programs are no longer only theoretical issues. The school system's concern in this regard is how to position the organization and the human resource function so that whatever health maintenance strategies are adopted, they will result in closing performance gaps at individual, group, and organizational levels.

Service Benefits

Recent organizational trends in benefits have led to an expansion of what has been defined as employee service benefits. Three classes of service benefits include job-related services; personal services; and perquisites. Some examples are:

Cafeteria plan	Flexible work arrangements
Child care	Food service
Computer equipment	Legal insurance
Counseling	Outplacement counseling
Dental plan	Parking
Educational subsidy	Retirement counseling
Equipment purchase	Service-seniority awards
Expense account	Supplemental insurance
Extended leave	Transportation
Family leave	Travel allowance

Since the current cost of indirect (benefit) compensation amounts to nearly 40% of base pay for every employee on the payroll, benefit management needs to consider how strategic benefit plans relate to employment continuity; how benefits can be effectively structured and cost controlled; how to communicate the real costs and benefits to system personnel; and how to utilize forms, records, and computer-based systems to realize the strategic aims of personnel continuity.

Temporary Personnel

Temporary personnel, also referred to as *substitute, part-time,* or *contingent employees,* are defined in general terms by the U.S. government as those employees who work fewer than 35 hours a week. Part-time employees in school systems may be categorized as those who (a) are regularly employed on a part-time basis (e.g., cafeteria, transportation, and communications personnel and those who regularly render legal, engineering, architectural, or medical services); (b) are temporarily employed for short periods of time (e.g., clerical, substitute, and consultant services personnel); (c) are phasing out their careers by making the transition from full-time to part-time work to retirement; and (d) share a full-time position on a part-time basis (e.g., traffic, security, and teaching aides personnel).

Because of unprecedented changes taking place in all work organizations, the human resource function has been forced to reconsider strategies for recruiting, selecting, inducting, developing, and appraising persons employed less than full time. One of the roles of the human resource function is to meet the challenges posed by employment continuity. Addressing the task of obtaining, maintaining, retaining, and developing a qualified work force from a strategic standpoint demonstrates that the school system approaches the continuity objective with awareness of its emerging marketplace importance; treats it as an ongoing process rather than a periodic event; and stresses that the concept of continual staff improvement provides strategic and psychological advantages. Contemporary experience indicates that management of temporary personnel can be improved through:

• Development of a framework, as illustrated in the following example, for classifying types of temporary personnel and for allocating administrative responsibilities.

Classification of Temporary Personnel	Employment Status	
Professional instructional	Regular (part time)	Short term
Professional noninstructional	Regular (part time)	Short term
Support instructional	Regular (part time)	Short term
Support noninstructional	Regular (part time)	Short term

• Formulation of a specific plan to be followed in administering the part-time program (including absence procedures for full-time personnel) and the application of all personnel processes as they apply to replacements or substitutes.
• Written specifications for employment of part-time personnel.
• Development of plans to improve position satisfaction and assimilation of substitute teachers into the system.
• A permanent, specialized corps of replacements to meet minimum system needs, to be composed of competent personnel selected and trained to deal with special problems of substitution (a salary incentive is suggested because of the exacting nature of the assignment).
• A second group of temporary personnel to be employed seasonally when the demand for replacements cannot be filled by the permanent corps; this group should be recruited and selected on the basis of criteria for personnel able to perform in this capacity.

•   Clear definition of responsibilities for carrying out details of the replacement plan, including development, assignment, and full utilization of the permanent corps, as well as recruitment, selection, orientation, supervision, and appraisal of temporary personnel.

•   Experimentation with alternatives for replacing absent teachers either in addition to or in place of substitute teachers, the use of professional and career persons from the school community, incentive plans for teachers to save on the costs of substitute teachers by advance preparation for absences, a planned enrichment program of events to act as a replacement for teachers, use of high school honor students, and greater use of educational television and films.

•   Preparation of a handbook for temporary employees routinizing procedures to be followed and helping to define and minimize problems usually encountered when regular personnel are absent.

•   Advance planning in each building unit by the principal and regular staff regarding preparation and maintenance of plans to be used by temporary personnel (this point is important because continuity of instruction can be enhanced by clear directions).

•   Continuous appraisal of the replacement plan (records of the daily, monthly, and yearly absence rates are necessary to improve various aspects of this service, such as the predictable need for temporary personnel and effects of whatever plan is employed on the quality of instruction).

•   Differential pay scales for short- and long-term substitutes and for substitutes with different educational backgrounds.

•   Use of computer technology to facilitate the search for and selection of the best possible teacher for the assignment at hand.

The need for temporary help is not confined to professional instructional personnel; there are occasions when professional noninstructional personnel are needed to render legal, medical, architectural, engineering, and other forms of advisory or consultative services. Temporaries are needed occasionally to supplement the regular support force during work peaks, to temporarily fill a position that has been vacated while a study is made to determine whether the position should be continued, or to tentatively occupy a position being developed until such time as the position description is formally developed and written.

For a school system to manage the temporary personnel sector effectively, all aspects of designing, directing, and controlling it should be integrated into a master plan. This requires the human resource function to be upgraded so that (a) all of its processes contribute to program strategies, (b) all forms of temporary work are identified and creative ways found to attract a qualified work force, (c) alternatives are examined to determine which approaches to part-time employment will have the greatest impact on performance expectations, and (d) uncertainty is reduced regarding the manner in which every aspect of the operation will be carried out.

The increased use of temporary personnel in all types of organizations is undeniable. Their employment has proven to be a cost-effective method for filling positions through temporary, part-time, contract, and consulting assistance. Temporary help agencies, it should be noted, are capable of responding quickly to school system personnel needs, especially for support positions.

Absenteeism and Lateness

Absenteeism and lateness are directly related to steady-state staffing plans. There are various kinds of absences (such as arranged, excused, occasional, and chronic), but the focus of this discussion is on the habitual absentee, the individual who chronically stays away from work for reasons not beyond his or her control. *Lateness* may be defined as arriving for work after the designated starting time.

Reasons for absenteeism and lateness are almost as varied and fanciful as excuses given in court for traffic violations. The impact of these two conditions on the operation of the system, however, can be significant. The administrator, teacher, secretary, custodian, bus driver, or cafeteria worker who is absent or late impairs the work of the school and interferes with the daily routine of other staff members. The cost to the system is poor instruction, work delay, frustration, and high work imbalance even when absentees are not paid. It is essential to reduce to a minimum avoidable absence and lateness rates in the school system. One viewpoint considers absenteeism to be a cultural problem. To deal with it, a cultural solution is needed, one that involves changing the norms of the organization that are traceable to leadership, environment, and group expectations.

Redesign Features

Although much has been written about the problem of absenteeism and numerous ideas have been offered to resolve the dilemma, more analyses need to be made of the root causes of the absenteeism culture, how various facets of the culture interact, and how problem resolution can be linked to its major causes. Figure 9.3 presents a model based on the premise that the desire to come to work is influenced largely by two factors: *job satisfaction* and *pressure to attend.*

It is clear from a review of the literature that an absenteeism culture has significant organizational, psychological, social, and pupil learning costs. The problem goes beyond position dissatisfaction and the view that liberal benefit provisions permit system members to work whenever they choose to do so. There are basic societal, individual, and organizational forces that underlie and, indeed, contribute to high rates of absenteeism. Major innovative efforts are needed to deal with such contributing factors as weak or indefinite administrative approaches to the problem, social tolerance of absenteeism, abuse of leave benefits, low work motivation, immaturity, a stress-prone society, alcoholism and drug abuse, and lenient supervi-

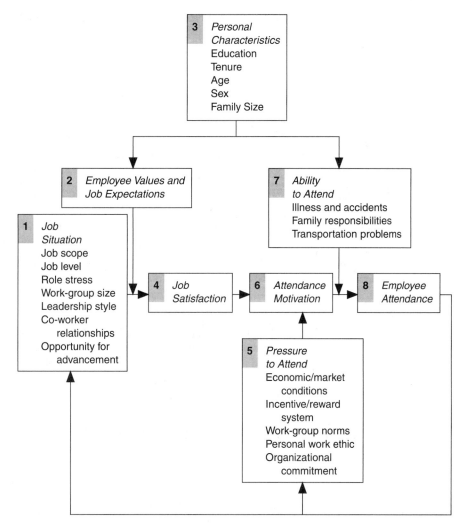

Figure 9.3   Major influences on personnel attendance.
(*Source:* Reprinted by permission of publisher, from Personnel, Nov/Dec 1980 © 1980. American
Management Association, New York. http:www.amanet.org. All rights reserved.)

sion. Redesign efforts tend to avoid piecemeal approaches and rely more heavily on
a coordinated or systems approach to achieve a lasting impact in improving individual and organizational effectiveness.

Systemic and comprehensive design efforts to improve individual productivity
and reduce absenteeism include the following:

• *Definition*—Absenteeism is defined as any failure of an employee to report for
or remain at work *as scheduled,* regardless of the reason. This excludes vacations,
holidays, jury duty, and excusable absences.[3]

- *Analysis*—Review of the prior absence record of new applicants. Employ medical services to consider medical treatment of or consultation with chronic offenders. Absenteeism relates less to illness than to dissatisfaction with work, low morale, and impossible demands by unthinking supervisors. Most absences attributed to illness are not caused by it.[4]
- *Communication*—Incorporation of rules in the personnel handbook governing absence or lateness.
- *Proactive provisions*—Creation of an attendance-oriented culture; payment for unused sick leave; creation of a sick leave bank; provision for physical examinations, exercise, and counseling programs.
- *Cost improvement*—The cost of unscheduled absence in the United States in 1997 dollars, varying from about $290 to $630 per employee per year.[5] Absenteeism behavior costing focuses on system data to be applied to developing improved solutions for employee continuity. This includes information on the extent of absenteeism, workplace sources of chronic absences, and analysis of system personnel records, medical records, and files for valuable data on absenteeism.
- *Control*—Review of collective bargaining agreements to identify sources of absence abuse due to contractual terms; review of state laws to ensure that payments for sick leave are legitimate and permissible; centralization in the personnel office of records and reports on absenteeism. The absentee rate can be determined by dividing the number of absences by the number of workdays in a given period multiplied by the number of payroll employees.[6,7]

Internal Staffing Decisions and Employment Continuity

The remainder of this chapter considers the internal staffing aspects of employment continuity. Internal staffing includes policies, practices, and procedures relating to promotion, transfer, demotion, resignation, disability, retirement, severance, and death. Figure 9.4 presents the continuing and enduring internal staffing decisions in every facet of the school organization. Personnel employment continuity, through day-by-day actions, focuses on its steady state as well as its growth; demands administrative strategies for coping with human problems in a workplace setting; and requires conscious forethought about who will do what effectively with whom, in what circumstances, in order to realize individual, work unit, and system objectives.

Promotion

Promotion is generally taken to mean an advance in status or position. Frequently, it implies a change in duties, responsibility, and compensation. It belongs to the cluster of administrative problems relating to movement of personnel into and out of the organization—recruitment, selection, placement, transfer, and separation. Pro-

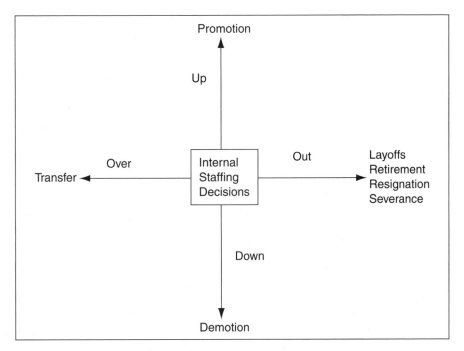

Figure 9.4 Illustration of internal staffing decisions and employment continuity.
(*Source:* Adapted from W. F. Cascio, *Managing Human Resources,* 5th ed. New York: McGraw-Hill, Inc., 1998, p. 357. Reproduced by permission of The McGraw-Hill Companies.)

motion is a significant aspect of personnel administration. The system is dependent on availability of qualified replacements at all structural levels. Opportunity for promotion is related to recruitment and retention of personnel. It is also necessary to maximize realization of the desires and interests of personnel.

Major issues involved in personnel promotion are (a) seniority or position fitness, (b) internal or external promotion, (c) formal or informal promotion, (d) past performance or future position potential, (e) promotion criteria, and (f) negative effects. Forming a school system promotion policy also involves consideration of the following:

• Because of the small size of most school systems in the United States, as well as the limited availability of positions to which members can be promoted, the potential for advancement through career paths is extremely limited.
• Until contemporary models of career development replace traditional practices, the likelihood of individuals progressing through predictable and satisfying career stages is not high.
• Competition for administrative positions, with their higher compensation, has resulted in a loss of excellent classroom teachers.
• Development or career ladders for classroom teachers are often centered on preparing for administrative positions rather than improving teaching performance or the educational program.

• Extensive encouragement of classroom personnel to prepare for administrative positions precludes maintenance of a superior teaching staff.

Throughout this text, the importance of designing and implementing a proactive human resources strategy has been stressed. One aspect of this strategy is getting the right people into the right positions. Promotion policy should be shaped to advance individuals who have the abilities, skills, attitudes, and commitment to enhance strategy. Under this arrangement, promotions are bestowed on those who not only meet but exceed performance standards. Promotion criteria help to identify people whose strengths are needed to achieve position and system aims and to place such individuals where their strengths can be fully exercised.

Promotion policy should avoid practices that place less emphasis on performance strengths and more stress on political, union, special interest, minority, ethnic, and seniority considerations. If organizational culture is performance based, the promotion decision issues (seniority, internal–external, formal–informal, and negative effects) can be dealt with more decisively.

Once the practice of fostering promotion strengths is established, administrative specifics are needed for its operation. These may be expressed in several ways. The first step is to analyze those positions to which applicants will be promoted in terms of strengths needed to fulfill position expectations. The second step is to develop profiles of persons within the system who have the potential to perform effectively in those positions. The third step is to match positions and profiles, aided by data derived from the personnel information system and related channels. Part of the assessment involves analysis of applicant–group compatibility. When such factors as loyalty, friendship, consistent agreement with official viewpoints, exhibitionism, and favoritism are excluded from promotion practices, those who have not been promoted have little basis for grievances, court suits, and charges of discrimination. Through a carefully planned career development program, officials can identify persons with promotable capabilities within the system, provide opportunities to assess such capabilities, and establish a talent bank from which to fill vacancies as they occur. Such a program tends to minimize the issues mentioned above because it complements the human resources strategy, which aims at preparing personnel for position advancement when the opportunity arises.

Transfer

Transfer, promotion, and dismissal of personnel are closely linked to one aspect of human resources planning: the need to shift position holders within the system to staff vacancies, place personnel in positions in keeping with their interests and abilities, and correct staffing errors. The term *transfer,* as used here, refers to movement of personnel from one position, office, department, or school to another. The movement is generally horizontal and may or may not involve increased responsibilities or compensation. Transfer should not be confused with *reassignment,* which means a change

TABLE 9.2
Reasons for Personnel Transfer

Transfers Initiated by the Administration (Involuntary)	Transfers Initiated by Personnel (Voluntary)
Overstaffing in certain units	Desire to work in a new school
Enrollment increase or decrease	Personal friction
Changes in the organization of instruction	Physical reasons
Unsatisfactory service	Blind alley jobs
Technological advances in maintenance and operation affecting the workload of support personnel	Monotony and stagnation
	Desire to work in schools that are not in low-income areas and that are not obsolete
Deterioration in personal relationships	Desire for advancement in status or compensation
Planned experience for future administrative service	
Efforts to identify future administrative talent	Desire to work closer to home
Gender, racial, talent, and experience balance	Contract rights to more favorable working conditions (seniority)
More appropriate placement	
Needs of the system	
Closing and opening of facilities	
Court decisions	
Staffing a new program	

in assignment within the same office, department, division, or school. In general, transfers are initiated either by the administrative staff (involuntary) or by organization personnel (voluntary) and affect both professional and support employees.

Transfer of personnel is an important aspect of school administration, one that deserves more attention from a policy standpoint than it is usually accorded. Some understanding of the extent of the transfer problem can be gained from Table 9.2. This table shows that every school system should establish personnel transfer policies and procedures. The central consideration should be the welfare of school children. A plan that places senior members of the faculty in favored schools and inexperienced teachers in difficult schools does not meet this criterion.

Although it is not the purpose of this discussion to prescribe what type of transfer plan should be established in a given district, certain important decisions need to be made in developing a course of action. These relate to questions such as the following:

• What forms of employee transfer are officially recognized in the system's transfer policy (employer initiated, employee initiated, work unit initiated, temporary, indefinite, permanent)?

• What are the conditions of transfer (seniority, promotion, demotion, compensation)?

• What criteria shall apply in evaluating employee transfer requests?

• What contractual considerations are involved in employee transfer?

• What system policies and procedures govern transfer relative to position openings?

• What arrangements exist to consider personal reasons of employees who request or refuse transfer?

- For what reasons will transfers be made? It is advisable to establish a minimum length of service that personnel must render in a general assignment before a transfer can be effective. Underlying reasons for establishing control of the transfer process are to enable the administration to appraise the performance of the individual, determine suitability of the original placement, and avoid interruptions in the instructional program.
- What are the circumstances or conditions for which transfer requests will be considered? Conditions under which transfers will be granted should be clearly defined. The plan should set forth circumstances under which the administration may initiate transfer, as well as when personnel may do so.

It is important for these conditions to be publicized in the personnel manual or through other media to minimize misunderstanding. Under the typical collective bargaining agreement, the initial assignment of personnel is the responsibility of the central administration, subject to constraints imposed by the location of vacancies after voluntary internal transfers have been made. Once initial assignment has been made, involuntary transfer of personnel is limited under many existing agreements. For example, a teacher may be reassigned satisfactorily in one situation but not in another. Without widespread understanding among administrators of the aims of the transfer plan, its chances for success are minimal.

Transfers should be encouraged whenever they are in the interest of the individual and the system. Transfer is a valuable administrative device for improving staff development and flexibility. It should be construed as a means of putting into practice the concept that administration has a continuing responsibility for matching persons and jobs.

Continuous appraisal of transfer policies and procedures should make it possible to improve the operation. It should help administration to secure information on the scope of the transfer problem, the effect of transfers, improvement of service, and those aspects of the transfer plan that are effective as well as ineffective. Appraisal of personnel performance is fundamental to the success of the transfer plan, for the information it yields is essential in making judgments and decisions about transfer problems.

Many transfer problems focus on what is referred to as the *dislocated individual,* one who has become a marginal performer because the position outgrows the person or because of other reasons, such as aging and senility, professional obsolescence, low work motivation, and rejection by peers. Several options are available to the system in dealing with the dislocated individual. These options include carefully planned trading between organizational subunits, retraining, demotion, transfer, and dismissal. If the decision is made to retain the individual in the organization, it is essential that whatever approach is adopted should be based on the objective that the individual must attain and maintain a prescribed level of performance. A plan not aggressively pursued will not alleviate problems generated by dislocated personnel.

Demotion

Demotion has been defined as a form of transfer or reassignment involving a decrease in salary, status, responsibility, privilege, and opportunity. Some demotions are beyond the control of the individual, especially in the case of staff reductions. Others have a variety of reasons, such as overqualification for the position, marginal performance, disciplinary action, or to correct an error in initial placement. Forms of demotion include lowered job status with the same or lowered salary; same status with lower compensation; being bypassed in seniority for promotion; moving the person to a less desirable job; keeping the same formal status, but with a decreased span of control; being excluded from a general salary increase; insertion of positions above the person in the hierarchy; moving to a staff position; elimination of a position and reassignment; and transfer out of the direct line for promotion.

From the standpoint of the system, one of the most important aspects of demotion is that appropriate procedures for such action are established and adhered to scrupulously. Due process violations in demoting personnel are numerous, and they occur because of failure to observe individual rights guaranteed under the First, Fifth, Sixth, and Fourteenth Amendments to the U.S. Constitution. In addition, use of legal counsel prior to action on personnel demotion is advisable, because ignorance of the law is not an accepted excuse for violating it.

Behavioral aspects of demotion are also important considerations when such action is contemplated. To many individuals, work is the most important element in their lives. To be subjected to a demotion is to most persons a rejection, a crushing blow, one that is likely to generate the severest kind of antiorganizational behavior. For long-time employees or for those who have performed faithfully and effectively, demotion may not be the appropriate action if certain responsibilities of such individuals can be shifted temporarily to other positions. Other alternatives include transfer to a less demanding position without loss of pay or status or providing incentives for early retirement. Such solutions are preferable when they can be arranged without interference with system operations and without creating role inequities that may lead to conflict.

As noted in previous chapters concerning conditions of leave, performance effectiveness, and various forms of employee benefit provisions, a precise definition of control terms that make clear the framework governing demotion is imperative from legal, moral, ethical, employee, and employer standpoints. The main reasons for demotion are considered to be *ineffectiveness* or *inefficiency*, although others have been invoked, including conflicts regarding employee behavior and performance standards, behavior reflecting poorly on the institution, individual–organizational ideological differences, employee–system differences about management conduct, layoff, and position elimination.

Whatever the reasons for demotion, the decision should be based on a clear definition of what kinds of behavioral or system circumstances may lead to demotion.

Given these definitions, the system is then in a stronger position to use demotion appropriately. In any event, an act of demotion deserves system attention to determine the underlying causal conditions and to what extent, if any, there are weaknesses in the policies and procedures that have been established to prevent such management actions as demotion.

Resolution of demotion-related problems may include these actions: (a) informing the employee of the intent to demote; (b) providing options, where feasible, such as transfer to a position of lower status, responsibility, and salary readjustment; (c) endeavoring to negotiate a settlement acceptable to both parties; (d) formalizing and informing the individual of the reasons for demotion; (e) notifying concerned parties of the official starting date; and (f) prescribing new position responsibilities.

Separation

School systems consist of people who work together to achieve a common goal. People create a viable organization, breathe life and purpose into its structure, and give it color, depth, and vibrance. Personnel processes discussed throughout this text are means by which a steady state in the number, quality, and motivation of personnel is achieved. As illustrated in Figure 9.3, one of the subprocesses of the human resource function is designed to effect a high degree of staff continuity, which requires attention to the problems of people who enter the system, those who remain, and those who, for various reasons, are separated.

To provide the reader with a perspective on personnel separation, it is useful to consider separation as either no-fault or individual fault. The discussion that follows is devoted to the termination of employment for reasons beyond the control of the individual (no-fault). Permanent separation, usually referred to as *discharge*, is generally the result of some behavioral inadequacy of or offense by the individual (individual fault). This aspect of personnel separation is examined in Chapter 10.

The following discussion focuses on the insights, practices, and problems to be considered if personnel separation is to be performed humanely, effectively, and purposefully.

Resignation

One of the most common forms of personnel separation is *resignation,* an action initiated by the individual rather than by the system. Some resignations are frequently beyond the control of the system for a variety of reasons, such as opportunities for higher compensation, illness, promotions, relocation, and maternity. Certain resignations, however, are controllable, especially those associated with poor supervisory practices and unsatisfactory working conditions. Whatever the reasons for resignations, the impact on the system is sizable in recruitment, development, and replacement costs, as well as in interruptions in the teaching-learning process. Consequently, resignations from the system, or **turnover,** call for some form of analysis. This analysis is usually referred to as *turnover analysis* (the patterns of movement of the work force into and out of the system). The turnover rate in school systems can be calculated as the ratio of separations to the total work force $\times$ 100 for a given period. Calculating turnover on the basis of accessions rather than separations focuses attention on costs. The formula is:

$$TR \text{ (turnover)} = [A \text{ (accessions)} \div F \text{ (total work force)}] \times 100$$

Related approaches include:

- Exit interviews (questionnaires sent to terminees six months after departure).
- Statistical analysis (total attrition rates, as well as rates by age, unit, and position).
- Comparison of terminees by categories (such as "those we hate to see go and will miss," "those we will not miss," and "all others").
- Analysis of those areas where there is little turnover.

Every separation from the system should involve some sort of procedure carefully adhered to for numerous reasons. In the case of resignations, the procedure involves (a) notification by the staff member of the intent to resign; (b) documentation (in the form of a letter) by the school system that the resignation is voluntary; (c) notification of persons in the system who need to know about the resignation; (d) processing of paperwork related to resignation; (e) the exit interview, results of which are analyzed by the system to determine the extent to which the causes are controllable, and what action, if any, is in order; and (f) careful record keeping for a variety of reasons, including legal challenges and unemployment compensation.

It should be noted that there is a positive side to turnover. There are occasions when personnel separations provide strategic opportunities to fill positions with new talent with desired behavioral attitudes, needed skills, motivation, and enthusiasm to enhance strategic outcomes. Some research supports the premise that there are benefits to turnover and that it might not be cost effective to reduce the level of responsible voluntary turnover. Some organizations, under certain circumstances, would benefit if the employment of disruptive and unsatisfactory employees came to an end.

Reduction in Force

Sometimes the school system needs to reduce the size of its staff. Forces generating reduction in force, both internal and external, include declining enrollment, declining revenues, increasing costs, public concern about the total costs of government programs, reduction of educational programs and services, and conflict over which government plans should receive which priorities.

Legal, administrative, educational, and human implications of reduction in force (RIF) actions are such that school systems need to give considerable attention to the systemwide planning involved in RIF programs. Table 9.3 illustrates the kinds of decisions involved in designing RIF policies and procedures. This table indicates the nature and extent of problems generated by RIF actions, to which boards of education need to respond.

One comprehensive study of work force reductions indicates that the process consists of three phases:

- *Recognition period*—The organization confronts the need to reduce its work force.
- *Actual downsizing*—The organization reviews or establishes severance policies and procedures.
- *Forward motion*—The roles of remaining employees are restructured, often with broader roles for key players.

Even though school systems often decide unilaterally what criteria will be employed in the layoff of unorganized personnel, a systematic approach for dealing

TABLE 9.3
Policy and Procedural Elements to Be Considered in Developing RIF Programs

Policy Elements

Conditions under which RIF is initiated
Forestalling and minimizing layoffs
Due process to be followed
Individual rights to be protected
Adherence to federal and state laws and union contracts
Seniority (sole factor, primary factor, secondary factor, or equal with other factors)
Notifying and consulting provision
Work sharing
Staff and program needs of system
Equity of results for pupils and teachers
Quality of programs and services protected
Fair basis of reduction (same ratio of minority-majority employees and male-female employees)

Procedural Elements

Personnel groupings and subgroupings (bases for RIF)
Service computation date
Bumping and retreating rights
Vacancies
Notification
Appeal procedure
Status during layoffs
Reinstatement procedure
Rights after reinstatement
Termination
Employment of new personnel
Future changes in policies and procedures (board and individual rights)

with layoff problems is an organizational necessity. The procedure should be designed to resolve layoff issues equitably and efficiently, regardless of the presence or absence of a union. This means that for personnel who may be affected by a layoff, the system needs to decide in advance and communicate to personnel conditions that will govern layoff (the essence of which is outlined in Table 9.3).

Disability

Physical disability of personnel over a protracted period of time is another kind of separation problem relating to personnel continuity. Major problems connected with physical disability include (a) deciding whether an individual is physically incapable of fulfilling the assignment because of illness or injury, (b) establishing the amount of time a disabled individual is to be kept on the payroll, (c) timing of replacement, and (d) provisions for lessening the financial impact of physical disability. Again, system guidelines need to be established and communicated in advance to all personnel so that indecision and inequity will not occur when disability problems arise.

When personnel suffer disabilities, handicaps, and long illnesses, numerous questions arise that should be referred to qualified professional medical personnel. Medical problems, ranging from heart disease and cancer to full and partial physical immobility, raise questions about whether an individual should return to work and under what conditions. In other cases, malingering may be suspected. Consequently, the system's responsibility in matters of incapacity involves gathering evidence, consulting with medical personnel, and assessing prospects for return of the employee and for the level of performance anticipated. Most disability problems are extremely sensitive, especially the affected employee's perception of the treatment and sympathy provided by the system. Terminal illnesses and permanent physical immobility are matters deserving careful attention, especially with regard to the timing or replacements. Collateral benefits are of financial assistance in disability cases. In addition, insurance plans for long-term disability now exist and are becoming a standard feature of collateral benefit plans.

The Americans with Disabilities Act (ADA) of 1990 was referred to earlier in this chapter in connection with leaves of absence. The range of provisions in the ADA is extensive and should be taken into consideration in administration of the human resource function. Provisions include:

- *Planning process*—Definitions, policies, and procedures for accommodating persons with disabilities.
- *Recruitment*—Discrimination in hiring.
- *Selection*—Types of tests applied, that is, preemployment medical examinations.
- *Induction*—Position placement.
- *Development*—Shaping programs to meet disability needs.
- *Appraisal*—Position standards.

- *Justice*—Complaint procedures, equal opportunity, fair treatment.
- *Continuity*—Performance effectiveness, leave provisions, transfer.
- *Information*—Legal compliance records, accommodation documentation.
- *Compensation*—Equal pay.
- *Bargaining*—Contract adherence.

In addition to the ADA, there are other protective provisions in most state laws, Title VII of the Civil Rights Act, and the Rehabilitation Act of 1973. The implications for organizational accommodation of the legal employment rights of the disabled are extensive and, as noted above, require inclusion in the several processes of the human resource function.

Career Passage: Retirement and Beyond

Retirement may be viewed as a process in passing from one life stage into another or a withdrawal from one's position or active working life. In the 1990s, there was heightened interest in the significance of retirement education as a human resource issue. Retirement planning comes within the purview of the human resource function as one of the four stages of personal and career development: *establishment, advancement, maintenance,* and *retirement.* Retirement planning is also concerned with a fifth stage, referred to here as *postretirement living.* Special needs of individuals nearing the retirement age require retirement education programs to assist employees in making the transition from work life to after-work living. This is the theme of the following discussion.

Institutional retirement programs of the twenty-first century will be different from earlier ones. The changes concerning retirement have been propelled by prospective retirees concerned about how to deal with the problems of retirement. These problems include health maintenance, financial security, what to do with retirement time, early or mandated retirement, taxation of the elderly, medical reform, where to live comfortably and securely, stability of the state retirement system, benefit adequacy, and the extent to which retired persons will be affected by political, social, and economic uncertainties.

The retirement planning framework presented in Figure 9.5 includes six components:

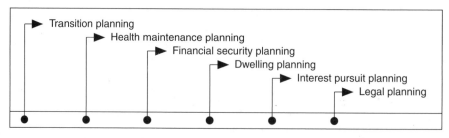

Figure 9.5   Retirement program planning components.

Organizational retirement planning includes development of flexible ways of moving out of the system people who, for a variety of reasons, are no longer capable of performing effectively or whose services are no longer needed. Consequently, the system is interested in career-change programs for its personnel from two standpoints: (a) developing better methods of helping staff members make the adjustment from a working to a nonworking or part-time employment status and (b) developing approaches that will motivate people to separate themselves from the system both for their own welfare and for the good of the system. Decision making concerning early retirement often involves consideration of the questions, Is early retirement favorable or unfavorable to the organization? To the individual?

Personnel retirement preferences vary. There are those who elect to retire early, those who opt to remain until the traditional specified age of 65, and those who choose to work until the age of 70. These choices, coupled with contemporary retirement legislation, have created various kinds of legal issues.

Managing Separation

In reviewing staffing decisions cited in Figure 9.4 (layoffs, retirement, resignation, severance), involuntary resignation merits consideration. This form of personnel **severance** is referred to variously as *termination, discharge,* and *firing.* The following discussion centers on the context in which separation from employment occurs. Personnel separation is also considered in Chapter 10.

From a management standpoint, the approach to involuntary resignation needs to be considered in terms of behavioral standards.

• External and internal standards of conduct (external example: off-duty illegal, immoral, inimical conduct). Each is considered a breach of societal mores.
• System policy standards of conduct. Employee behavior does not conform to the system's policies, rules, regulations, standards, operating procedures, practices, and ethical expectations (internal example: unauthorized distribution and use of system personnel records).
• System professional ethical standards of conduct (internal examples: a union leader incites members to engage in illegal acts; a business manager extorts money from out-of-state contractor; an employee lies about her citizenship status).
• Position performance standards of conduct (internal examples: a history of suboptimal performance; poor knowledge of and low skills in position performance; low dependability; no motivation to improve performance; position–person mismatch).
• Two categories of personnel behavior are linked to termination decisions. The first is defined as **misconduct** in the workplace—employee behavior that is disruptive, detrimental, or destructive to other individuals or the organization or a violation of organization rules. The second category includes individuals judged to be seriously deficient in performance.

_____ Administrative Responsibilities	_____ Ensurement of Termination Facts
_____ Approval (management involvement)	_____ File Disposition
_____ Attorney Review and Opinion	_____ Legal Protection (system)
_____ Collective Bargaining Agreement Review	_____ Legal Vulnerability (system)
_____ Conflict of Interest Policy	_____ Prior Notice (formal)
_____ Counseling (prior)	_____ System Policies, Rules Review
_____ Documentation (complete and accurate)	_____ Termination Records and Record Keeping
_____ Employee Rights	_____ Termination Records (protection)
_____ Ensurement of Fairness	_____ Termination Terms

Figure 9.6   _Checklist of termination activities._

- Procedures for tenured personnel (state-system regulations).
- Procedures for nontenured personnel (state-system regulations).
- Procedures for noncertificated personnel (state-system regulations).[9]

Management plans for dealing with the challenges posed by the behaviors mentioned above involve a termination checklist including items such as those outlined in Figure 9.6.

Voluntary and involuntary terminations occur in every school system. Reasons range from serious employee infractions to school system inaction and unsatisfactory personnel supervision. The school system's investment in time, treasure, and talent is lost when termination action is taken. Departure of an employee may be advantageous or disadvantageous to both parties. Every termination is somewhat of a dilemma for a school system. The likelihood of negative effects of termination, as well as retention of a loyal individual who cannot meet performance expectations, requires a choice between equally undesirable alternatives.

Death

Death of a member of the school system involves the following minimum responsibilities for the human resource function: (a) reporting responsibility, (b) representation responsibility, (c) fiscal responsibility, and (d) replacement responsibility. It is generally the responsibility of the administrator in charge of the function to notify relevant persons and organizations of termination in the case of the death of a staff member. These parties include the retirement system, the Social Security agency, the union organization, the unit administrative personnel to whom the deceased was assigned, and the unit within the system responsible for personnel payroll and benefits. The reporting responsibility also involves preparation of information, usually in the form of a memorandum to the school staff that includes whatever details are appropriate.

Contact with the deceased employee's next of kin or estate is an essential personnel activity. The assignment is usually delegated to a staff member who will represent the school system in providing whatever information, communications, or services are needed to expedite details relating to benefits, monies due, and incidental matters.

Various fiscal problems arise in connection with the termination of any staff member, including salary due, retirement, and benefits. Although all financial procedures relating to termination are usually established in advance, legal questions may arise in connection with fiscal payments, especially when no beneficiary has been designated by the deceased.

Review and Preview

This chapter has dealt with organizational provisions designed to retain personnel and foster continuity in personnel service. Analysis of the personnel continuity process indicates there are two clusters of activities: one is concerned with the health and mobility of continuing personnel; the other is focused on members who leave the system voluntarily or involuntarily.

As outlined in this chapter, the process for maintaining continuity of personnel service stresses the need for a projected course of action based on a series of decisions relating to what plans for personnel continuity are expected to achieve; types of plans needed to realize expectations; and program organization, administration, and control. Expectations or results that the system derives from plans for service continuity are both long- and short-range and include improvement of the system's ability to perform its mission; improvement of individual effectiveness; and improvement of the system's physical, psychological, and organizational environments. Models have been included to examine the employment continuity process, continuity policy, time-related benefits, absenteeism and lateness, reduction in force, and retirement. Other continuity aspects treated include employee assistance programs, health maintenance, temporary personnel, promotion, transfer, demotion, disability, and death.

The importance, design, and operation of an organizational justice system is the subject of Chapter 10.

Discussion Questions

1. There is strong support in the human resource literature for the premise that the school system's culture has a considerable impact on employment continuity. What system characteristics should be considered in making judgments about the cultural impact of the organization?

2. How can a school system reduce personnel costs? (Estimated direct and indirect costs for one person for a single day's absence average more than $150.)

3. What are the school system's expectations in return for making large outlays for indirect compensation such as health programs, disability, retirement costs, time off, staff development, and education-related expenditures?

4. How can school systems improve the quality of employment continuity?

5. What priority should a school system give to seniority-based promotions? Seniority-based pay raises?

6. What reasonable accommodation should be made for applicants or employees with disabilities?

7. What is the main reason for a school system to establish an employee assistance program?

8. Give four reasons why terminated personnel win a majority of the court cases contesting their dismissal.

Notes

1. Adapted from Anita Engleman, "Employee Benefits," in William R. Tracey, ed., *Human Resources Management and Development Handbook,* 2nd ed. (New York: American Management Association, 1994), 560.

2. P. Lombino, "An Ounce of Prevention," *CFO* (1992), 15–22.

3. Wayne F. Cascio, *Managing Human Resources,* 5th ed. (New York: McGraw-Hill, Inc., 1998), 617.

4. Louis Tagliaferri, "Cost Improvement," in Tracey, op. cit., 349.

5. Cascio, op. cit., 617.

6. Tagliaferri, op. cit., 349.

7. For a discussion of the price of neglecting school system employment continuity problems, see "What Makes a Good School," *Time* magazine Special Report, 1997, 90–91.

8. American Management Association, *Responsible Reduction in Force* (New York: The Association, 1987), 11.

9. National School Boards Association, *The School Personnel Management System,* rev. ed. (Alexandria, VA: The Association, 1996), 546.

Supplementary Reading

Andrew, Lloyd D. *Administrator's Handbook for Improving Faculty Morale.* Bloomington, IN: Phi Delta Kappa, 1985.

Flygare, Thomas J. "Mandatory Retirement Is Fading Fast: Will Tenure Be Next?" *Phi Delta Kappan* 59, 10 (June 1978), 711–712.

Friewald, J. Leo. "Tenure: Another Sacred Cow About to Bite the Dust." *Phi Delta Kappan* 59, 10 (June 1978), 711–712.

Hazard, William. "Tenure Laws in Theory and Practice." *Phi Delta Kappan* 56, 7 (March 1975), 459–462.

Lang, Theodore H. "Teacher Tenure as a Management Problem." *Phi Delta Kappan* 56, 7 (March 1975), 451–454.

Masters, Frank W. "Teacher Job Security Under Collective Bargaining Contracts." *Phi Delta Kappan* 45, 7 (March 1975), 455–458.

National Institute of Education. *The Culture of an Effective School.* Research Action Brief Number 227. Washington, DC: The Institute, 1984.

Nilsen, Alleen Pace; and Sandra Leuhrsen. "How to Keep Even Your Best Friend from

Getting Tenure." *Phi Delta Kappan* 72, 2 (October 1990), 153–154.

Prince, Julian D. *Invisible Forces: School Reform Versus School Culture.* Bloomington, IN: Phi Delta Kappa Center on Evaluation, Development, and Research, 1989.

O'Neill, James M. "Pressure to Cut Costs Puts Tenure on the Block." *Philadelphia Inquirer* (June 1998), E4.

Reeder, Linda Swift. "The Price of Mobility: A Victim Speaks Out." *Phi Delta Kappan* 67, 6 (February 1986), 459–461.

Skinner, David C.; William T. Edwards; and Gregory L. Gravlee. "Selecting Employment Practices Liability Insurance." *HRMagazine* (September 1998), 146–152.

10 *Employment Justice*

CHAPTER OBJECTIVES

Consider strategies to be used in developing and implementing an organizational justice system.
Identify essential components of an organizational justice system.
Direct attention to administrative implications of tenure privilege, academic freedom, and the justice system.

CHAPTER TERMS

Academic freedom	Justice system
Due process	Misconduct
Employee misconduct	Procedural justice
Grievance procedure	Tenure

The concept of personnel justice, as discussed here, may be introduced by the observation that in the course of making a living, people are exposed to many kinds of employment insecurities. The threat of losing one's position, status, power, and relative freedom of action or speech has always existed in all types of organizations. To counteract threats to work security, workers have invented and struggled ceaselessly to put into operation a variety of protective arrangements. The scope of modern provisions for lessening work-related anxieties of individuals employed in the field of education can be illustrated by examining protections accorded the classroom teacher: constitutional protection of the First and Fourteenth Amendments, continuing employment (tenure), postemployment financial provisions (retirement benefits), protection from arbitrary treatment (grievance procedure); position and financial safeguards in the event of illness or temporary disability; and the support of unions or teacher associations to maintain and extend ways of continuing member security within the school system. Indeed, human craving for security has become so intense that for many its attainment appeared to be an end rather than a means to peace of mind. Preoccupation with position protection in recent years has been brought into focus by emerging developments in legislation, judicial and administrative decisions, collective bargaining agreements, and arbitration awards. Although absolute protection against economic hazards and organizational tyranny is impossible, the school system is obligated to make arrangements to protect its personnel from threats that affect both their productivity and self-realization.

It has been noted that the decade from 1965 to 1975 produced the greatest advances in the area of individual public rights since the birth of the nation; at the same time, it produced the greatest threat to the economic security of public employees. Three reasons have been advanced for this ironic development:

- The severe economic turndown forced employers to take a more rigorous approach to existing personnel practices within budgetary limitations. Thus, position retention by system personnel has taken precedence over customary demands for economic improvements.
- Inefficient personnel practices have been exposed; and public and management demands for productivity, accountability, merit pay, and subcontracting have been renewed.
- Federal and state policies have been established that require removal of employment discrimination barriers and establishment of affirmative action programs that seek to change the composition of both public and private sector work forces.[1]

Another aspect of position security for teachers emerged from United States Supreme Court landmark decisions in the Roth[2] and Sindermann[3] cases. These rulings, handed down on June 29, 1972, have had positive effects on teacher rights and due process. The Court reaffirmed the First Amendment rights of teachers to free speech and association. At the same time, it held that nontenured teachers are not automatically entitled to due process on dismissal or renewal of contract unless they can show that the actions of the employer deprived them of "liberty" or "property" interest. Thus, the U.S. Constitution was incorporated into the employment contractual relationship of teachers and the public educational institutions that employ them.

Contemporary Developments

New and unprecedented developments have taken place in both the public and private sectors to protect and enhance personnel employment rights. These include government legislation (i.e., EEO laws); union contracts that underscore a bilateral approach to personnel security matters; court decisions that have affirmed the civil rights of system members in such areas as privacy, freedom of inquiry, freedom of conscience, and due process; legal challenges to the doctrine that management has the right to discharge employees arbitrarily; and the evolving concept that employment is a right to which there must be a process with respect to removal.[4]

Figure 10.1 demonstrates the expansion of legally protected employee rights and the application of principles of corrective justice as noted in the preceding list. Examination of Figure 10.1 provides a perspective on one of the most important dimensions of the human resource function: corrective justice. Although the problems identified in this figure relating to system treatment for present and future personnel are appearing at a critical period in the history of American education, their resolution has an important impact on personnel motivation, attitude, and performance outcomes. One of the most vital contributions that the human resource function can make to organizational well-being is the advisory service regarding potential legal challenges to decisions issuing from the personnel-related matters listed in Figure 10.1.

Although school organizations need personnel practices that eliminate discrimination and other forms of unfair treatment in the workplace, most of them are presently restricted because of a variety of factors, including underrating the role of the human resource function; school system size and resources; failure to effectively integrate the personnel–legal relationship; ignorance of or indifference to the economic, legal, and human implications of personnel rights violations; and weak personnel professional practice. *Few school systems are large or affluent enough to afford full-time legal or personnel specialists.* Consequently, principals, department heads, supervisors, and other administrative officials must become fully involved in the process of the human resource function, especially as they relate to employee rights. There are several lessons to be learned from the host of contemporary challenges to personnel decisions, the high cost of flouting employee rights, and the refusal to accept the emerging legal climate in which school administration must be practiced. Foremost among them are:

Types of Grievance Issues	
Academic freedom	Medical examinations
Addictive behavior	Misconduct
Age discrimination	Obesity
AIDS policy	Overtime
Appraisal, performance	Personal lifestyle
Behavioral standards	Political activism
Civil rights	Polygraph examination
Collective bargaining	Position specifications
Compensation inequities	Pregnancy
Defamation	Privacy rights
Disability Act	Problem personnel
Discharge	Record keeping
Discrimination	Reference checks
Documentation	Safety (health)
Due process	Sexual harassment
Employment-at-will	Slander
Gender discrimination	Speech, freedom of
Handbook, employee	System rights
Information disclosure	Tenure
Interviewing practices	Time off
Layoff	Workers' compensation
Management improprieties	Workplace romance

Figure 10.1   Types of grievance issues about which corrective justice has been invoked.

•   The need for a comprehensive unifying concept of personnel rights that will replace the narrow traditional approaches that rely on reactivity rather than proactivity in thought and action, which tilt toward adjudication rather than passive problem resolution.

•   The design and description of explicit, workable, and multifaceted strategies to achieve sustainable personnel safeguards. In addition to enhancing personnel security, the long-term outcome of the approaches should be minimization of expensive litigation, absenteeism, work disruption, loss of personnel commitment and loyalty, and chronic dissatisfaction with employment conditions.

•   Generating a system culture that insists on prompt resolution of inevitable day-to-day conflicts, disputes, and contractual differences; providing system members with guarantees against arbitrary and capricious supervisory decisions; and encouraging the location, reporting, analysis, and treatment of security problem sources.

One design tool in the human resources justice system is illustrated in Figure 10.2. The intent of the illustration is to convey Riverpark school system's commitment to provide an orderly method for addressing and resolving employee grievances.

The human resources justice problems and issues listed in the following are those of which the Riverpark school system is fully conscious and morally committed to address through its justice process in a manner that is right and proper. Our way of achieving balance among conflicting interests is through dispassionate application of justice fundamentals to which we are pledged to adhere. Our framework of the justice process entails:

- Conducting an annual review of all member complaints, grievances, and charges of discrimination to ascertain sources from which they originate and for remedial action when this step is in order.

- Communicating to staff members and position applicants the system's stance on fair treatment for its human resources.

- Adhering to all regulatory requirements regarding discrimination.

- Consulting with legal counsel concerning legal ramifications of provisions in the justice process and its operation.

- Providing programs for administrators and supervisors regarding the justice process and the manner in which it is implemented.

- Establishing informal justice machinery such as appointment of an ombudsperson to resolve problems before further action is invoked.

- Encouraging position holders to report actions or events considered to be in violation of system justice standards, such as infringement of the system's code of ethics.

Figure 10.2   The justice process of the Riverpark school system.

Riverpark's adoption of a formal justice system focuses on aims such as (a) providing an outlet for employee concerns, complaints, and grievances with a systematic approach to problem resolution; (b) reducing the likelihood of a legal claim; (c) taking informal action in advance of a formal grievance invocation; (d) communicating to system personnel its pledge to abide by its own policies and rules; and (e) abiding by the terms of an employment contract.[5]

Individual, Group, and Administrative Behavior

For the purpose of this discussion, behavior is considered to mean what a person says or does. In a school system, behavior refers to specific position holder actions or desired results that meet defined expectations or achieve intended outcomes. Behavioral expectations are expressed and judged in terms of standards such as performance levels, policies, procedures, rules, recruitment and selection specifications, and professional ethics. To a considerable extent, the manner in which standards are defined is conducive to judging whether or not member actions or results are appropriate or acceptable.

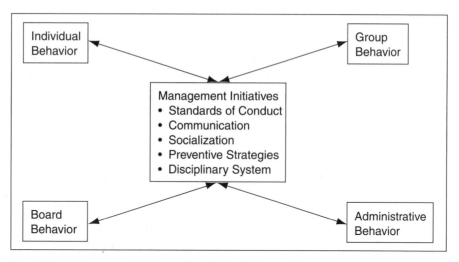

Figure 10.3   Factors involved in moral and ethical behavioral decisions.

Figure 10.3 draws attention to four forms of behavior involved in the operation of a school system—individual, group, board, and administrative. In addition, it identifies five key factors as being essential in influencing members to behave in ways that contribute to individual, group, and system effectiveness.

School Administration and Behavioral Influence

Attention is devoted to the importance of human behavior in the school organization and its relationship to school administration for a variety of reasons. It is taken for granted that the direction of a school system requires different ways of influencing member behavior in order to achieve individual, group, and administration objectives. The word *influence* is used in this connection to denote positive administrative actions in order to realize behavioral expectations. Administrative influence involves acts of generating desired effects without the apparent exertion of force or direct exercise of command. Here are some examples:

•   Setting performance standards, checking performance or conduct against standards, and taking corrective action.
•   Using positive approaches to influence personnel performance through a body of principles (sometimes called *doctrine*). This includes two-way communication, as well as using the personnel handbook to inform and explain doctrinal components such as strategic objectives, policies, purposes, practices, programs, job specifications, codes of ethics, collective bargaining agreements, and regulatory requirements.
•   Emphasizing the importance of proactive supervision to provide relevant information and guidance, relieving members of the sole responsibility for managing their positions and careers.

Employment Security and Employment Justice

Many initiatives to protect personnel from managerial abuses are rooted in the desire for employment tenure. Although the concept of employment security is a sound one and should become a fundamental component of personnel policy, when considered from an organizational viewpoint, there are several considerations regarding the concept and its implementation that should be noted. First, school systems want employment security to contribute to several objectives, among which are the inducement of qualified people to seek membership, develop creative solutions to position problems, contribute to attainment of objectives, and adhere to and enhance performance culture. Second, employment security and position security are not identical in meaning. The system cannot guarantee that certain positions will not be abolished; merged with other positions; or modified to meet changing economic, contractual, technological, and efficiency requirements. Employment security policy is based on the view that the system intends to make full employment available for position holders on the condition that they will be flexible and adaptable in order to accommodate changes that are inevitable in every position and structure. Third, employment security carries with it a quid pro quo. The system has certain behavioral expectations of its members, among which are loyalty, commitment, self-initiation of improvement in position performance, and acceptance and application of the most effective instructional technologies available. However, the history of union contracts indicates that employment security does not lead automatically to commitment to such expectations. In sum, employment security depends on the contributions individuals make to ensure its existence.

In the section that follows, a framework is presented to enable the reader to recognize salient elements involved in the justice process and to make the reader's understanding of its complexities more concrete. This area of the human resources function, it is worth noting, is one with a compelling need for reform, and one that poses challenges and presents opportunities for enhancing both individual and organizational aims.

Justice System Framework

Figure 10.4 presents a framework for viewing a human resource **justice system.** The structure is offered as a nucleus for identifying and defining elements involved in the justice process. Important points to note are that (a) the structure contains four elements that encompass virtually all aspects of position rights of system members; (b) when grouped together, the elements form the basis for an organizational justice system; (c) the structure includes both formal and informal grievances; (d) the thrust of a justice system is proactive, meaning that organizational culture focuses on identifying root causes of concerns and conflicts and resolving differences before they become formal grievances; (e) complaints or concerns extrinsic to

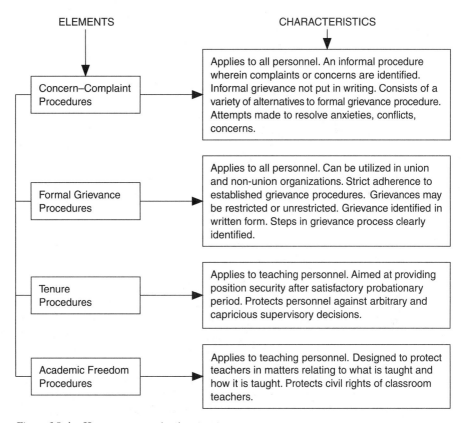

ELEMENTS   CHARACTERISTICS

Concern–Complaint Procedures

Applies to all personnel. An informal procedure wherein complaints or concerns are identified. Informal grievance not put in writing. Consists of a variety of alternatives to formal grievance procedure. Attempts made to resolve anxieties, conflicts, concerns.

Formal Grievance Procedures

Applies to all personnel. Can be utilized in union and non-union organizations. Strict adherence to established grievance procedures. Grievances may be restricted or unrestricted. Grievance identified in written form. Steps in grievance process clearly identified.

Tenure Procedures

Applies to teaching personnel. Aimed at providing position security after satisfactory probationary period. Protects personnel against arbitrary and capricious supervisory decisions.

Academic Freedom Procedures

Applies to teaching personnel. Designed to protect teachers in matters relating to what is taught and how it is taught. Protects civil rights of classroom teachers.

Figure 10.4   Human resource justice structure.

a contractual agreement are treated as though they are within the boundaries of contractual grievances; (f) the justice system encompasses all system members, although tenure and academic freedom matters involve professional personnel; and (g) concepts underlying the justice system, as well as their execution, represent a means by which to achieve personnel treatment that is right and just to all.

Nature of Concerns and Conflicts

Regardless of how well union contracts, personnel policies, codes of ethics, and personnel handbooks are written and understood by the system and its membership, complaints, concerns, and grievances will arise. The idea behind the structure depicted in Figure 10.4 is that organizational planning is basic to resolution of both trivial and serious disagreements that arise between individuals, groups, or the organization and the individual group. These differences between and among individuals, groups, and the organization are sometimes referred to as *conflicts of interest.*

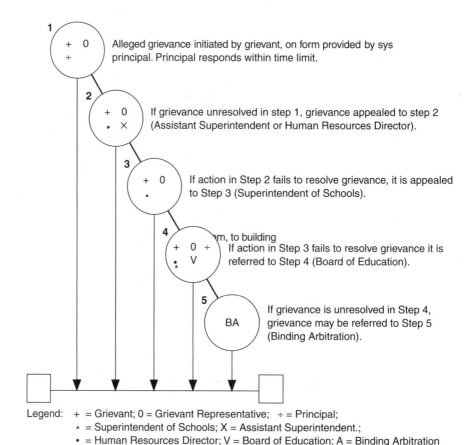

Legend: + = Grievant; 0 = Grievant Representative; ÷ = Principal;
          ▲ = Superintendent of Schools; X = Assistant Superintendent.;
          • = Human Resources Director; V = Board of Education; A = Binding Arbitration

Figure 10.5   A grievance procedure.

In Figure 10.4 there is an arbitrary division between complaints and grievances. A complaint, in the broadest sense of the term, is a concern, dissatisfaction, or conflict that is outside the area of a negotiated grievance procedure. A member of the secretarial staff may be concerned about or dissatisfied with work overload, which in his or her particular situation is not covered in the union contract. A grievance, on the other hand, as viewed in Figure 10.4, is a specified formal dissatisfaction expressed through an identified procedure (see Figure 10.5). A teacher who has been denied a leave to attend a family funeral (a denial that is in violation of the union contract) may be considered to have a grievance. Thus, a grievance in the narrow view is what the bargaining agreement construes it to be.

Identification of Complaints and Grievances

One of the important developments occurring in personnel security management, as indicated in Table 10.1, is the increase in the number of channels for identifying and dealing with complaints. The content presented in Table 10.1 relates the func-

TABLE 10.1
Internal-Informal Complaint Review Structure of a School System

Informal Situational Levels and Options	Complainant Review Options	Complainant Advisory Counseling Options	Informal Investigation Conciliation Mediation Adjudication Actions	Feedback to Executive Review Board
	A	B	C	D
Informal Situational Review: Levels and Options	Complainant Review Options	Complainant Advisory Counseling Options	Informal Investigation Conciliation Mediation Adjudication Actions	Feedback to System Executive Review Board
1 Supervisor	•	•		•
1 Human resources representative	•	•		•
1 Informal organization	•	•		•
1 Ombuds practitioner	•	•		•
1 Performance appraiser(s)	•	•		•
1 Union	•	•		•
2 Office above supervisor	•	•		•
3 Peer review panel	•	•		•
4 Panel resolution committee			•	•
5 System executive review board	•		•	

Note: Counseling with the complainant may occur on a confidential basis.

tions of a complaint system to each of the structures or procedures for dealing with personnel concerns. Some of the structures involve all functions; others have limited roles. Several of the more important channels for upward communication of personnel complaints are reviewed later.

Perhaps the most important element shown in any complaint system is the traditional **grievance procedure,** shown in Figure 10.5 as a multistep appeal system. Because of its importance in discovering and resolving serious conflicts of interest, more attention will be given to this procedure in the following section. Grievance administration comprises the greatest amount of activity in bargaining relationships and requires an understanding of how the procedure operates, channels for minimizing formal grievances, and complexities associated with their settlement.

In Table 10.1 various options are presented for identifying and settling disputes *before* they reach the formal grievance stage. One of these is *direct observation* by means of the *supervisory process* or through the *performance appraisal system.* Either approach provides the alert supervisor with clues to unusual or undesirable personnel behavior (such as chronic dissidence, protests, and emotional incidents) or information that brings to the surface perceived violations of an individual's rights. The ombuds practitioner is a person designated by the organization to receive and investigate concerns, complaints, disputes, frustrations, and feelings of unfair treatment or system injustices. Benefits that can accrue to the system from this approach are numerous, in many cases including eliminating the need for filing a formal grievance, enabling system members to talk freely and confidentially about complaints and feelings of unfairness, identifying and bringing to the surface incipient problems, and discovering inadequate personnel policies and procedures.

Other informal approaches to complaint handling include the *question* or *gripe box*, in which individual concerns are expressed anonymously. The *informal organization* or personnel network is a channel utilized on occasion to bring matters of concern to the attention of system officials. The *exit interview* has been utilized for complaint identification, especially when a member resigns because of failure to resolve a conflict of interest satisfactorily.

In addition to the structures mentioned for identifying real or alleged injustices, complaints, and trouble spots, the organization's *information system* should not be overlooked. A comprehensive information system will have records of formal grievances filed, ombuds reports, performance appraisal reviews, absenteeism and lateness, litigation against the system, resignations, transfers, union concerns about inequities or injustices, dismissals, and external complaints about system personnel policies and procedures. This information, when viewed in the aggregate, may reveal weak links in the organizational chain of components designed to prevent personnel injustice and inequity.

Informal Complaint Resolution

There are at least three alternatives to position holders for resolving conflicts, complaints, inequities, or dissatisfaction arising out of the employment relationship: (a) informal resolution, (b) grievance machinery, and (c) statutory alternatives to filing a grievance. Table 10.1 shows that informal resolution of complaints is an essential element of organizational justice and one which, when conducted properly, is generally beneficial to all concerned. Examination of Table 10.1 indicates various approaches to conflict resolution, uses of which are situational, depending upon the circumstances surrounding the complaint. In addition to alternative mechanisms for the complainant to pursue, there are opportunities to counsel with individuals or groups to solve an employment problem in the beginning steps of a complaint-grievance procedure. Complaints invoked may be due to various causes such as real or perceived pay inequity, personality clashes, discrimination, rejection of performance appraisal reports, or inattention by supervisors to violation of system employment practices and policies.

Equally important to the system is that most complaint problems are or can be resolved through informal communication. One of the key factors in complaint resolution is the skill and knowledge applied to problem resolution by those persons indicated in Table 10.1 as being charged with this responsibility. Although the use of complaint procedures will vary considerably among school districts, the benefits of informal resolution are too attractive to ignore. They include improvement of working relationships, minimization or avoidance of legal costs and personnel time loss, and those direct and indirect factors that accountants consider, such as the number of steps involved in resolving the problem, lost productivity, personnel involved, resolution time required, and salaries of those involved. Moreover, when the human stress and potential negative publicity factors are taken into consideration, informal resolution appears to have considerable advantages over the formal grievance procedure.

Grievance Machinery and Human Resources Justice

Although grievance resolution will be discussed in Chapter 11 in connection with contract administration, the subject is treated in this chapter as it relates to general provisions all systems need to enhance personnel security, regardless of stipulations in the negotiated contract for grievance arbitration.

The dictionary defines a *grievance* as a just or supposed ground of complaint. Every school system probably has its share of each. Whether a grievance is real or imagined, automatic means for addressing dissatisfactions are not yet available in every educational institution. Unless there are established procedures for recognizing and initiating action to deal with grievances, suppressed complaints may lead to poor morale and antiorganization behavior. Grievance procedures are usually contained in comprehensive agreements between boards of education and personnel representatives. Some states have teacher tenure laws that include provisions for appeal of school board decisions regarding the contract status of a permanent or tenured teacher. A review of state education collective bargaining laws by the Education Commission of the States indicates that grievances are frequently defined in state laws as complaints, by either party, related to application or interpretation of a bargained agreement.[6] Provisions in most state laws, according to the Commission's report, (a) grant public employees the right to discuss and file grievance complaints as individuals, not necessarily represented by the employee bargaining unit, and (b) allow for the inclusion of procedures, in bargained agreements, for the resolution of grievance complaints. A significant number of state laws require grievance procedures to be negotiated. Because a number of the state laws list "failure to comply with the terms of the bargained agreement" as an unfair practice, procedures for resolution of grievance complaints and unfair practices charges may be the same.

Causes of grievances are many, ranging from misunderstandings to neglect of human problems. The pattern of grievance in educational institutions differs somewhat from the patterns in the private sector. School personnel generally have greater job security than nonpublic employees. The nature of employment is different, as are the compensation structure, job classification system, objectives of the enterprise, and employer–employee relationship. Hence, grievance problems are different in educational institutions, but they do exist. Procedures for handling grievances in school systems vary widely. During the first half of the twentieth century, few school systems established formal grievance machinery of any kind for the examination and resolution of personnel complaints; most difficulties were handled by an open-door policy of the chief administrator. Unionization of public school employees, especially in the latter years of the 1960s, has done much to stimulate incorporation of formal grievance procedures into the collective bargaining process.

Purposes of the Grievance System

Generally speaking, a grievance is considered as an expression of disagreement or dissatisfaction about conditions of employment that is brought to the attention of management. The grievance process is an organizational justice system for resolving such disagreements, disputes, or conflicts. Grievance machinery serves various purposes; probably its most vital role is as a channel of communication for system personnel. Security of personnel is enhanced when they know there is a system of justice through which they can express discontent or dissatisfaction should the need arise. Moreover, the employee is assured that there will be no retaliation for taking an appeal through successive steps in the grievance process if this should be necessary. Several authorities insist that the psychological effect resulting from availability of grievance machinery to organizational personnel is more important than the degree to which it is utilized. When sincere administrative efforts are made to deal with personnel problems, the number of cases that run the line of appeal is likely to be reduced. This approach entails a willingness of administration to encourage personnel to identify sources of dissatisfaction and to enlist their judgment in remedying unsatisfactory conditions. Staff involvement in the development of appropriate procedures appears to be indispensable for dealing positively with grievances.

An equally important purpose of grievance machinery is to enable the system to identify potential sources of conflict between the individual and the organization. By examining the nature and incidence of grievances, an alert administration can correct conditions that portend conflict. If the grievance procedure brings to light problems, needs, and expectations of personnel that are not being met satisfactorily, the planning process can be employed to make necessary adjustments. The grievance system also serves as a check on arbitrary administrative action. The individual administrator is less likely to misuse authority when such behavior is subject to careful scrutiny at every level to which an appeal is carried.

The grievance procedure is an important facet of the collective bargaining process. It serves several purposes, such as providing a means whereby both parties can secure a measure of justice in administration of the agreement, clarifying terms of the contract, and identifying elements in the contract that need revision or clarification at contract renewal time. The procedure also serves as an effective channel of communication from personnel to management.

The Grievance Procedure

The anatomy of most grievance machinery is fairly simple and consists of a prescribed series of steps or line of appeals, beginning with presentation of the problem to the immediate supervisor. If the system member finds no redress at one level, he or she may take the case to consecutively higher officials in order of authority, for example, to the principal, superintendent, board of education, and finally the state education agency. There is usually a committee that acts in an advisory capacity and as a liaison between the aggrieved and the administration representative.

Figure 10.5 illustrates a grievance procedure, showing (a) the successive steps involved, (b) bilateral representation, (c) line of appeal, and (d) arbitration as a final step if actions taken in previous steps fail to resolve the grievance.

The number of grievance cases is lessened when administrators at the operating level closest to the employee are able to identify sources of discontent. Sensing an incipient problem and dealing with it promptly, tactfully, and informally often forestalls the need for complicated grievance procedures.

Foremost among the conditions necessary for dealing with staff discontent, complaints, misunderstandings, or dissatisfactions are the following:

- A policy declaration by the board of education that clearly indicates its intent toward expression and consideration of grievances (see Figure 10.6).
- Administrative procedures for implementing grievance policy. These include preparation of a personnel guide or handbook indicating what constitutes a grievance, how the grievance is presented, to whom it is presented initially, steps in the line of appeal with the routine to be followed in each step, and the time limits within which each phase of the grievance process should be completed.
- Constant assessment of conditions of employment so as to locate and deal with personnel problems.

The policy-procedural checklist shown in Figure 10.6 is intended to illustrate types of elements utilized to maintain an orderly method for addressing employment complaints and grievances.

Several approaches can be employed to reduce the number of personnel grievances. These include improvement of the total personnel process, conditions of employment, leadership styles of administrative personnel directly responsible for implementing collective bargaining contracts, and the manner in which any grievance within the system is processed.

In summary, systematization of grievance handling can help the system to minimize discontent and dissatisfaction and thus enhance personnel cooperation. Careful attention to individual grievances improves the chances that conflict will be dealt with in a positive manner and result in individual adjustment. Success in this effort will contribute to the ability of the individual school unit and the system to carry out plans.

- Has the school system established a formal policy for addressing employment complaints and grievances?
- Is there a union agreement establishing grievance machinery?
- Does the policy encourage consideration of any and all grievances?
- Do the policy and procedures provide ways of ensuring a receptive hearing for the grievant?
- What provisions are made for independent assessment of an issue not resolved to the satisfaction of either party?
- Is there a provision in the policy for discussing situations not covered in the agreement?
- Do system members in the resolution levels (Figure 10.5) have the knowledge and skills to interpret and apply resolution policies and procedures?
- Have criteria been established to determine whether the complaint or grievance is factual?
- Have criteria been established for determining whether there is a basis for the complaint?
- What procedures exist to deal with solution of potential problems before they become real problems?
- What procedures are established for presenting complaints or grievances to the system?
- Are time limits specified for filing a grievance at each level?
- Is the informal resolution stage written into both the system policy and union agreement?
- Does the system have checkpoints for reviewing answers to complaints and grievances?
- Are the system's policies and procedures for filing and handling grievances conveyed to all members on the payroll?
- What steps are taken to provide the grievant with assistance in presenting the claim in required form?
- What steps have been taken procedurally to ensure a receptive hearing for the grievant?
- Has the formal grievance process been reviewed independently for inclusion of norms and tests designed to meet courtroom standards?

Figure 10.6   Policy and procedural checklist for reviewing the grievance machinery of a school system.

Employee–Employer Conduct and Employment Justice

When we turn to the matter of human behavior in the school system, we must deal with two concrete realities. The first is that in every position in the school system there is a role expectation. The role expectation involves devotion to duty, decorum, and decency. The second reality is that organizational life is governed by an author-

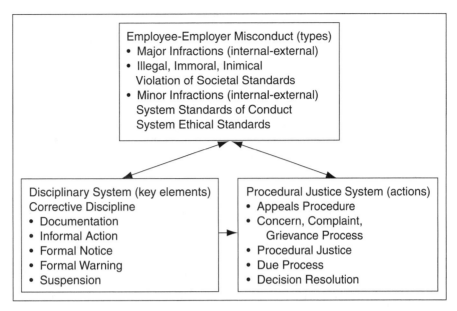

Figure 10.7   Characteristics of a personnel justice system.

ity system in either tacit, implied, or expressed form. When an individual decides to join a school system, for example, there is an implied assumption that he or she will accept the doctrinal components of the authority system (traditions, policies, rules, regulations, norms, job specifications, patterns of behavior, codes of ethics). There are occasions, however, when either the employee or the administration does not accept or consent to the bases on which authority rests. Under certain circumstances (Figure 10.7), the school system can exercise its authority to influence member behavior through the authority system.

Figure 10.7 portrays three facets of an authority system for dealing with **employee misconduct,** applicable to any member, regardless of status. These include major and minor infractions inside or outside of the school system. Key elements of the disciplinary system (Figure 10.7) include a set of stages ranging from corrective discipline to discharge. Protection of any member charged with violation of behavioral norms is managed through the procedural justice system. **Procedural justice** (due process) refers to the process of resolving fairness problems. *Justice* is a broader term used to describe the impartial adjustment of conflicting claims, merited awards, or punishment.

Throughout the twentieth century, a variety of internal and external forces have been used to effect mutual adjustment between individuals and employing organizations. These forces include regulatory actions, lawsuits, court cases, unionism, limitations on employer rights, changing environmental factors, changing membership challenges, and changing school system conditions. A review of relevant literature on organizational discipline systems in the workplace and its management indicates certain implications for school administration.[7] Among the more important are these:

- Define the school system's culture aimed at influencing and shaping member behavior. Elements include norms of behavior, codes of ethics, system policies, rules, and regulations. To these elements should be added justice and communication systems, as well as societal and professional responsibilities.
- Employ behavior-influencing strategies that are proactive and that emphasize preventive and progressive disciplinary approaches to problem resolution.
- Furnish and update member handbooks and manuals in order to communicate information and develop understanding of the disciplinary and justice systems.
- Make **due process** and procedural justice the cornerstone for dealing with complaints and grievances.
- Ensure that investigative actions relating to misconduct are carefully and fully documented, listing previous offenses and relevant administration actions. This information should be clearly presented to meet challenges such as grievances, lawsuits, unemployment compensation, severance claims, and contractual disputes.
- Take decisive action when the nature of the misconduct renders it necessary, in the judgment of school officials.
- Avoid reprisals for members invoking the grievance procedure.
- Set forth management responsibilities for enforcing disciplinary rules (who is responsible for doing what, by what process, for what reasons?).
- Provide an appeals procedure regarding disciplinary, grievance, and dismissal enforcements.
- Identify major behavioral infractions subject to summary discharge (done without delay or formality).
- Employ an attorney for on-call advice and service regarding disciplinary cases and pursuant actions. This attorney should specialize in labor law, with trial experience at all judiciary levels.

Tenure

Tenure, in the broadest sense, embodies a system designed to provide educators with continuing employment during efficient service and establishes an orderly procedure to be followed before services are terminated. Salient features of the tenure system include:

- Completion of a specified probationary period, construed to mean a temporary appointment during which time the individual is carefully supervised and appraised in terms of ability to render efficient service to the school organization.
- Automatic tenure status at the end of the probationary period to personnel who meet performance standards.
- An orderly procedure for dismissal of personnel. This includes provision for notifying the individual that his or her services are unsatisfactory, as well as a reasonable opportunity to show improvement before notification of intent to dismiss is given.

• Notification of the intent to terminate the services of the individual in the event that desired improvement in performance has not been attained. Written notice of the intent to dismiss details specific reasons for the contemplated action.
• A hearing before local school authorities that provides an opportunity for the affected staff member to defend himself or herself against the charges.
• The right to appeal an adverse decision to higher educational authorities and to the courts.

The meaning and operation of tenure laws are not always understood by some professionals or by many laypersons. Perhaps this misunderstanding has given rise to the relatively high incidence of tenure litigation, as well as to refusal of certain states to enact ironclad tenure legislation.

The following discussion considers the legal nature of tenure. In general, tenure is construed to be a privilege granted by the state rather than an obligation the state owes to the educator. The latter has no inherent right to permanent employment merely because he or she has complied with state certification requirements or served a probationary period during which satisfactory service has been rendered in the eyes of the employer. The courts generally hold that a tenure statute is not a contract between the state and the teachers affected by it, that an act of the legislature is only an expression of current legislative policy, and that the acts of one legislature do not necessarily bind future legislatures unless the intent to do so is clear.[8]

The phrase *permanent employment* is frequently the cause of many misinterpretations of tenure legislation. Customary practice is to grant permanent tenure after an individual has served a probationary period. Permanent tenure, however, does not necessarily mean that the local board of education has no authority to make changes affecting persons who have gained tenure status. It does not mean, for example, that the board, so long as its actions are not arbitrary and capricious, cannot transfer a teacher from one school to another. Tenure of employment and tenure of assignment are not necessarily synonymous. Nor does it mean that tenured teachers cannot be reassigned to different tenure positions. If the board decides to reduce the size of the staff because of declining enrollments, existence of tenure legislation does not prevent the board from taking such action. In brief, it is generally not the intent of tenure laws to prevent boards of education from making necessary changes involving tenured personnel. Permanent employment does not mean an absolute absence of change in conditions of employment. If this were so, administrators would be powerless to cope with the day-to-day personnel problems with which they are confronted.

Among the objectives most frequently cited for establishing tenure for professional educators are:

• Security of employment during satisfactory service.
• Protection of personnel against unwarranted dismissal.
• Academic freedom in the classroom.

- Permanent employment for best-qualified personnel.
- Staff stability and position satisfaction.
- Freedom outside the classroom commensurate with that of any other citizen.
- Liberty to encourage student freedom of inquiry and expression.

State activity in tenure legislation is generally defended on the basis of social benefit. The state seeks to improve the school system through the instrumentality of tenure, which is designed in part to protect the public and pupils from incompetent teaching. The state's purpose in protecting the teacher against arbitrary acts inspired by political, personal, or capricious motives is to grant the freedom required to render effective professional service. Tenure legislation is not intended to establish an occupational haven for the unqualified.

Numerous criticisms have been made of tenure laws. These include the harmful effect of the incompetent tenured teacher on the growth and development of pupils, the negative impact of the incompetent tenured teacher on total staff effectiveness, and impediments to system mission achievement created by tenure malfunction. The assault on tenure has been linked to the accountability movement, based on the hypothesis that tenure and accountability are incompatible. Critics of tenure view it as the "fool's fortress," irrevocable retention, leading to more complacency, having no contemporary relevance, and no counterpart in other professions.

The protections many teachers are now enjoying—*contractual protection* as well as *legislative protection*—appear to be in for increasing attack and probable modification. The American Association of School Administrators, noting popular as well as professional disillusionment with the consequences of teacher tenure, has advocated alternative measures to deal with tenure-related problems.[9]

Federal retirement laws may provide the final incentive to consider elimination of tenure. The unintended effect of the legislation is that lifting the retirement age will cause legislatures, school boards, and college and university governing boards to rethink their tenure policies. As courts in recent years have accorded all teachers the full protection of the First Amendment, one of the major reasons for the existence of tenure has been removed.

Tenure Law Developments

Data regarding tenure law status (1994) compiled by the Education Commission of the States indicates that:

- Forty-two states have teacher tenure or continuing contract laws.
- Six states have no tenure provisions.
- There are different rules for different cities with first-class designations.
- Some states provide continuing contracts only; there are no tenure provisions.
- Some states provide no tenure but establish continuing contracts after successful completion of a probationary contract.

• Four states have repealed tenure laws: Colorado, Massachusetts, New Mexico, and Oklahoma.

• In July 1998 New York State education officials approved a policy to abolish life-time licenses and to require 175 hours of courses every five years for new teachers.

• The tenure repeal provision of the Massachusetts Education Reform Act of 1993 has been described as a balance between the overriding interest of students not to be subjected to incompetent teachers and the significant interests of teachers in fundamental fairness.[10]

From the available data, it is becoming clear that gradual modifications are taking place in state tenure laws. Whether in the form of tenure repeal, tightening of due process requirements, or changes in other aspects of tenure privileges, steps are being taken to remove barriers to firing those individuals who cannot or will not meet performance standards.

Before conducting the last rites for the tenure system, with all of the abuses to which it has been subjected, this observation is worth making: although there is widespread discontent with tenure systems, part of the dissatisfaction arises from the assumption that tenure protects incompetents. The existence of incompetents in any organization, however, cannot be blamed totally on legislative provisions designed to protect the position security of teachers *as well as the school system.* Evidence indicates that inaction of school boards and administrators in dismissal and supervisory efforts deserves substantial blame. Tenure systems do not prevent school systems from designing effective appraisal and personnel development processes. They do not prevent the administration from taking action against incompetents. Both tenure laws and contemporary court cases reinforce the concept that teacher tenure establishes employment security within a framework of due process.

Unions, courts, governments, and school systems have gone to considerable lengths to provide for personnel security, which is one of the basic psychological needs of humankind. Tenure for educators, protection under civil service for many classes of noncertified personnel, contracts with seniority provisions, due process, and grievance systems are illustrative. Complete security for any individual, however, is an illusion. Fluctuations in the economic system, school closings and consolidations, individual health, and performance obsolescence all affect security. Without extensive opportunity for individual self-development and without better processes for staff liberation through motivation, security will become more of an illusion.

Symptoms of Tenure Malfunction

As the widespread call for educational reform in the United States has gathered impetus in recent years, one of the targets of school system change has been teacher tenure. Public and academic criticism of abuses generated by state teacher tenure laws has existed in some form throughout the latter half of the twentieth century (see Supplementary Reading). Here are some viewpoints that have been directed to the demand for tenure reform or abolition. Tenure discontent has grown in volume, in widespread disappointment with the quality of teaching in public education, and in emerging political endeavors to change the conditions under which incompetent teachers gain employment protection.

- The tenure concept—tenure and accountability are being viewed by critics as being incompatible.
- The deceptive interpretation of the concept of permanent tenure as a guarantee of effective performance.
- Teachers do not warrant both tenure and regulatory protection.
- Strategic focus—lack of official intent to employ strategic planning for recruitment, selection, and appraisal of personnel.
- Performance appraisal process—marginalization of the design and implementation of effective appraisal processes.
- Timing and feedback inconsistencies for performance appraisals.
- Appraisal plans not linked to work behavioral objectives.
- Pupil growth and development—condonement of poor teaching and its potential for affecting pupil growth and development.
- Management of tenure—inattention of school administrators to the important role of managing tenure and appraisal for maximum performance.
- School culture—system tradition and custom that defends tenure as an employment sinecure.
- Unionism—the charge that individual teacher responsibility has been replaced by organized collective dependence; the role U.S. teacher unions play in federal, state, and local politics; compulsory union dues for political purposes; union protection for teachers, right or wrong.

Termination of Service

From time to time, school districts will have reason to dismiss tenured personnel. In many cases, dismissal is not so much a reflection on the individual as it is on the recruitment, selection, placement, and appraisal processes. As almost everyone knows, there are personnel whose immoral, intemperate, or insubordinate behavior leaves the administration no choice but dismissal. Legal channels exist for accomplishing this purpose. But the individual whose regressive inefficiency becomes the cause for dismissal proceedings is another problem, especially if the incidence of such cases is excessive. Although the reasons why competent persons gradually become incompetent have not been clearly defined, there are grounds for assuming that some of the responsibility lies with the institution. Some staff members stagnate because of lack of opportunity; some become inefficient because of excessive teaching loads; some fail because of lack of proper supervision; some become embittered as a result of a lack of adequate grievance procedures; and some do not succeed in spite of their willingness. The point of concern here is that the

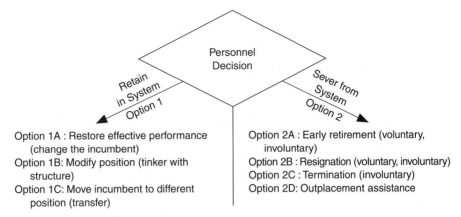

Figure 10.8   Model for a personnel retention-termination resolution.

organization must not fail in its effort to provide optimum climate and conditions of employment conducive to success. Until the organization does its utmost to match the person and the position and to create conditions requisite to success, dismissal is unjust. Termination of service should be regarded as a last resort, to be used only when all other remedies have failed.

Figure 10.8 illustrates a model for a personnel retention-termination resolution. If Option 1 is chosen as the solution, it involves at least three suboptions; if Option 2 is selected, several possibilities are available by which the decision can be implemented. Of the three possible courses of action that can be taken if a decision is made to retain the incumbent, the possibility of restoring the individual to a satisfactory level of performance cannot be overlooked.

Dismissal Procedure

The formidable array of constraints against severance of personnel makes development of and adherence to a systematic dismissal procedure an organizational obligation of high priority. Guidelines are outlined here and in Figure 10.9 to bring into focus the significance of the dismissal procedure to both the individual and the system. Examination of the model shown in Figure 10.9 indicates that it is based on these considerations:

• Implicit in every contract of service is the assumption that the individual performer will carry out contractual obligations.
• Implicit in every contract is the assumption that the system will assist the individual through supervision, facilities, and related means to perform his/her obligations.
• The system has a right and a responsibility to require that the individual effectively perform the services agreed to in the contract.
• The system has the right and responsibility to conduct its operations with maximum efficiency and effectiveness. In the event that individuals do not perform

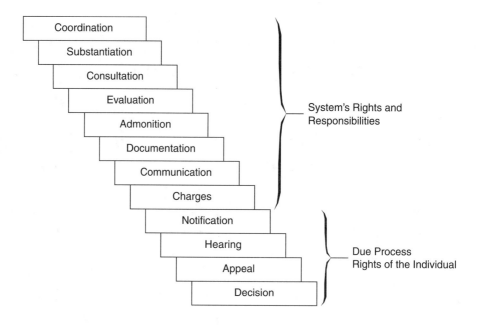

Figure 10.9   Model of the dismissal procedure.

according to expectations, the system has the responsibility to maintain and adhere to an orderly and equitable arrangement for personnel separation.

•   Protection of the rights of the individual through contractual, legal, and quasi-legal arrangements as well as through evolving social values has come to occupy a central position in any consideration of termination of the service agreement.

•   The system has the obligation to accord the individual due process in any action initiated to terminate services. **Due process,** as viewed by the United States Supreme Court in the landmark case of *Goldberg* v. *Kelly,* includes the following elements: (a) timely and adequate notice detailing the reason for the proposed termination, (b) effective opportunity to defend oneself by confronting adverse witnesses, (c) opportunity to cross-examine witnesses, (d) adequate notice before the hearing, (e) opportunity to be heard, and (f) assurance that the decision makers' conclusions will be based only on evidence presented during the hearing and that they will be impartial (*Goldberg* v. *Kelly,* 397 U.S. 254).

Academic Freedom and Employment Security

Free minds for free humans is in the tradition of the liberal democratic ideal. Accordingly, freedom of thought and expression is a crucial concern of education in a democracy and of the human resource function responsible for its attainment.

If children and youth are to be free to learn, the teacher must be free to teach. By protecting one freedom, the system seeks to ensure the other. Although data are not available to indicate the full extent of problems relating to **academic freedom** in educational institutions, there is considerable evidence that threats to the intellectual, political, and personal freedom of the teaching community do exist.

A Working Definition

The concept of academic freedom means different things to different people. To some it means absence of restraint on scholarship; to others it means the right to present conflicting and unpopular points of view in the classroom. Some would place certain limitations on academic freedom; others would not. Some maintain that academic freedom is a matter that concerns only university faculties; others hold that it refers to the liberty to inquire, to discuss, and to interpret any aspect of culture at all levels of instruction. Some believe it refers solely to teacher freedom. Increasingly, it is argued that student freedom is equally involved. Krug has suggested, for example, that the definition of intellectual freedom has two parts: (a) the right to believe what one wants on any subject and to express one's beliefs orally or graphically, publicly or privately, as one deems appropriate and (b) total and complete freedom of access to all information and ideas, regardless of the medium of communication used.[11] A statement by the American Civil Liberties Union on academic freedom reads as follows:

> Academic freedom and responsibility are here defined as the liberty and obligation to study, to investigate, to present and interpret, and to discuss facts and ideas concerning all branches and fields of learning. No limitations are implied other than those required by generally accepted standards of responsible scholarship. The right within and without institutions of learning to be free from any arbitrary limitations of investigations, expression, and discussion should be inviolate.[12]

These statements on academic freedom are buttressed by a decision of the U.S. Supreme Court, noted in Figure 10.10.

The concepts of both academic freedom and tenure are constantly undergoing redefinition. Both are interdependent and inseparable. Writings and court decisions, according to one report, "reflect oppositions to the excesses of absolute freedom and abandoned responsibility and provide a groundwork for narrowing the current broad definition of academic freedom."[13]

In the following discussion, *academic freedom* refers to the extent to which professional personnel are able to exercise intellectual independence and encourage it in the classroom. As such it is not to be considered a special kind of privilege for the educator but a condition essential to free inquiry for the student and the teacher, which is basic to freedom of learning. *Tenure* is construed to mean the right to protection against arbitrary or capricious reasons. Conditions of tenure do not carry

---

The U.S. Supreme Court on academic freedom

Our Nation is deeply committed to safeguarding academic freedom, which is of transcendent value to all of us and not merely to the teachers concerned. That freedom is therefore a special concern of the First Amendment, which does not tolerate laws that cast a pall of orthodoxy over the classroom. "The vigilant protection of constitutional freedoms is nowhere more vital than in the community of American schools" . . . The classroom is peculiarly the "marketplace of ideas." The Nation's future depends upon leaders trained through wide exposure to that robust exchange of ideas which discovers truth "out of a multitude of tongues, [rather] than through any kind of authoritative selection."

Keyishian v. Board of Regents, 385 U.S. 589 at 603 (1967)

Figure 10.10   U.S. Supreme Court decision on academic freedom.

with them the right to unbridled behavior within or outside the classroom. Tenure does not translate into sinecure or unlimited security.

It is no secret that some individuals and communities take issue with the concepts of intellectual freedom expressed in the preceding paragraphs. Efforts to ban ideas, limit information, remove textbooks, and censor libraries and school curricula are common. Examination of restraints and pressures on students, teachers, and administrators provides a wide range of illustrations. These include banning of classroom and library teaching materials, restrictions on teaching controversial issues, denying educators the right to hold public office, preventing school systems from inviting controversial guest speakers, and protests against curricula referred to as ultraliberal.

The following section presents in summary form the kinds of constructive action that can be taken by boards of education, administrators, and teachers to ensure freedom of thought and information.

Responsibilities of the Board

To an appreciable extent, establishment and maintenance of academic and personal freedom of school personnel depend on board of education leadership. This state of affairs is in keeping with the doctrine of organizational accountability, which is construed to mean the responsibility of authorities in an organization for the actions of personnel under their direction. If development and maintenance of intellectual independence in the school system are to be encouraged, the board of education must take certain steps to see that these conditions are established.

What steps can be taken by the board of education to encourage and protect the freedom essential to growth of the democratic ideal? Although the board can do many things, its first obligation is to understand clearly the purposes of education in a democratic society, for the events that take place in a classroom (the discussion, the methods, and the materials employed) must be appraised in terms of purpose.

Another step the board can take is to make clear the conduct it expects the staff to maintain within and outside the academic environment. Some of the problems that need to be resolved in doing so are suggested by the following questions: How does the board expect the staff to deal with controversial issues? Does the board feel responsible for institutionalizing the basic moral and intellectual commitments inherent in a democracy? Does the board perceive development of curriculum as a professional task? If the board is committed to this principle, does it resist pressures to eliminate certain textbooks? Does it resist attempts to change those parts of the curriculum not approved by the professional staff? Does the board support the principle that a teacher outside the classroom has no less freedom than any other citizen? Does it support freedom to express one's convictions on political, economic, and religious subjects? These and other issues call for policies by the board of education that will safeguard personnel in their responsibilities as teachers and citizens.

Responsibilities of the Administrator

The administrator has the difficult and delicate responsibility for maintaining the academic and personal freedom of the school staff. The task is to give support, meaning, and direction to principles of academic and personal freedom. This means, among other things, that the administrator:

• Understands and studies our civilization, its cultural heritage, values, and ideals; without this understanding, ability to provide democratic leadership is limited.
• Seeks diversity in employment of personnel, inasmuch as beliefs and attitudes of the teaching staff determine the extent to which free exercise of the intellect is achieved in the classroom.
• Exercises authority delegated to him or her as the system's educational leader to establish educational objectives, curricula, and methods that encourage development of intellectual independence.
• Clarifies for teachers their rights and responsibilities regarding academic freedom.
• Seeks adoption of policies that emphasize the professional prerogatives of teaching in the selection and utilization of instructional materials, as well as the right and responsibility of the school board and administrators to establish and protect curriculum standards.
• Resists attempts to limit or destroy intellectual freedom.
• Ensures that there is broad representation of pupils, parents, and staff in development and implementation of plans for academic freedom.
• Exercises leadership in promulgation of a written document or code governing teachers' rights inside and outside the classroom.
• Initiates programs to acquaint all personnel, parents, and pupils with the nature and intent of provisions for ensuring human rights.
• Interprets fully and clearly to the board, community, and school staff the role of academic freedom in ensuring the intellectual vitality of the school system.

•   Proposes for adoption by the board of education written policies and procedures for the selection and review of instructional materials utilized in the educational program.
•   Initiates a set of procedures for dealing with complaints, criticisms, and challenges relating to instructional materials.
•   Establishes a plan for keeping staff and citizens informed about the manner in which teaching and related materials are selected, the process by which challenges are dealt with, and the convening of public hearings to air viewpoints on the system's approach to the protection of freedom of thought and intellectual development.

Responsibilities of the Teacher

Two kinds of responsibility should be stressed in connection with the teacher and academic freedom. One pertains to the teacher's obligation to conduct the teaching-learning process in keeping with principles on which academic freedom rests. There is little point in establishing elaborate academic safeguards if the spirit of inquiry is not encouraged by the school staff. If controversial issues are ignored, if varying points of view are not tolerated, if the right to dissent is forbidden, if the teacher is careful not to bring up controversial topics, and if he or she evades an opinion solicited by students, where does this leave us? In certain respects, it leaves us with students who have little understanding of scientific inquiry or with citizens who are unable to make intelligent decisions because their education was conducted in an atmosphere in which the spirit of free inquiry was not encouraged.

This leads us to the difficult question of the levels at which such educational experiences are appropriate. As one author has pointed out:

> Until the learner has reached some stage of responsible maturity, not only must conduct be restrained to a larger extent than later, but the learning process must be affirmatively conditioned to secure the transmission to the newcomer of the prevailing cultural heritage. It is a delicate matter, as every parent and professional educator knows, to transmit the wisdom of the past and of the present consistently with freedom for the learner and with the attitude of devotion to basic beliefs, accompanied by tentativeness of view, that in our culture, must somehow be communicated. Yet, clearly, at an early age in the learner's course, the more certain knowledge and the relatively prevalent attitudes must be conveyed. Gradually criticism and questioning accompanied by methods of evaluation and of arriving at independent conclusions can be developed until the stage of complete freedom, testing all knowledge and all values without destroying them, is reached.[14]

This viewpoint reflects the essence of a 1989 Supreme Court decision confirming the right of schools to exercise ultimate editorial judgment over the content of school publications. In reality, adults have always exercised review and restraint over youth. The issue, it is argued, is not whether restraint should be exercised, but at what age this authority should be relinquished. Age distinctions and age-specific requirements are an essential part of our legal system in the forms of ordinances, statutes, and the U.S. Constitution. Thus, design of developmental processes whereby determination of the manner in which intellectual independence is established is one of the staff's most challenging professional responsibilities and opportunities.

Finally, there is another kind of teacher responsibility related to academic freedom: the self-discipline inextricably related to such freedom. It is the obligation to maintain those standards of personal and professional integrity in keeping with the noble purpose the teacher serves. The standards of teaching, learning, and scholarship to which he/she adheres must be conducive to attaining the aims of the educational system. This is, in essence, academic freedom's justification.

Review and Preview

Various arrangements evolved in the twentieth century to protect school personnel from internal and external threats to employment security. The scope of modern provisions for lessening work-related anxieties in educational institutions includes tenure, employment contracts, grievance procedures, due process, academic freedom, and policies for protection against arbitrary and capricious treatment.

This chapter has treated the role of employment justice as one of the human resource processes. Included in the presentation is a perspective on employment justice; individual, group, and management behavior as an aspect of the justice process; the organization's justice system; academic freedom; and the administrative implications of employment justice.

The chapter that follows considers collective bargaining as a human resource process, the gap between performance and promise in the public bargaining sector, elements of the bargaining process, and the strategic potential for improving public education through a cooperative union-system reform agenda.

Discussion Questions

1. Give two examples of situations in which informal disciplinary action is appropriate.

2. In a nonunion school system, how might problems such as the following be managed: contract disputes, performance-related incidents, progressive discipline, absenteeism, grievance procedures, due process?

3. What elements should a system checklist contain prior to initiating dismissal proceedings?

4. A voice system in school administration is construed as a number of ways in which system members or groups can communicate interests or concerns upward. Identify several voice system options.

5. What are the implications for school officials and the school staff regarding procedures governing sanctions taken against a faculty member? Types of sanction? Who initiates it? To deal with what forms of member behavior? Involvement in considering sanctions?

6. What are the positive and negative implications of numerous grievances filed annually in a school district?

Notes

1. 408 U.S.564 (1972).

2. 408 U.S.593 (1972).

3. Joseph Levesque, *The Human Resource Problem Solver's Handbook* (New York: McGraw-Hill, Inc., 1991).

4. The Equal Employment Opportunity Commission (EEOC) processes complaints of discrimination and issues written regulations to interpret regulatory antidiscrimination provisions of federal legislation.

5. Riverpark is a visionary school system designed to illustrate a justice process framework.

6. Education Commission of the States, *Cuebook: State Education Collective Bargaining Laws; Report F778–79* (Denver: The Commission, 1980), 7.

7. See the following sources for extended treatment of organization discipline systems: Wayne F. Cascio, *Managing Human Resources*, 5th ed. (New York: McGraw-Hill, Inc., 1998); William R. Tracey, *Human Resources Management and Development Handbook*, 2nd ed. (New York: American Management Association, 1994); National School Boards Association, *The School Personnel Management System*, rev. ed. (Alexandria, VA: The Association, 1996); Randall S. Schuler, *Managing Human Resources*, 6th ed. (Cincinnati: South-Western College Publishing Company, 1998).

8. William R. Hazard, "Tenure Laws in Theory and Practice," *Phi Delta Kappan* 54, 2 (October 1972), 54.

9. American Association of School Administrators, *Teacher Tenure Ain't the Problem* (Arlington, VA: The Association, 1972).

10. Education Commission of the States, *Teacher Tenure Continuing Contract Laws*, Clearing House Notes as Amended. (Denver: The Commission, 1994). Tenure trends and possibilities, published in April 1997 by the Education Commission of the States, defines types of tenure, options for change, models for change, viewpoints to address, options to consider, findings to consider, and related issues.

11. Judith F. Krug, "Intellectual Freedom and the Child," *English Journal* 61, 6 (September 1992), 805–813.

12. American Civil Liberties Union, *Academic Freedom, Academic Responsibility, and Academic Due Process in Institutions of Higher Learning* (New York: American Civil Liberties Union, 1996).

13. Allan Tucker, "Academic Freedom, Tenure, and Incompetence," *Educational Record* (Spring 1982), 22–25.

14. Ralph S. Fuchs, "Intellectual Freedom and the Educational Process," *American Association of University Professors Bulletin* 42, 3 (1956), 471–472.

Supplementary Reading

American Federation of Teachers. *The Truth About Tenure in Higher Education.* Washington, DC: The Federation, n.d.

Falcone, Paul. "The Fundamentals of Progressive Discipline." *HRMagazine* (February 1997), 90–94.

Flygare, Thomas J. "Mandatory Retirement Is Fading Fast: Will Tenure Be Next?" *Phi Delta Kappan* 59, 10 (June 1978), 711–712.

Friedman, Martha. "How Southern Illinois Broke 28 Tenured Contracts." *Phi Delta Kappan* 56, 7 (March 1987), 463–465.

Friewald, J. Leo. "Tenure: Another Sacred Cow to Bite the Dust." *Phi Delta Kappan* 61, 1 (September 1979), 50.

Hazard, William R. "Tenure Laws in Theory and Practice." *Phi Delta Kappan* 56, 7 (March 1975), 451–454.

Kessler, Robin. "Say Good-bye with Style." *HRMagazine* 43, 7 (June 1998), 171–174.

Lang, Theodore H. "Teacher Tenure as a Management Problem. *Phi Delta Kappan* 56, 5 (March 1975), 459–462.

Leonard, Bill. "Life at the EEOC." *HRMagazine* 43, 1 (January 1998), 83–91.

Levesque, Joseph D. "Discipline and Discharge: Controlling Performance and Conduct in the Workplace." In *Manual of Personnel Policies, Procedures, and Operations*, 2nd ed. Englewood Cliffs, NJ: Prentice-Hall, Inc., Chapter 29.

Lowery, Skip. "Censorship: Tactics of Defense." *Phi Delta Kappan* 79, 7 (March 1998), 546–547.

Lyncheski, John E. "Mishandling Termination Causes Legal Nightmares." *HRMagazine* 40 (May 1995), 25–30.

Masters, Frank W. "Teacher Job Security Under Collective Bargaining Contracts." *Phi Delta Kappan* 45, 7 (March 1975), 455–458.

McCarthy, Martha M. "The Law Governing Sexual Harassment in Public Schools." *Phi Delta Kappan Research Bulletin* 80 (May 1998), 15–18.

Montoya, John. "Who Should Investigate Sexual Harassment Complaints?" *HRMagazine* 43 (January 1998), 113–118.

Peck, Bryan T. "In Europe: A Europe Without Frontiers—the Prospect for Teachers." *Phi Delta Kappan* 74, 9 (May 1993), 736–739.

Reeder, Linda Swift. "The Price of Mobility: A Victim Speaks Out." *Phi Delta Kappan* 67, 6 (February 1986), 459–461.

Shaw, Margaret; Susan Mackenzie; Carol Wittenberg; and David Ross. "And Justice for All." *HRMagazine* 42 (September 1997), 131–137.

Werther, William B.; and Keith Davis. "Discipline." In *Human Resources and Personnel Management*, 4th ed. New York: McGraw-Hill, Inc., 1993, 548–550.

Zirkel, Perry A. "De Jure: A Chilling Effect on Evaluation." *Phi Delta Kappan* 71, 2 (October 1989), 164–165.

Zirkel, Perry A. "The Price of Due Process." *Phi Delta Kappan* 73, 3 (November 1991), 259–260.

11

Unionism and the Human Resource Function

CHAPTER OBJECTIVES

Sum up the historical basis and attendant developments of twentieth-century collective bargaining in public education in the United States.
Portray the importance of the human resource function in coordinating, systematizing, and administering the collective bargaining process.
Indicate why teacher unions should be a dynamic part of resolving public education problems in the twenty-first century.
Depict the elements of a model for the collective bargaining process.

CHAPTER TERMS

Arbitration	Negotiating modes
Collective bargaining	Negotiations
Collective bargaining process	Prenegotiations planning
Contract administration	Regulatory anatomy
Contract design	Scope of bargaining
Grievance procedure	Strike
Impasse	

Historical Perspective

The twentieth century has been referred to as the second great transition period in the history of humankind. This period has been identified as the time of transition from civilized to postcivilized society. The magnitude, rate, and scope of change in the affairs of humans during this era have been unprecedented. Vast changes have taken place not only in science and technology but also in social institutions, including modifications in the moral, religious, political, economic, and educational aspects of life. Educational institutions have not been excluded from this upheaval.

The first compulsory public sector **collective bargaining** law in the United States was enacted in 1959 by the Wisconsin legislature.[1] In 1962 Executive Order 10988 was issued by President John F. Kennedy, granting federal employees the right to bargain collectively. Several states enacted legislation shortly after the federal action enabling state and local public employees to organize and bargain or consult with their employers. Consequently, teacher groups began to organize extensively in protest against employment conditions. This movement has since led to widespread demands by educators for better salaries, protection from physical assault, economic and position security, freedom from paternalism, and the right to participate in decisions affecting conditions under which school personnel work. The collective bargaining movement in education is continuing to change rapidly and to bring about alterations in all types of educational institutions. Since the issuance of the 1962 federal executive order, the majority of states have enacted legislation granting public personnel the right to engage in a transactional relationship with governmental units.[2] School administrators, in response to the collective bargaining movement, have become increasingly cognizant of the need for continuing education relating to collective bargaining in the public sector in order to keep abreast of rapidly changing conditions and to learn to deal more effectively with the organizational impact of collective behavior.

This institutional revolution, considered to be one of the most significant legal developments in the twentieth century, has forced school systems to master collective bargaining procedures, just as they have learned to deal with other organizational problems imposed on them by a world in transition. School boards are rapidly gaining greater sophistication and acquiring those skills essential to cope with numerous complex issues posed by teacher unions. The initial collective bargaining movement in education found school boards and administrators generally unprepared to engage in the collective bargaining process. Some boards looked with incredulity on the use of collective behavior by teachers to define the conditions under which they worked. Further, they were stunned at the thought of having to deal with several types of unions or associations for both professional and support personnel. With the passage of time, however, there has been increasing awareness by school officials that application of collective bargaining techniques to school personnel problems requires boards and administrators to adjust to new and changing roles in order to establish conditions of employment for people under their jurisdiction.

Purpose Perspective

Collective bargaining may be defined as a process in which representatives of school personnel meet with representatives of the school system to negotiate jointly an agreement defining the terms and conditions of employment covering a specific period of time. The following summary statements are designed to identify important purposes and elements of the transactional relationship by which conflicting demands and requirements of both parties are reconciled. It is useful to review these propositions and to show their relevance to the human resource function before going on to a discussion of various steps in the conduct of the collective bargaining process.

• Members of school systems join unions for economic, psychological, political, and social reasons. The major goal of unions is to maximize opportunities and security for their membership, including a higher standard of living, financial protection, position security, employment rights, opportunity for advancement, maintenance of individual integrity, and attainment of status and respect warranted by members of any profession.

• A major objective of the administration of a school system is to operate the system effectively and efficiently in the public interest and to attain the authority and rights it needs to accomplish this purpose. Unions seek to restrict unilateral decision making by the board of education and to modify decisions so that they are in accord with the needs and desires of the membership. The school system resists moves that encroach on its prerogatives.

• The collective bargaining process in the public sector is influenced by a variety of interests that are portrayed graphically in Figure 11.1. The contract ultimately agreed to by both parties will be the result of the combined interaction of various forces, factors, and conditions. Over the years the public, courts, media, government officials, pressure groups, and students have become acutely interested in, drawn into, or attempted to influence the settlement of disputes between employees and employers in the public sector. It is also important to note that the conduct of the collective bargaining process (as indicated in Figure 11.1) influences the behavior of different interest groups, each of which brings its values to bear on the process.

• Collective bargaining goes beyond willingness of a board of education to hear from, listen to, or be consulted about conditions of employment. Collective bargaining means *codetermination* of the terms of employment, which, when mutually agreed to, bind both parties to those terms. It means the end of individual relations and the beginning of group relations between employee and employer.

• Formal acknowledgment (recognition) by a board of education of an employee organization to represent all employees of that jurisdiction (members and nonmembers) means acceptance by the board of the collective bargaining principle.

• There are differences in collective bargaining situations, the outcomes of which will be influenced by relationships between the parties involved, the social context of the bargaining situation, and issues to be negotiated.

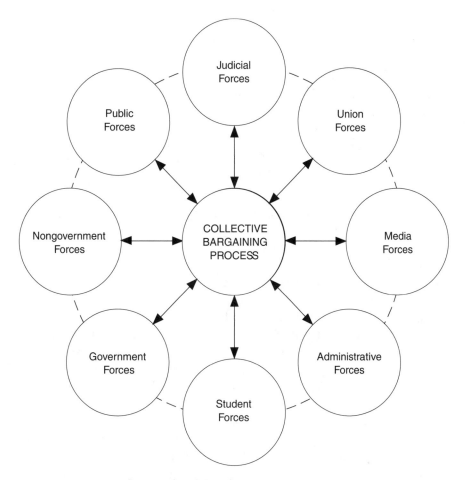

Figure 11.1   Forces influencing the collective bargaining process.

• Union behavior is likely to reflect or respond to system policies and practices. Likewise, approaches of the system to collective bargaining will determine the degree of cooperativeness of union leadership.

• The collective bargaining process involves new and emerging responsibilities for the system, modification of the administrative structure, extension of the human resource function, and different styles of leadership to deal more effectively with emerging employer–employee relationships, the new work ethic, and changing criteria for individual effectiveness in the world of work.

• Collective bargaining in the public sector gives the public employee the right to participate through a chosen representative in the determination of personnel policies and practices that affect conditions of employment. The extent of such participation and the principles and procedures governing its exercise are matters for which satisfactory solutions are yet to be reached.

• If more than one personnel association is recognized by the board of education, each of the units designates its bargaining representative separately. Large school systems, for example, may have one bargaining unit for teachers, one for maintenance personnel, and one for secretarial and clerical workers. Coalition bargaining involves a systemwide entity representing all personnel, even though they belong to separate units.

• Any negotiated agreement must be within the limits of the board's lawful authority.

• Even when the board adheres to the principles of collective bargaining, it may receive the views of individuals or other personnel groups not formally recognized as bargaining units. Agreement on the terms and conditions of employment, however, must be reached with the representatives officially designated by the recognized bargaining unit or units.

• Collective bargaining imposes restrictions on both the system and the personnel association or union. Unilateral action is prevented. The system must bargain with the official bargaining unit or units.

• The collective bargaining process, as outlined in Figure 11.2 (see p. 344), is one of several alternatives by which a contractual agreement between two parties can be negotiated. Adherence to the process obligates both parties to initiate and maintain bilateral procedures to resolve mutual organizational problems. Each grievance issuing from the contract is an extension of the collective bargaining principle through which both parties direct their efforts to establish terms and conditions of employment.

• Existence and acceptance of the collective bargaining principle by a school system does not imply abandonment of the twin objectives of organizational efficiency and effectiveness. The investment that a system makes in its human resources is considerable. The system should, therefore, focus its attention on controlling costs and maximizing the productive contribution of each of its members in exchange for the system's investment in pay, benefits, opportunities, and position-related satisfactions.

The ultimate goal of collective bargaining is to establish a sound and stable relationship between the system and its personnel. Only by participation of both parties in resolution of disagreements and by good faith on either side in yielding to reasonable demands can this end be achieved. Adherence of the board to its responsibilities to constituents is another essential ingredient of harmonious personnel relationships.

The Regulatory Anatomy of Bargaining

Public employment policy in the United States is defined by specific labor laws and enforced by administrative agencies and the courts. The nature of the external **regulatory anatomy** governing teacher union–school system employment relations, the policies by which they are shaped, the manner in which legislation is enforced, and judicial interpretations of such policy are of primary importance to the human resource function. The law must be considered by school officials in practically every personnel decision. Moreover, merging employment law into the human resource function frequently requires considerably more attention to the collective bargaining process and its derivatives than to pursuit of the organization's mission.[3]

State public sector bargaining laws, an external factor governing union–system employment relations, encompass such activities as recognition, bargaining rights, the bargaining process, impasse procedures, the right to strike, and contract administration. These features are outlined in the following text.

The term *recognition* refers to an aspect of labor law stating that collective bargaining cannot occur unless the bargaining unit is properly organized and certified. Most states having recognition provisions allow for exclusive representation.[4] Determination of an appropriate representation unit is decided by a voluntary democratic vote of eligible voters (members the union could represent if it wins unit determination) in a representation election. The range of *bargaining rights* encompasses (a) the right to submit proposals, (b) conferences with employers, and (c) full bargaining rights.[5] The *bargaining process* (which will be dealt with in a following section) consists of legal and quasi-legal arrangements that define when, where, and within what time frame bargaining takes place; composition of negotiating teams; authority of negotiating teams to reach a tentative agreement; proposal preparation; offers that can be both economic and noneconomic in nature; and strategies and tactics used in negotiating an agreement. *Impasse procedures* are those invoked when negotiations are deadlocked and the possibilities of reaching common ground for a new contract are unlikely. Mechanisms for breaking an impasse include mediation (bringing in an uninvolved third party to decide the issues), fact finding, and strikes. School personnel have the distinction of striking more frequently, losing more working days, and striking for longer periods than workers in other public sector levels (e.g., city, county, and special districts).[6] *Contract administration* refers to those activities involved in implementing the formal agreement. Disputes emanating from contract administration are resolved through grievance procedures, binding arbitration, and, on occasion, litigation.

Collective Bargaining and the Human Resource Function

As we examine the relationship of the human resource function to the collective bargaining process, it is worth remembering that negotiations result in economic decisions that have considerable significance for the system, its personnel, its clients, and the community. These decisions may have a profound effect on the extent to which aims of the function can be realized.

The human resources function should be designed to facilitate the collective bargaining process and its subprocesses. Personnel administration is concerned not only with protecting the interests of the organization so that established goals can be met but also with *taking advantage of opportunities* in the collective bargaining process to satisfy needs of individual staff members and to create a framework conducive to goal achievement.

There are at least four major functions in collective bargaining for which the personnel office is responsible for systematizing. The first is that of coordinating or facilitating the collective bargaining process, that is, organizing and administering the process so that problems can be identified, dealt with, and resolved. Included here is the coordination of central administration activities relating to bargaining goals, strategies, and tactics. An elusive but desirable state of organizational affairs is one in which the planning aspects of collective bargaining are linked to systemwide planning for human resources. If the central administration of a school system is committed to resolving human problems with which it is constantly confronted, chances for lessening union–system conflict are enhanced. The assumption that the antiunion/prosystem dichotomy is unsuitable has been challenged by many who believe that systematic planning approaches, when applied to the collective bargaining process in the same manner as they are directed to other facets of the organization, will minimize the need for personnel to seek assistance from unions to deal with dissatisfactions they experience while at work. The argument that the need for unions would diminish if the human resource function were properly planned and administered is not without substance.

The second function for which the personnel office exercises responsibility in collective bargaining is systematization of collecting, refining, storing, retrieving, and utilizing data essential to the conduct of bargaining. Without availability of current and relevant data, serious concession errors may result.

Next, the personnel office is centrally involved in administering the negotiated contract. This involvement includes keeping systematic records of experiences involved in contract implementation and processing grievances.

The collective bargaining process is closely interrelated with other processes included in the human resource function. Human resources planning (discussed previously) is a primary area of concern for collective bargaining because it establishes the future organization structure, the number of positions, the rules for promotion from within, transfers, staff curtailment, and the nature of the work to be performed. Similarly, matters pertaining to salaries, wages, and collateral benefits are of prime concern to both parties in the bargaining process. Security of and justice for professional personnel through tenure, academic freedom, retirement, termination, and protection from arbitrary treatment is another personnel process closely related to the collective bargaining process.

In attaining the goal of a competent and adaptable work force, system members are to be regarded as the school system's core constituency. If there is one defining reason for the operation of the human resource function, it is its contribution to generating strategies and practices to improve the quality of work life. This means exerting effort, through collective bargaining and other processes, to make the school environment more acceptable to those who render system service. Among the factors conducive to this end is the extension of means, through upward communication, to address direct and continuing personnel concerns; and to enhance member participation in the decision-making process in order to cope with ever-changing social, economic, organizational, political, environmental, and human conditions.

Twentieth-Century Collective Bargaining Developments in Public Education

To understand the current direction, key issues, and continuing problems in the evolution of collective bargaining in public education, it is helpful to review some of the salient developments that have occurred since the 1960s. These changes are noteworthy and include the following:

- The majority of states now permit collective bargaining for local and state government personnel, the laws for which generally follow the format of laws governing private sector bargaining.
- Membership in national organizations for educational personnel (e.g., the National Education Association and the American Federation of Teachers) has increased significantly, as have their resources and political influence.
- The negotiated agreement between school boards and teaching personnel has become commonplace.
- The growth of unionization and collective bargaining in the public sector has been accompanied by a substantial increase in strike activity.
- The collective bargaining movement in public education has resulted in legal issues that have kept legislatures, courts, school district representatives, and teacher unions constantly concerned with resolution of bargaining issues.
- The move toward administrative unionism in education has been spurred by (a) a concern that school boards are bargaining away the rights of middle-level school management, (b) fluctuating enrollments, (c) a desire of administrators for greater employment security, (d) affirmative action policies regulating promotion of administrators, and (e) economic pressures.
- Efforts have been initiated to secure a federal collective bargaining law for public employees.
- Statewide, regional, council, multilevel, and multilateral collective bargaining notions have been introduced as solutions to personnel issues in education.
- The scope of negotiations, whether the subjects are mandatory or permissive bargaining issues, continues to be controversial. Major trends in teacher agreements include provisions relating to compensation, grievance procedures, school calendar and class hours, class size, supplementary classroom personnel, evaluation of teachers, assignment of teachers, transfers, reductions in force, promotion,

in-service and professional development programs, instructional policy committees, student grading and promotion, student discipline and teacher safety, and federal programs.

•   Using a dual strategy of collective bargaining and political action, organized teachers have secured contractual gains locally and simultaneously have achieved political success at higher levels of government. Although these gains are neither total nor universal, teachers have acquired a number of noncompensation items that limit the flexibility of school management and increase the cost of public education. At the same time, collective bargaining emerged as a tool for remedying decades of low salaries and arbitrary treatment by school officials.

•   One emerging pattern immediately discernible is the continually strengthening pressure for citizen involvement in the entire public school collective bargaining process.

•   Since 1974 there has been no dramatic increase in the number of right-to-strike laws.[7]

•   The number of third-party professionals (mediators, arbitrators, or fact finders) has grown rapidly. This group has a stake in maintaining the status quo in collective bargaining.[8]

•   Collective bargaining does have a significant impact on the allocation of resources in school districts. The link between inputs and student outcomes, however, is less satisfactory.

•   By mid-1998 the two national teacher unions were sending merger signals with regard to the educational excellence movement.

•   The resulting influence of teacher unions in the United States must be regarded as substantial. Its power goes beyond union membership. Union tactics and negotiated contracts are emulated across the nation, and federal, state, county, and municipal governments are helping to shape employment relations in education.

•   Studies by Mitchell and Kerchner describe the evolution of union–school system relations in terms of three generations: from relaying teachers' views on policy to school officials to the realization that collective bargaining is a useful way to formulate educational policy. Negotiations ought to and do concern the way schools are run.[9]

Manifestations of Imperfections in Teacher Unionism

To comprehend where teacher unionism ranked in organizational popularity in the United States at the turn of the twentieth century, it is instructive to consider the emergence of a variety of negative manifestations. These forms of negativity have been expressed editorially, in public viewpoints, reform movements, threats, speeches, legislation, litigation, and actions and inactions of school and union officials.

The reader is probably aware of the fact that the avalanche of teacher union criticism emanates from a variety of sources. These include the mass media, reformers, representatives of the political spectrum, and sources from within and outside the profession, as well as from union members. In some cases, conclusions about unions are designed to fit prejudices. Moreover, union critics focus on its limitations rather than its potential generative powers for school improvement. Unions are held blameworthy for various forms of collective behavior, notably for singular overexercise of legal, political, and financial power for economic gain, protection, and enhancement of its membership. To this can be added its adversarial tactics, its failure to rid its ranks of incompetents, and its rigid adherence to industrial forms of collective behavior. Consequently, these manifestations have translated into serious unrest in many quarters, especially concerns about unions moving away from rather than toward educational reform in the public sector.

It is difficult to generalize about the future direction of teacher unionism. It is not likely that public sector unionism is headed for abolition. Personnel unions, associations, or assemblies of one kind or another, whether in unionized or nonunionized school systems, are needed to promote and improve the human resource function.

A Perspective on Collective Bargaining in an Evolving Environment

Now that we have been witness in the United States to four decades of public sector bargaining, let's consider its impact on public education. The general purpose of collective bargaining is to accommodate the needs of both management and employees. Despite the limitations, abuses, and challenges in instituting and adhering to cooperative relationships between school management and unions, collective bargaining in some form has become fairly well established in the public workplace.

We begin our consideration of the current state of collective bargaining in public education by presenting several viewpoints regarding the less than effective performance of unions in improving underperforming schools, upgrading professional skills, and leading the charge to raise pupil achievement to higher levels. We then outline, in light of the sweeping changes taking place in both the internal and external environments in which school systems operate, features important for realizing common interests through a strategic approach to bargaining. Allegations and assertions regarding the social and educational consequences of contemporary union practices have raised various concerns about the weakening confidence in teacher unions as standard bearers for public school reform. Here are several expressions of concern:

Education Renewal Concern

The importance of renewing teacher unionism has been expressed by the president of the National Education Association in a 1997 speech entitled "Reinventing Teacher Unions for a New Era":

Today, however, it is clear to me—and to a critical mass of teachers across America—that while this narrow, traditional agenda remains important, it is utterly inadequate to the needs of the future. It will not serve our members' interests in greater professionalism. It will not serve the public's interest in better quality public schools. And it will not serve the interests of America's children, the children we teach, the children who motivated us to go into teaching in the first place. And this latter interest must be decisive. After all, America's public schools do not exist for teachers and other employees. They do not exist to provide us with jobs and salaries. Schools exist for the children—to give students the very best, beginning with a quality teacher in every classroom.[10]

Ambivalence Concern

In an article published by the *New Republic,* Peter Schrag has expressed concern about union ambivalence:

> But teacher unionism has always been an uncomfortable fit, producing no end of ambivalence among the rank and file, particularly among the members of the older and sometimes sclerotic NEA. Are teachers just another collection of blue-collar working stiffs, like steel workers or auto workers, or coal miners? Or are they professionals whose responsibilities transcend the limits of negotiated hours, working conditions, and seniority rules? That is, are they not properly subject to collective bargaining, rigid salary structures, grievance procedures, and so on?
>
> And, if they insist on the prerogatives and status of professionals, can they also behave like assembly line unionists—hitting the bricks and trying to shut down the enterprise, even as they claim to have only the children's interests at heart?[11]

Political Concern

Membership money is used for political purposes rather than for bargaining purposes. Also, the National Education Association has a tax-free status despite the reality of its current political and lobbyist focus.

Legal Concern

Bargaining violates the constitutional rights of system members. Laws do not force either side to settle their differences. Public sector bargaining is inconsistent with democratic government. Binding arbitration inhibits the right of public agencies to make policy decisions.

Educational Outcome Concern

As teachers' salaries increase, as lifetime tenure for teachers remains in place, and as protective teacher legislation is enforced, the poor quality of education and the lack of quality teaching become unacceptable.

Economic Concern

The public costs of teacher unionism are skyrocketing. Monetary costs are borne not only by union members and taxpayers, but also by state monitoring of collective bargaining activities. Moreover, there are time, treasure, and talent costs related to contract administration, grievance procedures, legal advice, litigation, and legislative pursuits.

School Board Concern

There is a strong belief that school boards have been less than effective in two areas of collective bargaining: (a) utilizing the bargaining process to achieve current as well as long-term strategic system objectives and (b) application of the board's legal powers to bargain on the basis of realizing the ends for which school systems are created and supported. Use of power in negotiations does not exclude specific demands, persuasion, and convincing the union that the school system is, first and foremost, in the public rather than in the private or corporate domain. The public interest, and those of the pupils who attend public schools, remain the union's imperative obligation. It is essential for the union to realize the importance of school system quality to be attained and retained in a changing society.

Improving the Collective Bargaining Process

The future role of teacher unions is generating a great deal of discussion and speculation in society. Most likely there will be varying responses to two questions: What should teacher unions do to improve their image? and What should school systems do to improve the collective bargaining process?

For school systems to be successful in the emerging environment, it is clear that they must be managed more systematically, more scientifically, and more strategically. Whether school employees decide to be unionized, decertified, nonunionized, or to operate under a psychological contract (an unwritten understanding between the system and its employees about mutual expectations), a relationship in some form between both parties is essential and inevitable to satisfy mutual expectations.

Whatever form of model or instrumentality is employed to bargain collectively, human resource considerations must be integrated within the framework of organizational decision making.

On the assumption that every school system will use some method to determine the conditions of work, the process will be facilitated to the extent that:

• The core consideration in the bargaining process becomes the school system's mission, and its derivative purpose, goals, and objectives are to be treated as paramount. The primary purpose of schools is to educate children effectively.
• The board of education initiates managerial decisions in the interest of the school system.
• Making bilateral determination work is a matter of public interest.
• Responsibility for developing the climate for bilateral determination of bargaining issues through acceptance of the free enterprise system is a top management priority. Development of confidence and respect in bargaining to promote mutual gains is an important aspect of climate setting.

• The school system's culture—its values and beliefs about its human resources—is linked to the collective bargaining process. Values are about behavioral ethics the system intends to adhere to in carrying out its mission. Beliefs are convictions about what work is to be done, how it is to be done, and the attitude personnel associate with their employment responsibilities.

• Employment decisions are related to cultural values that are transmitted in decision making in each of the human resource processes.

The Collective Bargaining Process

The text that follows considers the actual steps in the **collective bargaining process** by which the board of education and the authorized negotiating unit move from prenegotiation activities to a collective agreement. The framework in which the content of this section is presented is based on a model of the collective bargaining process illustrated in Figure 11.2. This model conceives the bargaining process as embodying three phases: *prenegotiations, negotiations,* and *postnegotiations.* Although the discussion that follows focuses on the various facets of prenegotiations preparation (Phase 1), reference will be made to the interrelationship of each phase to the entire bargaining process.

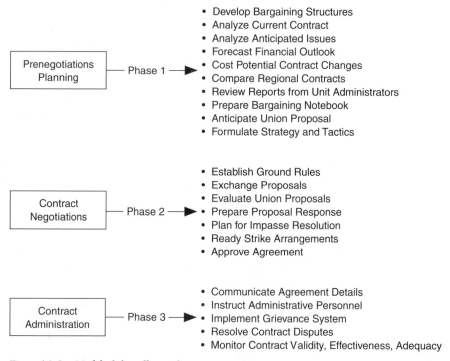

Figure 11.2   Model of the collective bargaining process.

The terms *collective bargaining* and *collective negotiations* are employed interchangeably in the literature. The term *bargaining,* as used here, refers to the *total bargaining process,* one phase of which is *negotiations.* At-the-table activities, as well as those directly relevant to them, are viewed as *negotiations.*

Prenegotiations Planning

Prenegotiations planning (Phase 1 in Figure 11.2) is a continuous activity. It begins with the signing of an agreement in anticipation of the next negotiation. One of the major reasons for the now generally recognized need for greater planning time is the complexity and number of issues to be negotiated. Although *economic issues* (such as salaries, wages, retirement, leaves of absence, group insurance, extra pay for extra work, and compensation incentives) usually constitute the core of agreement discussions, *noneconomic issues* (such as organizational justice, performance appraisal, nonteaching functions, and class size) have become equally important in the teaching profession. Moreover, the range of collateral benefits available to system personnel has increased substantially in recent years. The list of benefits provided for school personnel promises to multiply as the number and amount of benefits increase in the private sector of the economy. Finally, many recent social issues related to education now require resolution at the negotiations table, especially those involving civil rights. Integration, decentralization, transfer of teachers to inner-city schools, and community control of local school attendance units are illustrative agenda items. Accordingly, the need for sophistication at the negotiations table, based on extensive and careful preparation, is no longer debatable for boards of education; time is needed to gather facts, relate them to issues, decide strategy, and complete budget planning after contract settlement.

Ten Prior Planning Premises

Planning premises are advanced here to stress the importance of developing a system of plans and a planning process that will (a) strengthen the relationship between collective bargaining and student learning and (b) lead to an organization planning culture that methodically pulls together all of the strands of collective bargaining, which when entwined lend substance to system purposes, direction, and future generation of effective educational programs and services (see Table 11.1). Planning premises include:

- *Premise 1*—The organization's information system should be designed to facilitate effective strategic planning for collective bargaining (see Table 11.1).
- *Premise 2*—Political, governmental, technological, economic, and legal factors that affect the administration of modern educational organizations are rather complex and not readily resolved by simple, short-range plans (see Figure 11.2).
- *Premise 3*—The collective bargaining process encompasses a group of activities with considerable potential for exploring the broad range of opportunities and

TABLE 11.1
Outline of Information Related to Prenegotiations Planning

Illustrative Questions for Fashioning Bargaining Strategy	Bargaining Information Subsystems	Illustrative Information Sources
What is our current school productivity situation?	Pupil, teacher, work group, and organization productivity subsystems.	Local, state, and federal achievement data (pupil, teacher, work group, and system).
How effective are our current plans and programs for student learning?	Program evaluation subsystem.	Accrediting association reports, state agency reports, and evaluations of programs and services by central administration and work units.
How effective has the current union–system agreement been in achieving strategic aims for pupils and staff?	Contract assessment subsystem.	Policy committee appraisals, reports of chief executive and staff, and system intelligence sources such as media, union, staff mediators, and arbitrators.
What strengths and limitations exist in the current contract?	Contract assessment subsystem.	Evaluations by union and system regarding actual versus desired outcomes.
What changes should we anticipate in our internal situation? Our external situation?	Internal assessment subsystem. External assessment subsystem.	Community responses to contractual efficacy.
What major issues can we anticipate in the forthcoming negotiations?	Contract assessment subsystem.	Prenegotiation issue exchanges between union and system.
What do we want our future situation to be?	Strategic planning subsystem.	Strategic plans approved by the board of education.
What internal and external constraints may affect achieving the future we desire?	Internal and external subsystems.	Financial, demographic, political, economic, legal, and technological data having a bearing on system change.
What actions should we take to achieve the future we desire?	Strategic planning subsystem.	Strategic decisions approved by the board of education.
How shall we program the actions necessary to implement our plans?	Strategic planning subsystem.	Plans allocating responsibilities for implementing strategic decisions.

strategies in contriving to move the system from where it is to where it ought to be (see Figure 11.2).

•   *Premise 4*—A collective bargaining planning structure is an effective mechanism for implementing the strategic aims of the system (see Figure 11.2).

•   *Premise 5*—One of the objectives of prenegotiations planning is to generate plans for (a) development of new programs and services, (b) improvement of existing programs and services, and (c) divestment of nonproductive programs and services.

•   *Premise 6*—A collective bargaining policy, as illustrated in Figure 11.3, serves as a guide to thinking, discretionary action, and decision making, and provides a common premise for action and policy implementation.

•   *Premise 7*—The organizational right to engage in public bargaining is a long-standing public policy in the United States.[12]

Riverpark School System's Strategic Aims and the Collective Bargaining Process

Planning aspects of the collective bargaining process in the Riverpark School System focus on achieving strategic aims through three phases: (a) prenegotiations planning; (b) contract negotiations; and (c) contract administration. Action in each of these phases is brought to bear on these concerns:

- In the prenegotiations stage, designing a contract aimed at operating the system effectively and efficiently in the public interest and exercising authority to accomplish these aims.

- Establishing as a basis for negotiations the point of view that the strategic aims for the system as a whole, and for the human resource function in particular, can and should be furthered through the process.

- Taking the position that any negotiated contract places improvement of educational quality for every school attendee as an organization imperative.

- Stressing the premise that a negotiated contract represents an exchange in which the system creates conditions for adequate compensation, fairness, justice, opportunities for career development, and life satisfaction. System members, as partners in the exchange, are assumed to meet performance criteria; adhere to the system's code of ethics and loyalty expectations; contribute to resolution of disrupter problems noted below; and commit to realization of individual, group, and organization goals.

- Providing system members with employment rights such as position information, performance obligations, and supervisor quality; performance assistance, opportunities for career development, and upward mobility; performance recognition; and involvement in the system planning process.

- Employing negotiations to relieve conditions conducive to organization disrupters such as grievances, law suits, strikes, theft, turnover, absenteeism, abuse of benefit provisions, poor morale, alcoholism, drug abuse, and antiorganization behavior.

- Structuring the bargaining process to enhance strategic aims, including a negotiating team, good faith bargaining, resolving contract disputes, maintenance of a negotiations manual, and continuous monitoring of contract outcomes in relation to established objectives.

Figure 11.3   Illustration of a policy statement of intent regarding the conduct of collective bargaining.

- *Premise 8*—Responsible players in collective negotiations include three parties—employees, employer, and government. Each engages in protecting and promoting its fundamental objectives.[13]
- *Premise 9*—Gaining a thorough knowledge of the board's statutory powers and duties, and of laws and regulations that apply to bargaining, is an indispensible obligation of the board.[14]
- *Premise 10*—(a) Employing a qualified, experienced, external labor negotiator (exclude board or system members from the bargaining table); (b) limiting

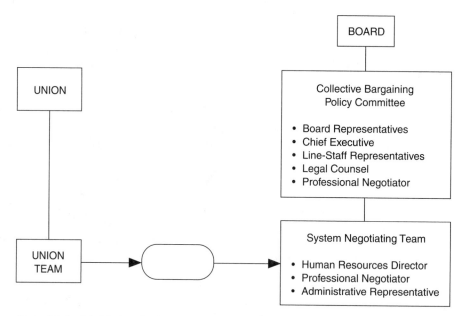

Figure 11.4   Model of a school system organization for negotiations.

negotiations to economic issues, grievances, and bargaining procedures; (c) being aware and wary of the bargaining term *working conditions* until its meaning is clear to both parties; (d) insisting on retaining the rights of the board as determined by governmental authority; (e) bargaining in good faith; (f) using win-win negotiations (side-by-side rather than side-against-side bargaining); and (h) bearing in mind that the board has no right to abrogate its legal authority are essential.[15]

Organization for Negotiations

In the preceding section we explored the planning aspects of collective bargaining. Illustrated were activities that relate to the specification of the belief system that governs **negotiations,** as well as the assembly, summary, and organization of information needed by the policy committee and the negotiating team. At the time the fact-gathering process is initiated, a concurrent decision is also needed to determine what agents will represent the system in negotiating with the teachers' association or, perhaps, the union representing custodial and clerical personnel.

Before representatives of both parties sit down at the negotiations table, it is essential that the system organize activities relating to collective bargaining, that is, that it decide what work is to be done, what mechanisms are needed to perform the work, and what the rules will be for individuals delegated to do the work. As outlined in Figure 11.4, one conceptual approach to a collective bargaining organization consists of two mechanisms: a planning committee and a negotiations team. The functions of each group will be examined in turn.

The Planning Committee

One approach to resolving the number and complexity of modern collective bargaining issues is a central committee that develops recommendations for consideration by the board of education. A major function of this group is to advise the board on systemwide personnel policies related to collective bargaining, such as compensation, security, promotion, transfer, and other conditions of work. A second function is to advise the board with respect to strategies and tactics that should be adhered to in collective negotiations sessions. Related tasks might include reviewing current agreements and proposing modifications, rendering advice and service on the formulation of system proposals, estimating the consequences of either system or union proposals, studying the long-term effects of agreements, and preparing background studies on various aspects of agreements or proposals.

The same logic should be employed in evaluating proposals made by personnel groups to the system. The system is interested in judging proposals on the merits of their contribution to the strategic aims of the total operation. The collective bargaining *planning committee* is one mechanism for strategic planning. It can recommend what proposals the system should make, identify and analyze proposals unions are likely to make, and suggest alternatives to both union and system suggestions.

Strategic plans will be affected by a variety of factors, including resources of the school system and attitudes of groups who influence plans (unions, boards of education, communities, and administrative personnel). There are many types of strategies a system can adopt, such as rigid resistance to negotiations, defensive negotiation, avoiding decisive commitments, and, finally, affirmative negotiations. The last strategy, that of keeping in advance of the other party, means that the best strategy for dealing with personnel groups in education is to view collective bargaining as a mechanism by which constructive steps can be taken to achieve for people working in the system those arrangements needed to integrate the individual and the organization and to achieve simultaneous satisfaction of both individual and institutional needs. The strategic plan in negotiations really boils down to how the system intends to treat the human resources in its employ. If properly planned, it can be advantageous to everyone.

Modes of Negotiating Behavior

The **negotiating modes** used in collective bargaining are the particular actions taken by either party to achieve strategic objectives. Some actions are taken prior to negotiations; most are taken at the bargaining table. Modes are the means by which policy goals are translated into attainable objectives on which the school system seeks to secure agreement with personnel groups.

The manner in which each of the three common negotiating modes—competitive, collaborative, and subordinative—is employed in system–union negotiations depends upon situational factors at the outset of Phase 1 (Figure 11.2). Comparison of the three modes leads to several observations about negotiations behavior. Collaborative (win-win) negotiations are based on the premise that through creative problem solving, both sides are satisfied and therefore winners. The competitive mode (win-lose) perpetuates the adversarial relationship. The subordinative mode leads one party to subordinate itself to the other's position.[16]

The planning committee may include representatives from the board of education, the chief executive, line and staff administrative personnel (such as principals, supervisors, and assistant superintendents), legal counsel, and professional negotiators or other consultants. No single model can be suggested for the planning committee. As a generalization, however, it should be noted that the board of education, the immediate superintendency team, and administrative extensions of the superintendency should have representation.

The Negotiating Team

Much attention has been devoted in the literature to the issue of who will represent the board of education at the negotiations table. Both theory and practice suggest that the conduct of negotiations has many ramifications and requires a combination of individuals with a variety of skills to resolve what often becomes a series of complex problems. Consequently, the model in Figure 11.4 indicates that a team rather than an individual should represent the system, even though responsibility for actual negotiations may be delegated to a single individual (the prime negotiator). The reasoning justifying such a position is that there are few individuals who can fully meet the following requirements:

- Understand the operation of the system in all its ramifications.
- Possess the knowledge to conduct negotiations within the established legal structure.
- Understand the needs of personnel groups and the ability of the system to satisfy those needs.
- Discern trends in personnel policies and procedures.
- Possess the ability to retain the confidence of the system and to make decisions in its behalf.

If the system chooses to have a team similar to the model shown in Figure 11.2, one of the consequences might be that the board of education must delegate considerable authority to the negotiating team. Negotiators for the system need authority to negotiate concessions at the propitious time, without requesting board permission. Further, round-the-clock negotiations are such that a board cannot be convened readily for review of every single item that arises. An illustration of bargaining responsibilities is shown in Table 11.2.

TABLE 11.2
Responsibility Matrix for Collective Bargaining Process for the Foxcroft School District

Collective Bargaining Process Time Structure

Responsibility	Phase 1 Prenegotiations Period —to—	Phase 2 Negotiations Period —to—	Phase 3 Postnegotiations Period —to—
Board of school directors	Creates planning committee and bargaining team. Identifies internal responsibilities and relationships. Approves alternate proposals to be designed and costed.	Approves all variances from negotiations plan. Ensures that all issues are resolved at the required levels. Reviews contract prior to approval.	Ratifies agreement. Incorporates agreement elements into official budget. Directs chief executive to communicate agreement details to appropriate parties.
Chief executive	Coordinates all planning responsibilities. Ensures that preparations are proceeding systematically. Prepares for possible strike. Keeps board informed about negotiations proceedings.	Serves as board liaison agent to planning committee and negotiations team. Coordinates all system activities related to bargaining process.	Coordinates communication of contract details to administrative staff. Coordinates implementation of contract.
Bargaining planning committee	Prepares bargaining strategy and negotiating plan for board review and adoption. Advises board on personnel plans related to negotiations.	Counsels with negotiations team on actual or anticipated negotiations problems, impasses, and disagreements. Appoints ad hoc committee(s) as needed.	Records experiences concerning planning and negotiating the agreement.
Bargaining team	Identifies strike issues for board. Establishes negotiations strategy and tactics.	Continues bargaining process in accordance with planning guidelines.	Communicates short- and long-term implications of contract (chairperson submits written report).
Professional negotiator	Assesses union motivation, strategy, and goals for impending negotiations. Counsels board on impact of union proposal in relation to system goals. Provides analyses of strengths and weaknesses of current contract. Counsels and drafts contract language on request.	Conducts bargaining process in accordance with board objectives. Focuses negotiations on problem solving. Counsels on request. Ensures that all contract items are in legal compliance. Advises board on third-party utilization.	Evaluates and submits in writing report on all aspects of various negotiations (within 45 days). Reviews contract for omissions, errors, and ambiguities. Counsels board regarding contract infractions and disputes about contract interpretation.
Director of business affairs	Provides comparative data on system's standing regarding economics, benefits, and other issues. Assesses impact of settlement costs of optional plans.	Evaluates union proposals relative to settlement costs. Renders general support service to negotiations team.	Transforms agreement into budgetary items. Administers fiscal aspects of agreement.
Director of personnel	Prepares strike manual. Provides current and historical information pertinent to planning. Prepares negotiations handbook. Reviews prior grievance and arbitration decisions.	Furnishes negotiations team with relevant information concerning key issues. Prepares press releases as directed by chief executive.	Records experiences concerning administration of agreement (disputes, infractions, and court decisions).
Secretary	Renders secretarial service to planning committee and negotiations team. Develops minutes, records, and reports for negotiations team.	Provides support service to system negotiations personnel.	Prepares official negotiations documents to be stored in information system.

Shaping the Human Organization Through Contract Design

By considering the collective bargaining process as a series of stages, one can identify several aspects of Phase 1 (planning) in which opportunities exist to develop plans for enhancing both individual and organizational effectiveness. Whether school system personnel are unionized or nonunionized, both the system and the position holders have expectations that must be incorporated into the **contract design.** The *formal contract* identifies what the individual and the organization will exchange; the *informal* (or *psychological*) *contract* is unwritten, but it is constantly in operation between the individual and the system. Both parties seek to have certain conditions of work satisfied.

Assume that a formal agreement is up for renewal. Long before the bargaining begins (Phase 2 of Figure 11.2), two matters need to be considered. First, shaping a new agreement involves consideration of two kinds of contracts: formal and psychological. The formal contract may be viewed as a short- or intermediate-range plan. The psychological contract is designed to sustain the exchange concept as a way of structuring continuing mutual expectations. Schein has described the psychological contract in the following terms:

> Whether people work effectively, whether they generate commitment, loyalty, and enthusiasm for the organization and its goals, and whether they obtain satisfaction from their work depends to a large measure on two conditions:
>
> The degree to which their own expectations of what the organization will provide them and what they owe the organization in return matches what the organization's expectations are of what it will give and get in return.
>
> The nature of what is actually to be exchanged (assuming there is some agreement)—money in exchange for time at work; social need satisfaction and security in exchange for hard work and loyalty; opportunities for self-actualization and challenging work in exchange for high productivity, high-quality work, and creative effort in the service of organizational goals; or various combinations of these and other things.[17]

The second concern is that changes of one sort or another occur during the contract agreement period. Board, staff, and administrative compositions change. External and internal environments change. People change. Contract provisions need to be changed. Consequently, feedback is necessary on the quality of the existing agreement, on contemporary conditions affecting a new agreement, and on changes that should be made to progress toward idealized aims for the system's human resources (Figure 2.3). In brief, prenegotiations planning should shape plans in the formal contract to advance the system from where it is to where management wants it to be, especially on such matters as the physical work environment, economic well-being, development and utilization of personnel skills, abilities and interests, individual involvement and interest, and supervisory and work-group relationships.

A. Are there clauses in the present contract that need modification?

B. What are the reasons for needed modifications? What information has led you to support the need for contract modification?

C. Has the agreement achieved those goals the school system expected to achieve as a result of its formulation and acceptance?

D. Is evidence available to indicate violation of the terms of the agreement?

E. What difficulties have been encountered in administering the agreement?

F. Have desirable items been excluded from the agreement?

G. Does the present agreement permit the flexibility required to administer the school system effectively?

Figure 11.5   Foxcroft school district questionnaire for reviewing current contract provisions.

Contract Reassessment

As depicted in Figure 11.2, prenegotiations preparation includes *analysis of the current contract.* This step is essential to secure information for the board, policy committee, and negotiating team relative to:

• Effectiveness of current contract provisions in achieving organizational objectives.
• New provisions needed.

Figure 11.5 illustrates one approach to current contract analysis. The figure shows a questionnaire sent to system personnel (board members, central staff, principals, and the chief negotiator) directly or indirectly involved in the bargaining process. The intent of the questionnaire is to secure facts and opinions regarding the operational impact of the current contract.

Responses to the questionnaire (Figure 11.5) from members of the planning committee provided information that formed the basis for compiling a *Planning Committee Workbook.* The workbook is conceived as a mechanism for systematizing the committee approach to Phase 2 of the bargaining process (Figure 11.2). One of the features of the *Planning Committee Workbook* of the Foxcroft school district is a set of strategic objectives, as well as subobjectives that are considered to be essential in the upcoming union–system contract.

Contractual Posture

Table 11.2 indicates that the planning committee in the Foxcroft school district is responsible for shaping elements of the proposed contract, which represents, in effect, the system's approach to resolving union–system contractual problems, including matters of educational policy, economic issues, personnel appraisal, and board rights and responsibilities. There are several advantages to the system in couching its posture in a verbal context:

- A proposal is an appropriate medium for communicating to system members the issues of concern and the position that the board plans to adopt.
- The proposal can be reviewed to determine whether the elements are legal.
- Preparation of the written proposal provides an opportunity to communicate the intent and expectations of the board's planning for human resources.
- In planning the proposal, there is time to test major decisions and contemplated action both internally and externally.
- Elements of the proposal can be linked to system and unit objectives that the board hopes to attain, either on a short- or long-term basis.
- Preparation of a proposal places the board in a proactive rather than a reactive posture. It is the board's approach to designing and finding better solutions to union–system problems.
- A proposal represents a planned strategy for initiating, implementing, and administering activities related to the master plan for the system's human resources.
- The proposal is intended to emphasize the board's responsibility for achieving a fair return on the community investment in education.
- Careful analysis of clauses in the current contract, as well as those in system and union proposals for the forthcoming contract, is possible prior to initiation of Phase 2 (negotiation) of the bargaining process.

Contract wording can be reviewed to test the extent to which the clauses in the proposal specifically and accurately express the system's intentions and expectations in a way that clearly reflects the values by which the organization intends to operate.

The discussion that follows is woven around salient features of Phases 2 and 3 of the bargaining process (negotiations strategy and contract administration) portrayed in the process model shown in Figure 11.2.

Negotiations Strategy

A *strategy* is one of the several different kinds of plans aimed at accomplishing a specific purpose. Decisions involved in developing a strategy are based to a considerable extent on anticipation of responses of those affected by the plan.

Negotiations strategy in collective bargaining (Phase 2 of Figure 11.2) is concerned with the kinds of educational services the system should deliver to its clients, procedures by which it should develop and deliver these services, and means for motivating personnel to cooperate voluntarily in accomplishing system goals. Negotiations strategy should focus on ways that enable each member of the system to derive from his or her work a suitable standard of living, a sense of dignity and worth, and meaning in a complex society. Thus viewed, collective bargaining strategy is one of several kinds of plans developed by the system to guide both its long-range and daily activities. Its primary intent is not to outmaneuver the other party at the negotiations table; rather, it is concerned with determining the extent to which and the manner in which the *strategic aims of the system can be furthered through the collective bargaining process.* To illustrate, the strategic aims of the system for its human resources may be to:

- Place improvement of the educational quality for every pupil at the top of the priority objectives list.
- Create a performance culture that will enhance educational achievement.
- Provide the best compensation and collateral benefits possible within the ability of the school system.
- Provide incentives to enable each to give his or her best efforts to the assigned role.
- Provide development opportunities to aid individuals to advance within the system.
- Provide leadership that enables each individual to do his or her best work.
- Establish working conditions, position security, and personal recognition that will make the system an attractive place in which to work and plan a career.

It is hoped that these are the kinds of conditions that the school wants to achieve for its staff, regardless of the presence or absence of a teachers' association or union. Moreover, if a system chooses to engage in collective bargaining, its *strategic planning* will consist in part of considering what proposals it plans to place on the negotiations table to achieve its long-term goals for its personnel and clients. Strategic planning also involves analysis of proposals to be made by the union, especially in terms of whether and to what extent such plans will assist the institution in attaining its purposes.

The central idea behind strategic planning for collective bargaining is that it offers considerable opportunity for both parties to achieve their expectations. It should also be noted that the link between the human resource function and the collective bargaining process is strong; the aims of the human resource function often coincide with those contained in proposals of teacher groups or supportive personnel.

Strategy planning in collective bargaining is essentially a decision-making process consisting of four phases: (a) defining the problem, (b) finding alternative solutions, (c) analyzing and comparing alternatives, and (d) selecting the plan or course to follow. This is to say that plans for achieving system goals for human resources through the collective bargaining process must be based on a definition of what the system intends to achieve, identification of the obstacles involved, examination of alternative courses of action available, and evaluation of the consequences of each suggested plan.

Modes of Negotiating Behavior

Three common negotiation modes are described as competitive, collaborative, and subordinative.

Competitive—Both parties focus on gaining dominance over the other.
Collaborative—A win-win negotiating environment is designed and maintained. Each party enhances its bargaining objectives.
Subordinative—Party Y subordinates its status and negotiating approach to those of Party X.

Comparison of the three bargaining modes leads to several observations regarding the conduct of negotiations.

First, it brings into bold relief the fact that each mode varies from the other in intent, tactics to be employed, planning activities, risk calculation, and outcome predictability.

Second, it brings into bold relief the fact that each negotiations mode varies from the other in intent, tactics to be employed, planning activities, risk calculation, and outcome predictability.

Third, it supports the premise that there is no universal method for planning and controlling the collective bargaining process. Relationships that exist between the two parties as they enter into negotiations, the economic scene, and the outcome produced by the previous agreement are illustrative of factors that will affect the negotiations mode.

Fourth, and perhaps most important, the type of negotiations mode to be employed is situational, which requires a careful examination of the circumstances affecting negotiations and the application of those tactics that will likely be effective in a given situation. Each or all of the modes may be utilized, depending on the circumstances. Although the shift from the competitive to the collaborative mode (minimization of conflict) is a desirable form of relationship, its attainment requires both parties to put greater emphasis on mutual goal orientation as well as value and attitude modification.

If the system adopts an affirmative strategy to improve conditions under which its personnel perform services, it is clear that this cannot be accomplished in a single agreement. Tactics may well be concerned with securing agreements on a series of subgoals that contribute to the broad strategic aims mentioned earlier. For example, it is difficult to improve a faulty compensation structure through a single agreement. Extensive improvements in the several elements that make up the compensation structure, such as salaries and wages, collateral benefits, extra pay for extra work, overtime, and noneconomic provisions, are generally not realized simultaneously.

Much has been written about the tactics of negotiations, but there is no pattern of tactical activity applicable to every negotiating situation. Let this be clear: when two parties come to a negotiations table, the facts of the situation are paramount. Neither side can choose freely the issues to be negotiated or the tactics to be employed in settling them. Different objectives require different tactics. Some problems are long-standing, arising again and again. The facts or conditions pertaining to current problems and issues will determine the kinds of negotiations that take place and their final outcome.

When the formalities of certifying a union as the exclusive unit bargaining agent for any group of school personnel are completed, both parties (the union and the system) are required to negotiate collectively. Bargaining issues are commonly described as *mandatory, permissive,* and *illegal.* Mandatory issues refer to conditions of work (e.g., compensation or working periods), permissive issues are those outside the mandatory category (e.g., educational policy), and illegal subjects are those in conflict with regulatory provisions.

Modes of negotiating behavior are influenced by a variety of factors, such as governmental restraints, economic conditions, bargaining strategies, bad-faith bargaining, dispute mechanisms, and court injunctions. The ultimate aim of collective bargaining is to arrive at an agreement to which both parties are signatories, the terms of which they are obligated to follow for a specified period. Strategies invoked at the time of negotiations determine not only the duration of the bargaining period but also the number and kinds of dispute mechanisms employed for resolution purposes.

Scope of Bargaining

The substance of what is to be negotiated at the negotiations table may be classified as economic or noneconomic issues, although they are not completely separable. Many noneconomic provisions have attendant costs, either direct or indirect. Economic issues relate to the level, form, structure, and method of compensation and collateral benefits. Noneconomic issues generally include those relating to such matters as management and union rights, nondiscrimination clauses, hours of work, vacations, sick leave, leaves of absence, seniority, grievance procedures, and terms of the contract (dates).

The **scope of bargaining** has been a negotiating issue fraught with conflict throughout the history of public sector bargaining. At the core of the matter is the question of what is bargainable, especially as it pertains to noneconomic issues. Unions have sought to extend their sphere of influence into the policy role of organizations by insisting that the scope of negotiations include items traditionally considered to be organizational prerogatives. It is not uncommon for unions to include in agreement proposals provisions pertaining to the curriculum, the instructional system, the performance appraisal system, transfer, promotion, seniority, residency requirements, discipline of union members, termination, and staff development. Institutional efforts to blunt union incursion into policy matters usually take the form of (a) a management rights clause asserting that control and operation are matters vested exclusively in management, except for those limited by provisions in the agreement, or (b) a clause listing all matters not subject to joint determination.[18]

The problem of what is bargainable is fraught with complexities. How to draw the line between mandatory and voluntary demands is not clear and remains fluid, shifting and changing with administrative rulings, legislation, and court decisions. Expanding the scope of bargaining to include educational policies (especially those that are not conditions of employment) is criticized on the grounds that it is undemocratic, constituting the negotiations of public policies with one interest group while other interest groups are systematically excluded.[19]

The last word has not yet been spoken or written on the scope of bargaining. Problems stemming from the union concept of equalizing the power of the public employee and public employer are numerous, raising questions as to whether collective bargaining in the public sector is desirable public policy, whether public policy on personnel matters should be a joint determination, and whether the present system of public sector bargaining is the best that can be devised to serve the interests of individual system members, the union, the school system, and the public. Experience has indicated that current approaches have not been able to meet all of these conflicting goals. Unless there is greater concern for a balancing of the public interest, what can be anticipated is greater public insertion into the collective bargaining process through various entries to ensure that its interests are served.

Impasse Resolution and Strikes

The collective bargaining process, as illustrated in Figure 11.2, involves two parties who make and live with an agreement in the form of a written contract. In negotiating the terms of a future contract and in living with an existing contract, disagreements and disputes are inevitable. Disagreements arise over (a) matters of interest (i.e., matters of concern to both sides in negotiating a new agreement) or (b) matters of right (i.e., those that relate to interpretation of provisions in the existing contract). There are occasions when proceedings reach an **impasse** or deadlock and neither side will move from its stated position. At this point in the process, various methods of resolving disagreements may be employed. The following text focuses on methods of dispute resolution.

Trilateralism

When two parties are unable to resolve a dispute, either over matters of interest or over matters of right, public employment policy, either in the form of federal or state legislation, provides for a third party to enter the controversy. The third party may be either a mediator or an arbitrator (often a government official), who helps the disputants to reach an agreement. Activities of a mediator center on efforts to stimulate, persuade, and influence the parties to reach an agreement; the mediator or conciliator has no authority to decide the issues involved. Moreover, the mediator's activities are centered on negotiations involving a new contract. In

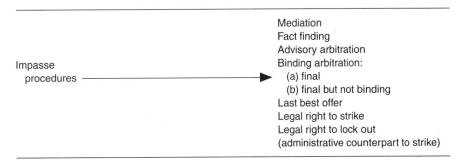

Figure 11.6   Procedures utilized to resolve union–system impasses.

effect, most mediation is new-contract mediation, not grievance mediation under an existing contract.

Arbitration, it should be noted, is primarily concerned with matters of right, that is, interpreting provisions in the existing contract. When the two parties involved cannot agree on how to resolve an issue stemming from the existing agreement, the procedure most commonly employed is referred to as arbitration, of which there are two types: voluntary and compulsory. Arbitration, generally speaking, is a process that involves the use of an impartial third party who collects pertinent facts from the disputants and proceeds to make a decision, which is usually binding. Compulsory arbitration usually involves both compulsory submission of the dispute to arbitration and compulsory acceptance of the decision. Thus, arbitration is the terminal step in the contract's grievance procedure. Under voluntary arbitration, either side may initiate action to take the unresolved grievance to arbitration. Under compulsory arbitration, especially in disputes in the public sector, the dispute resolution is transferred to a government-appointed agency. Legislative provisions often establish a fact-finding procedure, which is the designation of neutral third parties to assemble facts and make recommendations based on these facts. This procedure may help the parties involved reach an agreement voluntarily, which they might not do were not such facts and recommendations set forth.

Figure 11.6 lists procedures that are available and have been employed in union–system negotiations to resolve impasses. The procedures are listed in terms of frequency of use.

Mediation and fact finding appear to be the procedures most frequently found and utilized in settling union–system disputes. The final impasse procedure (after bargaining, mediation, and fact finding have been exhausted) may be the right to **strike,** or it may be one of several forms of arbitration that the parties have agreed to as an alternative to a strike. Experience in the public sector with binding arbitration has resulted in such criticisms of its employment as the following:

• The authority of arbitrators to order the expenditure of school district funds with no accountability to the public is tantamount to taxation without representation.
• Binding arbitration usurps government authority.
• Binding arbitration subverts the very purposes for which government was designed.
• The arbitration process is not conducive to good-faith collective bargaining.
• Permitting third parties not accountable to the electorate to engage in the process is an illegal delegation of legislative authority.
• Binding arbitration violates the one-person, one-vote standard mandated by the Fourteenth Amendment.
• Third-party appointees frequently do not represent the public interest.

When an impasse occurs between the board and the teacher union in public education, state controls govern the resolution process. The following provisions are representative of state controls:

• An orderly procedure has been established by state law, setting a deadline for the commencement of bargaining, with an impasse procedure included in the legal provisions.
• Impasse resolution procedures allow the parties of interest to come to agreement with voluntary mediation. In cases where this is not successful, or if specified deadlines are not met, state-level procedures are invoked.
• Impasse procedures include mediation, fact finding, and compulsory arbitration.
• A grievance procedure is mandated as a part of any agreement, with a definition of grievance limited to the interpretation or application of the agreement.

One of the state controls that usually governs public sector strikes is that they are lawful only when the fact-finding process is completed. Strikes, it would appear, have become an integral part of the bargaining process in the public domain. Although strikes are extremely unpopular with the public (and they are not typical results of negotiation), they and efforts to abolish or eliminate them must be anticipated.

As an alternative to the prohibition against school employees having the right to strike, the American Association of School Personnel Administrators has proposed the following resolution for states considering ways of dealing with strikes against the public and its governing representatives:

• A prohibition against retroactive contract settlements if there is a strike.
• A state procedure for a secret ballot election for all individuals in a bargaining unit to accept or reject the board's last and final offer on all issues. If accepted by the employees, the contract becomes binding on all parties; if rejected, the employees would follow the strike vote procedure or continue negotiations.
• A state-required procedure that governs how and when strike votes would be conducted and a mandatory cooling-off period. The state would select a fact finder or fact finders to hear the impasse issues and make recommendations for settlement. If the report was rejected by the parties, the strike would be allowed.[20]

TABLE 11.3
Illustration of Service Areas and Types of Emergency Prearrangements Needed in Anticipation of a Strike

Support Services	Instructional Services	Administrative Services
Food	Instructional plans	Public relations
Transportation	Substitute service	Record keeping
Security		Picket lines
Building maintenance		Staff meetings
Relations with suppliers		Board meetings
		Law enforcement
		Documentation of events
		Suspension of compensation, benefits

Problems involved in preparing for a strike include what to do about various services, as illustrated in Table 11.3. Preparation of a strike manual by a committee assigned to the task of deciding in advance what arrangements are needed is a desirable practice. The strike manual automatically becomes the controlling document if a strike occurs and may contain two categories of information: (a) what system procedures and responsibilities will be used if operations continue during a strike and (b) procedures to be employed if the system ceases operation for the duration of a strike. The manual may also include instructions to system administrators about their roles, as well as about the conduct of operations to bind the wounds when the strike is over.

The major limitation of current approaches to resolving impasses in public sector bargaining is the ambiguity about whether the third party is a fact finder, mediator, conventional arbitrator, final offer arbitrator, or mediator-arbitrator. The search continues for means different and more creative than current public sector impasse techniques that will lead to more constructive union–system relationships through satisfaction of mutual interests.

Paramount to any approach designed to correct current drawbacks in impasse procedures is the recognition of the right of personnel to negotiate the terms of employment, commitment to the public interest principle, cooperative system–union contract planning, and awareness of the union–system obligation to develop a partnership of responsibility.

Contract Agreement

The agreement arrived at by the school system and the personnel negotiating unit stipulates in writing the nature of the relationship that will exist between the two parties for a specified period of time. The agreement generally consists of four functional categories, each of which has a specific purpose: (a) security or rights of both parties, (b) compensation and working conditions, (c) individual security, and (d) administration of the agreement. Each of these divisions of the agreement will be discussed briefly in the following text.

Security of Both Parties

One of the first steps in collective bargaining is to settle the extent of recognition to be accorded bargaining units representing teachers or other personnel in the school system. Security clauses in agreements covering personnel groups negotiating with the school system may include such matters as the description of the bargaining unit, duration of the agreement, degree of recognition of the union or association, avoidance of discrimination based on union membership, permissible union activity on school premises, and access to school executives by union officials.

Prerogatives of the school system in the agreement are intended to affirm the rights the system must have to discharge administrative functions with which it is entrusted. Collective bargaining is a two-way street, and the system must have flexibility to administer the enterprise properly. When it bargains its rights away, the system renders itself incapable of carrying out its responsibilities. Protective clauses in agreements reserve to the system discretion in such personnel matters as size of staff, position content, teaching or work schedules, promotion, transfer, discipline, dismissal, staffing assignments, appraisal, and leaves of absence. In addition, the system may demand clauses stipulating protection of personnel from union intimidation, exercise of good faith in the use of privileges granted, restraint in publishing false or misleading information about the system, and a zipper clause that ensures that negotiations will not be reopened for a specified period of time. In short, the system must clarify in the contract what it considers to be its rights and privileges.

Compensation and Working Conditions

The core of any agreement negotiated collectively between two parties is the individual personnel contract. The school system, under the terms of the agreement, agrees to provide certain remunerations and to establish working conditions for employees in exchange for specified services. In recent years, considerable debate has taken place with respect to what is negotiable between the two parties. High on the list of items frequently considered at negotiations sessions are salaries, wages, collateral benefits, class size, consultation in setting school calendars, lunch and rest periods, adequacy of physical facilities for teachers, transfers, teacher planning time, protection of teachers from physical assault, nonteaching functions, control of student behavior, school closings at noon before holidays and vacations, academic freedom, and recruitment of unqualified personnel.

Pressures from personnel groups to increase the scope of bargaining must be anticipated as standard procedure. There is nothing wrong with conducting bargaining that includes a wide range of matters of interest to personnel. Two criteria against which the negotiability of any item should be tested are (a) its relationship to the strategic aims of the system for its human resources and (b) its impact on the prerogatives the system must retain to administer the institution effectively.

Individual Security

Clauses in the agreement that cover the security of an individual member of the staff are designed generally to protect him or her against arbitrary treatment from the school system, the union or association, other personnel or personnel groups, and community groups. This type of security is of as much concern to the system as to the individual or the personnel negotiating group.

Protection against arbitrary acts of the system is provided by an appeals system or grievance machinery. As a matter of sound personnel policy and with or without collective bargaining, the system should establish grievance procedures to protect the individual against arbitrary treatment in such areas as salaries, wages, transfer, promotion, and dismissal.

Protection of the individual against arbitrary acts of the union or association is provided by including clauses in the agreement covering these matters. The right of an individual, for example, to belong or not to belong to the union and to be free from intimidation by the union is generally guaranteed by the system in its prerogative clauses.

Protection from pressure groups within the community needs to be guaranteed by both parties. In recent years, during attempts to decentralize urban schools, some members have been threatened by arbitrary demands for their removal without recourse to an appeals system. As the struggle for control of education in attendance units goes on, the need for both the union and the system to join hands to protect the security of individuals should be self-evident.

Problems that impinge on the security of personnel are so complex that protection of the individual is not possible without cooperation of both parties. A system consists of individuals bound together, willingly or not. Accordingly, on issues such as individual security, there is much to be lost by failure to agree. It is worth noting, however, that there are some things that agreement between the parties cannot achieve in and of itself. The right of an individual to progress within the system according to his or her initiative and ability cannot be guaranteed by the union. Moreover, effective supervision, leadership, and exercise of individual initiative can be fostered most effectively by the system. It goes without saying that when the system is stripped of its right to administer functions for which it is held responsible, rights of the individual are certain to be lost in the process.

Day-to-day administration of the agreement negotiated by the two parties is based on application of grievance machinery, which is intended to settle violations of the agreement promptly, deal with disputes relating to the interpretation of specific clauses in the agreement, or handle problems arising in areas not covered by the agreement. Grievance procedures, including steps to be taken, time limitations, and provisions for arbitration, are discussed briefly in the following section.

Contract Administration

After the agreement has been ratified by both parties, each has a responsibility to make the contract work. Although the rights and obligations of both the system and the union are specified in agreement clauses, disputes are certain to arise over the meaning of the language in the agreement, as well as over methods employed to implement the contract. Because numerous disputes arise from the interpretation of contractual language, care should be taken to use language that will minimize misinterpretation, and the agreement should be reread carefully before it is signed.

It is conceivable that problems will arise from practically every provision in the agreement. When they do occur, the contractual means designed for their resolution is the **grievance procedure.** A grievance is a wrong, real or fancied, considered as grounds for complaint. The grievance procedure provides system members the right to appeal what they consider to be a violation, misinterpretation, misapplication, or inequitable or improper application of any provision of the existing union–system contract. In some contracts, a grievance is defined as a conflict arising from interpretation of a negotiated agreement, whereas a complaint is construed to be a conflict arising from the interpretation of policies, rules, and regulations not in the negotiated agreement. Practice varies with regard to grievance and complaint procedures. In brief, a formal grievance is an allegation that a provision, or provisions, of the agreement have been violated.

Characteristics of a formal grievance procedure, include a series of steps through which a grievance may be appealed to several levels of the administrative structure for settlement; stated time limits for presentation of grievances, rendering of decisions, and taking of appeals; and provision for arbitration as the final step in settling an unresolved grievance. Actually, the possibilities for settlement of a grievance are the same as those available for settling an impasse in negotiations. These include arbitration, mediation, and striking.

The grievance procedure has been referred to as the heart of the agreement. This is because the practical test of an agreement lies in its day-to-day application. Either side may attempt to adjudicate through grievance machinery differences of opinion arising out of meaning, interpretation, and application of various provisions of the agreement.

Effectiveness of the grievance procedure, as with any other step in the collective bargaining process, depends on those responsible for its administration. During administration of the agreement, the personnel director or his or her counterpart is able to perform various functions essential to making the contract a positive force for advancing the interests of both parties in the relationship. These functions include:

•   Recording and reporting to the superintendent of schools progress and problems encountered in administering the contract.
•   Interpreting the agreement to the administrative staff.
•   Providing ways of instructing line administrators to follow grievance procedures built into the agreement. Administrators at the operating level, for example, will need counseling in problems relating to work assignments, discipline, and performance appraisal.

- Recording experiences concerning administration of the agreement.
- Meeting frequently throughout the contract period with union or association representatives. The purpose is to inform each other of problems encountered, examine ways of improving the administration of the contract, discuss revision of those provisions that are ineffectual because of semantic weaknesses, or discuss failure to cope with unexpected contingencies.
- Coordinating efforts to make the grievance arbitration process an instrument for achieving and maintaining organizational justice.
- Identifying trouble spots within the system.

It has been said that there is more to a marriage than a wedding. So it is with collective bargaining. When the high drama of negotiating an agreement has passed, the problem of two parties learning to live together begins. What both parties do in the process of administering the agreement and how they do it become important to maintenance of sound relationships between the system and its personnel groups.

In summation, **contract administration** (Phase 3 in Figure 11.2) includes four elements: implementation, conflict resolution, enforcement, and evaluation. Few negotiators are blessed with the wisdom to foresee every problem, every conflict, and every clause with a potential for misinterpretation. Essential to positive agreement outcomes is the establishment of a union–system plan for resolving disputes and minimizing their effect on organizational operations.

Appraisal is one of the functions of the administrative process designed to see how well performance conforms to plan. It is concerned with the effects of all plans and procedures in relation to their contribution to system purposes. Appraisal of the collective bargaining process is an absolute necessity. The system, for example, wants to know:

- Strengths and weaknesses of the existing agreement.
- Sources of disputes in administering the agreement.
- Effectiveness of the negotiating team and its individual members.
- Impact of the agreement on the motivation of personnel.
- Desirability of modifying the negotiations strategy and tactics of the system.
- Steps that should be taken to improve the bargaining process.
- Whether the contract promotes attainment of strategic goals.

Coordination of appraisal activities relating to the negotiations process, like other matters pertaining to the conduct of the human resource function, is a responsibility of the individual in charge of the function. This includes the tasks of recording experiences and gathering facts and observations vital to the preparatory stages of the next agreement to be negotiated.

In sum, the collective bargaining process is a tool by which the system and its personnel solve problems growing out of their relationship. Its future direction in public education is something only time can tell. Its strength lies in providing an opportunity for improving organizational democracy and in providing a fundamental human relations tool for the betterment of education.

Review

This chapter is focused on five principal aspects of collective bargaining as it relates to public education in the United States:

•   The historical basis and attendant developments of public sector bargaining for education in the twentieth century. One late development of note at the turn of the century is the potential merger of the National Education Association and the American Federation of Teachers, which would become the nation's biggest and by far the nation's richest union.

•   Elements of a model for the collective bargaining process.
•   The behavior of three predominant players in public education collective bargaining—employer, employee, and government.
•   The important role of the human resource function in coordinating, systematizing, and administering the collective negotiations process.
•   Opportunities for the school system to employ collective bargaining to further its strategic objectives.

Discussion Questions

1. What are the prospects for cooperative relationships becoming institutionalized in the culture of modern school systems?

2. Identify positive and negative behaviors of negotiators conducive to win-win or win-lose modes of negotiating.

3. Compare and contrast each of the following impasse procedures: mediation, fact finding, advisory arbitration, binding arbitration.

4. If the right of teacher unions to call a strike is abolished, what alternatives should be considered as viable substitutes?

5. Do the costs of collective bargaining justify the alleged view that as bargaining costs increase, educational outcomes decrease?

6. Should collective negotiation sessions for teacher contracts be open to the public?

Notes

1. Public Service Research Council, *Public Sector Bargaining and Styles* (Vienna, VA: Public Service Research Council, 1978), 1.

2. Education Commission of the States, *State Education Collective Bargaining Laws* (Denver: The Commission, 1984).

3. See Vida Scarpello and James Ledvinka, "The Regulatory Environment," in *Personnel and Human Resource Management* (Boston: PWS-Kent Publishing Company, 1988), Chapter 6.

4. John A. Fossum, *Labor Relations: Development, Structure, Process* (Dallas: Business Publications, Inc., 1982), 419.

5. Ibid., 419.

6. Ibid., 426–427.

7. Grace Sterrett and Antone Aboud, *The Right to Strike in Public Employment* (Ithaca: New York State School of Industrial and Labor Relations, 1982), 3–4.

8. Vernon H. Smith, "Fuel for the Coming Battles Over Public Sector Unions and Bargaining," *Phi Delta Kappan* 62, 5 (1981), 402.

9. Douglas E. Mitchell and Charles T. R. Kerchner, *The Dynamics of Public School Bargaining and Its Impact on Governance, Administration, and Teaching* (Washington, DC: National Institute of Education, 1981).

10. National Education Association, *Reinventing Teacher Unions for a New Era* (Washington, DC: The Association, 1997), 4.

11. Peter Schrag, "Divided They Stand: Merger Mania Hits the Teachers' Unions," *The New Republic* (May 25, 1998), 17–19.

12. Richard E. Dibble, "Labor-Management Relations," in William R. Tracey, ed., *Human Resources Management and Development Handbook*, 2nd ed. (New York: American Management Association, 1998), 634.

13. Ibid.

14. National School Boards Association, *The School Personnel Management System*, rev. ed. (Alexandria, VA: The Association, 1996), 134–135.

15. Ibid.

16. Ibid.

17. Edgar H. Schein, *Organizational Psychology* (Englewood Cliffs, NJ: Prentice-Hall, Inc., 1980), 99.

18. Dale Beach, *Personnel: The Management of People at Work* (New York: Macmillan Publishing Company, 1980), 113–114.

19. Myron M. Lieberman, *Public Sector Bargaining* (Lexington, MA: Lexington Books, 1980), Chapter 4; Myron M. Lieberman, "Unions and Educational Quality: Folklore by Finn," *Phi Delta Kappan* (January 1985), 342.

20. American Association of School Personnel Administrators, *Trends in Collective Bargaining in Public Education* (Seven Hills, OH: The Association, 1978), 7.

Supplementary Reading

Chavez, Linda. "Denied the Political Punch of a Merger, Maybe Teachers Can Try Tending the Schools." *Philadelphia Inquirer* (July 8, 1998).

Clay, Mark Van. "A Collaborative Approach to Collective Bargaining." *American School Board Journal* 3, 54 (March 1997), 19.

Dunlop, John T.; and Arnold M. Zack. *Mediation and Arbitration Disputes.* San Francisco: Jossey-Bass, 1997.

Egler, Theresa Donahue. "The Benefits and Burdens of Arbitration." *HRMagazine* (July 1995), 27–30.

Keane, William. *Win-Win or Else: Collective Bargaining in the Age of Public Discontent.* Thousand Oaks, CA: Corwin Press, 1996.

Lancaster, Hall. "You Have to Negotiate Everything in Life, So Get Good At It." *Wall Street Journal* (January 27, 1998).

Lewis, Anne. "Pussycat or Tiger?" *Phi Delta Kappan* 79, 7 (March 1998).

Lieberman, Myron. *Public Education: An Autopsy.* Cambridge, MA: Harvard University Press, 1993.

Mezzacappa, Dale. "Teachers Reject Union Merger." *Philadelphia Inquirer* (July 6, 1998), A1–A5. "Teachers Send a Message." *The Wall Street Journal* (July 7, 1998), A16.

Muagusson, P. "Is the NEA Getting on the Reform Train?" *Business Week* 84, 96, 70–73.

Pfandenhauer, Diane M. "Selecting and Using Labor and Employment." *HRMagazine* (March 1998), 119–126.

Thompson, Robert W. "HR Issues Fill Congress' in Box." *HRMagazine* (1998), 70–73.

Schrag, Peter. "Divided They Stand: Merger Mania Hits the Teachers' Union." *The New Republic* (May 25, 1998), 17–19.

APPENDIX

Reaches of the School System Mission

The aim of this appendix is to develop an appreciation of the organizational potential of a school system's mission. The significance of designing, implementing, and adhering to the intent of the system's mission is becoming apparent and clearly relevant as we come to recognize its impelling force when school systems confront challenges posed by a changing social order. Mission statements and their implementation are often viewed as sufficient unto themselves, as pious platitudes, however well crafted. A new era has arrived, however, when the system mission needs to be considered for its far-reaching organizational value in coping with educational change.

Mission defined.
A school system's mission is an expression of the reasons why the system exists, the purposes it is designed to serve, and the boundaries or constraints of its application.

Mission statement.
A mission statement serves four primary functions:
•   Communicate to its internal and external environments the general legislative and collateral purposes the system is designed to serve.
•   Provide a frame of reference for making decisions and assessing intended outcomes.
•   Identifying what the system will or may come to be.
•   Set forth values to which the system intends to adhere in its mission undertakings.

In the text that follows, an outline of four reaches of a system mission is presented to demonstrate that mission serves as a thread connecting the primary elements of planning and operational endeavors. Every organizational decision, major or minor, has its roots in the system mission and must be considered in terms of its impact on the mission.

The Purpose Reach

•   Fulfill legislative and regulatory mandates.
•   Provide the broad context for developing an underlying pattern of the core domains on which the constituent parts of the school teaching and learning processes are based, such as the academic domain, the social domain, and the personal domain.

The Strategic Reach

- Investing in processes and practices to enhance student learning.
- Investing in personnel capable of and committed to enhancing the teaching and learning processes, who are effective in using and inventing tools and techniques for improving teaching and learning.
- Designing plans to enable students to realize the fullness of the learning domains (academic, social, personal).
- Making effective educational uses of information technologies.
- Enlisting cooperation and support from external entities (families, private domain, political entities, community and governmental agencies).

The Environmental Reach

- *Internal reach*—focusing attention on union–system cooperation to realize the purposes of the mission.
- Designing plans for internalizing members' commitment to fulfilling established cultural expectations.
- *External reach*—being responsible to external interests and concerns about school system effectiveness.
- Providing channels whereby members participate in organizational decisions that affect them.
- Enlisting the support of community agencies to play an integral part in mission accomplishment.

The Functions Reach

As noted in Exhibit A on page 371, the major functions of a school system are identified as the educational program, environment, logistics, planning, and human resources. These functions are considered operational components designed to plan, implement, and realize mission intent through short-, intermediate-, and long-term considerations for the benefit of the students, the staff, the system, and society.

Exhibit B.   Illustration of mission statements

School system. The mission of school system X is to develop and enhance the academic, social, and personal needs of its students.

Corporation. The mission of company X is to achieve and retain global leadership as a total quality supplier of superior products and services.

Retirement community. The mission of retirement community X is to serve the physical, emotional, recreational, social, religious, and health needs of residents in a professional and caring manner. These services are to be provided effectively and efficiently within a financially stable organization.

Publisher. Our mission is to publish books that empower people's lives.

Military. The mission of Corps X is to destroy the enemy in Corps X's zone. Mission execution factors: enemy, terrain, time, troops (yours).

Exhibit A.   Illustration of Organized Entities That Give Direction to the School
System Mission

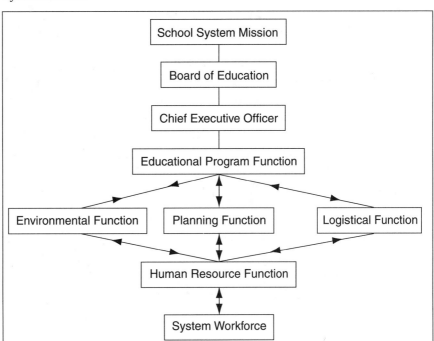

Christian School. Our mission is to educate students who will serve God and
impact the world through biblical thought and action.

National park. The mission of Valley Forge Park is to preserve and commemorate
for the people of the United States the area associated with the heroic suffering,
hardship, determination, and resolve of General George Washington's Continental
Army during the winter of 1777–1778 at Valley Forge.

Internal Revenue Service (IRS 1998). The mission of the IRS is to provide America's taxpayers with top-quality service by helping them understand and meet their
tax responsibilities and by applying the tax law with integrity and fairness to all.

Exhibit C.   Potential mission outcomes
Throughout this book the authors have tried to link the importance of a school system's mission to its organizational culture. This realization and the leadership to act
on it become the foundation of school system decisions, both basic and support.

Because of its fundamental importance, the discussion that follows extends the
treatment of an organizational mission as a key force in defining boundary planning limits and in defining what decisions are made, why they are made, how they
are made, and for whom they are made.

It is useful to consider the potential return when you combine mission and leadership action. As indicated in the discussion that follows, some of the possibilities are:

- A system focusing on its mission through its primary functions (educational program, logistical, planning, environmental, human resource), as portrayed in Exhibit A).
- The outstretched hand of the human resource function to bring the school staff to provide unified support of outcomes deriving from the intent of the system's mission (Figure C1).
- Linking the human resource function to other organizational functions so that they become boundaryless entities to be employed in achieving the strategic intent of the system.
- Maximizing the potential of the human resource function regarding its role in mission attainment (attracting, retaining, developing, and improving the system's human capital; employment law; employment justice; employment values; system culture, information technology; aligning work, performance, and compensation; strategic planning; and unionism).

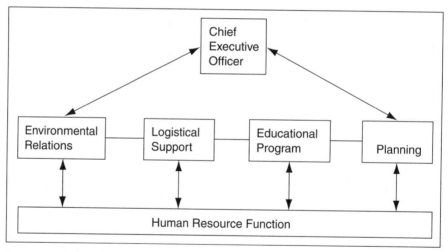

Figure C1.   Illustration of the outstretched hand of the human resource function to other organizational functions regarding its role in:
- *Mission attainment*
- *Attracting, retaining, developing, and improving its human capital*
- *Employment law*
- *Employment justice*
- *Employment values, ethics, and system culture*
- *Information technology*
- *Aligning work, performance, and compensation*
- *Strategic planning*
- *Unionism*

- A management focus, day by day, year by year, living by and for the mission's spirit and intent.
- An aggressive alternative to routine school system management that offers something better, more responsive, and more productive in educational outcomes.

Exhibit D.   School system values and mission attainment

In order to realize the mission of system, there are core values to which we are committed and are pledged to exemplify. Values represent our beliefs about system management for which we have an affectionate regard. Our values are translated into ethical behavior in the form of behavioral norms or standards that set the tone and boundaries in the treatment of our employees and our external claimants in carrying out our mission.

Concerning our personnel. We consider our personnel to be the most valuable of our system assets. In order to attract, retain, and develop our people, we will employ the human resource function and its several processes to establish and enhance a work force that is essential to move the system from its present state to a desired state.

Concerning our external environment. External forces that govern, regulate, have an interest in, transact business with, and desire to influence system operations include the media, parents, the political world, private entities, courts, parents, and community agencies. Our policies are designed to nurture external relationships by plans and actions that contribute to our mission interests.

Concerning organizational justice. Our justice system is designed to protect individual members from arbitrary, capricious, or unfair treatment. Fair treatment and fair process form the bedrock of our justice system.

Concerning disciplinary action. Our disciplinary system is crafted to protect the interests of the school system, as well as the rights of our personnel. Proactive measures include preventive as well as progressive disciplinary measures and predisciplinary procedures.

Concerning system rights. The system reserves unto itself those prerogatives essential to its legal, ethical, and stewardship obligations.

Concerning unionism. We view collective bargaining as one of the key processes of the human resource function that has considerable potential, through intelligent direction, for contributing to the wellness of the system mission. We view bargaining as a useful way to formulate educational policy and to influence the way public schools ought to be managed. Public policy regarding unionism is to protect *persons, income, jobs, and rights.* We consider such protection a legitimate subject for public concern and for mission aims. As employers, we assume that a negotiated contract represents a fair exchange, based on good-faith bargaining and proactive contract resolution. The exchange acceptance is based on the premise that both the system and the union are obligated to realize the system's strategic aims, which is the primary purpose for which public education and its school systems have been brought into being and furnished public support.

Concerning the way we behave. We are conscious of our responsibility for stressing, through various channels of system communication, the obligations of administrative, supervisory, faculty, and support personnel and the propriety of both internal and external behavior. This includes individual behavioral acts considered to be illegal, immoral, contrary to system and public interests, and, in some cases, ill-considered and senseless. Failure to separate personal and individual interests crosses the line of prudent discretion, leading to undesirable individual, system, and social consequences and infringement of our value system. We expect our personnel to perform effectively and, in so doing, strive to be the best people they can be.

GLOSSARY

Absenteeism formula. (Total hours of absence) ÷ (Total hours scheduled) × 1000

Academic freedom. The ability of professional personnel to exercise intellectual independence and to encourage it in the classroom without impediment or undue restraint.

Administrative theory. A set of concepts that guides administrative behavior and influences choices from among alternatives for deciding on courses of action.

Adverse impact. A management practice that has a disproportionate effect on a protected class group.

Affirmative action. Employment practices designed to afford certain protected class persons preferential treatment within the employment process.

Age Discrimination Employment Act of 1967. Prohibits employment discrimination against persons aged 45–65 regarding selection, compensation, termination, and related personnel practices.

Americans with Disabilities Act of 1990 (ADA). States that employers may not discriminate against an individual with a disability in hiring or promotion if person is otherwise qualified for position.

Application form. An instrument design to collect preemployment information from applicants.

Application ratio. The number of applicants applying for each position (10:1, 20:1, etc.).

Appropriate labor market. A policy decision focusing on the identification of comparable organizations.

Arbitration. Process that involves an impartial third party who collects pertinent facts from the disputants and proceeds to make recommendations based on the findings.

Archives. Storage arrangement for retention of records having historical importance.

Authority. Empowerment vested in school officials to create and modify formalized conditions of employment and to encourage and uphold adherence by system members.

Base pay. The amount of pay generally reflected on a salary schedule for a position, excluding any forms of supplemental pay.

Base rate. The percentage of employees who would perform successfully if a predictor were not used to select employees.

Behavior tolerance zones. Zones of behavior tolerance that the organization will accept from a system member. This concept can be illustrated in terms of a continuum arbitrarily divided into two kinds of behavior: productive and counterproductive. The line of demarcation is established to assist the organization in evaluating the acceptability of past, present, and predicted future behavior.

Benefits. A form of compensation in addition to base pay that can be either direct or indirect, such as vacation and insurance.

Bona fide occupational qualification (BFOQ). A skill or trait that is absolutely necessary for effective job performance.

Cafeteria benefits plan. A benefit plan in which position holders elect benefits they will receive within a specified dollar amount.

Career. The sequence of positions experienced throughout an individual's working life.

Career development. Activities pursued by individuals based on specific career objectives.

Career ladder. Vertical progression from one position to another.

Career path. Movement upward, downward, or across levels in the organizational structure.

Career planning. Organizational programs to assist position holders in considering their interests, capabilities, personality, and objectives in relation to career opportunities.

Career stages. Stages through which a position holder passes from career outset to retirement. These stages have been described as establishment, advancement, maintenance, and withdrawal. Career stages have been compared to life stages, identified as early adulthood, mature adult, midlife, and withdrawal.

Civil rights. Individual rights created by federal and state constitutions, statutes, and court decisions, one element of which is employment.

Civil rights Act of 1964 (CRA). Prohibits all forms of discrimination on the basis of race, color, religion, sex, or national origin.

Civil Rights Act of 1991 (CRA). States that the employer must demonstrate that educational requirements, physical requirements, and so on, are job related.

Cohort. A group of individuals having a statistical factor (e.g., age or class membership) in common in a demographic study.

Cohort survival ratio. A factor expressing variation in the number of individuals within a cohort from one accounting period to the next. For example: 550 individuals enrolled in Grade 10, having been preceded by 500 in Grade 9 enrolled during the preceding year, would yield a ratio of 550:500, or 1.10.

Collective bargaining. The process by which a teacher union and the school system negotiate a contract for a stipulated period of time regarding compensation, benefits, work periods, and other conditions of employment. The terms *collective bargaining* and *collective negotiations* are employed interchangeably in the literature. *Bargaining* generally refers to the total bargaining process, one phase of which is negotiations. At-the-table activities, as well as those directly relevant thereto, are viewed as *negotiations.*

Collective bargaining process. One of the processes in the human resource function embodying three phases: prenegotiations, negotiations, and postnegotiations.

Comparable worth. Refers to discrimination against women through pay practices. Embraces the position that women should receive the same compensation as men for holding positions of comparable worth as well as equal worth. Work assignments not equal in content but providing equal value to the system warrant equal compensation.

Compensation equity. Conformity to principles of fairness and impartiality in deciding the economic worth or value of positions and position holders. *Internal equity* refers to equal pay for equal work and performance outcomes under similar working conditions. *External equity* refers to internal compensation that is comparable to that of other school organizations with which the system competes for personnel.

Compensation index. A plan for establishing base salaries for administrative and supervisory personnel by transforming responsibility levels into dollar values.

Compensation planning tools. These include the position guide, organization chart, structural analysis diagram, and compensation scattergram.

Compensation structure. Interrelated provisions governing salaries, wages, benefits, incentives, and noneconomic rewards for school personnel.

Compensatory model. An empirical procedure for combining information about an employee's performance on each dimension when a minimum level of performance is required on each dimension.

Compensation policy. A formal statement that reflects the goals and intentions of the board of education in regard to a system's compensation practices.

Compression. A percentage that reflects the function growth potential associated with a particular salary range.

Computer. (a) An electronic machine that, by means of stored instructions and information, performs rapid, often complex calculations or compiles, correlates, and selects data; (b) a programmable electronic device that can store, retrieve, and process data.

Concentration statistics. An index that reflects the distribution of protected class persons across different job categories within an organization.

Confidential information. Maintenance of information about system personnel within the limits of the Privacy Act of 1974.

Content validity. An analytical paradigm for assessing the appropriateness of a measure or process.

Contingency plans. Plans established to resolve a possible but uncertain occurrence, such as a budget rejection by the board of education or community, a teacher strike, new legislation affecting the system, a court decision, or a school merger.

Contingent personnel. Temporary, part-time, and substitute professional or support personnel. Defined in general terms by the U.S. government as those who work fewer than 35 hours per week.

Contract administration. Day-to-day administrative negotiations between the union and the school system. Grievance machinery is employed to resolve contractual disputes.

Contract design. The elements of a written contract proposal concerning system–union relationships, compensation issues, and contractual disputes.

Control. Evaluation of the extent to which progress is being made according to plan (objectives). When results deviate from standards, corrective action is initiated to ensure success of the operation. Some form of control is essential to every organizational undertaking, regardless of its scope.

Criterion. A standard, benchmark, or expectation by which to evaluate personnel performance, policies, processes, procedures, and organizational outcomes.

Criterion contamination. The degree to which job tasks and behaviors are unique to the actual criterion and the predictor.

Criterion deficiency. The degree to which job tasks and behaviors are unique to the actual criterion.

Criterion-referenced. The level of job performance exhibited by an employee compared to an external standard independent of the level of job performance exhibited by other employees.

Criterion-related validity. A set of paradigms used to assess the relationship between a measure of procedure and a known standard.

Criterion relevance. The degree to which job tasks and behaviors are reflected by the ultimate criterion, actual criterion, and predictors.

Culture. Values shared by system members that produce norms shaping individual and group behavior.

Data (plural of *datum*). (a) Known, assumed, or conceded facts developed to establish a verifiable record of some past happening or event; (b) facts or figures from which inferences are made or conclusions are drawn; (c) individual facts and statistics capable of being converted into information.

Data base. (a) A collection of organized data, especially for rapid retrieval; (b) mass data in a computer arranged for rapid expansion, updating, or retrieval.

Data processing. The conversion of raw data to machine-readable form and its subsequent processing.

Development appraisal. Designed to improve performance or potential for performance; identifies areas for improvement or growth.

Development process. A process designed to assist position holders to raise their level of performance in present or future assignments to performance expectations.

Discrimination. Employment practices that have a disproportionate impact on certain individuals.

Dismissal. A personnel action initiated by the system to sever an employment relationship.

Diversity. Composition of a heterogeneous work force in terms of position, race, ethnicity, national origin, gender, age, religion, language, skills, disabilities, aspirations, personal idiosyncrasies, behavioral preferences, and lifestyles. Diversity management involves what to address and through what human resource functions.

Due process. A process that protects system members or union protection against infringement on employment rights. Requires showing of "just cause" and the use of "rules of reasonableness."

EAPs. Employee assistance programs. Plans designed to assist members with resolution of personal problems (e.g., alcohol or substance abuse) affecting position performance.

Eclectic model. An empirical procedure for combining information about an employee's performance on dimensions of job performance utilizing certain aspects of the multiple cutoff and compensatory models.

EEOC. Equal Employment Opportunity Commission. Established as the administrative agency for Title VII (Civil Rights Act of 1964).

Effectiveness. The degree to which organizational, group, or individual aims or intended effects are accomplished.

Efficiency. Outcomes or results evaluated in terms of organizational resources expended.

Elasticity. A percentage that reflects changes over time in the theoretical growth potential of a salary range.

Employee Polygraph Protection Act. States that employers are prohibited from requiring or requesting job applicants to take a lie detector test.

Employment communication. A two-way exchange or partaking of information between supervisors and subordinates, designed to achieve mutual understanding of roles and relationships underlying position performance.

Equal employment opportunity. Employment practices designed to be neutral with regard to the protected class status of an individual.

Equal Pay Act of 1963. A federal law requiring equal pay for equal work, regardless of gender.

External environment. Forces external to the organization over which it has no control, such as federal, state, and local regulations; court decisions; public opinion; economic fluctuations; and political movements or activities influencing system courses of action.

Face validity. An unacceptable measure of appropriateness based on unsubstantiated opinion.

Failure analysis. The process identifying the factor or combination of factors associated with ineffective performance.

Family and Medical Leave Act of 1993. A covered employer must provide up to 12 weeks of unpaid leave if the employee provides appropriate documentation substantiating the need for leave.

Feedback. Information received by position holders and/or administrators regarding position performance or planning outcomes.

Fiduciaries. Financial organizations entrusted with managing retirement funds and related assets.

File. A collection of papers or documents arranged systematically for reference.

Form. A standardized method of recording data.

Formative appraisal. Appraisals aimed at improving the performance of position holders.

Forms management. Responsibility for creating, revising, and controlling all school system forms.

Goal structure. A hierarchy of assumptions ranging from broad to narrow organizational intent (mission, purpose, goals, objectives, and targets). Developed to identify desirable future outcomes.

Grievance procedure. A prescribed series of steps or a line of appeals designed to resolve a disagreement, dissatisfaction, dispute, or conflict concerning conditions of employment.

HMO. Health maintenance organization. The Federal Act of 1973 requires employers to offer an HMO (medical organization) to their employees as an alternative to conventional group health plans.

Human resource function. Personnel is one of the major functions of school administration, including these processes: planning, bargaining, recruitment, selection, induction, development, appraisal, compensation, justice, continuity, and information.

Impasse. A situation existing when negotiations are deadlocked and the possibilities of reaching common ground for a new contract are unforeseeable.

Incentives. Forms of compensation in addition to base salary that link rewards to outstanding performance.

Induction. A systematic organizational plan to assist personnel to adjust readily and effectively to new assignments so that they can contribute maximally to the work of the system while realizing personal and position satisfaction.

Information. Knowledge consisting of facts that have been analyzed in the context of school administration. Information consists of data that have been refined.

Information system. A systematic plan designed to acquire, refine, organize, store, maintain, protect, retrieve, and communicate data in a valid and accurate form.

In-service education. Planned programs of learning opportunities afforded staff members for the purpose of improving the performance of individuals in already-assigned positions.

Internal consistency. A criterion for evaluation of compensation systems that focuses on the interrelationship among positions.

Internal environment. Forces within the school system, such as mission, goals, processes, performance culture, and leadership styles, that influence organizational courses of action.

Job. A group of positions identical with respect to their major tasks.

Job analysis. A formal set of procedures used to identify and define job tasks and behaviors.

Job categories. Includes professionals, office and clerical personnel, skilled and semi-skilled operatives, unskilled laborers, and support personnel.

Job content. Tasks and behaviors required to perform a job.

Job criteria. Actual indicators of tasks and behaviors necessary to perform a job.

Job evaluation. The process by which jobs are compared in order to determine compensation value and ensure pay equity.

Job predictors. Assessment instruments used to measure tasks and behaviors required for job performance.

Job satisfaction. Individual inclination, expression, feeling, or disposition relative to a work assignment and the environment in which it is performed.

Job simulations. A set of job tasks designed to approximate actual job behaviors and duties.

Job specification. A statement setting forth the personal requirements or capabilities entailed in performing the work of a position.

Justice. An inclusive term covering, completely or broadly, organizational maintenance of what is just by impartial adjustment of conflicting claims, rights, misconduct, or system personnel abuses.

Justice system. Organizational provisions by which personnel actions (individual and organizational) are determined as right or wrong. Rewards and penalties are allocated impartially according to principles of equity or fairness.

Learning curve. A graph depicting proficiency rates over periods of time.

Management by objectives (MBO). A narrative system of performance appraisal that focuses on establishing and assessing goals mutually determined by the employee and employer.

Mentor programs. Programs established by a school system to enable outstanding experienced teachers to serve as coaches, guides, and/or role models, especially for beginning teachers, teachers changing from one grade position to another or to another school, and to enhance the performance of other experienced teachers. Mentor programs entail special incentives for those serving as mentors.

Minority. Part of a population differing from others in some characteristics (cultural, economic, political, religious, sexual, or racial) and often subjected to differential treatment.

Misconduct. Deliberate violation of system employment standards relating to felony, insubordination, embezzlement, exceeding authority, misappropriation of funds, drug and alcohol abuse, off-duty conduct, and employment creating a conflict of interest to or detrimental effect on the system.

Model. A tentative description of a system or theory that accounts for all of its known properties. Models for the human resource function, for example, are conceptual frameworks designed to isolate key factors in personnel programs, processes, or procedures to show how these factors are related to and influence

each other. A model helps to visualize or portray plans that cannot be visualized directly or readily before adoption.

Modeling. The use of models to create, pretest, diagnose, and monitor various kinds of school system plans (structures, instructional systems, human resource processes, pupil forecasts, and compensation designs). Models are employed frequently to design and test the reasonableness of new plans or to diagnose the worthiness of those already in operation.

Motivation. Internal or external forces that influence an individual's willingness to achieve performance expectations.

Motivation theories. Assumptions regarding determinants that influence personnel to cooperate in putting their abilities to use to further organizational aims. Among those cited in the literature are two-factor, social comparison, consistency, reinforcement, and expectancy theories. Beliefs school officials hold about motivation influence personnel decisions.

Multiple cutoff model. An empirical procedure for combining information about an employee's performance on each dimension when a minimum level of performance is required on each dimension.

Narrative systems. A family of self-referenced systems that compare different dimensions of job performance as exhibited by a sample employee.

National Health Care Insurance. A variety of national health care insurance plans were introduced in the 103rd Congress in 1994 without reaching the enactment stage. These ranged from reliance on tax incentives for individual insurance purchasers, to employer-mandated contributions to health care costs, to establishing a national health insurance system.

Need. A discrepancy between an actual and a desired state. Objectives are the counterparts of needs and are employed to translate problems into programs.

Negotiating modes. Three common modes of negotiations are generally described in the literature: competitive, collaborative, and subordinative.

Negotiations. School system professional contracts are commonly negotiated by a single union and a single employer. In some situations, different contract negotiations are agreed upon for different groups of support personnel.

Negotiations strategy. Plans that establish the kinds of educational programs and services the system will make available for its clients, procedures by which these programs and services will be delivered, and means for motivating personnel to cooperate voluntarily in making the delivery system effective.

Norm-referenced. The level of job performance exhibited by an employee compared to the level of job performance exhibited by other employees.

Norms. Unwritten group rules or values shared by members regarding work behavior. Statistical norms are averages sometimes construed as standards (goals).

Objective theory. A theory for recruitment that focuses on the economic incentives associated with jobs/organizations.

Objectives. What is to be accomplished, for what purpose and to what extent, by whom, with what resources, and within what time frame. Objectives should be measurable and linked to broad system aims and strategies.

Organization. A group of individuals systematically united to achieve a particular method or objective, such as a military, educational, religious, or commercial organization.

Organization chart. A graphic representation of functions, accountability, responsibility, relationships, and levels of various positions in the organizational structure.

Organization culture. Values, standards, and attitudes of appropriate conduct and fair treatment established and reinforced by the organization and system members.

Organization manual. A document (handbook) describing the formal organization structure and related policies, processes, programs, rules, and regulations.

Organization structure. A framework for assigning roles, responsibilities, relationships, and decision-making authority among system members.

Organizational development (OD). Most definitions include (a) a planned, systematic intervention (b) to shape a more desirable organization culture (c) by improving individual, intragroup, and intergroup attitudes, shared beliefs, and norms (d) employing theory and technology of applied behavioral science.

Organizational elements. Key elements include structure, design of positions, power, and staffing.

Organizational influences: external. Among the external, uncontrollable elements influencing the human resource function are the regulatory environment, legal precedents, political climate, federal and state legislation, community population patterns, cultural/social change, technological developments, economic change, school enrollments, and union culture.

Organizational influences: internal. Among the internal elements influencing the human resource function are the financial condition of the system, quality of information flow, structural setting, quality and quantity of school personnel, individual behavior, group behavior, and nature of formal and informal organizations.

Performance appraisal. The process of arriving at judgments about a member's past, present, or predicted future behavior against the background of his or her work environment or future performance potential.

Performance appraisal system. Techniques and procedures used by an organization to assess the job performance of employees.

Performance criteria. Criteria used to measure or evaluate the position holder's performance. They include trait, behavioral, or outcome criteria or any combination of the three.

Performance culture. Established patterns of behavior deemed essential to fulfillment of agreed-on position, group, and organizational values, standards, and attitudes.

Performance effectiveness. The level of performance that the position holder is expected to achieve.

Performance effectiveness areas. Key results areas or components, specified in a position description, in which the incumbent should be investing time,

energy, and talent to achieve position expectations.

Performance objectives. A statement containing information relative to what a position holder is expected to accomplish and how well it is to be accomplished.

Personnel administration. Refers to the range of personnel activities involved in achieving individual, group, and organizational aims through proper use of the system's human resources.

Personnel continuity process. A series of managerial tasks and provisions designed to retain competent personnel and foster continuity in personnel service.

Personnel development needs. Development needs that surface at various levels (organizational, unit, and individual), at different times, for varying reasons.

Personnel development process. Formal and informal activities aimed at improving the abilities, attitudes, skills, and knowledge of system members.

Personnel information. Information about individuals who apply for employment and enter, work in, and leave the system.

Personnel information modules. Units of personnel information arranged or joined in a variety of ways with the specific purpose of contributing to administration of the human resource function.

Personnel information process. An organizational process through which efforts are made to achieve a desired state relative to personnel information. Steps in the process include diagnosis, preparation, implementation, evaluation, and feedback.

Personnel policy. A written statement expressing general aims and intentions of the board of education with respect to working conditions and relationships that are intended to prevail in the school system.

Personnel protection. Protection of persons, jobs, income, and staffing.

Phased retirement. Opportunities for personnel nearing retirement to reduce their workload through leaves of absence; part-time employment; and reduced work days, work weeks, or work years.

Placement. The assignment of an individual to a specific position within an organization.

Planning. Deciding in advance of action those objectives to be achieved and developing strategies to achieve them.

Planning tools. A set or collection of management mechanisms that belong to or are used together. For example: (a) *mission* refers to the primary purpose for which schools are established; (b) *strategy* refers to the use and allocation of system resources to guide action toward long-range objectives; (c) *policies* are the express system intent and boundaries within which actions are permitted or expected; (d) *aims, goals,* and *objectives* refer to desirable future results; (e) *programs* and *projects* are plans designed to achieve objectives; (f) *procedures, rules,* and *regulations* are specific instructions that guide actions and performance behavior essential to attainment of objectives; and (g) *controls* are management arrangements designed to compare planned and actual results; (h) *budgets, audits, standards, inventories,* and *research studies* are types of controls employed to compare and correct deviations from plans.

Planning vision. An idealistic image of the school system or its components in a preferred future state. A vision of the future state of the human resource function, for example, incorporates the long-run changes deemed essential to achieving the desired image.

Policy. Broad statements of organizational intent that establish guidelines to govern the scope and boundaries of administrative decisions. There are, for example, compensation policies to govern base pay, addends, benefits, temporary hires, and pay levels comparable with other employers.

Position. A collection of tasks constituting the total work assignment of a single worker.

Position guide. A statement describing both position requirements and position holder requirements. Useful in the recruitment, selection, induction, compensation, and development processes.

Position-holder value. Economic worth of individuals who occupy positions in the system.

Position value. The relative importance of a position in the organization structure. Positions involving greater responsibility and difficulty are valued more highly and should receive more pay than those of less responsibility and difficulty.

Power. The degree to which an individual can influence others.

Power bases. Five power bases are described as reward power, coercive power, referent power, legitimate power, and expert power.

Practice significance. The functional utilization of a process, procedure, or practice to achieve a purpose.

Predictive validity. An empirical paradigm for assessing the appropriateness of a measure or process.

Pregnancy Disability Act of 1978 (PDA). Prohibits discrimination in employment practices on the basis of pregnancy, childbirth, or related medical conditions.

Prenegotiations planning. Initial phase of the collective bargaining process, which includes such activities as developing the bargaining structure, analyzing the current contract, anticipating issues, preparing the financial outlook, developing the bargaining handbook, and formulating strategy and tactics.

Privacy Act of 1974. Federal legislation that places limits on the collection and dissemination of personal information of members of affected organizations.

Problem personnel. System members who are unable or unwilling to meet organizational standards of performance or behavior.

Procedural justice. Refers to organizational procedures employed to arrive at impartial adjustment of conflicting claims, rights, or adherence to employment standards. Focuses on conformity to truth, fact, or reason.

Professionalism. The standing practice or methods of a professional as distinguished from an amateur. Involves professional character, spirit, and methods. Expertise is currently assumed to be the defining element of professionalism in areas such as law, medicine, academe, nursing, and teaching.

Professional staff size index. The number of professional staff members per 1000 students.

Program structure. Parts of an educational program arranged in some way, such as curricula; courses of study; electives; and instructional objectives, outcomes, and practices.

Protected class status. Protection of specific groups of individuals from discrimination in employment on the basis of group characteristics (age, sex, race, etc.).

Psychic income (also referred to as *noneconomic perquisites*). Includes a variety of privileges incidental to regular salary or wages. Granted voluntarily, beyond position requirements, usually in recognition of, in return for, or in anticipation of some service to the school system (recognition, appreciation, status symbols, special commendations, transfers to more attractive work, psychological security, or special arrangements related to work or working conditions).

Psychological contract. A conceptual view of an unwritten employment transaction between the system and its members in which the position holder exchanges certain types of position behavior (cooperation, continuity, and adherence to position requirements) in return for compensation and other sources of job satisfaction (rights, privileges, and position control).

Quality of organizational life. The extent to which conditions or arrangements in the school system maximize opportunities for the position holder to assume a personalized role conducive to satisfaction of position performance, growth, initiative, and flexibility.

Ranking systems. A family of norm-referenced systems that compare the job performance of one employee to the job performance of other employees.

Rating systems. A family of criterion-referenced systems that compare the job performance of an employee to external standards.

Rationality. Pertains to an expected salary differential between a supervisor and a subordinate.

Record. (a) A written entry or memorial for the purpose of preserving memory or authentic evidence of facts or events; (b) accumulation and organization of data regarded as being of more than temporary significance.

Records center. A central storage area for school system inactive records.

Records inventory. The records the school system maintains, by categories, their location, retention, disposition, and management responsibilities.

Records policy. Guidelines for directing, controlling, and auditing the school system's records program.

Recruitment. The administrative task performed by an organization to attract applicants for employment consideration.

Recruitment message. The communication between an organization and an applicant independent of mode.

Reference. Information obtained from external sources about applicants, which can be either professional or personal.

Regulatory environment. Outside forces that govern and influence virtually all personnel processes (e.g., the U.S. Constitution, congressional acts, executive orders, state and local legislation, and judicial systems).

Reinforcement. The process of modifying behavior by arranging positive consequences for desired behavior and negative consequences for undesired behavior.

Reliability. Refers to those measures that give consistent results either over periods of time or among different raters.

Reports. Utilization of records to communicate information.

Resignation. A voluntary decision by a position holder to sever an employment relationship.

Retention-ratio projection. An estimate of the future number of individuals in a cohort, derived by multiplying an existing number by the mean survival ratio experienced over a selected number of time intervals.

Retroactive enrollment ratio. A factor expressing variation in the number of individuals enrolled from the present accounting period to the preceding period. The ratio is derived by dividing enrollment in a grade during a given year by enrollment in the next higher grade during the following year. For example: 500 individuals enrolled in Grade 9, having been succeeded by 550 individuals enrolled in Grade 10 during the following year, would yield a ratio of 500:550 or .91.

Salary. Amount of money received for services rendered by employees exempted from the Fair Labor Standards Act of 1938.

Scope of bargaining. The substance of economic and noneconomic issues to be negotiated at the bargaining table.

Security process. Arrangements designed to protect system members from internal threats and anxieties that occur in organizational life.

Selection. The administrative task performed by an organization to choose among applicants for employment purposes.

Self-referenced. One dimension of job performance exhibited by a single employee is compared to another dimension of job performance exhibited by the same employee.

Socialization process. Formal and informal experiences through which members become adjusted to the values, roles, relationships, and culture of the organization. A formal socialization process (induction) is aimed at assisting members to make a productive start in their positions.

Span of control. Ability to manage a given number of people.

Spreadsheet. A computer program used to analyze numbers in a row and column accounting format. Useful in budgeting, collective bargaining planning, forecasting school enrollment, and staff projections.

Staff development. Systematic means for continuous development of performance capabilities of system personnel. The philosophical underpinning of staff development is that anyone who keeps a job should keep proving and improving himself or herself every day.

Standard of comparison. The criterion to which an employee's level of job performance is compared.

Standards. Criteria against which to judge or measure the acceptability of performance or service. These measures include quality, time, cost, and personnel ratios.

Stakeholder. One who has a monetary, share, personal or emotional concern, or involvement in the well-being of an educational enterprise.

Statistical significance. The empirical utilization of a process, procedure, or practice to achieve a purpose within the bounds of certain probabilities.

Stock statistics. An index that reflects the degree of utilization of protected class persons relative to their distribution in the labor market.

Strategy. Development or employment of overall plans, sometimes referred to as *grand designs*, in order to achieve goals, planned effects, or desired results. Considered a technique of total planning that encompasses the overall aims of the system and establishes functional strategies (e.g., educational program, personnel, logistics, and external relations) to achieve them. Each functional area is broken into individual modules to create an overall strategic plan for the organization.

Stress interview. A recruitment-selection technique designed to identify candidates who are capable of reacting in a calm and composed manner in tense, uncomfortable, and pressure-driven situations.

Strike. To quit or cease working in order to compel employer compliance with a demand.

Subjective theory. A theory for recruitment that focuses on the psychological rewards associated with jobs/organizations.

Summative appraisal. Personnel appraisal focused on decisions involving compensation, tenure, dismissal, promotion, and reemployment. Does not occur simultaneously with formative appraisals.

Support personnel. Employees who perform work for which no educational certification is required and who do not participate directly in the educational process.

Systems concept. A concept that embraces the interdependence among system components and the internal and external environments in which they operate.

Technical rationality. Judicious use of techniques, operations, resources, knowledge, and know-how to improve, sustain, and encourage effective performance.

Tenure. An official status granted after a trial period to a teacher or a member of another covered professional class to protect the individual from summary dismissal.

Termination. Severance of an employment relationship.

Termination at will. The absolute right to discharge, with or without cause, in the absence of a written contract.

Theories of learning. Assumptions regarding the process by which new behaviors are acquired.

Theory. (a) A proposed explanation to describe or account for a phenomenon; (b) an individual view, speculation, or hypothesis. Theories in the literature describing certain aspects of the human resource function include behavioral, organization, equity, motivation, administrative, and communication theories.

Turnover. Changes in the composition of the work force due to resignation, transfer, retirement, or behavioral reasons. Generally expressed as the rate of turnover—the number of persons hired within a period to replace those leaving or dropped from the work force.

Uniform guidelines of 1978. Federal guidelines covering employee selection procedures.

Unionism. A school system or other organization in which the terms and conditions of employment are fixed by legal forces between employer and teacher union. Modern unions rely heavily upon the political process at all levels of government to realize their objectives.

Validity. The degree to which an instrument measures what it is designed to measure.

Values. Ideals, customs, and beliefs of system members for which a group has an affectionate regard.

Variable. A quantity susceptible of fluctuating in value (e.g., test scores, performance rank, and absentee rate).

Wage. Amount of money received for services rendered by employees covered by the Fair Labor Standards Act of 1938.

Work-force analysis. Analysis of the composition of the work force with respect to balance in the number and percentage of minority as well as male and female personnel currently employed, by level and position classification.

Work itself theory. A recruitment theory that focuses on duties and job tasks associated with jobs/organizations.

AUTHOR INDEX

SUBJECT INDEX